PIETIST AND WESLEYAN STUDIES
Editors: David Bundy and J. Steven O'Malley

This monograph series will publish volumes in two areas of scholarly research: Pietism and Methodism (broadly understood). The focus will be Pietism, its history and development, and the influence of this socio-religious tradition in modern culture, especially within the Wesleyan religious traditions.

Consideration will be given to scholarly works on classical and neo-Pietism, on English and American Methodism, as well as on the social and ecclesiastical institutions shaped by Pietism (e.g., Evangelicals, United Brethren, and the Pietist traditions among the Lutherans, Reformed, and Anabaptists). Works focusing on leaders within the Pietist and Wesleyan traditions will also be included in the series, as well as occasional translations and/or editions of Pietist texts. It is anticipated that the monographs will emphasize theological develop-ments, but with close attention to the interaction of Pietism with other cultural forces and to the sociocultural identity of the Pietist and Wesleyan movements.

1. Gregory S. Clapper, *John Wesley on Religious Affections*. 1989.
2. Peter Erb, *Gottfried Arnold*. 1989.
3. Henry H. Knight III, *The Presence of God in the Christian Life: John Wesley and the Means of Grace*. 1992.
4. Frank D. Macchia, *Spirituality and Social Liberation: The Mes-sage of the Blumhardts in the Light of Wuerttemberg Pietism*. 1993.
5. Richard B. Steele, *"Gracious Affection" and "True Virtue" according to Jonathan Edwards and John Wesley*. 1994.
6. Stephen L. Longenecker, *Piety and Tolerance: Pennsylvania Ger-man Religion, 1700-1850*. 1994.
7. J. Steven O'Malley, *Early German-American Evangelicalism: Pietist Sources on Discipleship and Sanctification*. 1995.
8. R. David Rightmire, *Salvationist Samurai: Gunpei Yamamuro and the Rise of the Salvation Army in Japan*. 1997.
9. Simon Ross Valentine, *John Bennet and the Origins of Methodism and the Evangelical Revival in England*. 1997.
10. Tore Meistad, *Martin Luther and John Wesley on the Sermon on the Mount*. 1999.
11. Robert C. Monk, *John Wesley: His Puritan Heritage*. 1999.

Martin Luther and John Wesley on the Sermon on the Mount

Tore Meistad

Pietist and Wesleyan Studies, No. 10

The Scarecrow Press, Inc.
Lanham, Maryland, and London
1999

SCARECROW PRESS, INC.

Published in the United States of America
by Scarecrow Press, Inc.
4720 Boston Way
Lanham, Maryland 20706

4 Pleydell Gardens, Folkestone
Kent CT20 2DN, England

This work is based on "To Be a Christian in the World: Martin Luther's and John Wesley's Interpretation of the Sermon on the Mount," Ph.D. dissertation, University of Trondheim, 1989.

British Library Cataloguing in Publication Information Available

Library of Congress Cataloging-in-Publication Data

Meistad, Tore, 1942–
    Martin Luther and John Wesley on the Sermon on the mount / Tore Meistad.
        p.   cm. — (Pietist and Wesleyan studies ; no. 10)
    Based on the author's thesis (Ph. D.—University of Trondheim, 1989) presented under title: To be a Christian in the world : Martin Luther's and John Wesley's interpretations of the Sermon on the mount.
    Includes bibliographical references and index.
    ISBN 0-8108-3567-3 (cloth : alk. paper)
    1. Wesley, John, 1703–1791. 2. Luther, Martin, 1483–1546. 3. Sermon on the mount—Criticism, interpretation, etc.—History. I. Title. II. Series.
BX8495.W5M39   1999
226.9'06'0922—dc21
                                          98-45129

Contents

Editors' Foreword

Luther and Wesley are two of the towering figures of Christian theology. It is clear that Wesley drank at the wells of various branches of Continental theology including Luther and Luther's heirs. That trans-historical relationship was seldom comfortable for John Wesley whose major theological commitments lay in other directions. Significant effort has been made to examine the relationship of Wesley with the Moravian, Pietist, Catholic, Reformed, Quietist, and Eastern Christian traditions. Finally with the work of Tore Meistad, *Martin Luther and John Wesley on the Sermon on the Mount*, one has a carefully defined comparative study that explores the trajectories of Luther's and Wesley's thinking about a biblical text, the Sermon on the Mount. In the hands of Meistad, this provides a lens through which primary theological themes of these two important theologians can be examined and compared.

One of the goals of the *Pietist and Wesleyan Studies* series is to contribute to the project of understanding the historical, social, and institutional development of the two related traditions. Meistad's book elucidates the thought of the founders of the Lutheran and Wesleyan traditions in new and interesting ways.

Professor Meistad is well qualified to provide this work on Luther and Wesley. An earlier version of this work served as his doctoral dissertation at the University of Trondheim (1989). Between the earlier and present versions of this work, he has written or edited twenty-one books and booklets, many of which explored facets of the issues discussed in *Martin Luther and John Wesley on the Sermon on the Mount*. Among these are *John Wesleys tolkning av Bergprekenen* (Oslo: Norsk Forlagsselskap, 1984) and *Studier i wesleyansk teologi* (Alta, Norway: ALH-forskning, 1994). Meistad was graduated from the United Methodist Theological Seminary, Göteborg, Sweden (1966)

(M.Div.), and pursued additional studies at the University of Bergen. After founding Soltun People's College and serving as Dean and Lecturer in Religion and Psychology, he turned again to the study of theology and was awarded degrees from the University of Trondheim in 1983 (M.A.) and 1989 (Ph.D.). He is presently Associate Professor of Religion at Finnmark State College of Higher Education, Alta, Norway, where he serves as Head of the Department of Religion.

We are pleased to publish Meistad's study of Martin Luther and John Wesley as a volume in the *Pietist and Wesleyan Studies* series.

David Bundy
Associate Professor of Church
   History and Librarian
Christian Theological Seminary
Indianapolis, IN

J. Steven O'Malley
Professor of Church History and
   Historical Theology
Asbury Theological Seminary
Wilmore, KY

Foreword

Martin Luther was basically a 16th-century man (1483-1546), just as John Wesley was a man of the 18th century (1703-1791). Thus they lived about two hundred years apart, in two different countries, under different political and social circumstances, and different church relations and problems. When the idea of comparing the views and thinking of these two giants in the history of the church is being proposed, the question inevitably arises: Can there be an acceptable basis for a comparison of the theology and ethics of two persons under such different circumstances? Dr. Tore Meistad's answer is clearly "yes." The writer of these lines tends to agree with him. We must also accept Meistad's decision at this point, first of all, because the theologies of both men are still highly relevant within the respective churches of their heirs and followers. It is, furthermore, a meaningful task because human beings are in essence the same: lost sinners in need of reconciliation with God and with one another. Finally, such an endeavor is both necessary and meaningful because, as is becoming more and more clear, their thinking is not only interesting but useful and relevant for Christians and their life in the world of today.

Although both men share the important Protestant view of salvation by grace through faith, there are many differences between them. One of the most crucial differences, perhaps the most important one, lies in their anthropology. Both Luther and Wesley hold the doctrine of the believer being *simul iustus et peccator*, but the content and meaning of this concept is quite different for the two men.

For Luther, the Christian person has Christ's righteousness imputed to him or her and stands therefore before God without guilt, justified by grace through faith, and is now living the life of faith in the world. But even this person is and remains a sinner.

This status does not really change. He or she still lives the Christian life in trust and in faith under the guidance and power of the Holy Spirit. Luther's view of *simul iustus et peccator* is a static one: there is, therefore, a definitive need for daily repentance and commitment.

Wesley, on the other hand, while fully accepting that the Christian is both sinner and justified at the same time, strongly emphasizes the human situation as being much more dynamic: the believer receives forgiveness (Christ's righteousness is imputed), but Wesley immediately adds the second aspect of this one event, namely that of the New Birth. Not only is the guilt removed, but the Holy Spirit takes a dwelling within the believer. There issues a New Creation, a New Being, God's life in the human life. This life has the qualities of all life: it must grow or die (cf. *WW*, 1:432 ff.). Consequently, Wesley teaches not only *imputed* righteousness, but *imparted* righteousness as well (sanctification—Christian perfection). Thus the Christian is formed into being like Christ, in His image. Wesley writes: "Scripture perfection is, pure love filling the heart, and governing all the words and actions ... Pure love reigning alone in the heart and life,—this is the whole of Christian perfection" (*WW-J*, 11:401).

The Augsburg Confession speaks of Christian perfection in a different way:

> For this is the Christian perfection: that we fear God honestly with our whole hearts, and yet have sincere confidence, faith, and trust that for Christ's sake we have a gracious, merciful God; that we may and should ask and pray God for those things of which we have need, and confidently expect help from him in every affliction connected with our particular calling and station in life; and that meanwhile we do good works for others and diligently attend to *our* calling. (Article XXVII, *Book of Concord*, Philadelphia, 1995, pp. 78-79)

The emphasis is here on trust in God's mercy and providence, and proper ethical behavior. Wesley focuses on love (i.e., God) reigning in the heart, from which all good deeds and actions flow.

Dr. Meistad develops these thoughts and much more in this book. He has chosen to delimit his study to the two men's treatment of the Sermon on the Mount. While this may seem to limit the basis for his conclusions too much, and while he still occasionally feels compelled, for the sake of clarity, to refer also to other writings of the two men, he still has been able to give a comprehensive treatment of Wesley and Luther, pointing out the similarities in their views, as well as their differences. Meistad's study is a welcome addition to our understanding of the thought of Wesley and Luther. The comparisons are especially welcome at such a time as the present, where all distinctions seem to fade away or are simply neglected.

Ole E. Borgen, Ph.D.
Bishop emeritus of the United Methodist Church

Preface

This book is based on my doctoral dissertation, "To Be a Christian in the World: Martin Luther's and John Wesley's Interpretations of the Sermon on the Mount" (1989, University of Trondheim, Norway). While the presentation of Luther's and Wesley's exegesis is a summary of the dissertation, the chapters discussing their systematic theologies are completely rewritten. It has been necessary to remove most footnotes with information on the background of their exegeses, critical evaluations, etc. The readers will have to consult my dissertation for a more detailed discussion.

Outline and Contents

In the first part a brief introduction clarifies backgrounds and presuppositions of my study. A broad presentation of recent research on Luther's and Wesley's theologies is not included, nor any extensive discussion of method.

I then offer a brief analysis of Martin Luther's interpretation of the Sermon on the Mount. After introducing the backgrounds of his exhortations on Mt. 5-7, I point out the main distinctives of his exegesis. I then conclude on the structure of his hermeneutics and systematic theology implicit to his biblical interpretation.

In the third part I analyze more in depth John Wesley's interpretation in similar ways. Because my primary concern is to investigate Wesley's exegesis and theology, his interpretation is discussed in more detail in light of its historical context.

The fourth part offers comparisons of the exegesis and theologies of Luther and Wesley. The nature of differences of interpretation is discussed. In this part I aim to describe the structure of Luther's and Wesley's theologies and ethics, as they are implied in their Sermon on the Mount exegesis. The differences of theological and ethical positions are compared and discussed from the structural perspective of their theologies.

Please notice:

(1) The primary aim of this study is to investigate Wesley's biblical interpretation as well as his theology. The comparison with Luther is used methodologically to clarify Wesleyan distinctives. It is not my intention to offer new scholarly insights in the biblical exegesis and theology of Luther.

(2) Nor do I intend to offer a comprehensive presentation of the theologies of Luther and Wesley. I restrict my presentation to issues that are focused in their expositions of the Sermon on the Mount.

Comment on References

Whenever I quote or refer to Luther's works in my dissertation, I give full references to the *Weimarer Ausgabe* (*WA*). Significant passages are quoted in their original text, in German or Latin. In this book I restrict all references to the American edition of *Luther's Works* (*LW*). Only when the text is not translated, I refer to *WA*. Cross references to various editions of Wesley's works are given in the dissertation, but in this book I restrict references to one source only and always to the bicentennial edition of *The Works of John Wesley* (*WW*) whenever possible.

Acknowledgments

Many persons have contributed to this work. They are all mentioned in my dissertation. This manuscript has become possible because of research time offered by Finnmark College, Alta, Norway, and a grant from the Norwegian Council of Research. I am also grateful to the editors of the *Pietist and Wesleyan Studies*, Scarecrow Press, who encouraged me to revise my dissertation for publication in the series. Dr. Ole Borgen has, besides writing the foreword, given most valuable comments on the manuscript as well.

Once more I want to express my deep gratitude to my family and to my parents in particular, Alma and Alf-Erling Meistad, for their generous encouragement of my studies.

Abbreviations

ANF: *Ante-Nicene Fathers: Traditions of the Writings of the Fathers down to A.D. 325*, 10 vols., Alexander Roberts and James Donaldson, eds. Grand Rapids, Michigan: W.M.B. Eerdmans Publishing Company. American reprint of the 1867 Edinburgh edition, 1981.

Arminius: *The Works of James Arminius*, 3 vols., the London edition, translated by James Nichols and Williams Nichols, with introduction by Carl Bangs. Grand Rapids, Michigan: Baker Book House, reprinted, 1986.

Creeds: *The Creeds of Christendom: With a History and Critical Notes*, 3 vols., Philip Schaff, ed. Grand Rapids: Baker Book House, sixth ed., 1931, reprinted.

Discipline: *The Book of Discipline of the United Methodist Church*. Nashville, Tennessee: The United Methodist Publishing House, various years.

EWM: *Encyclopedia of World Methodism*, 2 vols., Nolan B. Harmon, ed. Nashville: United Methodist Publishing House, 1974.

Institutes: Calvin: "Institutes of the Christian Religion." *The Library of Christian Classics*, vols. 20-21, John T. McNeill, ed. Philadelphia: The Westminster Press.

LV: *Martin Luther Verker i utvalg* ("Martin Luther: Selected Works"), 6 vols., Sigurd Hjelde, Inge Lønning and Tarald Rasmussen, eds. Oslo: Gyldendal norsk forlag, 1979-1983.

LW: *Luther's Works*, Helmut T. Lehmann, general ed. Philadelphia: Fortress Press and Saint Louis: Concordia Publishing House, 1955-.

NPNF: *A Select Library of the Nicene and Post-Nicene Fathers of the Christian Church*, 14 + 14 vols., Philip Schaff, ed. Grand Rapids, Michigan: W.M.B. Eerdmans Publishing Company, 1981.

Introduction

The Aim and Design of the Research

In the history of the church, the Sermon on the Mount has been a significant scripture as a basis for theological and ethical considerations. This scripture has been decisive for the interpretation of the ideal Christian attitude to society, as well as for the more basic issue of the relation between faith and ethical action.

The history of the exegesis of the Sermon on the Mount demonstrates that the variety of options for interpretation as well as possible patterns of social and ethical action implied in these interpretations is almost limitless.[1] One question that arises is, how can it be possible to interpret one biblical text in so many different ways? But more basic problems need to be considered:

1. How is a theological system developed on the basis of the biblical exegesis of the interpreters? For instance, what are their philosophies, methods of hermeneutics, and other basic presuppositions?
2. What is the relation between biblical exegesis and the historical context of the interpreters? Are religious, social, cultural, eco-

nomic and political structures decisive for their interpretations? How?

3. What possibilities and/or limitations may a theological system promote in the interpreting process with regard to the dialectics between the biblical text and the actual social and historical frame of reference of the interpreters?

All these issues need to be discussed. My primary aim is, however, to study how the structure of John Wesley's theology and ethics is revealed through his interpretation of the Sermon on the Mount. To highlight this structure, I will analyze and compare Luther's and Wesley's exegesis and hermeneutics of the Sermon on the Mount in light of their historical contexts. A secondary aim is to study the influence of the historical context on the biblical exegesis of Luther and Wesley.

Methods

Comparative Analysis

Comparative research may have different goals. My goal is to study the distinctive features of Wesley's theology and ethics that are focused when compared to Luther's.

A direct comparison between the theologies of Luther and Wesley is not simple. In general, Luther and Wesley use the same theological concepts, for instance, "justification by faith." But is it certain that this concept functions in completely the same way in Luther's and Wesley's theological systems? Because of this uncertainty, I need to examine the meanings as well as the functions of similar concepts, and determine whether they are actually compatible or not.

My hypothesis is: The problems involved in comparing Luther and Wesley indicate that they represent two different paradigms in theology. The differences in their theological systems show up especially when they interpret the relation between salvation and ethics. How should their theological paradigms be characterized?

Luther and Wesley faced different historical situations to which they responded in their exegeses of the Sermon on the Mount. These historical situations provided distinct religious and social challenges. The main reason for the shift of focus of Luther's theology in relation to the traditional theology of his time is his discovery of new answers to the spiritual needs of ordinary people. He therefore introduces a truly new theological paradigm.

Wesley shifted the focus of Reformation theology from its preoccupation with a formal relationship between God and humankind, to a new concern for how God transforms creation into God's own likeness. By doing so, he developed a theology with a systematic structure which should be characterized as a new theological paradigm, compared to Luther's. The consequence is that a comparative analysis of Luther and Wesley needs to realize that a direct and simple comparison hardly is possible; the comparison should be performed on a paradigmatic rather than on a detailed level. The different structures of their respective theological systems must be taken into consideration before a valid comparison is possible.

Contextual Analysis

Through comparative analysis my design is to observe and describe how Luther's and Wesley's theologies and ethics are elaborated from their different contexts. My preliminary position is that their interpretations differ because their scriptural exegeses are related to different philosophical, theological, and other factors, particularly their unequal historical, economic, and cultural contexts.

For this reason, contextual analysis will be necessary. Luther's and Wesley's exegeses must be understood in light of the specific religious, economic, and social situations in which they were elaborated.

Hermeneutical Analysis

This investigation presupposes that any biblical interpretation is dependent on a basic theology with a systematic structure. My aim is to analyze and describe the systematic structures of Luther's and Wesley's theologies that are foundational to their scriptural inter-pretations.

Neither Luther nor Wesley is generally supposed to be a "systematic theologian" in the traditional meaning of this concept. They never actually attempt to do theology in the tradition of the scholastic theology, that forms the ideals of systematic theology. On the contrary, both reject explicitly this kind of theology.[2] This does not at all mean that their theologies have no inner structure. An analysis of their hermeneutics will reveal the implicit structure of their theologies. As a matter of fact, without understanding the systematic structure of their theologies, our insights into their bib-lical interpretation will seem superficial.

In my interpretation Luther and Wesley I in general follow the flow of their own ideas, particularly as they are presented in their discourses on the Sermon on the Mount. Though the text will seem repetitive at some points, my aim is to demonstrate how they are building up their ideas.

Previous and Comparative Research on Martin Luther and John Wesley

Comparative research on Luther and Wesley started as psycho-logical investigations of their religious experiences.[3] Theological comparisons of Luther and Wesley came on the agenda as a result of the Ecumenical movement. The goal of this phase was either apologetic in order to prove that Wesley, in spite of his popular and "unsystematic" form of theological statements was an accept-able theologian after all, or, to harmonize Wesley with Luther for ecumenical purposes.[4] The objective of this method was to defend Wesley by showing that his theology essentially had the same evangelical basis as that of Luther. On the other hand, I know of no investigation that assesses Luther on Wesley's terms.[5]

Thor Hall (1988; cf. 1963) indicates that a new way of com-paring Luther and Wesley is about to be introduced. Hall rejects the earlier tendency to emphasize similarities between theologians in order to hide the dissimilarities. Using Luther, Calvin, and Wesley as examples, he offers a method of analyzing different theological types and proposes a typological perspective that can clarify the distinctive character of each type. His aim is to focus upon the particular contribution each has made to the ecumenical understanding of Christian faith and life (Hall 1988:46).

Hall indicates that traditional comparative analysis is not very effective because it chooses to focus on single-point criteria (for instance, justification) or dialectical criteria (for instance, theocentricity and egocentricity) instead of considering a larger number of dynamic dimensions. Consequently, he suggests a method of theological comparison with the help of a three-fold dynamic:

1. The dimension of **time—eternity** (earth—heaven, or nature—transcendence);
2. the dimension of **motive—action** (inward—outward, or faith—works);
3. the dimension of **sacred—secular** (church—world, or religious community—society in general. (Hall 1988:47, 59)

Hall concludes that, with regard to their interpretations of the Christian life, Luther and Calvin in general are at opposite ends of all three continuums,[6] while Wesley resides at the center between the extremes.

Though my objective is not to compare Wesley to Calvin but to limit the comparison to Luther, Hall's analysis indicates the need to take multiple factors into consideration. Several dimensions of the theologies of Luther and Wesley will therefore be considered.

NOTES

[1.] In my MA dissertation (Meistad 1983) I discuss various traditions of interpretations of the Sermon on the Mount.

2. Luther condemned reason as a whore whenever used as a source of theology. Wesley regarded scholastic theology as pure "metaphysics" or "speculative theology" in contrast to his own "practical divinity" (Cushman 1989:59-60).

3. Lockyer (1922:22) in his book, *Paul: Luther: Wesley: A Study in Religious Experience As Illustrative of the Ethic of Christianity*, suggested that the study of types of religious experience could be compared with prevalent types of contemporary ethics. The comparative study of Luther and Wesley started, therefore, as studies of their ethics by help of psychological method (Lockyer 1922:22). Anker Nilsen's *The Idea of God and Personality Integration with Special Emphasis upon Self-Evaluation As a Deciding Factor—an Historical, Clinical, Experimental Approach* (1952), includes a similar comparison but from an empirical psychological point of view.

4. Direct comparisons are few. Hildebrandt's, *From Luther to Wesley* (1951) is a classic, though its theological analysis is rather superficial. The only other investigations I have identified are Schmidt's, *John Wesley* (1966; particularly vol. 2, chapter 7), Rupp's, *John Wesley und Martin Luther: Ein Beitrag zum lutherischen-methodistischen Dialog* (1983), and Marquardt's, "Gewissheit und Anfechtung bei Martin Luther und John Wesley" (1988).

Examples of apologetic comparison of Luther and Wesley are, Cell, *The Rediscovery of John Wesley* (1935); Lindström, *Wesley and Sanctification* (1961); Carter, *The Methodist Heritage* (1951); and Colin Williams, *John Wesley's Theology Today* (1962). All to some degree defend Wesley's theology by establishing his basis in the Protestant theological tradition.

Runyon (1981:19-20) explains this apologetics of Wesley by indicating that as neo-Reformation thought became the norm in the Protestant ecumenical movement, any interest in religious experience was labeled "Schleiermachian." The doctrine of Christian perfection was regarded as superficial because it was not considered to pay sufficient attention to the doctrine of sin. In the view of Continental Protestant theology, Methodists had no theology that could interest the ecumenical discussion.

5. A possible exception is Ole E. Borgen (1972), who occasionally compares the two theologians on Wesley's terms, cf. pp. 69-70 (notes 71, 78), 131 (note 35), 166, 203, 268-269 (critique of Hildebrandt's comparative approach), 277-278 (notes 34, 36, 38), and 280-281.

[6.] Hall's results are in agreement with Sauter's analysis of the crucial differences between the theologies of Luther and Calvin. Though they hold basically the same ideas on the doctrine of predestination, their theologies are nevertheless different because of the different function this doctrine has in their respective theological systems. While Luther uses the doctrine of predestination to safe-guard against works-righteousness, its function for Calvin is to express the final sovereignty of God and the certainty of salvation (cf. Maddox 1984:10).

Martin Luther's Interpretation of the Sermon on the Mount

Historical and Text-Critical Remarks

From the end of October 1530 until late April 1532, Martin Luther preached regularly from the Wittenberg pulpit. He filled in for its ordinary pastor, Johannes Bugenhagen. (Pomeranus), who then lived in Lübeck organizing the Reformation there. On Sundays he preached over the lectionary, while on weekdays he was free to choose his own scriptures. On Wednesdays he preached a series of sermons or Bible studies on the Sermon on the Mount (Mt. 5-7; *LW*, 21:3-294; *WA*, 32:299-544).

Luther wrestled with issues raised by the Sermon on the Mount all through his career as a preacher. This was especially true in connection with the events leading up to the Peasants' War and until the middle of the 1530s. There are 790 references to Mt. 5-7 in the American edition of Luther's works. In addition come his discourses on the Sermon on the Mount in volume 21.

Unfortunately, the original text of Luther's *Wochen-Predigten* does not exist. Perhaps there was never an original text at all, as he possibly exhorted on the Sermon on the Mount without using a

complete manuscript. In that case, the sermons were transcribed by
one or more of his listeners and compiled into the text which is
transmitted to us.[1] Georg Rörer and Veit Dietrich[2] may have been
responsible for this work (*LW*, 21:viii).

Luther's commentary on the Sermon on the Mount was first
published in three editions, 1532, 1533, and 1534. In the 1534
edition certain revisions of the text appeared, apparently due to the
editor's intention to downplay some of Luther's opinions or
phrases (*LW*, 21:xx-xxi). The most obvious reason is that his polemics were too sharp for his friends (cf. *LW*, 15:X).

The text in the editions of Luther's works probably does not
follow his original outline in detail. It is not always easy to understand the motivation behind the editor's outline for the published
text. For that reason the outline of the text is an uncertain source to
Luther's thoughts.

These uncertainties make it necessary to handle the text with
some caution. The editor, or editors, probably took certain liberties
when transmitting Luther's words and thoughts. There is no reason
for the extreme skepticism of some scholars, however, who doubt
the reliability of the commentary. There are too many parallels
with other works by Luther, in both terminology and contents, to
question the origin of his teaching in these sermons. My conclusion is that the text gives a reliable expression for Luther's views.

Exegesis

The Scriptural Context (Mt. 5:1-2; 7:28-29)

Luther's first aim for his sermons on Mt. 5-7 is to offer a doctrinally authentic interpretation and to present their "true, pure, and
Christian meaning" (*LW*, 21:3). The aim of the Sermon on the
Mount is to reestablish doctrinal orthodoxy. Christ corrected the
Jewish distortions of religion, and Luther intends to correct his
contemporary Scribes. For this reason his commentary is contex-
tually related to a specific historical situation. His second aim is to

teach how Christians should live and act according to the Sermon on the Mount.

Roman Catholic theologians are attacked for their "Double Standard" doctrine, that implies the interpretation of Mt. 5 as "evangelical counsels" (*LW*, 21:4) reserved for persons who stretch out for a higher level of perfection than other Christians. This makes salvation dependent on works and the works of the Sermon on the Mount optional. Though salvation is granted by grace and not merited by works, it is essential to Luther to insist that the Sermon on the Mount should be observed by all Christians.

Luther is also confronted with an opposite error, the absolutist observance of the Sermon on the Mount. Many Baptists[3] of his time reject the participation in public life such as owning private property, swearing, holding office as a ruler or judge, and defending oneself.

The Sermon on the Mount is distorted from two sides. Luther concludes that their error is basically the same, "they do not recognize any difference between the secular and the divine kingdom, much less what should be the distinctive doctrine and action in each kingdom" (*LW*, 21:5). In both cases the divine order is attacked.

Luther here introduces his doctrine of the two kingdoms as the hermeneutical key to the Sermon on the Mount. Roman Catholics and Baptists alike, he holds the distinction between the divine and the secular kingdoms. Both groups confuse the two kingdoms with one another, each in its own way. It is paramount to him to show how important it is to distinguish between the kingdoms while simultaneously holding them together in a creative tension. The sermon has a purely soteriological nature, it "is intended to teach how we are to come to that other life" (*LW*, 21:9). His distinction between the divine and the secular kingdoms corresponds with two distinctive sources of religious and ethical knowledge. The revelation through Christ is valid for the spiritual kingdom, and the natural enlightenment through the human reason is valid for the secular kingdom.

According to Luther, Christ in the Sermon on the Mount reveals the relationship between spiritual and secular spheres of life. The sermon deals with the spiritual life of the Christian. The works by Christians in the stations are considered to be fruits of faith, too. They do not merit salvation, and they are informed by reason, but they have their energy from their relationship to God through Christ.

The issues of faith and works, grace and merit, faith and fruit, are focused in the Sermon on the Mount. Basic misconceptions have led Luther to present what he regards as the authoritative interpretation on this scripture. His basic statement is, "it must be maintained that faith or being a Christian is quite distinct from its fruit" (*LW*, 21:285). He refuses to describe the character of a Christian on the basis of the differences of fruits or outward tasks, for this character ought to be described from the common faith in Christ, "with no one elevated above the other" (*LW*, 21:287). The fact that salvation is received freely and by grace, does not in Luther's thought lead to antinomianism. Any person who is "in grace" and who is a child of God, ought to "do his duty" and be repaid in the kingdom of heaven (*LW*, 21:290). For this reason, the Sermon on the Mount deals with how to live as a Christian.

In his further discussion of merits, Luther introduces the idea of consolation. Merits can never make a person a child of God, for "He is not teaching me where to build the foundation of my salvation, but giving me a promise that is to console me in my sufferings and in my Christian life" (*LW*, 21:292). Consequently, the gospel does not transform sinners nor social structures, it rather consoles believers in their hope for a future redemption.

The Beatitudes (5:3-12)
The Poor in Spirit (5:3)
The poverty of spirit is to be understood spiritually and not economically. Luther's distinction between spiritual and secular poverty is based in his idea of the two kingdoms: "Christ ... wants to discuss only the spiritual kingdom—how to live before God [*coram Deo*], above and beyond the external" (*LW*, 21:12). Whenever

the believer is a spiritual beggar, it is evident that salvation is worked by God's grace. But material resources are necessary for the sustenance of life. It is "before God" that we should be spiritually poor. No lord nor prince nor a head of any household can be poor, for they shall take care of the people or their households. The basis for secular power is the creating and sustaining will of God.

Luther identifies two foci in his theology that must be held together but not confused. In the spiritual kingdom salvation is given unmerited by God's grace, in the secular kingdom political and economic power is given for the sustenance of God's created order.

Luther's polemics are directed against spiritualist positions of his time, represented by the monastic orders as well as by the Baptist movements: "We are not to run away from property, house, home, wife, and children, wandering around the countryside as a burden to other people" (*LW*, 21:14). His basic objection is that they confuse the spiritual and secular kingdoms. To correct this confusion he draws a dividing line in the midst of the personal life of the Christian. As a citizen in the world the Christian is obliged to adjust to social regulations in order to maintain the social order. But when it comes to the Christian's uttermost loyalty, this should be to God alone and not to secular regulations.

In his further criticism of voluntary poverty and the Baptist position, Luther argues that Christ's idea is, "we should use all temporal goods and physical necessities, the way a guest does in a strange place, where he stays overnight and leaves in the morning" (*LW*, 21:13). Though temporal values are good and necessary for the physical life of the human being, they have no ultimate value. His expectations of the immediate *parousia* of Christ and his idea of the Christian life as a pilgrimage on earth may have contributed to a reduced concern for the ethical aspects of the Christian life to some of his followers.

Those Who Mourn (5:4)

All Christians will experience mourning. Christ therefore offers consolation. Luther now clarifies that the secular kingdom is not identical with "the world." The world is the stage of a metaphysical struggle between the powers of God and the devil; it is the scene of two kingdoms, the secular kingdom of God and the kingdom of the devil. It is the kingdom of the devil that causes the afflictions and sorrows of Christians.

The Meek (5:5)

Luther's issue is how to link spiritual poverty to inheriting the land. The creating will of God is that a man should have "wife, children, cattle, house, and home ... so that he can stay on the land where he lives and have dominion over his possessions" (*LW*, 21:22). The life in the secular stations and the right to hold earthly possession should be exercised with meekness. His basic hermeneutical intention is reinforced:

> Christ ... is only talking about how individuals are to live in relation to others, apart from official position and authority ... we must sharply distinguish between these two, the office and the person ... Here we have two different persons in one man ... once we are born, God adorns and dresses you up as another person. He makes you a child and me a father, one a master and another a servant, one a prince and another a citizen ... He is not talking about this person here, letting it alone in its own office and rule, as He has ordained it. He is talking merely about how each individual, natural person is to behave in relation to others.
>
> Therefore if we have an office or a governmental position, we must be sharp and strict, we must get angry and punish; for here we must do what God puts into our hand and commands us to do for His sake. In other relations, in what is unofficial, let everyone learn for himself to be meek toward everyone else, that is, not to deal with his neighbor unreasonably, hatefully, or vengefully. (*LW*, 21:23-24)

Four significant aspects of Luther's theology are here demonstrated: (1) The Sermon on the Mount neither deals with situations that activate any official station nor to persons in their relations to the stations of the secular kingdom. (2) The dividing line of the two kingdoms runs in the midst of each person; the Christian is spiritual and secular at the same time, and the outward relations determine which kingdom is in charge. (3) The norms of conduct for the two kingdoms differ and may be contrary to each other; the meekness of the individual Christian is supposed to be in relation to non-official situations only. As officials the Christians must be strict. (4) The Christian officials should not direct their actions according to the norms of the Sermon on the Mount, but follow the laws of society and govern according to them. Their punishments should be strictly impersonal and exclusively related to the demands of their offices. This implies that the virtues of the Sermon on the Mount should prevail in the secular kingdom, too, not as rules for the secular society but as basic attitudes of the hearts of the Christians.

Luther argues that Christ's teaching on meekness is a reasonable pattern of conduct to the neighbor. Attitudes of love are possible because "This sermon is intended only for those who are Christians, who believe and know that they have their treasure in heaven, where it is secure for them and cannot be taken away" (*LW*, 21:25). The Sermon on the Mount informs Christians in the secular kingdom, but it never was intended as a general law for the society.

Those Who Hunger and Thirst after Righteousness (5:6)

Affirming good works as fruits of faith, Luther affirms that the works are entirely products of God's undeserved grace. A dilemma arises when a believer searches for righteousness, thus contradicting the imputed righteousness as an unmerited gift. He maintains that the human part of justification is totally passive and something which happens to the sinner. Christ in this beatitude addresses the Christian's own and outward righteousness in the secular kingdom rather than the alien righteousness of the sinner, that is graciously given by God without human merits.

Luther at this point must abandon his general interpretation of the beatitudes as related to the spiritual life. There are two kinds of righteousness, one for each kingdom, the "own" righteousness related to the secular world, and the "alien" righteousness that belongs to God. Observing the dissolution of the social order of his time, the concern to maintain the society influences his theology. He therefore admonishes his audience to be loyal to the social system. The secular righteousness is nothing but faithful obedience of the stations and the offices: "What is the righteousness of the world except that in his station everyone should do his duty?" (*LW*, 21:26).

The Merciful (5:7)

Speaking of the holiness and righteousness manifested in the life of the stations, Luther states that "If a man deals with his neighbor in an effort to help and correct him in his station and way of life, he should take care to be merciful and to forgive" (*LW*, 21:29-30). Nor is this beatitude related to the spiritual kingdom but restricted to the secular kingdom. Consequently, the two kingdoms are related dialectically and not dichotomously. The spiritual and secular kingdoms are distinguished but not separated, and the life in one kingdom influences the life in the other.

The Pure In Heart (5:8)

Holiness is not an issue of "outward cleanliness of body" (*LW*, 21:33). The purity of which Christ speaks has nothing to do with the withdrawal from this world. Husbands, wives, and children, are living pure lives, for "Whatever God has commanded cannot be profane (Acts 10:15)" (*LW*, 21:32). The world is pure as created by God. Though the stations of family life are secular, they are divine. Nothing unclean in this world can destroy the inward purity of heart. The Christian remains pure by keeping firmly to God's Word in two ways: Faith in God restores the sinner in the state of God's favor through justification, that will purify the heart. Secondly, to be obedient in one's station, implies the adaptation to God's order in this life, that is pure from creation. Both ways are necessary aspects of a true Christian life.

Luther distinguishes between the kingdoms in two ways. First, the spiritual kingdom is concerned with the purity of heart. In this respect, the believer is directed by "the Word of faith," which is revealed by God through grace. Secondly, the secular kingdom is concerned with the relationship "toward his neighbor in his station" (*LW*, 21:34). In these relationships reason will direct the believer. The doctrine of the two kingdoms therefore has implications at several levels, for instance, to soteriology, to ethics, and to the issue of religious and moral recognition.

Purity has to do with the believer's relation to God. Luther's concern is that the purity of the heart is based in the pure Word of God. Good works will come as secondary effects of this purity. He therefore affirms the duty to "Honor your father and your mother" by staying with them over against the practice of the monks, who "flee from their parents" (cf. Ex 20:12; *LW*, 21:36). The pure heart "functions completely on the basis of the pure Word of God," and it "will also manifest itself outwardly in this life" (*LW*, 21:37), that is, in the life of the offices and stations.

The promise of this beatitude is to "see God," which may be fulfilled by recognizing God "as a gracious and faithful Father, on whom you can depend for every good thing", that happens only through faith in Christ, and by living "in your station with your husband, wife, child, neighbor, or friend" "according to God's Word and command" (*LW*, 21:37-38). To "see God" is to have faith in God as a loving father as well as to perform one's duties in the civil stations. In this way a specific historical structure of society is tied together with religious fulfillment, a fact that may explain why the Reformation historically did not have the transforming impact on the society which might have been expected (cf. Rublack 1985:237, 266-267).

Concluding the interpretation of Mt. 5:8, an assurance of faith is implied. Assurance was a vital religious issue in the 16th-century. The Council of Trent rejected that any assurance of final salvation could possibly be infallible. Contrary to this, Luther affirms that anybody "who takes hold of the Word of God and ... who remains in faith" can rely on the hope for salvation (*LW*, 21:39). This discussion reveals a fundamental change of piety from an emphasis on ritual action to knowing and knowledge (cf. Rublack 1985:251-252). It is a turn away from a piety of religious achievement within the liturgical framework over which the Ro-

man Catholic church had absolute control, to a Lutheran orientation of religious abstraction and cognitive training. This change
opens up for a limited assurance of faith that is related exclusively
to faith as an acceptance of the Word of God, interpreted in cognitive terms. No concept of experience interpreted in emotional
terms is implied. He warns explicitly against evaluation of one's
state before God on the basis of feelings.

The Peacemakers (5:9)

Luther's definition of a peacemaker is founded in the active waging of peace. He attacks both priests and princes for being too
quick to start wars. The peacemakers "try to make peace, not only
in their own lives but also among other people ... and try to avoid
and prevent war and bloodshed" (*LW*, 21:39).

Luther accepts the idea of "just war" but he restricts the use of
it. No cause is ever "just" enough to start a war for any individual
because that can only be done by the authorities. Nor should a
prince, who has the authority to start war, do that easily, until negotiations for the purpose of peace have broken down and the
enemy starts the war. But in case of an attack from an enemy, the
Christian prince is obliged to defend his land and people.

These rules apply for the princes. But what can a person do if
being attacked or violated in some other unjust way? Luther admonishes that the Christian should as a start try to bear it and keep
peace without hitting back. If the attack is unbearable, however,
"leave the vengeance and punishment to your judge, who has the
command; it is against him that your enemy has done wrong" (*LW*,
21:40).

Luther distinguishes between the rights of the person and the
authorities of the appointed leaders of the society. It is important to
keep the relations between individuals and society in a proper
perspective. The authority to punish is given to the proper offices
and authorities only. But the commandments of love and peace
should be observed in both kingdoms. Though Christ's teachings
are for the Christian life and not for civil affairs, the Christian
official still is a Christian and accountable to God. In cases with

conflicting rules and expectations, the secular laws govern the behavior when a Christian is in office, and the laws of God when he or she is out of office.

Most of Luther's comment on Mt. 5:9 deals with the issue of evil speaking of other people. Any Christian should be "a reconciler and a mediator between ... neighbors" (*LW*, 21:43). He defends himself from accusations of speaking badly about his opponents by indicating that he has been peaceful as long as he could, and implying that the evil is widely spread and "does public damage." Besides, his public office provides him with the authority to speak up. Lastly, he adds, "Christ is not talking here about public office, but in general about all Christians insofar as we are all alike before God" (*LW*, 21:44). His basic defense is that his harsh polemics is performed in the public office of preaching and therefore acceptable.

Those Who Are Persecuted for Righteousness' Sake (5:10-12)

Luther reminds the reader that the Sermon on the Mount deals with the life of the heart only. He regards the beatitudes as elements of "a Christian's way of life and the spiritual fruits" (*LW*, 21:45). The soteriological basis is justification by faith alone, "in his own person" the Christian in relation to God is nothing but a poor beggar. But in relation to others the Christian has reason and free will to act and live according to God's ordinances within the stations like any other human. The ethical implications of salvation by faith are worked out in the secular kingdom. Religion and ethics are intimately related, and the Christian existence in one kingdom is closely linked together with the life of the other.

Any person who chooses the Christian way of life will be the object of attacks of the devil and must prepare for persecution. In other words, it is a consequence of discipleship. That is exactly why faith is so necessary. When persecution is a fact, the eye of faith only is able to see that it is "for righteousness' sake." Not every persecution has, however, a "genuine divine cause" (*LW*, 21:47). The persecution Christ speaks of is not for moral evils but

for good works. To Luther, the aspect of righteousness and inno-
cence in the midst of persecution is most significant for his interpretation of the Sermon on the Mount. Christ "is not teaching me
where to build the foundation of my salvation, but giving me a
promise that is to console me in my sufferings and in my Christian
life" (*LW*, 21:293). The principal aim of the Sermon on the Mount
is to bring comfort and consolation to Christians who faithfully
live according to God's will, that is, faithfully in the civil offices
and stations.

Another comforting thought is that the origin of this kind of
persecution is the devil. He presupposes a dualism between demonic and divine powers. The struggle against the demonic powers is projected to the performance of one's duty in the secular
world on the one hand, and to the preaching of right doctrine in the
spiritual kingdom on the other. In the secular kingdom, the end is
to sustain the created orders. God's support is expressed through
consolation in suffering, a consolation which is anticipating the
recompense to be given at the final judgment.

To Luther, the social structures are basically good by themselves. Encouragement is strongly given to suffering and patience,
but not to the transformation of the social structures that are causing evil.

Admitting that a Christian may be perfect in the midst of persecution, Luther trusts in God's "equipping and preparing His
Christians to live and suffer in the world." Ending his exhortations
on the beatitudes, the doctrine of the two kingdoms establishes the
criteria of how perfection is established: (1) Living a decent life in
the stations of the secular kingdom. (2) Suffering for righteousness' sake. (3) The proper administration and life in one's office,
which is to use it in the service of other people.

The Salt and Light of the Earth (5:13-16)

Luther defines the salt as "the office" of the Christians. This salt is
for "the whole world." For that reason, the Christians should be
ready "to be poor, miserable, thirsty, and meek, and to suffer all
sorts of persecution" (*LW*, 21:54). This general "office" of Chris-

tians is facing the world "in person," that is, in the spiritual king-dom. God is ruling in the spiritual kingdom by the revealed Word, and Christian love should penetrate all the offices of the world.

Because the earth is corrupt before God, Christians should be "a salt to everything that the world is" (*LW*, 21:55). This statement should not be understood in contrast to Luther's understanding of the created world and society as God's world. He directs this say-ing toward forces of the world that are not based on the Word of God. The statement is polemics against the self-claimed "saints" of his contemporaries, namely the monks and perhaps the Baptists, whom he regards as diabolic spirits.

The salt has a cleansing effect. The Gospel should be preached in a sharp way that rubs salt into the wounds of the sinners. Preachers have by their expositions of orthodoxy a particular re-sponsibility to prevent sectarian movements of any kind; he fears that "the true doctrine of faith is destroyed, Christ is lost, and eve-rything is ruined" (*LW*, 21:56-57). He states that "The real salt is the true exposition of scripture, which denounces the whole world and lets nothing stand but the simple faith in Christ" (*LW*, 21:59).

The salt of Mt. 5:13 is the doctrine of salvation by faith alone: "This is why I have always admonished, as Christ is doing here, that the salt should remain salt and not lose its taste, that we prop-erly teach the chief article of faith" (*LW*, 21:59-60). This is in harmony with the preface to Luther's discourses on the Sermon on the Mount, in which he repeatedly emphasizes his aim to restore the pure teaching of Christ, giving his interpretation its distinctive doctrinal and apologetic character.

While the salt is the negative proclamation of what Christian theology is not, and the apologetic correction of false doctrine, the light is the positive preaching "to instruct souls and guide them to eternal life." This interpretation allows Luther to reinforce his polemics against the Roman Church. The "light of the world" of which Christ is speaking, "must be authoritative and adequately enlighten the whole world," while the Roman Catholic teachings he regards as "merely human regulations" (*LW*, 21:61).

Luther requires this ministry of light to be public and not secret in any way; he is here speaking of the preaching office only.[4] He attacks both targets for his general polemics, the Roman Catholics and the Baptists. Though the Roman clergy are properly called for their ministry, they are unfaithful stewards of their calling. The Baptists are attempting to exercise a ministry they are not properly called to, for which reason they are "schismatic spirits" (*LW*, 21:63). The true ministers of Christ work in the tension between the proper calling and commissioning on one side, and the proclamation of true doctrine on the other. The constitution of the Christian minister is neither any kind of new character of the minister bestowed in ordination (cf. Roman Catholics), nor a spiritual equipment (cf. Baptists), but a public commissioning by the Church.

Interpreting Mt. 5:16, Luther is critical of the way works are discussed in the synoptic gospels. A dichotomy is established between faith and works. He finds that St. John and St. Paul are more basic, "First and highest is the proclamation about faith and Christ, then comes the emphasis upon works" (*LW*, 21:65). His aim is to give a balanced assessment of the four gospels in their interrelations as well as their relations with the Pauline writings. According to his *ordo salutis*, faith has the absolute primacy. This fact does not completely eliminate the impression, however, that the biblical authors which are emphasizing works more strongly than faith, have a lesser value to him than do the others; "the profound doctrine of Christ" apparently implies a stronger emphasis on justification by faith alone, than he observes in the gospel of St. Matthew.

Luther does not exclude works from the Christian life, his concern is rather to define their character as fruits of faith. It is particularly important that works are not separated from faith as their source: "You must always connect them with faith and incorporate them in it, making them a result and a concomitant of faith" (*LW*, 21:65). These works do by no means come from any inherent holiness of the Christian, however, they are the results of the believer's relationship to God. He is here reinforcing the theological basis for his doctrine of the Christian as *simul iustus et peccator*.

The light of the world, too, has to do with doctrinal teaching about how the Christian life is to be, that is, to remain hidden and secret. This light is the expression of orthodoxy, it is a cognitive response to the gospel, and it is reserved for the limited number of properly called preachers.

The intention is not to isolate doctrine from life. On the contrary, Luther concludes his interpretation of the pericope: "First we should constantly teach and emphasize faith, and then we should live according to faith" (*LW*, 21:67). He here repeats his point from the interpretation of the beatitudes, that Christ in the Sermon on the Mount first deals with spiritual life and faith in God, and, secondly, that this faith should be expressed faithfully in the civil stations of the secular kingdom. The life "according to faith" is loyalty to God's created order, faithful government of superiors, and obedience to superiors.

The Law (5:17-20)

To Luther, Christ here rejects the moralists "who are teaching God's commandments and performing holy acts of worship every day," namely, "the pope and his mob" who are "denouncing us and accusing us of heresy for prohibiting good works" (*LW*, 21:67). He feels that the historical situation is compatible with the religious situation predicted by Christ, but the Reformation has come to fulfil the Law and the Prophets. The Roman Catholics are about to abolish the law, but the Reformation restores its true meaning.

The problem is, the Roman Catholics as well as Luther "are appealing to the same scripture and laying claim to one Gospel and one Word of God" (*LW*, 21:68). What is right? The situation described by Matthew is parallel to his own:

> He [Christ] is not denying that they are God's people and that they have the Law, the fathers, and the prophets. Nor are we condemning or denying that under the pope there were Christians or Baptism or the Gospel, but we are saying: "What we have is the right Baptism and Gospel." We protest against ... the demonic addition of their cowls, tonsures, indulgences, purgatory, and sacrificial masses (*LW*, 21:68-69).

The dividing line between Roman Catholicism and the Reformation is the issue of right and pure doctrine. The continuation of the Reformation, which started in Wittenberg 1517, is basic to Luther's interpretation of the teaching of the Law. He does not reject the papal church as non-Christian but attempts to highlight abuses that need to be changed.

Luther is critical of Augustine's interpretation of the Sermon on the Mount on this point. Augustine affirms that the fulfillment of the law implies to supplement its deficiencies, and to carry out its content (Augustine, 28). Luther rejects the first point made by Augustine, for "no one, not even Christ Himself, can improve upon the Law" (*LW*, 21:69). Nor can it be any higher teaching than that of the First Commandment of loving God wholeheartedly (Deut. 6:5). What remains is Augustine's last implication, to carry out the content of the law. In order to avoid the Scholastic teaching of grace, which actually is "supplementing" the Law, Luther insists that Christ here is talking of "that fulfilling which takes place through teaching" (*LW*, 21:69).

To imply that grace supplements the human capacity in order to secure salvation by the merits of the law, is a semi-Pelagian distortion of the gospel. To Luther, Christ's intention is not ethical but cognitive and doctrinal, the teaching of the right doctrine of the law. What this right teaching of the Law is, he will establish through his comments on the antitheses.

Luther interprets Mt. 5:18 by referring to his own historical context. He attacks the Roman Catholic abolishment of the basic Christian doctrine, justification by faith in Christ. He also relates this attack to his criticism of the double standard doctrine. These issues are interrelated.

In the first place, Augustine introduces the double standard model of interpretation precisely at this point. He first prepares the ground by referring to "the things which are added to bring about perfection" (Augustine, 29), and then, in commenting on the first antithesis (Mt. 5:21-26), he uses the double standard doctrine as his hermeneutical key.

As Luther views it, the basis of the double standard doctrine is that there are various levels of perfection. The evangelical counsels are for those persons who aspire for a higher level of perfection, but these works are not required for salvation. Contrary to this position, Luther insists that the outward fulfillment of the law in no way merits salvation. Justification is wrought by faith and grace only. Once justified, the believer is fully perfected in the same moment because of the imputation of the perfection of Christ. No levels of perfection exist, because the only perfection one can speak of in the spiritual kingdom, is the perfection of Christ.

Luther's comments on Mt. 5:19-20 are determined by his polemical position against the Roman Catholics. He refers to the Diet of Augsburg (1530), where the opponents of the Reformation admitted that "our [the Lutheran] confession is purely scriptural and does not conflict with any article of faith" (*LW*, 21:71). The debate rather was concerning "the additional things that have been decreed for them by the councils and the popes" (*LW*, 21:71), and that he considered to be amendments to the gospel. This is a serious accusation, because he can never be reconciled with persons who neglect pure Christian doctrine as well as its consequences, the life of the stations and offices:

> Since they ... want to make us forsake Christ and pure doctrine which they themselves cannot criticize, we repudiate them ... In short, everything that the Lord demands here on the basis of God's commandment they have made nonobligatory, as if these were merely bits of good advice or works of supererogation. (*LW*, 21:71-72)

Luther concludes his interpretation of Mt. 5:19 by commenting on how the law is to be fulfilled "at the same time we teach that no man can fulfil it," stating that,

> We cannot be justified or saved through the teaching of the Law, which only brings us to the knowledge of ourselves ... Once we have become Christians through Baptism and faith, we do as much as we can. Still we can never take our stand before God on this basis, but we must always creep to Christ. He has fulfilled it all purely and perfectly, and He gives Himself to us, together

> with His fulfillment. Through Him we can take our stand before
> God, and the Law cannot incriminate or condemn us. So ... all
> must be accomplished and fulfilled even to the smallest dot, but
> only through this one Man. (*LW*, 21:72-73)

The "great chief doctrine" referred to is the doctrine of justification. Christ is here speaking about the role and function of the law
in the economy of salvation. The law cannot provide salvation, it
can only give us a recognition of sin. Nor is any help of the law
necessary for the work of salvation, because it is fulfilled by
Christ. Whatever human beings do according to the commandments of the law, it does not improve their status before God. Luther consequently removes the law from the sphere of soteriology
(Lerfeldt 1977:57). The Mosaic law is applicable only when it
overlaps the natural law (Edwards 1975:54).

Luther's interpretation of the law is most significant for his
theology, forming the image of God, Christology, anthropology,
soteriology, the relations between gospel and law, and ethics. Salvation is necessary as well as possible because God is just. God is
dishonored because the holy law is violated. Humanity is without
capacity to fulfil the requirements of the law. The law must therefore be fulfilled by a perfect human being on behalf of humanity;
that is what happened in Christ. Here are elements of a theory of
atonement and of a Christology that focuses on the human side of
Christ and his capacity to do what the law requires; Christ is in this
context pictured as a perfect ethical human being. There is no need
to fulfil the law because Christ has done so on behalf of the sinners. He affirms, "It is true that the law must be fulfilled to the
smallest jot, but only through this one man Who has fulfilled it
purely and perfectly, and Who gives Himself to us with His fulfillment" (Siggins 1970:102, with reference to *LW*, 21:72-73).

The Antitheses (5:21-48)
Luther introduces his exhortations on the antitheses by commenting that Mt. 5:21-48 teaches the kind of righteousness which exceeds that of the scribes and Pharisees, "to illumine for them the
real piety which the Law demands, as Christ will now show" (*LW*,

21:73). This piety is doctrinal in character: "Here He [Christ] begins the correct explanation of several of the Ten Commandments" (*LW*, 21:74). It will be established that the antitheses have great impact on his interpretation of the Sermon on the Mount as a whole. The exegesis of the antitheses actually contributes significantly to the development of his theology and to his ethics.

On Anger (5:21-26)

Luther accuses "our papists" for eliminating the implications of Christ's word. By interpreting the commandment in a strict literal way they particularly fail to take their hatred into consideration. He rejects their interpretation of the antitheses as evangelical counsels, advised for those who aim at a higher perfection only. Real holiness should take the law of God seriously, he insists.

But Luther himself faces hermeneutical problems in recommending Christian officials to sentence criminals to death, and Christian soldiers to kill their enemies, however, without hatred in their hearts (for instance, *LW*, 21:113). Explaining why his rejection of the scholastic argument does not destroy his own interpretation, he admits that sins must be punished, and that "the government must be angry" in order to protect the social order. There is "an anger of love, one that wishes no one any evil, one that is friendly to the person but hostile to the sin" (*LW*, 21:76).

According to Luther's hermeneutics, the doctrine of the two kingdoms establishes the dividing line between right and wrong exegesis. In the spiritual kingdom the commandment is to be understood literally as taught by Christ. But in the secular kingdom it is different. Christ's teachings do not apply to everyday life in the world where reason and the imperial law rather than the Sermon on the Mount govern Christian conduct.

This hermeneutics of the two kingdoms is basic to all of Luther's writings. For instance, his catechisms and his sermons are based on the two kingdoms doctrine, too (*LW*, 51:152-153). He there condemns persons who do not prevent evil-doing against their neighbor. In such cases love is expressed through the use of violence, though not performed in anger and hatred.

In the commentary to Mt. 5:25-26, Luther focuses upon the person being persecuted: "the injured party should also be willing to be reconciled and to forgive" (*LW*, 21:82). The only exception is when the secular kingdom is involved. Victims of persecution or violence should be revenged and punished "where your office requires it, there you must be angry, even though no injury has been done to you personally" (*LW*, 21:83).

There is no doubt, the hermeneutical key for his interpretation of the first antithesis is the doctrine of the two kingdoms. One might expect that the same is the case for the rest of the Sermon on the Mount.

On Adultery and Divorce (5:27-32)

Because of their neglect of the adultery of the heart, Luther accuses his opponents of making adultery easier (*LW*, 21:85-86). He condemns both the narrowest and the broadest interpretations of Christ's saying. On the one hand, he emphasizes that the commandment should include more than the physical commitment of adultery alone, as the issue is the adultery of the heart. On the other hand, he does not give credit to persons who run away from situations where the commandments are tested in real life, but he protests against the monastic demand for chastity. What Christ forbids is not the looking at women, but the lusting:

> He does want us to distinguish between looking and lusting. You may look at any woman or man, only be sure that you do not lust. That is why God has ordained for every person to have his own wife or husband, to control and channel his lust and his appetites ...
>
> When a man does not look at his wife, on the basis of the Word of God, as the one whom God gives him and whom He blesses, and when instead he turns his gaze to another woman, this is the principal cause of adultery. (*LW*, 21:86)

Luther here reveals that his prime rationale for marriage is the containment of sexual desires. He regards marriage to be essentially remedial, and never upgrades the social partnership as a principal aim (Rublack 1985:267). As a contribution to his contemporary discussion whether it is "sinful for a man and a woman to desire each other for the purpose of marriage," he comments that, if it were not for the sexual lust, the husband and the wife would have more frequently left each other. For that reason we can understand "that the sexual union of husband and wife is also most pleasing to Him [God]" (*LW*, 21:89; 373).

A distinction is also made between involuntary or accidental evil thoughts, and habitual lusting. Luther agrees with Thomas Aquinas' statement that "If an evil thought is involuntary, it is not a mortal sin."[5] He makes his point by quoting one of the Church Fathers, "I cannot keep a bird from flying over my head. But I can certainly keep it from nesting in my hair or from biting my nose off" (*LW*, 21:88).[6] The issue is not how to keep evil thoughts and temptations away, but how to "Keep them from taking root" (*LW*, 21:89).

Luther follows the same hermeneutical course as he continues his discussion of divorce. His general view is that this issue belongs to the lawyers and governments of the secular kingdom,

> For marriage is a rather secular and outward thing, having to do with wife and children, house and home, and with other matters that belong to the kingdom of the government, all of which have been completely subjected to reason. (Gen. 1:28; *LW*, 21:93)

Significant ideas are implied: (1) Matters concerning marriage and divorce ought to be regulated by civil legislation because they are related to the life in the stations. Marriage is a divine ordinance however set in worldly law as a part of the charge God has independently given to the secular government. (2) Christ is not prescribing laws but instructing the consciences of how to deal with civil law. Civil marriage and divorce legislation, as well as the pattern of coupling between man and woman, basically are in harmony with the will of God. (3) Christian ethics is here related to the revelation of Christ exclusively and not to reason. By making this distinction he implies that there are two different sets of Christian ethics. There is one universal ethic for the entire humanity that is based on the natural recognition of God's will by reason, and one ethic which is revealed to Christians only. Regarded as ethics, the Sermon on the Mount belongs to the last set. Therefore, it offers no ethics for the world but for Christians-in-person only.

Luther's general view on divorce and remarriage probably is in harmony with the absolutist hermeneutical tradition, emphasizing that divorce from the beginning was contrary to the original will of God, but permitted for the sake of "your hard hearts" (Mt. 19:8; *LW*, 21:94).

In Luther's understanding adultery is a legitimate cause of divorce. Within the context of the Mosaic legislation, which punished adultery with death (Lev. 20:10), the admission of remarriage is self-evident, because the death of the adulterous spouse has abolished the first marriage (*LW*, 21:96). At first he takes a rigorist position on the issues of divorce and remarriage. He then declares that the secular law ought to be followed in these matters, regardless of what they may prescribe. A genuine Christian attitude is expressed by the forgiveness of an adulterous spouse without using the legitimate right to divorce. The issue of remarriage, however, is not a matter of spiritual ethics but should be left to the civil authorities.

On Oaths (5:33-37)

Luther rejects a general and absolutist interpretation of this antithesis because of the necessity of an accurate distinction between the two kingdoms. He repeats that

> Christ has no intention here of interfering in the order of the secular kingdom, nor of depriving the government of anything. All He is preaching about is how individual Christians should behave in their everyday life. Therefore swearing should be thought of as forbidden in exactly the same sense as killing or looking at a woman and desiring her was forbidden earlier. Killing is right, yet it is also wrong. Desiring a man or a woman is sinful, and it is not sinful. That is to say, we must take the proper distinction here. (*LW*, 21:99)

Each of the two kingdoms has its separate regulations and rules for ethical conduct, and these demands may be contradictory. Luther replaces the Roman Catholic double standard doctrine, which reserves the commandments of the Sermon on the Mount for the persons seeking for a higher perfection, with a double standard doctrine of his own. The double standards he is teaching are not related to different persons but to the same person in different situations or relations. When the Christian is "individual," that is, "in person" and not "in office," she or he has the obligation not to kill, not to look at the other sex with lust, and not to swear. When the Christian is "in office," however, the Christian judge and soldier must kill, the Christian husband and wife should have sexual desires for their spouses, and the Christian citizen is required to swear oaths for the court.

Luther's criticism of the Pharisees is that "they had developed a distinction between oaths that were valid and those that were not, thus allowing people to swear freely" (*LW*, 21:100). He, too, distinguishes between valid and invalid oaths, but the difference is that he does not allow "people to swear freely" (*LW*, 21:101). When it comes to the official responsibilities of the Christian, however, the situation is different. The needs of the neighbor, too, may call for oaths at occasions.

Luther here introduces two new principles. He is stating explicitly that the government and the offices of the secular kingdom are not to be confused with the Gospel. On the contrary, he strongly affirms the autonomy of the secular institutions and regulations over against the spiritual kingdom. In addition to the oath sworn when required by the civil court, love, too, may claim an oath of a Christian. To act in love in the spiritual kingdom is superior to the outward observance of the law, provided that Christ's commandment may be understood as "law" at this point. In the secular kingdom, love does not exclude civil laws and regulations, however, love is the motive of the heart while carrying the laws out into practice.

On Retaliation (5:38-42)

Luther joins a long exegetic tradition affirming that the last two antitheses of Christ's exposition of the Decalogue, Mt. 5:38-48, contain the sum of the Sermon on the Mount, or at least they are providing the key to their hermeneutics. Luther shares this tradition. The issues of non-violence and love to the neighbor probably raise the exegetic paradox that leads him to formulate the doctrine of the two kingdoms as the solution of this dilemma.

On Violence (5:38-41)

Luther is not happy with the traditional exegesis of this scripture. His polemics is on the one hand directed against the Roman Catholic confusion of the kingdoms because of the church's desire to exercise temporal power. On the other hand, it is also directed against the Baptist confusion of the kingdoms by applying God's law, the Sermon on the Mount included, to the secular kingdom. A pure Christian theology must distinguish carefully between the two kingdoms. This doctrine is as decisive for Christian orthodoxy as the doctrine of justification by faith. Christ's exegesis of the ten commandments should not be understood as related to the secular kingdom but to the spiritual kingdom exclusively. He particularly rejects political ambitions of the common people,[7] "For we have been transferred to another and higher existence, a divine and an eternal kingdom, where the things that belong to the world are unnecessary" (*LW*, 21:106-108).

The rationale for Luther's position at this point is his eschatology. The last quote should not be understood as escapism from this world, as numerous sayings elsewhere prove that he definitely roots the human life into the life of the world. Because human beings are created beings, a life apart from this world will deny the will of the Creator. His point is that salvation has nothing to do with this world; his "otherworldliness" is purely soteriological and not social. The works in this world can never merit salvation, nor can salvation change the order of the life in the world.

Salvation concerns persons and this world deals with offices. The aim of salvation is not to govern the world, for the created order is perfect in itself. The written law of God is given for sote-riological purposes only by its constant reminding of Christians of their total inability to earn their righteousness before God, and not for the purpose of civil administration. Business is left to the of-fices that are authorized to deal with matters of that kind. To sup-port the social structure is a significant concern to Luther. God is calling all Christians to sustain the created order by faithful work in the offices and stations. In this way everything will be according to the will of God.

The distinction between the person and the office is crucial to Luther. The justified Christian's attitudes to society and to social behavior are basically unchanged. But the life of the world has nothing to do with the spiritual life. The reason for this is the theological concern to avoid a "false righteousness," or, the confu-sion between the unmerited and alien righteousness of the Chris-tian and the proper righteousness that the Christian has as a human being and a citizen in the world. Consequently, the doctrine of the two kingdoms has soteriological significance as a safeguard against the false conception of meritorious works.

At the same time the doctrine provides the mandate for the ethical obligations of the Christian to the world, implying works of the Christian but without confusing them with the righteousness belonging to the spiritual kingdom. The only link between the two righteousnesses may possibly be that, according to Luther, the reborn Christian reinforces his or her motivation to enter the duties of secular society faithfully because of the deepened recognition of the created world and secular society as ordered by God. The good Christian, therefore, faithfully performs his or her responsibilities in the stations and offices.

Luther's presupposition is that no Christian is entirely spiritual; he or she also belongs to the world and the secular society with their regulations. The Christian therefore is two persons in one. As a secular person she or he is ruled by the laws of the civil world, and as a spiritual person he or she is ruled by the commandments of the Sermon on the Mount.

Christ's command to turn the other cheek raises the issue of pacifism over against the use of violent means in conflict solving in Luther. His tracts *Against the Robbing and Murdering Hordes of Peasants* (*LW*, 46:45-55; cf. his letter to John Ruehel, May 4, 1525; *LW*, 49:106-112) and *An Open Letter on the Harsh Book against the Peasants* (1525; *LW*, 46:57-85) and *Whether Soldiers, Too, Can Be Saved* (1526; *LW*, 46:87-137) reveal his practical use of the doctrine of the two kingdoms on this point. In the first tract mentioned, he condemns the peasants because of their violation of the social order:

> they are starting a rebellion, and are violently robbing and plun-
> dering monasteries and castles which are not theirs; by this they
> have doubly deserved death in body and soul as highwaymen
> and murderers. ... Therefore let everyone who can, smite, slay,
> and stab, secretly or openly, remembering that nothing can be
> more poisonous, hurtful, or devilish than a rebel. It is just as
> when one must kill a mad dog; if you do not strike him, he will
> strike you, and a whole land with you. (*LW*, 46:50)

"The temporal authorities" must realize that they are in the place of God. Therefore there should be "no place for patience or mercy. This is the time of the sword, not the day of grace." Besides, "anyone who is killed on the side of the rulers may be a true martyr in the eyes of God" (*LW*, 46:52-53).

In his second tract Luther does not weaken this strict position. On the contrary, he reaffirms that the punishment of the peasants is the duty of the government as the representative of the secular kingdom. The last tract concludes, on the basis of the doctrine of the two kingdoms, that the sword is the instrument of the secular kingdom: "there is no doubt that the military profession is in itself a legitimate and godly calling and occupation" (*LW*, 46:100).

To be a Christian is to be a spiritual person ruled by the teachings revealed in the Sermon on the Mount. At the same time, the Christian is also a civil person with specific offices in relation to other persons. The rules of the offices have a totally different character. They are the civil laws and regulations of the society. When the Christian is in-person, he or she is controlled by the spirit and the ethos of the Sermon on the Mount. Consequently, the Christian

has to be related to, and regulated by, two different and often contrasting sets of rules. The relation to other persons determine
which norms are actually in function. In the spiritual kingdom,
when the Christians are in-person, her or his conduct is regulated
by the commandments of the Sermon on the Mount or other parts
of God's revealed will. In the secular kingdom "the imperial or the
territorial law" provide the guidelines (*LW*, 21:109-110). Luther
presupposes that an identity exists between the natural law, human
reason, and the secular law. Because they all are made by God,
they are serving as proper standards for the ethical life in the
world. There is no Christian ethics apart from the natural law.

From the standpoint of the secular kingdom, there is no difference between Christians and heathens. There is a difference between them in the spiritual kingdom only: Christians are righteous
in both kingdoms; in the secular kingdom they have their own,
proper righteousness according to the faithful obedience of the
civil authorities. In the spiritual kingdom they have been imputed
God's righteousness as their alien righteousness because of their
faith in Christ. Heathens are, no less than Christians, righteous in
the secular kingdom.[8] In their outward ethical conduct Christians
and heathens follow the same codes. But in their judgments or in
their punishing acts, Christians carry neither hatred nor vindictiveness in their hearts. Outwardly, they are basically the same, but
inwardly Christians are driven by love.

Luther also distinguishes between the heart and the outward
life. The purity of the heart is a matter of love or hate. A pure heart
is filled with love. In that case, "everything is right and well done,"
either when the Christian is in-relation or in office, or the Christian
is in-person. If the heart is filled with hatred or vindictiveness, it is
not right, whether the Christian is in office or not.

Luther's solution of the dilemma of combining two different
and contradictory sets of rules in one and the same person, is to
distinguish between the "heart" and the outward behavior. When a
Christian-in-person seeks revenge, it is a violation of the secular
order. But for a Christian-in-office to go to court is a social obligation, because this contributes to protect the society from a
threatening chaos. The spiritual kingdom is significant by influ-

encing the heart of the Christian as a public person; the Christian judge or soldier carries the punishing sword, but with a loving heart without hatred and revenge. When it comes to the outward life, however, the spiritual kingdom has no influence upon the actual behavior. Then the rules of the secular kingdom are in function.

A significant function of the doctrine of the two kingdoms is that it makes it possible to isolate issues like violence, military, police, etc., from the spiritual domain. These issues have to do with the protection of social order. In any situation where the Christian is in-relation, he or she is both secular and spiritual at the same time, spiritual when it comes to attitudes and compassions, secular when it comes to actual behavior. The same is the case with issues like division of property, trade, and other matters of business. All these issues are to be dealt with according to reason, secular regulations, and ordinary capitalistic-monetary rules.

If the secular authorities are unjust and contrary to the will of God, Luther answers: "We have to suffer anyway, since as individual persons we have no power or defense against the government if it should set itself against us" (*LW*, 21:115). When the secular law is turned against the Christian, she or he has to suffer without resistance. The only possible reaction is obedience and submissiveness.

On Economy (5:42)

By interpreting this scripture Luther engaged in a historical situation still being in transition.[9] He no doubt contributed significantly by settling some of the burning issues in the field of economics. Apart from the references to these problems in his discourses on the Sermon on the Mount and other places, he explicitly deals with them in his tract *Trade and Usury* (*LW*, 45:231-310).

Luther states that Christ in this scripture is not preaching about the general distribution of money and property and about rules for business, for this is regulated by reason and the secular or imperial law. Christ does not deal with the division of property, or with business, but how a Christian-in-person should respond to begging for alms. In such cases the Christian should give and lend willingly and happily. But the Christian must take care that she or he is not abused by scoundrels who are too lazy to work for their own food. This concern occupies about two-thirds of his commentary on the verse. He introduces the idea of a church-related secular office with the authority to control who may be declared to be worthy beggars. It is hard not to get the overall impression, however, that his major concern is to limit as much as possible the number of persons who qualify for alms.

Luther's attitudes to the poor are not revealed in fullness in these comments. The true imitation of Christ is to become a servant, like He was, and give oneself to the neighbor in sacrificial service. He describes elsewhere this relationship between Christ and the neighbor as a sacramental and covenantal community, the basis of which is "Christ's sacrifice of love, making the believers one body or 'loaf' with Christ and therefore also with each other" (Althaus 1981:304).

The reason why Luther deals so much with unworthy beggars is his specific historical context, particularly that the number of persons who were voluntarily poor for religious reasons increased enormously in 16th-century Germany (Scharffenorth 1982:318). For instance, he is concerned with the left wing of the Reformation, the Baptists and the spiritualists among the peasants.

Some spiritualists interpreted the Sermon on the Mount to be a literal law for this world (G.H. Williams 1962). The Amosites interpreted its message to make suffering and poverty basic Christian virtues. The Waldensians claimed that the Christians' private property ought to be sold and given to the poor, after which Christian communes should be established. The Hutterites believed that the unity with Christ and the true imitation of him could not be achieved without giving up private property. According to their terminology, *Gemeinschaft* connoted both fellowship and the community of goods. The church was regarded as a provisional paradise. The Taborites, due to their religious expectations of a prospective society of sharing, attempted to transfer God's commandments to the laws of society. As a matter of fact, they grounded their insistence on community of goods in the oneness of

Christ with the Father on one hand and the oneness of Christ with his followers on the other. Their ideas were not very far from Luther's in their origin. But he could neither approve their claim of poverty as a virtue, nor could he accept their violations of the economic order.

Historical evidence indicates that social problems were created by the Baptist ideals of poverty. They came on the top of the old problems caused by the mendicant monks. Luther restricts, therefore, the obligation of giving and lending, because he is concerned that the Christian should not give or lend to people who ought to be able to take care of themselves. He stresses the importance of refusing alms to "lazy bums" to the degree that he proposes to seek assistance from "your secular person," or that the church in "every city should have church officials to determine who these people are and how they live, so as not to let any of the lazy bums become a burden to other people" (*LW*, 21:118). Consequently, it is hard to resist the impression that keeping away from the "unworthy" beggar is more important to Luther's understanding of Mt. 5:42 than the positive commandment to give to the "worthy" neighbor who has legitimate needs.

On Love for Enemies (5:43-48)

The issue of this antithesis is the disposition of heart with which the Christian should meet the world. Luther now states that it is also necessary to distinguish between the person and the office because the office does not belong to the person, but to God. The person who carries an office is merely an instrument in God's hand. It is therefore wrong for a person who is commissioned, not to administer the office. The offices are ordered by the Word of God, and God's Word has to be placed above everything else.

These considerations lead Luther to affirm that the commandment of love for enemies is not to be understood absolutely. A personal enemy of the Christian should be loved, but there is no commandment of loving the enemy of God and God's Word.

Luther defines love "to be good-hearted and to wish the best, to have a heart that is friendly, kind, and sweet toward everyone"

(*LW*, 21:122), to be friendly, and to do "cordial works" (*LW*, 21:123). This love, however, is limited to the personal life of the Christian; the dominant issue is not the dichotomy between spiritual and secular, but that between person and office.

Being in conflict, the secular regulations are prior to the spiritual. No personal suffering should be revenged by the Christian, because God will take care of it. The punishment should be left to God who has authorized instruments for that, namely, the offices of the secular kingdom. A Christian should meet personal attacks and violence with non-resistance and love. But as the holder of a judging office, the very same Christian has to represent God's punishment of the evil-doer. The point is that the Christian "in person" accepts evil and loves her or his enemy, while "in office" the enemy is judged and punished for the protection of God's created order. By the Christian's administration of the office with a loving heart this administration is completely free from revenge and hatred. Love is made the basic principle for the conduct in both kingdoms, even if the actual conduct is to punish the evil-doer.

At the end of the antithesis, Luther comments upon the perfection taught in Mt. 5:48. He rejects the interpretation of the canonical scholars, who apply perfection to the monastical and ecclesiastical hierarchies, thus causing that "perfection" becomes completely inapplicable to the ordinary Christian way of life, as if such people could not be called perfect or be perfect. But Christ is actually, he insists, "talking here ... to all Christians who are His pupils, who want to be called the sons of God" (*LW*, 21:128-129). By this comment he returns to the theme introduced at the beginning of his discourses; the Sermon on the Mount is to be applied to every Christian person and not to a limited group of clergy only. Perfection is, consequently, applicable to any Christian. He explains further that perfection is not a state without sin but, first, a perfection of doctrinal purity, and, secondly, a perfection of life. On this doctrinal basis Luther interprets perfection in categories of love, being "an entire, whole, and undivided love, where one loves and helps his enemy as well as his friend" (*LW*, 21:129).

Luther defines perfection negatively as not being sinless, and positively as being undivided love. He seems to imply a plea for human efforts in the search for perfection, that is more obvious in the German text than in the English translation: "Only we must keep striving for it, and moving and progressing toward it every day" (*WA*, 32:406; *LW*, 21:129). Rather than implying an inherent holiness, however, his concern is doctrinal perfection, as his theological basis is the doctrine of *simul iustus et peccator*:

> This happens when the spirit is master over the flesh, holding it in check, subduing and restraining it, in order not to give it room to act contrary to this teaching. It happens when I let love move along on the true middle course, treating everyone alike and excluding no one. Then I have true Christian perfection, which is not restricted to special offices or stations, but is common to all Christians, and should be. It forms and fashions itself according to the example of the heavenly Father. (*LW*, 21:129)

Christian perfection is here not a question of renewal of human nature, but the domain of the spiritual powers over human flesh. The sin remains, but it is controlled by the spirit.

Furthermore, perfection is not, according to Luther, tied to "special offices or stations" but "to all Christians." This is an attack on the specific ecclesiastical offices. Contrary to the canonical scholars he places the life of Christian perfection in the life in the secular offices and stations. The same he does with the concept of holiness; cf. his comment on perfection to Mt. 6:14-15: To be perfect is to love and to believe correctly. He here designs a hierarchy of orders in which love is made a "general order" with priority before the natural orders of preaching, family, and government. This is in full harmony with his hierarchy of ethical norms as it is observed above.

The Three "Works" (6:1-18)

A shift in the outline of the Sermon on the Mount occurs between the 5th and the 6th chapters of Matthew. Luther describes this shift by observing that Christ attacks the good works of the Pharisees.

Consequently, the shift in outline resembles a shift in polemics, from doctrine to Pharisaic styles of life. His suggested outline of Mt. 6:1-18 indicates that he still operates within the frame of "public and private" (*LW*, 21:155), or within the doctrine of the two kingdoms.

Alms-giving (6:1-4)
Luther observes that Christ does not reject alms-giving in itself but the "purpose and aim" of the Pharisees' alms-giving (*LW*, 21:131). He implies that people are too much concerned about being honored for their generosity and thereby ruin the intentions of the alms-giving, which is to give for God's sake out of a pure heart. Again, he is critical of the hermit monasticism.

Because of this emphasis on motivation "no one can do a truly good work unless he is a Christian" (*LW*, 21:134). This saying is related to the spiritual kingdom, for within the secular kingdom men and women have their own righteousness with a full capacity to do good works. Good works are works without the slightest intention of gaining merits. Probably, Luther refers to persons who hold the doctrine of salvation by faith alone. His ethics is an ethics of intention and not one of consequence, the focus is on the motivation and purpose of the heart.

Prayer (i) (6:5-15)
Luther defines praying as "another work that is appropriate to the Christian." It is a good work because of its motivation; it is not looking out for one's own advantage (*LW*, 21:137). But for that reason "praying is a rare work, which no one does but Christians. At the same time, it was very common in the world ... There is no shortage of praying" (*LW*, 21:138). The Roman Catholic clergy is the target of his attack, especially because of its economic exploitation of the people. He already indicates this criticism by the publication of the 95 theses October 31, 1517 (*LW*, 31:175, 176, 206, 208, 247).

According to Luther, the theory as well as the actual experience of being a Christian *simul iustus et peccator*, provides the best incentive for prayer. Because the Christian remains a sinner, "the praying should continue in the heart almost without interruption." Christ condemns neither formal praying nor formulated prayers but "the false motive of praying for sake of the appearance of reputation or anything of that sort" (*LW*, 21:139). He calls the daily prayers "a precious thing and a powerful defense against the devil and his assaults" (*LW*, 21:140). At this point he replaces the ritual praying of the clergy with that of the household. The notion of prayer as a mystical force against the powers of chaos, which were connected to the instant ritual praying, he applies also to family praying.

The components and characteristics of "every real prayer" are, the urging of God's command to pray; God's promise to listen to prayers; the examination of our burdens, which we carry to God and pour out before him; true faith, based on God's word and promise.

Luther now implements the characteristics of prayer mentioned above on the practice of prayer of the contemporary clergy. He rejects formulated prayers which are not related to the actual needs. That kind of praxis actually distorts prayer and turns it to be "merely slave labor of their mouths or their tongues" (*LW*, 21:142). By the same reason there is no necessity for long prayers; their quality is far more important than their quantity.

Luther then turns to the issue of why prayer is necessary. It is not necessary to inform God, who is all-knowing. "By praying, therefore, we are instructing ourselves more than we are Him. It makes me turn around so that I do not proceed as do the ungodly, neither acknowledging this nor thanking Him for it" (*LW*, 21:144). The basic need for prayer is the need for self-instruction, particularly focusing on the Christian as a sinner with a need for daily conversion.

In general Luther replaces liturgical prayers of the Church with family prayers. In his introduction to *The Lord's Prayer*, he emphasizes its functions within this context. For the detailed interpretation of the Lord's Prayer, Luther refers to his comments elsewhere.[10] He summarizes some basic ideas that need to be considered. First, the Lord's Prayer has two main parts, the first part related to the spiritual kingdom, and the second to the secular kingdom. The distinction between the kingdoms does not exclude the possibility that the description of the needs of the secular kingdom are penetrating even the petitions of the spiritual kingdom. He identifies in the Lord's Prayer "three most important elements" (*LW*, 21:146), which are: The doctrine of salvation by faith alone is related to the spiritual kingdom only. Secondly, the dwelling of God's kingdom in us refers to God's dominion in the secular kingdom as well, which is God's kingdom no less than the spiritual kingdom. Even if the spiritual kingdom is primary in the prayer, there is also an implied reference to the secular kingdom. Thirdly, the interrelation of the spiritual and the secular kingdoms is apparent; God has established the secular kingdom in order to secure that God's will is done in the world and society. In conclusion, Luther's faith in the kingdom of God aims at bringing humanity closer to this world thus making us more concerned about how to realize the will of God on earth.

Luther in the first main part of the Lord's Prayer points to the contrast between God's kingdom and the evil or demonic powers of this world. The first part of the prayer on the spiritual kingdom is penetrated by the secular world, and the second part of the prayer on the secular kingdom is penetrated by the spiritual. The first and third parts are dealing with "our daily bread—that is, everything necessary for the preservation of this life," and, "is brought on by the fact that we are living on earth." The second part is, on the contrary, dealing with the forgiveness of our trespasses. "The glory" he interprets as the honor and praise which "belongs only to God," adding that God may be honored through holders of God's offices, too. When I honor my father and mother, "I am not doing this to a human being but to a divine office, and I am honoring God in them. Wherever there is authority and power, therefore, the glory and the praise belong to him" (*LW*, 21:148). He comes close to identifying God's rule with the government of the lords in the world at this point. He makes God a part of the power systems of the world by joining the Roman Catholic tradition before him. On the other hand he identifies the civil authorities with the representatives of God's power, over against the church.

Luther now raises the notion of Christian perfection, and he reinforces his views observed to his interpretation of Mt. 5:48 (cf. *LW*, 21:129). He avoids the notion of merits, suggesting that Christ, by

> connecting the forgiveness of sin with our forgiving ... had the special purpose of making mutual love a Christian obligation, and the continual forgiveness of the neighbor the primary and foremost duty of Christians, second only to faith and the reception of forgiveness. As we live in faith toward Him, therefore, so also we should live in love toward our neighbor ... When this is the case, the Christian man is perfect, he believes correctly, and he loves correctly. Whatever other faults he may have, these are to be consumed in his prayer, and it is all forgiven and remitted. (*LW*, 21:149)

Luther's concept of perfection is based on forgiveness rather than growth in grace and does by no means include sinless perfection. Its basis is a doctrinally correct faith. This perfection is based in its relation to Christ and it is actual in its relation to neighborly love. He conceives perfection as related to the Christian as *simul iustus et peccator*, as there is a "close connection between forgiveness and our works ... we should confirm our possession of faith and the forgiveness of sin by showing our works, making the tree manifest by means of its fruit" (*LW*, 21:149-150). Together with his preference of orthodoxy in doctrinal matters, good works are estimated in a positive way, provided they are understood as fruits of faith and not as merits for the purpose of salvation.

In *The Freedom of a Christian* (1520; *LW*, 31:327-377), Luther develops ideas on a triangle of God, the Christian, and the neighbor, defining the Christian as "a Christ to the other" (*LW*, 31:368), concluding that a Christian lives not in himself, but in Christ and in his neighbor. Otherwise he is not a Christian. He lives in Christ through faith, in his neighbor through love. The remission of sins is entirely worked by God through faith and grace. If justification is not followed by the Christian's forgiveness of the neighbor, however, this lack of human forgiving probably is an indication of lack of a truly justified state. Justification is no automatic act following any kind of faith produced by human beings. There is a distinction between "genuine faith" as justifying faith producing forgiveness of the neighbor as its fruits, and other kinds of faith which do not work forgiveness due to the fact that no justification has taken place.

Luther in this chapter has spoken of the works as fruits of faith in relation to forgiveness and in this relation only. When he has discussed the concept of fruits of faith earlier, he has done so only in relation to the loyal performance of the duties in the offices and stations of the secular kingdom. So even at this point the possibility of contradictions of rules and expectations easily occurs. For instance, he admonishes that a Christian judge should obediently condemn a murderer to death according to the laws of the civil society, but with a forgiving heart according to the laws of the spiritual kingdom (*LW*, 21:113, cf. 152).

The means of grace are then discussed. Listing up baptism, eucharist, prayer, and absolution, Luther emphasizes that the means partly are accessible outside of the church; God has not made the means of grace dependent on the clergy. In spite of the fact that he names exactly the same means of grace that are listed in the Augsburg Confession (articles nos. 9-11; *Creeds*, 3:13-14), he has not given an extensive list of the means of grace. First and foremost, he does not mention the Word of God, which he elsewhere names as the primary means of grace. By including absolution he indicates that his intention is to attack the abuses of this means of grace in the Church only, not the means itself.

Regarded as works, the means of grace, confession included, are not human undertakings, but "a divine sacrament and a great and powerful comfort that you can attain to the grace of being able to forgive your neighbor" (*LW*, 21:152). The human aspect diminishes as these acts "are all linked together" in a way that everybody who has the forgiveness of God are obliged to forgive their neighbor (*LW*, 21:152).

There are two kinds of sins only, affirms Luther, "one kind is confessed, and this no one should leave unforgiven; the other is defended, and this no one can forgive, for it refuses either to be counted as sin or to accept forgiveness" (*LW*, 21:153). But if your neighbor "confesses his sin and begs your pardon but you refuse to forgive him, you have loaded the sin upon yourself, and it will condemn you as well" (*LW*, 21:153). So there is an intimate relationship between grace and forgiveness; neither of them has anything to do with human merits, only with God's mercy through Christ.

Fasting (6:16-18)

Christ's intention is to restore proper fasting. The Pharisees had their own fasts because they needed to show their higher level of spirituality and perfection by fasting at times when nobody else did. By doing that, they made a show of their pretended piety. Christ did the opposite, he fasted secretly rather than "for the sake of acquiring a reputation" (*LW*, 21:155-156). A similar problem is visible in Luther's own time; the fasts in the papal church are turned into excessive feasts of eating and drinking without devotion. The custom to fast by replacing meat with fish is especially criticized.

Luther recommends three annual periods of fasting over a few days prior to the three main feasts, Easter, Pentecost, and Christmas, "so people can learn to keep track of the seasons" (*LW*, 21:159). Additionally, he personally is in favor of fasting every Friday evening. But he insists that fasting remains completely voluntary. His reasons given for fasting are rather pragmatic. He mainly talks of training for a less excessive life, and he wants to help people to learn the seasons. When coming to his understanding of what "true Christian fasting" is, his aims are basically the same (*LW*, 21:160, 162).

Because of its abuses, Luther is reluctant to admit that fasting is religiously significant. The problem is that the fasting may, consciously or not, encourage a pelagian soteriology. But fasting by itself can never improve a person's status to God. Fasting is actually a possible "enemy of faith and love" and not of faith only. Faith is frequently taken in the strict sense, *sola fide*, contrasting works (of love) in order to reinforce the exclusiveness of faith in

Christ as the mediator of justification. When he here mentions "faith and love" together, including justifying faith plus works of love as the fruits of the justifying faith, he implies a hierarchy of problems affecting true soteriology. Fasting is more of an enemy to an evangelical soteriology than other good works.

The functions of works of love and those of fasting are not the same; love to the neighbor is a fruit of faith in Christ, while fasting is rather instrumental in the disciplining of the body. Fasting has no soteriological function, while works of love are regarded as fruits of faith.

In medieval piety, the sacrament of penance provided absolution to the penitent sinner. The penitent had to make satisfaction and atonement through works like fasting, alms-giving, pilgrimages, etc., according to the judgment of the confessor. The abuses occurred when church leaders got the idea that the system of penance could be exploited for financial purposes. It was primarily the abuses that arose from the sale of indulgence letters, that were attacked by Luther from the beginning. Later he attacked the basis of the sacrament of penance as well, indicating that the unmerited grace of God is its foundation (*LW*, 48:64-70). The outward practices of penance were not compatible with the gospel. On this background his depreciation of fasting is understandable because it was too involved with the abuses of the Roman Catholic Church.

Treasures upon Earth, in Heaven, and Anxiety (6:19-34)

Luther first summarizes the contents of the previous passages. He identifies the nucleus of the Sermon on the Mount as Mt. 5:21-48, and he regards Mt. 6:1-18 as the practical application of the antitheses. The beatitudes have no substantial importance to the Sermon on the Mount. Christ's intention is to restore orthodoxy as well as orthopraxis. Orthopraxis comes out of orthodoxy and not the other way round. Only in light of orthodoxy, which here is primarily justification by faith alone, can orthopraxis be understood correctly, namely, as good works stemming from faith like fruit coming from a good tree.

Luther's intention is to interpret the rest of the Sermon on the Mount as an apology for the teachings of orthodoxy and orthopraxis dealt with above. Exegetically, the dividing line between Mt. 6:18 and 6:19 is more fundamental for the interpretation of the Sermon on the Mount than that which may be drawn between 5:48 and 6:1; a right understanding of the relationship between faith and works makes works valuable when regarded as fruits of faith. Secondly, Mt. 5:3-20 should be regarded as an introduction to the main teaching part of the Sermon on the Mount, which is defined as Mt. 5:21-6:18.

Treasures upon Earth and in Heaven (6:19-23)

The first issue that Luther deals with is greed. In his interpretation he uses the dialectics between faith and works introduced above. He acknowledges that one reaction to the Reformation, however distorted, has been greed. The historical background for this comment is apparent. He may hinting to some Lutheran princes who, by supporting the Reformation, were more interested in getting hold of the property of the Church than in the faith, however, the greed of the Lutheran princes was not fully apparent until later in the 1530s.[11] He also may refer to his general criticism of the economic exploitation by the Roman Catholic Church; his text is crowded with metaphors implying polemical attitudes against the papal church. He implies, for instance, that the Pope is not the universal Lord that he claims to be, for "Christ shall be a King and Lord over the whole world" (*LW*, 21:167). Most likely, he attacks greed among Roman Catholics and Lutherans alike.

Luther's conclusion is that "those who do not have many treasures are the best off, for they do not have many rats to feed and do not have to be afraid of thieves" (*LW*, 21:169). That does not mean generally, however, that treasures should not be collected. In that case, "The lords and the princes have to get and store provisions for their land and people ... This concedes that he may gather treasures in moderation" (*LW*, 21:169). Treasures may be collected for the purpose of redistribution. According to his understanding, therefore, Christ does not condemn the collecting of treasures on earth by princes who collect moderately and for the sake of the people only.

In the continuation he elaborates the implications of his doctrine of the two kingdoms in more detail:

> a sharp distinction must be made between the Christian and the man of the world, between a Christian person and a secular person. For a Christian as such does not bear the title male or female, young or old, lord or servant, emperor or prince, peasant or townsman, or anything else that can be named as belonging to the world. He does not have a "person" or mask, and he should not have anything or know anything in the world but be satisfied with his treasure in heaven. (*LW*, 21:170)

Luther is here referring to the masks used in the Greek theatre, called *persona*. The actors changed characters by changing masks or *persona*. In the same way the Christian changes masks all the time according to the situation. The mask takes precedence over the person and rules the conduct because the Christian in office functions as "a mask of God, as an agent of God's ruling work through God's law" (Gustafson 1968:125):

> each status or office is properly distinguished from the other; and yet they are combined in one person and, so to speak, are contradictory ... Thus every human being on earth has two persons: one person for himself, with obligations to no one except to God; and in addition a secular person, according to which he has obligations to other people. (*LW*, 21:171)

Luther here carefully explains the basic implications of his two kingdom doctrine: (1) "Every human being on earth has two persons," one by nature that is secular and one spiritual person. The secular mask that is activated by the manner in which the human being is related to the challenges of the surroundings; the relational aspect is crucial. (2) "Each status or office is properly distinguished from the other," each with its own set of rules and regulations, attitudes and obligations. When being "in-person," the obligations are to God, when being "in-office," the obligations are to the secular law. (3) "Yet they are combined in one person," however, "contradictory", because the split of expectancies is running through the midst of the life of any person. When obligations conflict, the duties to the office are "above and beyond" the duties of the Christian.

Returning to his scripture interpretation, Luther reinforces that Christ does not imply any attack on the public finance of the princes. Christ's intention is rather to comfort Christians and admonish people to trust God by trusting that the prince as their universal father will take care of their needs. As the father is the head of the family, so is the prince head of the entire people. This position gives him the same responsibility of care for persons who are in need as a father has for his children. For that reason a prince may gather treasures on earth, however, at the same time his responsibility is to contribute to others in time of need. Every city should store away goods for the common welfare, and every parish should lay up a common treasury for the poor. What is wrong is gathering goods for the sake of greed and lust, not to fulfil one's obligations as a secular citizen. The comment, "In your outward and secular life you may lay up as much as your relation with God and your honesty permits" (*LW*, 21:172), reveals how intimately the two kingdoms are interwoven.

Taking practical consequences of his ideas, Luther makes proposals to establish a public system of poor relief. Eleven years previously he made a proposal to forbid begging, with clear reference to the begging monks;[12] at that time begging was still accepted socially (Imsen 1984:44). He now repeats his proposal, as he also does as a part of his comments to Mt. 5:42. The Christian-in-person should not care about the worldly needs but leave this anxiety to the temporal offices authorized for taking care of the provisions needed for the society. To rely on God is the same as relying on the civil authorities. But human greed is a problem. He quotes the German proverbial expression, "Money is his heart" (*LW*, 21:175), concluding that "money and property are not my heart's treasure" (*LW*, 21:176).

To Mt. 6:22-23 Luther observes that St. Paul (in Eph. 5:5; Col. 3:5) identifies this particular vice as "idolatry" because it is in direct conflict with faith, which is the true worship or honoring of God. This is a serious accusation, because greed, as the idolatry of Mammon, is a neglect of the first and foundational commandment. He then applies his discussion to Christ's proverbial saying "The eye is the lamp of the body." The meaning is to apply a realistic assessment of the actual personal status versus the laws of the spiritual kingdom. A greedy person should not believe that he or she is a good Christian, because greed is an expression of idolatry and not of a genuine fear of God.

Luther points to the fact that the secular laws, too, aim to restrict the greed in commerce so that individual monopolies are avoided for the common good. On the one hand, he insists, "we still have to let the world remain the world." On the other hand, "whoever really has the Gospel in his heart becomes mild." The saying is directed against greed and lack of mercy. In society everybody ought to behave like citizens with obligations to the emperor and not to Christ, and still, in their "hearts," the love and forgiveness of the Gospel remain.

In the end of his comment to Mt. 6:22-23, Luther strongly admonishes his people to be content with the "spiritual possession and the heavenly blessing" (*LW*, 21:185). By doing that, he adds another perspective, namely, the advice against seeking a raise of status and rank before God. Greed also may be expressed through social ambitions. People who intend to advance themselves or their children "into a higher and more honorable rank" so that they can "provide for them generously only in order to improve and exalt their social position" (*LW*, 21:185) have no support in him.

To keep social stability is a primary goal to Luther, however, the goal of social stability is not to secure the privileged classes, but to comfort the people who suffer. His perspective is clearly that of the people. Nevertheless, though he has sympathy for their struggle for social justice, he is not willing to attack the hierarchical structure of stations and orders. When experiencing injustice from a ruler, suffering and patience are the remedies recommended, for the reformation of the civil society is the responsibility of the government and not of the individual and certainly not the Christian. A typical historical example of his politics in these matters is his *Admonition to Peace: A Reply to the Twelve Articles of the Peasants in Swabia* (1525; *LW*, 46:3-43), where he lays out the principles of his thinking on the conflict leading to the Peasants' War. As a start, he declares the twelve articles to be "their intolerable grievances" (*LW*, 46:17); the peasants, according to his opinion, confuse the spiritual and the secular kingdoms by supporting their temporal claims by scripture quotations (cf. *LW*, 46:34). But at the same time, he admits that the claims of the peasants are actually just. He accuses the princes of abuse of power, indicating, "as temporal rulers you do nothing but cheat and rob the people so that you may lead a life of luxury and extravagance. The poor common people cannot bear it any longer." They should rather accept the revolt as wrath from God as a punishment for their evils. When addressing the princes he declares that the twelve articles are "fair and just," and "the people cannot tolerate it very long if their rulers set confiscatory tax rates and tax them out of their very skins" (*LW*, 46:22-23).

On addressing the peasants, Luther admits that the princes "have sinned so greatly against both God and man. And they have no excuse." But he is not for that reason prepared to support the peasants: "Nevertheless, you, too, must be careful that you take up your cause justly and with a good conscience" (*LW*, 46:23). His objection to them is, with reference to the use of violent means in order to obtain their ends, that they should not call themselves Christians and transgress the divine law expressed through the social order at the same time. Furthermore, "The fact that the rulers are wicked and unjust does not excuse disorder and rebellion, for the punishing or wickedness is not the responsibility of everyone, but of the worldly rulers who bear the sword. True "Christians do not fight for themselves with sword and musket, but with the cross and with suffering, just as Christ, our leader, does not bear a sword, but hangs on the cross" (*LW*, 46:32). His concluding reply to the peasants is, therefore,

> You ... have ... undertaken to compel the rulers to give you what you wanted by using force and violence. This is against the law of the land and against natural justice ... To sum up, everything

is concerned with worldly and temporal matters. You want power and wealth so that you will not suffer injustice. The gospel, however, does not become involved in the affairs of this world, but speaks of our life in the world in terms of suffering, injustice, the cross, patience, and contempt for this life and temporal wealth. (*LW*, 46:34-35)

In spite of the facts that Luther condemns both parties in the conflict and that his sympathies are with the peasants, he actually takes sides with the princes against the peasants. He tells the peasants that "[you] are much worse than these [the princes], because you rage and struggle against the divine and natural law, which all the heathens keep" (*LW*, 46:27). To him, the orders of the secular kingdom are expressing "the divine and natural law," for what reason any person should accept and subject to them.

Care and Anxiety (6:24-34)

Christ's restriction of the laying up of treasures is an attack on "greedy bellies" in all times. Luther insists there is no criticism against the doctrine of the two kingdoms in Christ's teaching. He then turns to the problem of corruption, concluding that those who belong to mammon are God's enemies. On the other hand, to do one's duty properly in the stations in the secular kingdom is the same as being in God's service. This close relationship between service and the secular offices makes it natural to view the successful life in the stations as a gift of God. The two kingdoms are interrelated and influence each other mutually.

Money becomes the master of the Christian in the moment money is served instead of used for service. When money takes control over human lives it corrupts and becomes mammon and thereby an enemy to God. When money is loved, the Christian has lost control and serves mammon. "Whatever I love, that is my god," he quotes. But when mammon is loved, God is hated. But the possibility of serving mammon should not cause a fear of money as such. The solution is not to give it away, as the monks and Baptists did, for the money is given by God in order to serve humanity. Therefore, greedy people are no better than heathens:

"Baptized or not, therefore, no greedy belly can be a Christian: but he has certainly lost Christ and has become a heathen" (*LW*, 21:201). Baptism by itself does not guarantee a Christian life. He apprehends the actual life of the Christian to be a criterion of Christian faith as much as baptism.

In his comment to Mt. 6:25 Luther reveals the basic reason why money is a temptation. The human body "is still in his [the devil's] kingdom," and human beings are sinners. To serve mammon is the result of a deep-going corruption of the heart which makes humanity inclined to be its own God.

After this consideration of the soteriological aspects of the desire for riches, Luther once more warns against the confusion of the two kingdoms. Talking of neighborly love he actually is talking about the obedient and faithful performance of the duties of the civil offices and stations. In this respect the life in the stations is "something divine and Christian" because it expresses the concern for God's ordering of the human society. By doing that, he upgrades virtues as loyalty and obedience to superiors so that they become crucial for the life of the Christians. The results are, on the one hand, a static and hierarchical society, and on the other hand, the possibility of the rulers' abuse of the loyalties of their subjects.

The foundational motive for Christ's preaching of the Sermon on the Mount was the "seeking the kingdom of God." Luther asserts that the kingdom of God is entirely different from the "filthy and mortal kingdom of the belly" with its anxiety. It "is divine and imperishable and ... gives me eternal life, righteousness, peace, joy, and salvation" (*LW*, 21:203). This kingdom, however, primarily belongs to the coming world. Because this kingdom is not of this world, its accompanying righteousness is different, too. For this reason, the kingdom of God should be regarded as a present realization of salvation. To live according to the gospel means "doing good works, fulfilling your station of office diligently and faithfully, and undergoing all sorts of suffering for the Gospel" (*LW* 21:205). Luther's vision of salvation has here its focus in the present; salvation works an actual change in the life of the believer, enabling Christians to do their duty in the stations.

According to Luther, the kingdom of God and the kingdom of the world have two distinctive kinds of righteousness. He develops his theory of the two kinds of righteousnesses in his sermon, *Two Kinds of Righteousness* (*LW*, 31:293-306) as early as in 1519. In this first sermon on the subject, however, the rationale for the theory of the two righteousnesses is different from that of the discourses. Its conclusion is derived from the fact that "man's sins are of two kinds" (*LW*, 31:297).

The ideas of the last quotation resemble Luther's sermon of 1519. The foreign righteousness of the sinner is Christ's righteousness imputed by faith. It removes the guilt of sin in a moment. At this early stage of his theological development he believes that this kind of righteousness makes progress in the life of the believer until it is perfected in eternal life. In a paradoxical way he holds together the absolute freedom of sin and a progressing liberation from sin. The proper righteousness "is that manner of life spent profitably in good works "by self-discipline, love to one's neighbor, and meekness and fear toward God. It appears that his distinction between the two kinds of righteousness in this early sermon of 1519 is based upon the distinction between a theological ("foreign") and an actual ("proper") righteousness, the last following as the fruit or consequence of the first. He also describes the development of the proper righteousness until it is "transformed into his likeness ... It is precisely this that Christ requires" (*LW*, 31:300). Obviously he in 1519 regards both kinds of righteousness to be parts of the kingdom of God.

In 1531 Luther declares "In the kingdom of Christ is half sin and half holiness," and, "what is still our own remain sinful." He has now left the notion of an inherent and progressing righteousness. In the kingdom of God there is one kind of righteousness only, the righteousness of Christ that is accounted as well as imputed to the believer, but without being actual in an ontological sense. It is actual, however, in an epistemological sense. The sins of the Christians need to be "put to death ... daily" (Billing 1917:84-86). In 1519 he anticipates a gradual mortification of actual sin in the Christian, by 1531 he replaces it with the daily mortification of the guilt of sin. It is significant that what is "continual progressing" is no longer conceived as a growth in actual perfection but rather a growth in a cognitive, doctrinal understanding and acknowledgment of the believer's relationship to God, that Christ "is ours through faith and who lives and works in us" (*LW* 21:205). His anthropology and the *simul iustus et peccator* doctrine are still basic, however, "For our condition in the kingdom of Christ is half sin and half holiness" (*LW* 21:205). At the same time, he reserves the foreign righteousness for the spiritual kingdom and the proper righteousness for the secular kingdom.

In his comment to Mt. 6:34, Luther insists that God "wants to be generous to you, but not on account of your being concerned or even on account of your working," for "God gives a free gift without our anxiety" (*LW*, 21:208). The natural response is therefore, to answer the calling from God implied in the stations: "The kingdom of God requires you to do what you are commanded to do, to preach and to promote the Word of God, to serve your neighbor according to your calling,[13] and to take whatever God gives you" (*LW*, 21:209).

Religious Duties (7:1-12)
Judging Others (7:1-6)
Christ here preaches about "another great and dangerous vice, called 'self-centered wisdom,' which judges and criticizes everyone" (*LW*, 21:210). His criticism of judging does not neglect the authority of the courts of this world, however, for he addresses his message to the disciples only. Consequently, the seventh chapter of the gospel of Matthew, too, is interpreted by Luther within the context of the doctrine of the two kingdoms. The disciples should not judge, but holders of a secular office "cannot avoid judging and punishing." This is all part of the secular kingdom.

The confusion of the kingdoms causes schisms among Christians and between churches. If every Christian should have the opportunity to judge in matters of doctrine and Christian life, an impossible situation would occur. Without doubt, Luther is referring to his problems with the Left Wing of the Reformation movement. But he may also refer to the Swiss reformers, Zwingli and Calvin. Negotiations between the German and Swiss wings of the Reformation were attempted but finally broke down in 1929, the year before his Sermon on the Mount discourses began.[14] The history of the Reformation actualized the issue of who should receive authority in doctrinal matters. His solution was that Christ by his teaching in Mt. 7:1-6 was "instituting the office of the ministry" (*LW*, 21:228). The exegetical basis for this supposition is uncertain; however, it is a logical and consistent statement considering his doctrine of the two kingdoms.

Originally, Luther took the radical stand that every Christian should have the right to interpret the scriptures and the biblical message (Imsen 1984:209). This position came out of his rejection of the authority of the tradition of the Church, which he replaced with the absolute authority of scripture. His doctrine of the general priesthood of all believers corresponded to this principle. He actually abolished the ministry of the clergy for some time (cf. Haendler 1981:41-42, 47-49, 59). He abandoned this radical view as he realized that the need for a general doctrinal uniformity required a specific office of preaching ministry as well as a liturgy for the service of the Word; probably this was caused by his experiences with the Baptists and the Peasants' War. A preaching ministry with authority to interpret the scriptures, in order to judge in doctrinal matters, was necessary.

Luther identifies the public character of this ministry and its official authorization as crucial points. He has already rejected the non-authorized preaching and teaching. He now adds a rejection of unauthorized judging. Not to judge others should be regarded as "a commandment" (*LW*, 21:229). The transgression of it is a serious sin, bringing the Chritian under the judgment and possible condemnation of God.

Self-adoration is identified by Luther as the source of judging. Judging therefore reveals "ingratitude to God," and the disastrous effect will be that "the person who does the judging is usually stuck deeper in sin and vices than other people" (*LW*, 21:217). It is a certain way to alienate "both God and your neighbor," because "you lose both the grace of God and the Christian life simultaneously, and you become worse than a heathen who knows nothing about God" (*LW*, 21:219). The better way is to give active support to the neighbor.

Mt. 7:6 is one of the most debated scriptures in the history of interpretation of the Sermon on the Mount (Betz 1985:93, note 24). Luther relates its meaning to the protection of doctrine, asking, "who are the ones that trample on what is holy and turn against us?" Answering, "the false teachers ... our sectarian fanatics," or, the Baptists, his "worst enemies on earth" (*LW*, 21:224). When it comes to life, however, Christ is referring to corrupt preachers who have made themselves servants of the civil authorities or princes "so that they have to preach and do what he wants" (*LW*, 21:224). Serious Christians must avoid throwing the Gospel "before swine and dogs," or the Baptists, "the schismatic spirits" (*LW*, 21:225).

Persons with a "schismatic spirit" should be separated from the church, and persons who hold doctrines deviating from Luther's own theology should be denied the means of grace. Conversion to right doctrine again can only be accepted after a doctrinal judgment performed by himself or by a minister authorized by him. From the history of the Church he has learned the need to protect right doctrine. The tradition of interpreting Mt. 7:6 as an admonition for the total exclusion of unbelievers from the means of grace is a radical position which is quite seldom taken. However, he has some support in the ancient exegetic tradition for this interpretation.[15]

The fruits of the "sectarians" are probably a primary reason why Luther despises them. They threaten to dissolve social order because they give up their properties, resist carrying arms, and question the authority of the officials of society. These evil fruits indicate to him that their gospel was not right, "Because the Gospel has been refused and even persecuted in our Germany, the corners are full of sectarians, fanatics, and Baptists; and there is nothing anyone can do to prevent it" (*LW*, 21:227). He did not fully realize the significance of the revolutionary socioeconomic forces that existed in support of the Reformation. But these people were not content with his ideas of right doctrine as long as they experienced social and economic injustice, and he was unable to meet their concerns because of his loyalty to the princes.

Prayer (ii) (7:7-11)

Luther acknowledges that Christ addresses the entire Christendom, saying, "I have given you instructions about how you ought to live and what you ought to watch out for" (*LW*, 21:229). He now gives "an admonition to prayer," that is "second to the office of the preaching, prayer is the chief work of a Christian and an inseparable part of the sermon" (*LW*, 21:228-229).

Though God's initiative is the basis of salvation, Luther acknowledges that some sort of human response is necessary: "You will have need of asking, seeking, and knocking" (*LW*, 21:229). The context for his thoughts on prayer is the struggle against sin and evil. The beginning of the work of grace in the sinner is entirely the initiative of God. The continuation of it is dependent on human activity, however not understood as merits.

Luther has reason to fear that the people of the Reformation are neglecting prayer after the destruction of the Roman Catholic practices. The admonition to prayer is therefore more than an admonition, it is "a commandment, as much as ... 'Judge not' is a commandment." Any Christian "should know that he is obliged to practice this Christian work" (*LW*, 21:229).

Prayer is not merely a commandment, it is attached to promises, too. Luther suggests that the existence of natural evil and the weak faith of human beings indicate that human lives are invaded by the devil. The primary strategy of the devil is "to extinguish the Word in me again and to smother it"; no wonder that "we have a continual reason for prayer and invocation" (*LW*, 21:231). The need for praying will not disappear until the Christians are in heaven. Thus far, the daily life is crowded with afflictions of all kinds causing new need for prayer.

Luther admits that the life in the two kingdoms is filled with more conflicts than a person could bear were it not for God's assistance. The duties from the two kinds of righteousness, God's righteousness and the civil righteousness, are bound to conflict because the natures of the two kinds of righteousness are basically contradictory. He describes the housefather's relation to his household as a matter of "control." He probably realizes that any hierarchical system of social stations and offices, superiors and subjects, ultimately will lead to the need for the superiors' "control" of their subjects.

Praying is an opportunity indicating that we should not take care of our afflictions on our own: "We should develop the habit, whenever we see anguish or need to fall on our knees immediately and to spread the need before God, on the basis of this admonition and promise" (*LW*, 21:232). Prayer never fails, he insists, as long as Christ has taught "you what you should believe from your heart, to make you certain that your faith, Gospel, and Christ are correct and that your station in life is pleasing to God" (*LW*, 21:232). The power of as well as the motivation for prayer comes from the Word of God. The effect of prayer also comes from using of scriptures and relying on their promises. Orthodoxy and orthopraxis are both necessary elements in the Christian religion, according to him. They are interrelated and interdependent, making orthodox belief irreligious as long as it is not situated in the life of the heart of a believer. In that case it is turned into mere philosophy. On the other hand, if right doctrine and the religion of the heart do not lead to obedient life in the stations, they may be turned into revolutionary politics.

Luther's concluding remarks on prayer reinforce the necessity of prayer for the continued state of salvation. What is necessary for a healthy spiritual life is that the believer responds to God's grace in prayer.

The Golden Rule (7:12)

Christ with the words of the golden rule "concludes the teaching He has been giving in these three chapters." It is a summary of the entire law and a conclusion at the same time. Observing this rule, "We could be our own teachers, teaching ourselves what we ought to do" (*LW*, 21:235, cf. 236-237). Consequently, Mt. 7:12 as well as the ten commandments is an outstanding expression of the natu-

ral reason or natural recognition of morals. Because it is in ourselves, "Why do you refuse to obey your own rule?" If we examine the second table of the ten commandments we "will find that
this is really the summary of all possible sermons ... Thus this is
properly termed a short sermon" (*LW*, 21:236). He speaks of
God's will as something "written in his [the believer's] own heart,
in fact, in his whole life and activity" (*LW*, 21:236), affirming that
"you are your own Bible, your own teacher, your own theologian,
and your own preacher" (*LW*, 21:236-237). He also affirms that
the Christian has

> a daily sermon in your heart. From it you can easily learn to un-
> derstand all the commandments and the whole Law, how to
> control and conduct yourself personally and socially. On this ba-
> sis you can decide what is right and wrong in the world. (*LW*,
> 21:239)

Luther here describes a natural recognition of ethics based upon
principles of the natural law. This is, to him, a divine code of morals fully satisfactory for the life in the secular world. As citizens,
people are their own bibles. In other places he completely dis-
charges the guidance of reason, and the revelation through scriptures is the only guidance: "If you cling to the Word, guiding
yourself by it, and not by what your eyes see, He will certainly be
next to you" (*LW*, 21:246, cf. 254).

This paradox of contradiction is present in Luther's mind without being harmonized. A radical implication of his teaching that
"you are your own Bible" would be that the scriptures are not necessary at all, and he certainly does not draw that conclusion. Nor
does he accept the scriptures as an exclusive source for knowledge
about the life in this world. On the contrary, he states that "the
Bible," which does not mean the holy scriptures but the natural
reason, "has been put into your workshop, into your hand, into
your heart. It teaches and preaches how you should treat your
neighbor" (*LW*, 21:237). He is here possibly referring to the special revelation of God's love in Christ in the spiritual kingdom as a
source of inspiration for neighborly love in the secular kingdom.

But when it comes to daily ethics, the norms are to be deduced by reason.

One problem with Luther's teaching on natural law is that it may end up in a subjective understanding of ethical recognition. Another problem is how it relates to what he has stated earlier about the public ministry of preaching, allowing no others to interpret the scriptures than the minister who is properly called and authorized. Suggesting the following solution, he is obviously aware of the problem himself:

> Christ names the Law and the Prophets in direct contrast to the Gospel or the promise. He is not preaching here about the sublime doctrine of faith in Christ but only about good works ... He is discussing only the commandments of the Second Table. (*LW*, 21:239-240)

In his attempt to solve the conflict, Luther separates faith from ethics. By this separation he causes another contradiction, that between "works" in the secular offices and works as fruits of faith, a distinction that is established earlier. At this point he turns their relation the other way round: "By your example you may prompt other people to do good to you in turn, even those who used to do you damage before" (*LW*, 21:240-241).

All doing good has a religious basis. The power necessary for the fulfillment of the golden rule will come from the piety inherent in the believer. Luther thus takes his theology to the edge of the confusion of the two kingdoms that he struggles to avoid. But the strict distinction of the kingdoms should not be pushed to its extreme. There are relations between the two which are destroyed if it comes to a complete separation between the kingdoms (or righteousnesses, or ways of recognition).

The golden rule has to be taken as a serious commandment, for "He will not let it be made free or optional" (*LW*, 21:238). This commandment has a divine origin and purpose, but it is beyond the laws of the bible because of its roots in the natural law. It is, therefore, general and less specific than is the case with many laws in the bible. This fact indicates to Luther that the scriptural laws are not to be taken literally.

Exhortations (7:13-27)
The Narrow Gate and the Narrow Way (7:13-14)
Christ now has finished preaching, his aims are accomplished. Now come the final "warnings, to arm us against all kinds of hindrances and offenses of both doctrine and life that we confront in the world" (*LW*, 21:241).

Luther suggests that Mt. 7:13-14 contains a warning against conformity to the world. To be a Christian is not easy. For that reason it is most significant to avoid the temptation of thinking that others, who are in the majority or in positions of authority, must be right. He insists, "If you want to be a Christian, then be one!" (*LW*, 21:245).

False Prophets (7:15-20)
False preachers are not necessarily preachers with a false doctrine. Luther's primary objection is that they come secretly and "under the pretext of the Gospel but ... introduce another Gospel and thus distort and destroy both doctrine and life" (*LW*, 21:247-248). False preachers may represent true doctrine; for instance, it is possible that they teach salvation by faith alone. Teachers who arise "secretly," however, are preachers who are not authorized by a public calling. Therefore, they represent a threat against the social and ecclesiastical structures and a violation against the doctrine of the two kingdoms. Characteristically, they do not arise from outside the Church, but from inside.

There are false prophets of two kinds, those with a commission to preach and those who have established themselves as preachers or teachers. Luther despises the latter category in particular, because they violate the social order. The issue of social order is at this point taken to a doctrinal level similar to that of soteriology; to have a proper office counts more than to profess a sound doctrine:

> Even if they taught correctly, they would be intolerable. They try
> to meddle in other people's office and commission, in defiance
> of the ordinances of the government ... God has instituted this
> office, as He has others; therefore we should not act in opposi-
> tion to it. (*LW*, 21:250)

Who is the object of Luther's polemic at this point? The issue
under discussion is more typical of the Baptists, but the description
of these preachers as "tramps" indicates mendicant orders may be
in his thoughts as well. So does the reference to their ascetic
works. Most probably he includes both of these groups.

Luther does not give any specific clue for the detection of false
prophets who have their commission as authorized preachers on
behalf of the church. Because they appear "in sheep's clothing ...
they are irreproachable and outwardly indistinguishable from
genuine preachers." They do tremendous damage because, "they
have the valid office, and in addition they give such a beautiful
impression and appearance that no one can say anything except
that they are true, pious preachers, interested in everyone's salvation" (*LW*, 21:251).

The problem is how to detect who is a false prophet and who is
not. A criterion is their use of the scriptures. Christians who are
concerned about the genuine doctrines of the gospel will therefore
easily detect false preaching. Luther is confident that the orthodox
interpretation of Christian theology provides the valid criteria for
doctrinal judgment of the "prophets," and that his interpretation is
the right understanding. The final criterion is "whether or not he
agrees with my Gospel" (*LW*, 21:253).

I have indicated above that Luther sometimes almost replaces
the institutionalized doctrinal judgment of the church with the
subjective judgment of the believer. The last quotation is an example of his thinking in this respect. It should be observed that the
phrase "my Gospel" is not related to every believer but only to
Christians who take the gospel seriously, which probably means
believers who are firmly based in an orthodox faith. Additionally,
he balances the subjectivity of doctrinal judgment against the official judgment of the preacher authorized for this responsibility by

a public commission. In his opinion, he himself is properly commissioned for the office of preaching. Therefore he has the authority to make doctrinal judgments.

Turning to the Baptist heresies, Luther is more specific in his criticism of the message of these "false prophets." His basic criticism of them is connected to their rejection of the social order. He questions their fruits and regards them as enthusiasts or *Schwärmer* because "they lead the people away from the stations" (*LW*, 21:258).

Luther's violent rejection of the Baptists has its basis in his doctrine of the two kingdoms. To be a Christian can mean nothing else than to stay in one's station, he affirms. If a person leaves his or her station, this person can be no Christian. It is even worse when certain Baptists oppose the civil authority and encourage people to leave their stations. They then are disclosed as false prophets and teachers. He offers another alternative:

> you must hold on to [1] the chief part, the summary of Christian teaching and accept nothing else: That God has sent and given Christ His Son, and that only through Him does He forgive us all our sins, justify and save us. Then if you open your eyes, [2] you will see all sorts of differing situations and ways of life ... and whatever stations and offices there may be in the world. (*LW*, 21:254-255)

This statement of Luther is most significant for the definition of the structure of his theology. In its basis, it has two foci: (1) justification by faith in Christ alone, and (2) the doctrine of the two kingdoms. The Baptists agreed wholeheartedly with the first part of this bifocal theology of Luther but they disagreed with the second part. As he continues his discussion, he reinforces these two foci:

> we must be careful ... to be correct in [1] the chief doctrine about Christ. [2] Then we can make right judgments about all the outward masks and ways of life, and the Spirit will teach us and lead us well. Thus any individual who wants to be pious will find enough genuine good works to do in his own station, and he

will not have to go looking for anything special. (*LW*, 21:255-256)

These two foci are not to be understood as equally important for justification. Faith in Christ is the sole basis for salvation. But the life in Christ will necessarily take shape, and the Spirit will lead the true Christian to accept the obedient life in the stations of the secular kingdom. In terms of how salvation is imputed, the doctrine of justification by faith alone is basic. In terms of how the Christian life ought to be structured, the doctrine of the two kingdoms is basic. There is no need to look for the doing of God's will outside the stations, offices, and occupations. An idea like that is likely to turn the attention away from the duties as citizens.

Luther uses the doctrine of the two kingdoms at this point as a check-point for the validity of a believer's salvation. If salvation is legitimate and truly based on the unmerited gift through Christ, the doctrine of justification by faith by necessity will carry fruit in the offices and stations. Both doctrines therefore have a soteriological function. The doctrine of justification by faith builds the foundation. The doctrine of the two kingdoms determines what fruit is good and what is bad. He insists that the life in the stations is the best Christian life, because the stations are ordered by God. Therefore all the stations are necessary and equal in value. The stations should therefore be honored and faithfully practiced. Through them the Christian is certain to be in the will of God, wherever the occupation is placed in the hierarchical structure of society.

In his discussion of fruits (Mt. 7:16-29), Luther states that this scripture must be given "a spiritual understanding on the basis of the Word of God" (*LW*, 21:260-261). The false teachers, however, are misleading because they are more rationalistic in their understanding.

It is not easy to follow Luther's logic at this point. He argues with scripture in opposition to reason in two ways. Against the Baptists' literal understanding of the ethics of the Sermon on the Mount, he claims that reason informs us of how to behave in the world. Secondly, he senses a confusion between the two kingdoms in Roman Catholic as well as in Baptist theology. Against their emphasis on fruits apart from the stations he points to the necessity of a spiritualized understanding of salvation, completely apart from works of any kind. The works never merit salvation, they are fruits of the Spirit, and true fruits are observed when they take shape out of loyal conformity with the roles of the secular stations only.

Luther is positive that his understanding of the stations of the secular kingdom has a solid basis in the scriptures, though he does not give too many scriptural proofs for it in his discourses on the Sermon on the Mount. The doctrine of the two kingdoms is used as a comprehensive interpretation which is generalized to a hermeneutical principle. By help of this hermeneutics the details of the entire scripture are interpreted. The good works that can be recognized as fruits of faith are the works performed in the life of the civil stations and occupations, provided they are motivated by Christian love: "If you have Christ through faith, then let everyone be obedient and subject to the government (Rom. 13:1) and practice mutual love in your station (Rom. 13:8-10)" (*LW*, 21:262).

No one who is not "obedient and subject to the government" can be a Christian, and good works are only essentially good when performed within the stations. It does not matter that many offices and stations are filled with "rascals" and other people misusing the stations for their own purposes. The stations are given by God, who expects Christians to do their duty within their own station. As example he refers to the station of a housewife, and he absolves her from criticisms of the surrounding world. The simple fact that she is in her station is an apology for whatever she is doing, good or bad, because the good about the works is essentially coming from the station and not from faith. The monk, on the other side, is constantly living in opposition to God's commandment. If he had remained in his station or office, however, he could not have been a bad tree, for "we cannot do wrong" as long as "we are in a station," that is equal to "live according to the Word of God and do what we have been commanded to do. ... In other words, you cannot ruin it [your life], since you are living in the divine office and in the Word" (*LW*, 21:267).

Faith and station are two sides of the same reality. Christians express obedience to God as faith in the spiritual kingdom and by submitting themselves to the life of the stations in the secular kingdom. The link between the two is the love of the heart, a love which is expressed equally to God and to the neighbor. In this context, sin is to transgress the limits of the stations, in which one is living. If works are performed in office, they are good fruits because they are functions of the office, regardless of their results.

The Two Foundations (7:21-27)

Luther's concern is the eternal destiny of the monks. "It is a frightening judgment," he comments, "that no one is deeper in hell than the great servants of God, the most saintly monks." For, "those who brag about being the greatest saints shall not enter the kingdom of heaven" (*LW*, 21:268). How can he pass this sentence?

It all depends upon Luther's interpretation of how God's will is best performed. According to him, the Carthusians, one of the stricter monastic beggar orders, do not do the will of God in spite of their rigorous ascetic discipline. He refers to this order a number of times throughout his discourses, and each time with disgust and rejection.[16] His concept of doing the will of God is different because it comes out of his two-kingdom doctrine.

The monastic *regula* reduces the opportunities of doing God's will. The message of the "schismatic spirits" does the same (*LW*, 21:270). To do God's will means, first, to believe in Christ. Secondly, it means to be in a calling, which in this context refers to the obedient life in a station. The calling is not reserved for the monastic and clerical people. The truly religious character of everyday life in the stations is emphasized by his use of "calling" in this respect.[17] Thirdly, to be in a station; with station he means the specific public roles that every person has in relation to other persons in society. The most usual stations are, emperor, prince, judge, soldier, preacher, teacher, husband, wife, father, mother, children, master, servant, etc. Persons are in these stations related to others in a way which creates a specific responsibility. For a scriptural basis, he points to the relations between the stations and the ten commandments on the one hand, and to the fulfillment of love to the neighbor on the other.

On Mt. 7:22-23 Luther comments that the final judgment is met with surprise because it is passed against "really high and outstanding people" (*LW*, 21:270) who are "pleased with" themselves. He is replacing the common searching for the miraculous event with the discovery of God's activity through the stations in everyday life. Although this life is not counted much, God truly reveals God's will it.

As Luther continues, he particularly attacks the popular piety of Roman Catholicism. Indicating that it is neither directed to Christ nor to the neighbor. Along with the essentials of justification, the stations of the secular society are made a significant criterion for his rejection. The works of the stations are the greatest ever possible for a Christian. The stations are necessary for the propagation of the Christian message, too; although the preacher is "an unbelieving and wicked man," "he brings you to faith, rescues you from the power of the devil and from eternal death, and leads you to eternal life in heaven." This by far surpasses all outward signs and wonders. The conclusions of the Donatist struggle is here used in support of his doctrine of the two kingdoms. The office itself is above the person who is in office, because the instrument in God's hand is the office and not the person. He is convinced that God does not ask about the faith of the preachers, because "the office is right and good nevertheless, since it does not belong to man but to God himself" (*LW*, 21:277).

To Luther, the dynamism of God's work is exclusively bound to what happens "within the limits of their office" (*LW*, 21:278). In the moment the limits of an office are transgressed, that very office is distorted as an instrument of God's will and purpose. The offices of the secular and the spiritual kingdoms should be carefully separated, because each of the kingdoms has its own hierarchy of offices. The secular kingdom must take care of the government of political issues, and the family in issues of household, and the spiritual kingdom must take care of the proclamation of the Gospel by help of the ministry of Word and sacraments.

Another careful distinction is now made between "the office and the person" (*LW*, 21:278). Luther indicates that good works are done by pious Christians, whether being in person or in office, or by wicked persons being in an authorized office. Works done by wicked persons in office are good, because the office makes them God's works. Any work made by a holder of an office should advance faith; because it is an act of office, it should reveal God's creating will. If a different kind of worship is established, however, or if pure doctrines are forsaken, there is reason to reject the preaching of a certain "prophet ... though it were snowing miracles" (*LW*, 21:279).

According to Luther, Mt. 7:24-27 serves as "the conclusion and the end," indicating that "the doctrine is a good end and a precious thing, but it is ... preached for the sake of ... action and its application to life. ... Therefore we must not only hear and be able, but actually *do* and *fight*" (*LW*, 21:281). Basic to his interpretation of the Sermon on the Mount is his doctrine of justification by faith in Christ alone. There is no way to be saved by works. When he now emphasizes the need of works, he explains carefully the proper understanding of them. They do not merit anything, but they may express the love which is the response of grace or fruit of faith.

In the end, Luther comments on the assurance of faith by pointing to his own experience seeking assurance as a monk, and to the example of St. Bernard. Both references serve the same purpose, to elevate "the doctrine about Christ," in whom the believer has confidence. The main thing is to "stand on the rock, that is, on the doctrine about Christ" (*LW*, 21:282).

Hermeneutics

Luther's hermeneutics is discussed by several scholars. They generally agree that he looks for his understanding within the scripture itself and not elsewhere as, for instance, in the Church, or in the tradition. Pelikan (1959:81) discusses the relations between scripture and tradition in Luther, concluding that he basically understands the writings of the church fathers as expositions of the scriptures, while his Catholic opponents seemed to make them extensions of the scripture. He was not the first to stress the supremacy of scripture, he rather "continued a trend present throughout the medieval church, one which had been articulated by some of the outstanding scholastic doctors" (Pelikan 1959:74). But he put the doctrinal authority of the scripture over against the Church in a much more radical degree than what had been seen before.

Hendrix (1983:234) characterizes Luther's biblical hermeneutics as a search for "the legitimate meaning" of the biblical texts. In general Luther uses grammatical and historical analysis as his tools, but if necessary, he also makes use of the classical allegorical and christological methods of interpretation. He uses the method best fit to highlight the significance of the text and its historical perspectives. He neither makes a hermeneutical distinction between the historical and present meaning of the text, nor does he ignore this distinction completely. He "could leave the meaning of a text at the level of historical or theological analysis" at the same time as "he often utilized personal experience and his diagnosis of the contemporary church to make the text speak immediately to his own day and thus to reveal its meaning". Hendrix concludes that Luther's hermeneutical contribution lies "in the discovery of the legitimate meaning, based on grammatical and historical analysis, informed by the theological reflection and applied to one's own life and the church of the present" (Hendrix 1983:238).

Pelikan (1959:107-108) observes that Luther's understanding of historical and literal exposition of the scripture is not quite the same as our understanding today. With the historical context of the scripture he primarily understands "the history of the people of God." For that reason allegorical and typological methods of interpretation are not incompatible with a "historical" understanding of a text. Pelikan's observation that Luther's concept of history is different from ours is supported by my research. Stronger than Hendrix, Forde (1983:247) insists that "The literal and historical sense is the only legitimate meaning" to Luther.

Luther's starting point for his Sermon on the Mount hermeneutics is that the antitheses, particularly the last two (Mt. 5:38-48, on the issues of hatred, revenge, non-resistance, and love), cannot be applied to human and social life. His intention is to interpret the biblical text literally, but he finds the consequences of a literal interpretation to be impossible as a theory of how to live as a Christian in the world. For that reason, he is compelled to find his hermeneutical key outside the text of the Sermon on the Mount.

Approaching the Sermon on the Mount Luther faces a double hermeneutical problem. A theological problem is that Christ in the Sermon on the Mount is speaking of works and rewards in a way that he finds to be incompatible with the grand doctrine of the Reformation, justification by faith and grace alone. No human works can merit salvation. This concern is the christological or soteriological part of his hermeneutical problem. Another and practical problem is that an absolutist or rigorist understanding of the two antitheses mentioned above will have dramatic consequences for the stability of human society. If evil acts are never to be resisted, social and economic structures will dissolve. Behind this practical problem is another theological concern, namely, that of creation; he considers the social structures as expressions of God's will in creation and that they were established for the good of humanity.

Luther solves these problems by giving the literal understanding a special meaning. The first and soteriological problem he handles by inserting the doctrine of justification by faith as the key hermeneutical principle, and by accepting the works of the Sermon on the Mount as fruits of faith in Christ. The rewards of the Sermon on the Mount he interprets as words of consolation, reminding the faithful Christian of the recompense that will be given in heaven. Therefore, the teachings of Christ about works and rewards in the Sermon on the Mount do not imply that human activities merit salvation. Human works cannot improve one's situation before God, only faith can do that. Salvation is entirely wrought by the grace of God, and works are acceptable as fruit only. His conclusion is that the Sermon on the Mount teaches what the fruits of a genuine Christian faith ought to be.

In order to draw this conclusion, it is necessary for Luther to introduce scriptures in addition to the Sermon on the Mount as keys of interpretation. The large number of these texts are Pauline. First and foremost he points to the theology of justification, which is deduced from the epistles to the Romans and Galatians in particular, as the following example, taken from his comment to Mt. 5:19, will show:

> He [Christ in the Sermon on the Mount] is not dealing with the great chief doctrine of what He is and what He gives. We cannot be justified or saved through the teaching of the Law [Rom. 3], which only brings us to the knowledge of ourselves, the knowledge that by our own ability we cannot properly fulfil an iota of it [Gal. 3:19ff]. Once we have become Christians through Baptism and faith, we do as much as we can [Rom. 6; Gal. 5]. Still we can never take our stand before God on this basis, but we must always creep to Christ [Rom 7:24-8:4]. (*LW*, 21:72-73)

The second and practical problem Luther solves by inserting the doctrine of the two kingdoms as his second hermeneutical key. This doctrine makes it possible to distinguish between the Christian as a private and as an official person. By stating that the Sermon on the Mount is valid for the spiritual kingdom and ought to be understood literally by the Christian as a private person only, he avoids the problem of turning the other cheek to the evil-doer, giving willingly to people asking for temporal assistance, etc. By restricting its application to the spiritual sphere, he affirms the absolutist character of the commandments of the Sermon on the Mount, but he also removes their relevance from the secular kingdom. The scriptural basis for this doctrine is not argued for in detail in the Sermon on the Mount discourses, nor is the biblical basis for his hermeneutics of the Sermon on the Mount made clear by him.

My conclusion is that the hermeneutical keys for Luther's interpretation of the Sermon on the Mount are derived neither from the Sermon on the Mount itself nor from its immediate scriptural context. The keys are the doctrine of justification by faith and the doctrine of the two kingdoms. These doctrines make up the two foci upon which his theological structure is based, as it is revealed through his Sermon on the Mount exegesis. He uses them as his primary tools for his understanding of the Sermon on the Mount. From a strict biblical point of view, therefore, his conclusions may be valued as the result of *eisegesis* rather than *exegesis*.[18] In this case he is subject to his own criticism of an exegesis that determines the meaning of a text on the basis of generalities (Pelikan 1959:130).

This kind of eisegesis, however, is generally accepted in the history of biblical interpretation as the method of *analogia fidei*. This hermeneutical rule presupposes that there is a universal agreement on the doctrines applied to the text. Luther's doctrine of justification by faith no doubt qualifies for the use of *analogia fidei* according to this criteria. It is an open question if the doctrine of the two kingdoms is generally accepted. However, at least outside the circles of confessionally oriented Lutheran theologians, it is probably right to say that it is not accepted.

These two doctrines form the bifocal center of the systematic structure of Luther's exegesis of the Sermon on the Mount. Over and over again, he maintains that true orthodoxy consists of the dual focus on the doctrine of justification by faith and the doctrine of the two kingdoms.[19]

From a hermeneutical point of view, Luther's interpretation of the Sermon on the Mount provides an example of another of his general principles of biblical exegesis, namely, to let the pure message of Christ govern his exegesis.[20] To his own presuppositions, he protects "Christ" by the rejection of pelagian soteriology and by the formulation of the doctrine of the two kingdoms. If his theological presuppositions had less sharp distinctions between God's creating activity through the Father and God's saving work through the Son, his conclusions would possibly have been different. Now, this distinction leads, first, to a distinction between the spiritual and secular kingdoms, secondly, to a distinction between gospel and law. Because of his polemics against works meriting salvation, he is forced not only to hold that the place of the law is in the secular kingdom because it has nothing to do with grace, but also to state that the law is an enemy of the gospel. He is positive that he restores the genuine meaning of the law, as in this comment to Mt. 5:17.

Luther identifies the basic problem that Christ deals with in the Sermon on the Mount as the relations between gospel and law. In the Sermon on the Mount, the law part of the problem is focused; however, the meaning and the role of faith in the Christian's life are underlying. His exposition of the Sermon on the Mount is logically built up as an elaborated theological system for his understanding of the Christian in the world. The actual place of the law is removed from the Christian life in the spiritual kingdom, where law is considered to be an enemy of the gospel.

The historical context is paramount to Luther's exegesis. From the beginning, he presents his purpose as the reconstruction of right doctrine versus Roman Catholic theology and religious practice on the one hand, and the radical and absolutist approach to the Sermon on the Mount of the Baptists on the other. It is not possible to know how he would have interpreted the Sermon on the Mount in an unhistorical setting completely free of polemics. What is certain is that his polemics sharpens his theological foci.

The context in which an exegesis is performed therefore must be considered. This analysis informs why the emphases of a certain interpretation become foundational, and it throws light on the function of key concepts.[21] In conclusion, Luther's exegesis of the Sermon on the Mount is determined by systematic-theological considerations as raised polemically by his historical context. To him, the message of the Sermon on the Mount in a nutshell is faith and love. The life in the spiritual realm is organized around these two concepts. The relation to God is through faith, to the neighbor it is through love (*LW*, 21:149), however, only when the neighbor, too, is in-person (*LW*, 21:121). Luther here affirms that love has to reign in the heart of the Christian but is to be expressed, first and foremost, through civil stations and orders of the secular realm. Faith produces fruits, and the spiritual fruits are in general identical with the doing of one's duty in one's proper calling (cf. comments to Mt. 7:16-20; *LW*, 21:259-268; cf. *LW*, 21:291).

Luther never clarifies completely his conception of the outline of the Sermon on the Mount. My reconstruction follows below:

		LUTHER'S OUTLINE OF Mt. 5-7
I	5:3-7:12	CHRIST'S PREACHING / TEACHING
1.1	**5:3-20**	**Introduction**
1.1.1	5:3-12	The structure of pure doctrine and Christian life is organized around two foci, the doctrine of justification by faith, and the doctrine of the two kingdoms.
1.1.2	5:13-16	The preaching of orthodoxy.
1.1.3	5:17-20	The place of law within soteriology.
1.2	**5:21-6:18**	**Teaching: Orthodoxy**
1.2.1	5:21-48	The theological basis of pure doctrine: The doctrine of the two kingdoms.
1.2.2.	6:1-18	The significance of intention: The Christian life must remain hidden in the world.
1.3	**6:19-7:12**	**Application: Orthopraxis**
1.3.1	6:19-34	God's love to the world is expressed through its stations and offices.
1.3.2	7:1-6	The office of doctrinal judgment: Christ's ordering of the preaching ministry.
1.3.3	7:7-11	Basis for a Christian life (I): Prayer for divine power.
1.3.4	7:12	Basis for a Christian life (II): The use of human reason.
II	7:13-7:27	CHRIST'S WARNINGS
2.1	7:13-14	Warning against conformity to the world.
2.2	7:15-20	Warning against prophets whose fruits reveal false doctrine and/or life.
2.3	7:21-27	God's judgment upon teachings that are not orthodox.

Luther is not completely consistent in his outline, probably because he indicates different concerns in different scriptural contexts. The minor variation which exists is of little importance.

The suggested outline indicates that Luther regards the doctrine of the two kingdoms to be particularly significant as the theological basis for his general interpretation of the Sermon on the Mount. Though the introduction clearly establishes this doctrine as one of the two foci of his soteriology, it is nevertheless more basic to the exegesis of the Sermon on the Mount than the doctrine of justification by faith. For this reason his program of restoring pure doctrine does not reduce his concern for a pure life, and it definitely does not lead to antinomianism.

NOTES

[1.] That this practice was frequently followed, is indicated by a letter of November 1526 from Melanchton to John Agricola (*LW* 15:X).

[2.] Luther's lectures on Genesis were edited by Veit Dietrich, who put his own stamp on them (*LW*, 2:X). It is a well-known fact that Dietrich's editorial work was performed so liberally, that conflicts might occur for that reason (*LW*, 12:VIII-IX, cf. 18:X).

[3.] More often called "Anabaptists." Historically, this concept is accurate, because most of them were baptized as infants and rebaptized as adult believers. Nevertheless this is, as a characteristic of the theology of this tradition, rather imprecise. They should rather be named "Baptists" because they rejected infant baptism as valid; consequently, they themselves did not consider baptism of believers as a re-baptism. Nor should the nickname "Enthusiasts" ("*Schwärmer*") be used, because this concept implies a confessionally based judgment which is rather invalid in other contexts. Whenever I use the word "Baptist" in this book I refer to the Baptists of the 16th-century.

[4.] Cf. his interpretations of Mt. 5:9 (of the public character of the preaching office; *LW*, 21:44), and of Mt. 6:16-18 (of the secret character of the Christian life in general; *LW*, 21:163-164).

[5.] Thomas Aquinas, cf. his discussion, *Summa Theologiae*, I, II, Q. 6 and especially Q. 77, Arts. 7, 8 (*LW*, 21:88, note 33).

[6.] The saying is from the *Vitae Patrum*, reprinted in *Patrologia, Series Latina*, LXXIII, 940 (*LW*, 21:88, note 34).

[7.] Luther is concerned that Christians should not chase political power. He did not reject the demands for justice of the peasants in 1524-1525, but their demands for power (cf. *Admonition to Peace: A Reply to the Twelve Articles of the Peasants in Swabia*; *LW*, 46:35-44; *An Open Letter on the Harsh Book against the Peasants*; *LW* 46:57-86).

[8.] Cf. Luther's *Two Kinds of Righteousness*, 1519 (*LW*, 31:293-306).

[9.] In their comments on Mt. 5:42, the Church Fathers generally affirmed economic communism among Christians. The Medieval theologians gradually accepted commerce, the use of interest, etc., however, contradictory concerns influenced the economic doctrines of the Medieval ages. One tradition restricted the right of the individual to do business in a capitalist way in order to increase their own property. Thomas Aquinas disputed the right of any human being to hold private property; God is the sole owner of the created nature. Another tradition tolerated and encouraged economic freedom, the urbanization of society, and the bureaucratization of civil administration that created a need of monetary institutions. The Church soon participated eagerly in the economic life.

[10.] Luther's Catechisms; see even An Exposition of the Lord's Prayer for simple Laymen (1519; LW, 42:15-81).

[11.] The Reformation was carried through in Denmark-Norway, for instance, in 1537. On his introduction of the Reformation in Sweden 10 years earlier King Gustav Vasa confiscated both church property and the bishops' and the clergy's share of the tithes with the result that he almost quadruplicated his income from then on (Broch 1954, 3:80). It is highly unlikely, however, that Luther regarded this kind of policy to be a problem until the later part of the 1530s.

[12.] *To the Christian Nobility of the German Nation Concerning the Reform of the Christian Estate* (1520; *LW* 44:115-217).

[13.] The word Luther uses that is translated "calling," is *Beruff*, which originally meant a mission to which one is called, but in the ordinary language it was used for a secular profession or occupation.

[14.] The final break with the Roman Catholic church came in 1530. Luther never tried to join his forces with the Baptists. He was therefore isolated theologically in all directions at that time.

[15.] For instance, Tertullian (*On Prescription against Heretics*, # 26. 41; *ANF*, 3:255. 263; *On Baptism*, # 18; *ANF*, 3:677). *Didache, or The Teaching of the Twelve Apostles* (# 9:6; *ANF*, 7:380); Clement of Alexandria (*The Stromata, or Miscellanies*, # 1.12; *ANF*, 2:312); the pseudo-Clement *Recognitions of Clement*, # 2.4; *ANF*, 8:98); *Constitutions of the Holy Fathers* (# 3.1.5; *ANF*, 7:427); Augustine (*Augustine*, 154-155, 156; the *NPNF* text, 10:159); Hippolytus (*The Refutation of All Heretics*, # 5.3, 9.12; *ANF*, 5:55, 133); Methodius (*The Banquet of the Ten Virgins*, # 4.4; *ANF*, 6:324; *On Things Created*, # 1; *ANF*, 6:379); Cyprian (*The Treaties of Cyprian*, # 50; *ANF*, 5:546); *Revelation of John* (*ANF*, 8:586); *Martyrdom of Habib the Deacon* (*ANF*, 8:694).

[16] For instance, *LW* 21:35, 73, 80, 166, 266, 286.

[17.] Wingren (1948:193) has written the classical analysis of this subject. His conclusion is that, an "avocation" is to realize God's love in the daily life in the stations. By being in "vocation," the believers are God's partners in the world.

[18.] In his dealing with Luther's hermeneutical principles, Althaus (1981:77) emphasizes that his general rule is, "scripture is to be interpreted according to its simple literal sense ... unless a recognized article of faith compels us to another interpretation" (Althaus 1981:386). In his view, the principle of *analogia fidei* has primary emphasis on the general biblical message over against Luther's literal interpretation of scripture. In this case, *analogia fidei* primarily means the doctrine of justification by faith alone: "scripture is always to be interpreted according to the analogy of scripture. And this is nothing else than the analogy of the gospel. Christocentric interpretation for Luther thus means gospel-centered interpretation, understood in terms of the gospel of justification by faith alone" (Althaus 1981:79).

Pelikan (1959:112) affirms that the literal meaning is primary to Luther and that his basic hermeneutical rule is to use only the precise literal meaning of a scriptural text. When Luther is in theological controversy and in need for scriptural proof, the literal meaning of the text is the only valid one. Only "compelling reasons" could force Luther to leave an obvious, literal meaning of a text. For instance, "the statement of the text itself that it was not to be taken literally; the powerful indication by another passage to this same effect; the clash between a literal interpretation and 'a clear article of the faith' [i.e., *analogia fidei*]" (Pelikan 1959:126-127). Consequently, Pelikan, too, admits that Luther's biblical hermeneutics may be grounded in doctrine rather than in the literal understanding of the text itself.

[19.] It is crucial to understand Luther in light of both of these doctrines. The use of the doctrine of justification by faith helps Luther to affirm the Sermon on the Mount as a genuine part of the gospel, because this doctrine makes it possible to distinguish between *lex Christi* and *lex naturae* and settle the conflict between the *opus alienium* and the *opus proprium* (Bauman 1985:358). On the other hand, his vocational ethics build the bridge necessary between the demands of the Sermon on the Mount and creation ethics. It is absolutely necessary that the precepts of non-violence and non-resistance are restricted by the creation morality: "Since God created the world, he cannot therefore in the Sermon on the Mount intend that it perish. From that perspective, he [Luther] gains appreciation for the violence of government as divine service" (Bauman 1985:170-171).

[20.] My observation is confirmed by Althaus: "scripture cannot be in conflict with Christ its head, that is, with the gospel ... The interpreter has the right so to interpret all passages of scripture that they agree with the gospel, the obvious center of the scripture; that is, to apply Christ-centered and gospel-centered interpretation" (Althaus 1981:336). "Luther's ultimate authority and standard was not the book of the Bible and the canon as such but that scripture which interpreted itself and also criticized itself from its own center: from Christ and from the radically understood gospel. For Luther the authority of scripture is strictly gospel-centered. ... The canon itself was, as far as Luther was concerned, a piece of ecclesiastical tradition and therefore subject to criticism on the basis of God's word" (Althaus 1981:336). Wisløff explains this hermeneutics: "scripture is its own interpreter, for it brings the witness of Christ all through. Therefore we always ought to interpret scripture so that it is in harmony with its own testimony about the center of the Bible: Salvation by grace, through faith in Christ alone" (Wisløff 1983:72; cf. Pelikan 1959:86).

[21.] The significance of the historical context for Luther's exegesis leads Gritsch to state that "Luther was a contextual rather than a systematic theologian, a biblical scholar who felt constrained to relate his findings to concrete situations relating to the issues of his age" (Gritsch 1983:266).

John Wesley's Interpretation of the Sermon on the Mount

Historical and Text-critical Remarks

Wesley's journals and diaries frequently account that he preached on the Sermon on the Mount (Outler 1975:13; *WJ*, 2:486 note 1; cf. Doughty 1955:88). From the beginning of his field-preaching activities until he published the first *Standard Sermons* in 1746, he preached on these scriptures more than 100 times (*WW*, 1:467).

Wesley published his 44 *Standard Sermons* in four volumes in 1746, 1748, 1750, and 1760. In 1771 he added nine more sermons making the total number 53. Thirteen discourses on the Sermon on the Mount were included in the original four volumes (*WW*, 1:466-698). Together with his *Explanatory Notes upon the New Testament*, published 1755, these discourses provide the basis for this analysis of his interpretation of the Sermon on the Mount.

A list of Wesley's 13 discourses upon the Sermon on the Mount reveals that he for some reason did not include any sermon on the antitheses of Mt. 5:21-48, which are the most disputed parts of the Sermon on the Mount. Hermeneutically as well as theologically, it is of great importance to understand the reason for this omission.

No.	Script.	Title	Publ.
21	5:1-4	Upon Our Lord's Sermon on the Mount, I	1748
22	5:5-7	Upon [...], II	1748
23	5:8-12	Upon [...], III	1748
24	5:13-16	Upon [...], IV	1748
25	5:17-20	Upon [...], V	1748
5:21-48 **No sermons**			
26	6:1-15	Upon [...], VI	1748
27	6:16-18	Upon [...], VII	1748
28	6:19-23	Upon [...], VIII	1748
29	6:24-34	Upon [...], IX	1748
30	7:1-12	Upon [...], X	1750
31	7:13-14	Upon [...], XI	1750
32	7:15-20	Upon [...], XII	1750
33	7:21-27	Upon [...], XIII	1750

Why did Wesley dedicate as many as 13 sermons upon the Sermon on the Mount out of the original 44 *Standard Sermons*? This cannot be accidental and may indicate that they are the closest he ever came to writing a "systematic" or comprehensive presentation of his theology.

Wesley wrote his comments on the New Testament in 1754-1755, *Explanatory Notes upon the New Testament*; however, they have not been appreciated by Methodist theologians as a genuine source of his exegesis and theology. This work is often considered to be random comments of little value. Biblical scholars, even Methodists, seldom give it serious consideration for four reasons: Wesley's translation of the Greek New Testament deviates significantly from the King James Version and sounds unfamiliar; his terminology is popular and unacademic; a number of his exegetic comments are unusual, they might even seem to be rather awkward to some; he gives credit to Johannes Bengel for "many of his excellent notes" (*NT-Notes*, 7), which Wesley may have translated or abridged.

The appreciation of Wesley's *Explanatory Notes* is now growing. *The Cambridge History of the Bible* comments that Wesley's translation of the New Testament is based upon a fresh and independent study of the Greek text, and that his judgment with respect to the Greek text is generally sound. Most of his approximately 12,000 changes from the King James Version were accepted in the Revised Version in the 1870s (Greenslade 1963:3:368).

Wesley's unacademic style was the result of a deliberate choice. He wanted to avoid extensive commentaries, because his intention was "to assist the unlearned reader" (*NT-Notes*, 7). The same motivation is expressed in the preface of the *Standard Sermons* (*WW*, 1:104). He was a pioneer in the general enlightenment of the people (Prince 1926:9) and given an honored place in the history of education in Great Britain (*EWM*, 748). He intended to do theology for the ordinary people and for the revival movement and not for other scholars.

A number of sayings of Wesley indicate that the Sermon on the Mount has a special place in the biblical basis for his theology (for instance, *WW*, 1:470, 473-474, 475). In his journal he informs that he preached on "the Sermon on the Mount, the noblest compendium of religion which is to be found in the oracles of God" (*WJ*, 5:433). He here conceives the Sermon on the Mount as a summary of the Christian religion. For this reason one should not be surprised that his comments on the Sermon on the Mount constitute a significant part of the doctrinal basis of Methodism.[1] An analysis of his preaching on different scriptures from the Sermon on the Mount gives reason to believe that he used the Sermon on the Mount intentionally for the formation of his theology, particularly in critical periods of the history of the revival (Meistad 1983:99-109).

Outler's critical edition of the sermons of John Wesley has made his original text more easily accessible than it used to be. The sermon texts are reliable and undisputed by the scholars. Extensive genetic commentaries prove that he had access to classic commentaries by, for instance, Augustine, Luther, and Calvin.

There is no evidence that he uses any of these explicitly, for when he refers to the thoughts of these theologians, he normally uses other sources. More significant is the influence on his text from Anglican divines, for instance, bishop Offspring Blackall of Exeter, J. Blair, S. Collett and not least the Anglican homilies from 1547, as well as from the Eastern Antiquity. This means that he was more informed by Byzantine theological sources than by Western theologians.

The text of Wesley's *Explanatory Notes upon the New Testament* is more complex. Many editions were published in his lifetime, and he revised each edition before publication. The originality of the text is not in doubt, however, and the revisions therefore indicate the development of his exegetic insights. An example is that he originally translated the Greek term *makarios* into "blessed," the concept he also used in the discourses. In the 1770's he changed the translation to "happy." He obviously did not finalize his interpretation of the Sermon on the Mount by the time of the first edition of his sermons and exegetic comments, and for that reason it is also necessary to look into his later comments on the Sermon on the Mount.

A far more disputed issue is whether Wesley's exegetic works are reliable with regard to his theology. My conclusion is that, apart from his comments on the Revelation, his exegetic comments should be regarded a reliable source of his theology. He did not merely copy the works of others but used them critically, selecting and arranging them to serve his own purposes.

Historical Contexts of Interpretation Compared

Luther and Wesley basically deal with two different kinds of contexts. One is general and made up by the historical, cultural, philosophical, and theological traditions that compose the backgrounds of their training as theologians. The other is specific and made up by the historical, political, and social situation into which they intend to speak their messages.

Luther's general context is the first half of the 1500s in Germany, experiencing the breakdown of the Middle Ages and the transition to modern times. His theological training has its focus in the Scholastic theology, and particularly the Nominalist tradition. It is characteristic to his situation that he himself contributes to accentuate the transition from medieval to modern times. It is a time of revolution, and he is the revolutionary *par excellence*. He launches the earthquake that makes the most significant social and political institution, the Roman Catholic Church, shake in its foundations. By questioning its soteriology he threatens its power over the masses.

Luther's immediate context is revealed by his polemics, that in his Sermon on the Mount discourses mainly are directed in two directions. To the right he criticizes the Roman Catholic Church for its Pelagian soteriology and the religious customs coming out of it, as explained above. To the left his target was radical Protestantism, the spiritualists and the Baptists. His basic accusation is similar to both sides; because of their political aspirations they confuse the doctrine of the two kingdoms. The Roman Catholics seek a general dominion over the civil authorities, and the Baptists confuse the Protestant message of liberation from the guilt of sin with political liberation. It is important to keep in mind at this point that the Peasants' War, which was experienced by him as a national as well as a religious catastrophe, is a significant part of his immediate context; his discourses were delivered 5-7 years after this war.[2]

Luther preaches over the Sermon on the Mount with the purpose to eliminate this confusion, obviously because this scripture—according to his opinion—has been deeply misunderstood. His constructive contribution is to affirm that Christ's message was of a purely soteriological nature, dealing with the salvation of the soul and also with how a justified sinner should live accordingly in the world in love. In his discourses he pictures a system of soteriology that is made up by two doctrines, the doctrine of justification by faith alone, and the doctrine of the two kingdoms. The Roman Catholics need to hear both doctrines. The Baptists accept justification by faith, but they then distort the system by applying salvation to their social and political situation.

The doctrine of justification by faith is developed as an answer to what Luther believes is a distorted soteriology of merits of the Roman Catholic Church. He insists that the authority of the fathers and councils is subordinate to the authority of the Holy Scriptures (Steinmetz 1986:94). His exegetic studies had persuaded him that salvation depends on Christ's sacrificial death on the cross and not on human merits as defined by the church. God justifies by grace sinners who have faith in Christ. According to him, it is not the scriptures that need radical hermeneutical surgery but the scholastic theology (Steinmetz 1986:38). The works of the Christian should not be understood as merits for salvation but as faith that works by love. He at this point joins the Augustinian tradition focusing upon grace alone — *sola gratia* — to a degree that makes salvation dependent on God's election of the person.

Wesley's general context is the British rationalism. The age of reason dominates the cultural as well as the theological ideas; a great many Anglican divines, who are decisive to the theological agenda, are Deists. Wesley himself was, however, more influenced by his family's strong roots in the Puritan piety. For this reason, he as a young Anglican priest disputed the Deist theology by insisting on a close relationship between the Christian and God. This relationship should carry fruits in good works to the neighbor in need. For this reason his polemics was directed against the Anglican rationalism, the Lutheran antinomianism, and the rich Methodists who kept their fortunes to themselves rather than distributing their resources to the poor. His Puritan roots were more related to its life than to its Calvinist doctrines. He therefore attacks the doctrine of predestination, replacing it by the Arminian emphasis on the engraced free will. On the other hand he is deeply influenced by the philosophy of John Locke, whose empiricism he interprets in light of his own theological concerns. He focuses human reason and the necessity of experience as the basis of knowledge no less than Locke, but he also emphasizes that human reason is enlightened by God's grace.

Wesley lived at the dawn of British industrialism. He lived almost the entire 18th century and experienced dramatic changes of his nation socially and economically. The industries were growing fast and created masses of industrial workers, who at that early stage had not been organized in unions which could take care of their rights over against capitalist exploitation. Compared to our age, the political system of Great Britain hardly could be characterized as more than pre-democratic. In this historical situation he took sides with the poor against the rich, and he made the concern for the poor a theological proof of Christian legitimacy.

The formulation of the way of salvation is Wesley's primary answer to the challenges of his time. He suggests this way as a constructive theological contribution, focusing the union between creation and salvation in union, and sanctification by faith explained as a spirit-filled life (participating in the divine life) in love to God and neighbor (social-ethical and -political activism).

Exegesis

The Scriptural Context (5:1-2; 7:28-29)
Wesley defines the scriptural context of the Sermon on the Mount by asking: Who is speaking? What is he teaching? Whom is he teaching? And, finally, How is he teaching? He thus opens up for a systematic presentation of his soteriology and its implications.

WHAT is he [Christ] teaching?
Wesley answers: "The way to heaven ... to the kingdom ... the full and perfect will of God" (*WW*, 1:470). Christ's message is defined in developmental, eschatological, and ethical terms. He also expresses a strong belief that the bible contains the infallible revelation of salvation.

WHO is speaking?
Wesley describes the preacher of the Sermon on the Mount by presenting elements for an elaborated christology:

(1) "The Lord of heaven and earth, the Creator of all." Wesley identifies the savior with the creator who is the Lord of heaven and

earth at the same time. Most significantly, salvation is linked together with creation.

(2) "The Lord our *Governor*," who has the ultimate right to
dispose over everybody.

(3) "The great *Lawgiver*" could enforce all his laws upon humanity but he implements another plan of salvation.

(4) "The eternal *Wisdom* of the Father" is related to the concept
of peace, which is basic to Wesley's understanding of the biblical
vision of salvation. In Genesis the created world in its original
state is characterized by wholeness, the Hebrew prophets envision
the realization of peace in God's final restoration of cosmos, and
the Christian bible pictures Christ as the prince and pattern of
peace. Peace is the essence and goal of salvation, including the
natural, human, and social world. "The Wisdom of the Father" has
a triple emphasis; (a) the origin of humanity is the existence in
unity with God; (b) the "inmost frame of humanity" is a relation to
God, to fellow human beings, and to every creature; the individual
is always related to a spiritual and a social context; (c) the will of
God is to be adapted to all the circumstances of human existence.

(5) "The *God of love*," whose mission is to fulfil the prophecies
of Is. 42:6-7 according to Lk. 1:79, which is to realize peace in the
world.

(6) "The great *Prophet* of the Lord," referring to Deut. 18:19-
20 and Acts 3:23.[3]

(7) "*The Son of God*, who came from heaven, is here showing
us the way to heaven."

WHOM is he [Christ] teaching?
Referring to Mt. 11:29, Wesley relates *hoi mathetai autou* (his
disciples) to *hoi ochloi* (the people) taught by Christ to the mountain, as well as "all the children of men, the whole race of mankind, the children that were yet unborn — all the generations to
come even to the end of the world who should ever hear the words
of this life" (*WW*, 1:472). Against the Calvinist theology of predestination as well as the Roman Catholic "double standard" doctrine he insists that the concern of all parts of the Sermon on the
Mount is all humankind, "either all the parts of this discourse are

to be applied to humanity in general or no part," for "they are all connected together, all joined as the stones in an arch, of which one cannot be taken away without destroying the whole fabric" (*WW*, 1:473).

This systemic perspective of the Sermon on the Mount may indicate that Wesley's discourses are motivated by a concern for a more systematic presentation of his theology. His intention is to give a "systematic" synopsis of his theology by writing and publishing his 13 discourses on the Sermon on the Mount.[4] One of his basic hermeneutical principles is revealed, too, the analogy of faith, implying that the details should be interpreted in light of their wider scriptural and doctrinal context. This hermeneutical principle is particularly necessary for the interpretation of his dealing with the antitheses of Mt. 5:21-48.

Wesley uses the phrase "the way of salvation" (*WW*, 1:472). The traditional phrase is "the order of salvation," and his theology is often interpreted as a kind of *ordo salutis* (the order of salvation). With his concept he identifies salvation as a dynamic process rather than as a mechanical pattern of preset religious experiences.

HOW is he [Christ] teaching?

Christ's teaching has priority over the teachings of the apostles. They are servants only, but He is the Lord.

The Sermon on the Mount contains "the whole plan of his [Christ's] religion"; "a full prospect of Christianity," that describes "the nature of that holiness without which no man shall see the Lord" (Heb. 12:14). Wesley suggests that Christ in it delivers a unique message: "never besides here did he give, of set purpose, a general view of the whole. Nay, we have nothing else of this kind in all the Bible" (*WW*, 1:473). As the beatitudes are "The sum of all true religion" (*WW*, 1:475), he makes them the hermeneutical key of the Christian Gospel. They "constitute real Christianity ... [that is] holiness" (*WW*, 1:651) because they reveal God's will for humanity. They also re-create or restore the original relationship between God and humanity.

God's will is revealed with love, a divine love which particularly is expressed through the beatitudes as "The way of pleasantness; the path to calm, joyous peace, to heaven below and heaven above!" (*WW*, 1:474). He emphasizes "heaven below and heaven above" equally. According to the usual understanding at his time, the kingdom of God is far above the human world, but he also locates it to the present world. Whenever the powers of the kingdom are effective, it can be realized as a "heaven below."[5]

In its expression of the eschatological wholeness, harmony, and union between God, humanity, and nature, peace is the concept that more than others integrates the notions of creation, salvation and re-creation. Peace and love follow from the right relation to God, made possible by the atonement and faith in Christ. The restoration of the law to its proper place is implied. A tension exists between present and future perspectives with an emphasis on the present. Peace and love are described as order, harmony, justice, happiness, safety, health, prosperity, and absence of war and conflicts. His vision also stresses active non-violence and peacemaking, human friendship, assurance, power over sin, and renewal of ethical life, etc. His soteriology is rooted both in his theology of creation and in his visions of the new creation. The beatitudes reveal the way to the peace that God has designed for humanity.

Reinforcing the connection between creation and salvation, Wesley affirms that the sermon is divine: "It speaks the Creator of all—a God, a God appears! Yea, *ho on*,[6] the being of beings, Jehovah, the self-existent, the supreme, the God who is over all, blessed for ever!" (*WW*, 1:474).

Wesley offers another outline for the Sermon on the Mount based on exegetic observations (*NT-Notes*, 28):

Part	Script.	Contents
1	5:3-12	A sweet invitation to true holiness and happiness.
2	5:13-16	A persuasive to impart it [holiness and happiness] to others.
3	5:17-7:12	A description of true Christian holiness; in which, it is easy to observe, the latter part exactly answers the former.
4	7:13-27	The conclusion, giving a sure mark of the true way, warning against false prophets, exhorting to follow after holiness.

Wesley replaces Bengel's suggestion that Christ in the Sermon on the Mount teaches true righteousness with holiness, probably polemically against a Lutheran interpretation. His frequent use of "righteousness" in the discourses is usually synonymous with "holiness" (for instance, *WW*, 1:495-498). Theological implications are:

(1) The beatitudes are "invitations" to God's offer of salvation that is "holiness and happiness," expressions related to Wesley's exegesis based on peace. Salvation is described as "the way to heaven." Consequently, this way of salvation is not to be understood as dependent on human efforts and merits, but as a free gift offered by God.

(2) The twin parables of the salt and light demonstrate that God's gift is given for the purpose of being brought out into the world by the Christian.

(3) As the corpus of the Sermon on the Mount, Mt. 5:17-7:12 explains various aspects of the holiness as gifts and tasks at the same time. Mt. 7:12 is "exactly answering chapter 5:17," commenting: "This [Mt. 7:12] is the sum of all. ... The whole is comprised in one word—Imitate the God of love" (*NT-Notes*, 42). The peak of this part of the sermon is 5:48, corresponding to the central place given to perfection in his soteriology.[7]

Wesley's comment "in which ... the latter part exactly answers the former" explains why he eliminates 5:21-48 as scriptures for his discourses. He is inspired by Augustine: "The ... beatitudes are ... stages of Perfection" (Augustine, 6), who connects the seven stages of perfection with the seven gifts of the Holy Spirit modeled after Is. 11:2. The beatitudes therefore are "eight blessings ... [Christ] annexing them to so many steps in Christianity" (*NT-Notes*, 28). He follows Augustine by identifying certain antitheses as practical consequences of certain beatitudes (Meistad 1983:33, 87-88, 90-92). Because the beatitudes are interpreted as the way of salvation, each stage in the process of salvation may be described by certain characteristics. His interpretation of Mt. 5:21-48 therefore has to be studied in the light of his exegesis of Mt. 5:3-12.

(4) "The sure mark of the true way [of salvation]" is pointing to the second twin parable of the Sermon on the Mount, dealing with the Judgment: The Christians are holy people who do not only hear the message, but actually do it.

The Scriptural Context (5:1-2; 7:28-29) Compared

Wesley agrees with Luther in defining the Sermon on the Mount as a soteriological text. Because the context of his preaching is a revival, his focus is on the process of salvation: How can I be saved, and how should I live as a Christian? Though Luther's and Wesley's primary interpretations are parallel, their historical contexts make them to develop different soteriologies. Starting from the teaching, preaching, and healing ministries of Christ according to Mt. 4:23. Wesley's discussion is broader than Luther's, who limits his focus to the issue of relationship between faith and works (*LW*, 21:284).

Luther and Wesley have different starting points with regard to establishing a theological frame of reference for their interpretations of the Sermon on the Mount. Luther's aim is to imitate Christ's restoration of orthodoxy. This does not mean that his interest is purely doctrinal. He also carefully stresses the nature of Christian ethics as being fruits of faith, or as the true effect of this orthodoxy. Different from Wesley he rather quickly leads the attention to the stations and orders of his contemporary society, or, to his doctrine of the two kingdoms. Elements of a hierarchical structure of society are implied, particularly concerning the right of preaching.

In his postscript, Luther clarifies his position by discussing more carefully the issue of cause and effects in his soteriology. The doctrine of justification by faith is basic. The problem is, however, that Christ in the Sermon on the Mount speaks more of works than of faith. A tension exists between Paul and Matthew at this point. Therefore, he distinguishes sharply between faith *per se* and its fruits. Salvation is a divine gift by grace through faith. Faith necessarily leads to fruits, but fruits do not merit salvation. What Christ teaches in the Sermon on the Mount is not how to become a Christian, but the nature of the fruits coming from faith, and how Christians are consoled when their faithful discipleship causes hate, envy, and persecution from the world. Christians may then expect their recompense in heaven.

Wesley's starting point is that the Sermon on the Mount is a divine program explaining the comprehensive nature of salvation in light of the teaching, preaching, and healing ministries of Christ (Mt. 4:23). What needs to be restored, according to him, is not theological doctrines but God's creation. His soteriology is therefore concerned with the re-creation of humanity as well as the entire cosmos to its original state before the Fall. He describes salvation as a "way" to heaven. A heaven realized in the present world is implied. He anticipates that the divine powers shall transform human existence to the image of God, and societies to God's peace.

Luther and Wesley equally emphasize the eschatological context of the Sermon on the Mount, however, in different ways. While Luther's focus is on the present consolation in hope for future salvation, Wesley's is more on the present fulfillment of God's promise in terms of actual transformation of the human existence according to peace.

The Beatitudes (5:3-12)
The beatitudes are most significant to Wesley's hermeneutics. He regards them to be an accurate description of the different parts in the way of salvation, beginning with the poverty of spirit and leading to persecution of the faithful disciple. Consequently, he

finds the hermeneutical key for his understanding of the Sermon on the Mount in them.

The Beatitudes Compared

To Luther, the beatitudes remind the Christians that they exist in two kingdoms, the spiritual kingdom by faith and the secular kingdom by their social responsibilities. The beatitudes in general deal with the spiritual life, because nobody should be poor nor meek in their secular life. On the other sides, the spiritual attitudes described in the beatitudes should prevail in Christians' exercise of their secular offices as well.

Wesley ends his interpretations of the beatitudes by exhorting:

> Behold Christianity in its native form, as delivered by its great Author! This is the genuine religion of Jesus Christ ... What beauty appears in the whole! How just a symmetry! What exact proportion in every part! How desirable is the happiness here described! How venerable, how lovely the holiness! This is the *spirit* of religion; the quintessence of it. These are indeed the *fundamentals* of Christianity. (*WW*, 1:530)

To Wesley, the beatitudes are a summary of the Christian religion, they are "the whole." He admires the balanced and interrelated presentation of "happiness" and "holiness" of the beatitudes. On the one hand, they offer the free grace of God to be received by faith alone. On the other hand, they lead the believer on the way of salvation, including holiness interpreted practically and ethically. Experienced religion will have outward consequences due to the likeness with Christ. In short, the beatitudes reveal the complete way of salvation. They are eschatological promises of God's grace and invite the sinner to accept God's grace and enter into the life of discipleship.

On this basis Wesley uses the antitheses as examples of the kind of fruits of faith which may be expected at the various stages on the way of salvation described by the beatitudes. By doing that, he puts the emphasis on the reception of free and undeserved grace (the beatitudes), and works (the antitheses) as the fruits of faith. He makes these connections when the believer is under grace only and not under the law, thus repudiating any interpretation of works as merits providing salvation.

Luther and Wesley both interpret the beatitudes within the theological framework of soteriology. When spelling out its implications, however, they differ. To Luther, the need to protect the doctrine of salvation by faith alone makes him exclude soteriology from creation and the everyday life of the Christian. Another doctrine is therefore necessary to explain the relations between soteriology and society, namely, the doctrine of the two kingdoms. To Wesley, the soteriological work of God is viewed in line with his work of creation, thus implying that the experience of salvation brings a new relation to society as well. There is no other way to express this experience except socially.

The Poor in Spirit (5:3)

Wesley relates his understanding of spiritual poverty to spiritual development. The beatitudes are "the sum of all true religion" (*WW*, 1:475). Phrases like "begins ... goes on ...; come up higher" (*WW*, 1:475) imply that the beatitudes resemble a characteristic pattern of growth, of which the poverty of spirit is the first and foundational step. Each beatitude also indicates a specific "disposition of heart" (*WW*, 1:476) characteristic to the way of salvation.

This development is a growth in grace that takes place in the sinner from the natural state in sin to the imprinting of the image of God in the person. Wesley is at this point influenced by the Antiochean and Byzantine schools of theology. Consequently, his doctrine of sanctification should be interpreted in light of the Eastern-Orthodox concept of *theosis*, relating salvation to the actual change of the Christian as they share God's nature (2 Pet. 1:4).

The beatitudes are described by Wesley as "the sum of all true religion." The antitheses of Mt. 5:21-48 are later interpreted as works and attitudes that are described by the beatitudes. The Sermon on the Mount is therefore more than a collection of ethical commandments. First and foremost the beatitudes, in particular, are an outstanding revelation of "the way to heaven."

Poverty of spirit is the first step on this way of salvation.[8] The poor in spirit are "the humble; they who know themselves, who are convinced of sin; those to whom God hath given that first repentance which is previous to faith in Christ" (*WW*, 1:477); they are "unfeignedly penitent; they who are truly convinced of sin; who see and feel the state they are in by nature, being deeply sensible of their sinfulness, guiltiness, helplessness" (*NT-Notes*, 28). He never defends poverty as a virtue, nor does he regard poverty to be an expression of natural order. His point is that the experience of Christ's merits leads to humility.

Wesley's concept the "first repentance" reinforces the developmental structure of the process of salvation, as a "first" repentance by necessity requires a second.[9] Repentance is related to the acknowledgment of the totally corrupted state in which the human being is by nature apart from the grace of God. The original sin is conceived in organic and medical-therapeutic terms—favorite concepts of Byzantine soteriology—and affecting the total human existence; the person "has a deep sense of the loathsome leprosy of sin, which he brought with him from his mother's womb which overspreads his whole soul, and totally corrupts every power and faculty thereof" (*WW*, 1:477). His theology of original sin is not as much rooted in the Augustinian judicial paradigm as in a therapeutic view, more closely connected to the Eastern Fathers' concept of original sin as a disease. But he is also rooted in the Augustinian-Protestant tradition; the fall makes the divine atonement absolutely necessary, and the function of the first repentance is to lead the sinner to Christ, who is the only one to atone for human sin and redeem the guilt.

To the issue of repentance Wesley comments "that Christianity begins just where heathen morality ends" (*WW*, 1:480). The recognition of sin is basic to the progress on the way of salvation, for without it no person will feel the need of salvation. At this point, too, he deviates from the Augustinian-Protestant tradition, whose doctrine of Original Sin inevitably leads to a doctrine of predestination.[10] To him, God breaks this logical chain by enabling the sinner to turn to Christ for salvation through prevenient grace. In harmony with the Arminian tradition he includes the necessity of the sinner's use of the free will in turning to God.

In his *Explanatory Notes* Wesley translates the Greek *makarios* of the beatitudes with "happy *are,*" while he in his discourses uses the more common "blessed", without hyphenating "are". This difference indicates a change in his theological emphasis toward a more realized understanding of salvation as an eschatological blessing.[11] Salvation is a present reality to be experienced here and now. The poor in spirit as well as other persons are pronounced *makarioi*, they *are* actually happy. His interpretation of the kingdom of God has its emphasis in realized or, rather, inaugurated eschatology;[12] "it is heaven already opened in the soul" (*WW*, 1:481). His interest is in the fact that the heavenly kingdom is breaking into the present reality. The kingdom of heaven "which is within us" is characterized by "righteousness, and peace, and joy in the Holy Ghost," a phrase which he is using over and over again in all his writings. He defines righteousness as "the life of God in the soul, the mind which was in Christ Jesus, the image of God stamped upon the heart, now renewed after the likeness of him that created it"; peace as "that sweet repose in the blood of Jesus, which leaves no doubt of our acceptance of him"; and joy in the Holy Ghost as the divine person "who seals upon our hearts 'the redemption which is in Jesus,' the righteousness of Christ, imputed[13] to us for 'the remission of the sins that are past'" (*WW*, 1:481).

The fact that salvation is inaugurated in this world but completed in heaven reveals that sin will always remain in the life of the Christian. Wesley therefore relates the kingdom to the atonement. Original sin causes total depravity of soul and body. How can he connect sin with his realized eschatology? He answers by introducing the "second repentance," though the term is not used, indicating that, to live in the inward kingdom of heaven does not create a false sense of security but rather a deepened need to come closer to Christ:

> "Poverty of spirit," in this meaning of the word, begins where a sense of guilt and of the wrath of God ends; and is a continual

sense of our total dependence on him for every good thought or
word or work ... the conviction we feel of inbred sin is deeper
and deeper every day. The more we grow in grace the more do
we see of the desperate wickedness of our heart ... and the necessity of our being entirely renewed in righteousness of true
holiness. (*WW*, 1:482-483)

The Poor in Spirit (5:3) Compared

Luther and Wesley equally affirm that the poverty of spirit is a
religious and not an economic concept. To be poor in spirit implies
repentance and humility toward God. Both have polemical remarks against Roman Catholic ideals of voluntary poverty.

To Luther, the interpretation of this first beatitude exemplifies
the confusion of the two kingdoms made by the Roman Catholics
as well as by the Baptists. He affirms that the spiritual poverty of
the Christian does not exclude a proper financial basis for the execution of the Christian's duties in office. The kingdom of heaven
is a future reward for piety, and nothing to be realized in the present world. The dynamics of God's works in this world are God's
sustaining of creation. The civil stations and orders are means
ordered by God for this purpose. The result is that God works in
different ways in the two kingdoms. In the secular kingdom, creation is sustained, and in the spiritual kingdom, salvation is offered.
These two works of God have nothing to do with one another.

To Wesley, spiritual poverty is the initial step on the way of
salvation. His concern is not to separate the spiritual sphere of life
from the secular, but to understand salvation as a dynamic process
energized by eschatological powers realized within this world.

Three general differences between Luther and Wesley may be
deduced: (1) Their concerns regarding the secular and spiritual
aspects of life are different. Luther's concern is to distinguish between these two aspects and Wesley's concern is to unite them.
The reason is that Luther distinguishes between creation and salvation, while Wesley regards them to be the same work of God,
viewed from different angles. (2) Their eschatological emphases
are different. Luther's eschatology is oriented to the future, while
Wesley's eschatology anticipates the present realization of the

kingdom of God. (3) Their approaches to the society are different. According to Luther, the civil stations are founded in God's order of creation, and they ought to be observed until the *parousia*. Wesley has a perspective of development and actual change.

Those Who Mourn (5:4)

This second beatitude implies another step on the way of salvation. The sinner "begins to know the inward kingdom of heaven" (*WW*, 1:483) and experiences not only sin but a glimpse of redemption as well. Those in this state deepen the experience of guilt, adding mourning because of sin to the feeling of guilt. The mourning is related to the fact that the sinners have had a "taste" of "the pardoning word. ... But ... now ... they cannot see him [God] through the dark cloud" (*WW*, 1:483-484). God's grace has worked conviction of sin and longing for salvation, but the sinner has not yet experienced grace as a saving grace.

Christians will experience a "second mourning" no less than a second repentance. This second mourning is "for the sins and miseries of mankind", for "them that weep not for themselves," and for "the weakness and unfaithfulness of those that are in some measure saved from their sins" (*WW*, 1:486). It is caused by the sanctified Christian's caring for the soul of the neighbor. The eschatological context of the Christian experience makes Wesley haste in terms of active evangelism and caring for others.

Those Who Mourn (5:4) Compared

Luther relates mourning to the Christian experience in light of the encounter with the diabolic powers of this world. Wesley implies a relationship between mourning and the pre-Christian experience of personal sin under the influence of God's prevenient grace. Where Luther establishes a dialectic between external and internal life, Wesley's dialectic is that between the guilt-stricken sinner's mourning over the corrupted state on the one hand, and the experience of assurance of faith on the other.

The interpretations of Luther and Wesley are coming out of their soteriologies and constitute different theological paradigms.

Luther's paradigm is expressed by the concepts of the two-kingdom doctrine, while Wesley's paradigm is characterized by the view that the life of the Christian is in process, or growing in grace.

Wesley's developmental approach begins not very differently from Luther's habitual insistence on the experience of justification following the sinner's repentance, created by the spiritual use of the law. He differs, however, by sketching the further development of the Christian experience. While Luther insists on the *simul iustus et peccator* experience (for instance, *LW*, 21:129, 205), Wesley disputes that a reborn sinner by necessity "must come into a state of darkness" again. Referring to the parable of the child delivery in John 16:19-22, he comments: "They never need lose either their peace or love, or the witness that they are the children of God" (*NT-Notes*, 372).

In summary, Luther's and Wesley's interpretations of the "mourning" in Mt. 5:4 may be sketched like this:

Luther	*Blessed / Happy are they that mourn*	Wesley
The Christian's encounter with the diabolic powers of the world	**Context**	The Christian's encounter with personal and social sin
The doctrines of - The two kingdoms - Justification by faith alone: *Simul iustus et peccator*	**Presuppositions**	The way of salvation as growth in grace: Salvation from the guilt and the power of sin
External (public) and internal (personal) life	**Dialectical tension**	Experiences of sin versus assurance of faith

The "second mourning" is, to Wesley, linked theologically to the gap between the experiences of the majesty and holiness of God on the one hand, and to the sin in the world on the other. Affirming that the mourners are "grieved for the dishonour continually done to the Majesty of heaven and earth" (*WW*, 1:486), he emphasizes this gap no less than Calvin. He preaches the wrath of God and the possibility of damnation and hell in darker colors than usual for his time (cf. *WL*, 3:346). Nevertheless he parts from the Calvinists in his emphasis on God's dynamic acts of salvation in the midst of human life and society. His hermeneutics of peace makes him interpret God's wrath in light of the restoration of the fallen creation rather than the damnation of it. His image of God is one of closeness and love and not one of distance and revenge.

Consequently, Luther's and Wesley's exegeses reveal different eschatologies. If the chiliastic expectancies of Luther weaken his followers' concern about ethics, the opposite is true to Wesley. He, too, has a strong eschatological awareness: "God and eternity are real things. Heaven and hell are in very deed open before you: and ye are on the edge of the great gulf" (*WW*, 1:487). Their eschatological conclusions are also different when it came to living out the Christian experience in everyday life. Contrary to Luther's belief that the Christians will be comforted in heaven, Wesley insists that they will be comforted "More solidly and deeply even in this world" (*NT-Notes*, 29).

The Meek (5:5)

Wesley opens up for the next main part of the way of salvation: "'the winter is past' ... he that comforts the mourners is now returned" (*WW*, 1:488). The person who is poor acknowledges sin, the mourner mourns over the lack of salvation, and the meek is about to experience redemption. The turning-point is near.

Meekness is neither insensibility nor lack of emotions, nor apathy in the sense of the Stoics, nor being without zeal for God. It is but rather the avoidance of "every extreme," to "balance the affections," and it "poses the mind aright ... preserving the mean in every circumstance of life" (*WW*, 1:489; cf. *NT-Notes*, 29).[14] The echoes of Rationalism are recognizable. Wesley establishes meekness is an effect of the relation to God, primarily as a total surrender to God's will, next as governing the relations to the neighbor as "mildness to the good and gentleness to the evil" (*WW*, 1:490). The meek may experience suffering but live with it patiently. The meek are zealous, but their zeal is a divine temper regulated by faith and love.

Meekness implies the sinner's giving up the struggle against sin, making the justifying act of God possible. God is the only giver of salvation. The surrender to God's will is also an ongoing and deepening process in the Christian's life and a significant aspect of sanctification. Meekness is a property of love; "meekness and love" are "particular branches of holiness" (*WW*, 3:548). It therefore belongs to the initial phase of the way of salvation as well as to the way itself.

The promise of the beatitude, "*They shall inherit the earth*," means, "They shall have all things really necessary for life and godliness. They shall enjoy whatever portion God hath given them here, and shall hereafter possess the new earth, wherein dwelleth righteousness" (*NT-Notes*, 29). He does not devalue the life in this world, and the joy of it is part of the spiritual life. There is no separation between the secular and the spiritual, nor any denial of the joy of the world as such. Precisely because his primary focus is on the way of salvation, the life in the world is included.

At this point Wesley introduces the first antithesis in order to explain the implications of this beatitude. It gives guidelines for human emotions, as is shown by Christ's interpretation of the commandment "Thou shalt not kill": "Our Lord here ranks under the head of murder even that anger which goes no farther than the heart" (*WW*, 1:491). His interpretation follows the absolutist tradition. He reinforces his interpretation by omitting the Greek term *eike* (without a cause), that is used in a number of manuscripts.

An established relationship to God by necessity will lead Christians to their neighbors. Religion is founded on God's grace given freely to sinners apart from merits, but its effects will include the neighbor. True piety will lead to active caring for others. He rejects the egoistic piety where the believer puts his or her own salvation into focus in neglect of God's love for all humanity.

The Meek (5:5) Compared

Luther's and Wesley's interpretations logically evolve from the hermeneutics established. Luther bases his exegesis on the doctrine of the two kingdoms and finds that meekness is a virtue of the Christian person only. When the Christian is in office, the obligation is not meekness but anger and punishment on behalf of the civil law.

Wesley identifies meekness as the point on the way of salvation where the experience of justification by faith is at hand. The first meekness signifies the sinner's giving up the fight against sin. It is a human resignation that opens up for the divine saving work. The second meekness is the mind of gentleness given to the reborn sinner in his or her dealing with the world. So while meekness is separated from the life in the world by Luther, indicating that it is a virtue for the spiritual world only, it is integrated in the life of the world by Wesley.

A common concern is their positive valuation of the Christian's life in the world. No recommendation of withdrawal from the world is given. On the contrary, the will of God is that the Christian should live in the midst of the world. Another shared concern is their unanimous emphasis on how it is not possible to remain a Christian without loving one's neighbor.

Those Who Hunger and Thirst after Righteousness (5:6)

Wesley interprets this beatitude as a turning-point on the way of salvation. "The hindrances of true religion" (*WW*, 1:495) are left behind and replaced by the experience of Christ's righteousness, laying the way open for the continuous work of God. The basic term is righteousness, defined as "the image of God, the mind which was in Christ Jesus." His use of the term is rooted in the Byzantine tradition as well as in the Protestant. Righteousness is "every holy and heavenly temper in one; springing from as well as terminating in the love of God as our Father and Redeemer, and the love of all men for his sake" (*WW*, 1:495). Righteousness is in this scripture the same as sanctification.

Wesley observes "that hunger and thirst are the strongest of all our bodily appetites" (*WW*, 1:496). He criticizes folk religions that are concerned with outward deeds, and that lead to increased hunger and thirst. The "religion of the world" implies "the doing no harm, the abstaining from outward sin, the doing good; ... the using the means of grace." As an alternative he has established his societies, which general rules actually are designed after the same pattern as his description of "the religion of the world" above. What makes the program of his societies different from folk religions, however, is that they are for persons "who appeared to be deeply convinced of sin, and earnestly groaning for redemption." The societies are formed for people "having the form and seeking the power of godliness" (*WW*, 9:69; cf. *WW*, 11:322). The only condition for membership is a desire "to flee from the wrath to come, to be saved from their sins" (*WW*, 9:70).

To Wesley, the dividing line between the outside and inside of religion is neither the experience of sanctification, nor the assurance of faith, but the desire for salvation. The condition for membership in the Methodist societies is the seeking for "the power of godliness." He is positive that this desire will necessarily lead to the search for salvation by avoiding evil, doing good, and most important, using the means of grace in order to base salvation the divine reality. "The religion of the world," however, is based on human efforts rather than on God's grace. He replaces the religion of form with "the power of godliness" (*WW*, 1:497). The sinner searching for righteousness shall experience "his love ... the entire renewal of thy soul in that image of God wherein it was originally created. ... Let nothing satisfy thee but the power of godliness ... the dwelling in God and God in thee" (*WW*, 1:498). Consequently, to hunger and thirst for righteousness is to seek sanctification.

Those Who Hunger and Thirst after Righteousness (5:6) Compared

Neither Luther nor Wesley interprets the righteousness of Mt. 5:6 as a justified state viewed as a forensic concept. Luther takes it to be the human righteousness stemming from the life in the sta-

tions and the offices of the secular world: "What is the righteousness of the world except that in his station everyone should
do his duty?" (*LW*, 21:26). Wesley takes it to be the fruits of
God's transforming grace. The taste of this grace is exactly what
leads the believer to hunger and thirst for more, to be entirely
sanctified or "renewed after the likeness of him that created us"
(*WW*, 1:496).

A problem facing Luther is that a righteousness to be searched
for, as advised in Mt. 5:6, would be too dependent on human activity to fit his soteriology, as the imputed righteousness should be
completely passive in terms of human response. The active search
for salvation, which is supposed in the Wesleyan societies, is entirely foreign to his thought.

To Luther, to be a Christian means to be led back daily to the
point where the problem of guilt is overcome once again. To
Wesley, it means to continue on the way of salvation. The decisive
theological motive is the same for both, namely, to insist that salvation is worked through the merits of Christ by grace alone and
not by human efforts. They differ, however, in the consequences
which they draw from that basis. To Luther, the consequence is to
regard the Christian life under the perspective of *simul iustus et
peccator*. The proper way to meet the promise of God's grace is to
come back to the cross every day as a guilt-stricken sinner begging
for pardon. By necessity, the righteousness of this world has to be
distinguished from that of salvation, and the life of the Christian
has to be viewed according to two different sets of rules, one for
the secular life, another for the spiritual. To Wesley, the consequence is to view the Christian life under the perspective of
growth in grace. He regards the problem of guilt to be solved once
and for all at the moment of justification, and the proper way of
dealing with God's grace is now to live in it by being transformed
by it. He agrees with Luther that the righteousness of the Christian
actually is imputed by God from the beginning, but once given to
the sinner it becomes real in the reborn believer.

The theological differences between Wesley and the Lutheran
pietist and leader of the Moravian movement, count Zinzendorf, is
illuminating at this point. They had a number of conversations

including one on dealing with the issue of imputed righteousness
and its relations to sanctification. In the conversation of September
3, 1741, which is recorded by Wesley, Zinzendorf affirms that
"The best of men are miserable sinners till death." On the issue of
perfection he insists that "I know of no such thing as inherent perfection in this life. ... All our perfection is in Christ. All Christian
perfection is simply faith in Christ's blood. Christian perfection is
entirely imputed, not inherent. We are perfect in Christ; never
perfect in ourselves."[15] Contrary to this, Wesley's position is that,
"Christ's own Spirit works in true Christians to achieve their perfection". On Wesley's request Zinzendorf comments on the concept *imago Dei*. He accepts, it deals with holiness; however, "this
is mere legal, not evangelical holiness. Evangelical holiness is
faith."

As Zinzendorf rejects Wesley's notion of growth in love as
well as in holiness, the dividing line appears: They disagree fundamentally on the issue of whether an actual, religious growth in
the believer is possible or not. Zinzendorf affirms that the believer
is fully sanctified in the moment of justification. Wesley is open to
the idea of instant sanctification, but he distinguishes it from justification (*WW*, 2:153-169; 3:169-179). Zinzendorf accepts a growth
in grace, but not in holiness. This conversation illuminates
Wesley's position against the Lutheran, as he knew it. They do not
differ on the issue of imputed righteousness nor on the insistence
that the Christian life is a matter of how to bring the fruits of
God's righteousness out to the world, but of the issue of inherent
righteousness and sanctification.

Both Luther and Wesley affirm an inherent righteousness of the
believer, however, quite different ideas are actually implied. In
order to protect the pure doctrine of justification by faith, Luther
distinguishes between two kinds of righteousness. On the one
hand, he describes God's righteousness as being imputed by grace
but not imparted, which is the alien righteousness of Christians.
On the other hand, inherent human righteousness is the proper
righteousness of the human being as a citizen of the secular kingdom. For this righteousness the revelation of Christ adds nothing
substantial. Wesley recognizes one righteousness only, God's

righteousness imputed to the believer by grace through faith. This righteousness is imparted to the believer according to the image of God and regenerated in the life of the believer in order to be established in the world. Human merits are therefore out of question for Wesley no less than for Luther.

Comparing Luther's and Wesley's interpretations on the fourth beatitude, one more observation ought to be made. They both insist that the Christian's duty is "to promote general welfare" (*LW*, 21:26). They seem to be in harmony with each other, however, their basic presuppositions as well as their implications are actually different. This observation is most significant to understand the different theological paradigms the two are working with. To Luther, the justified sinner is called to serve God in the world through the created stations and orders. His basis is a theology of creation. Wesley's basis is a theology of salvation. For this reason, arguments that look the same from the outside reveal basically different traditions. Why cannot Luther's insistence on the righteousness of the world be understood as equivalent to Wesley's cry for social justice? Because the function of the stations and orders of Luther's secular righteousness is to restrict the evil in the world until the final consummation, while Wesley's orientation from *peace* implies an actual restoration of cosmos as a result of God's saving work.

This difference would not have been such a big problem, were it not for Luther's sharp distinction between creation and salvation. According to him, this distinction is crucial if the works of Christians should not be confused with salvific merits. For this reason he establishes two kinds of righteousness, one spiritual and one secular, one for God (the Christian's "alien" righteousness) and one for the world (the Christian's "proper" righteousness). From his point of view Wesley is subject to the same confusion between the spiritual and the secular that was characteristic of the Baptists of his own century.

Righteousness according to Luther and Wesley		
Luther		Wesley
The Secular Kingdom	The Spiritual Kingdom	The Total Social and Human Existence
Inherent righteousness	*Imputed righteousness*	*Imputed righteousness*
The proper righteousness of the Christian, who is to observe civil law and order	The alien righteousness of the Christian, who is *simul iustus et peccator*	The Christian is transformed to the image of God and thus made actually righteous by God's grace

The Merciful (5:7)

Supposing that the believer now is reborn and has the assurance of faith, Wesley continues his exhortation of the way of salvation. Because the believer's faith is filled with the life of God, it now carries fruit: "the merciful ... love their neighbors as themselves" (*WW*, 1:499).

The merciful are sanctified Christians. In a number of places Wesley identifies the process of sanctification with human experiences of the commandment of love as a gracious gift of God.[16] The love of God and the neighbor is the primary criterion for sanctification. To be merciful means to observe the golden rule and the double commandment of love.

Wesley describes holiness as tender-heartedness. God works empathic capacities toward the neighbor, enabling the Christian to sense the needs of other persons and of the surrounding world. This increased sensitivity is a fruit of faith nourished by the renewed image of God. He explains the practical-ethical implications of it by referring to 1 Cor. 13 as a model of conduct for the merciful.

Comparing the Western so-called Christian cultures (which he describes as "religion of form") with the truly merciful Christian (who has the "religion of power"), he finds a "loss of true genuine love in the earth" (*WW*, 1:507). He will not use "Christian" as a concept for institutions like kingdoms, nations, cities, families, and churches, because they all are corrupted by power. A Christian culture does not exist as an empirical fact. His criticism is that power may corrupt the best Christians is interesting in light of Luther's confidence in civil authorities; Luther conceives the power of temporal authorities to be instruments of God's wrath.

Wesley's alternative to the "Christian" establishment is a religion that has its nucleus in the experience of God's grace, and the active response of the believer in terms of active discipleship, that could be conceived as "responsible" or "responsive" grace (my terms). He is positive that in the last days—which are now—God will institute peace as a lasting dispensation. In sanctified persons who accept God's transforming acts, the promises are already fulfilled although preliminarily. He identifies the Methodist movement with the remnant. Contrary to the projectionist notion of "the little flock" of pietism with its tendency of withdrawal from the world, he insists on leading the movement into the active struggle against evil. His notion is, therefore, more closely connected to the idea of the remnant that gives new life to the tree (for instance, Is. 1:9; 4:2-4; 10:20-27, etc.), or to the idea of the remnant as the leaven. Consequently, he encourages the merciful to fight the evils of this world.

Wesley's criticism of the so-called Christian institutions makes him hope for God's future, however, he does not turn his back to this world. His hope is for its fulfillment realized in this world also. The "perfection" of the sanctified believers, who love the neighbor in this world, points to the future perfection in God's world; they are "the first-fruits, if the harvest is not yet." In the meantime,

> Do thou love thy neighbour as thyself. The Lord God fill thy heart with such a love to every soul that thou mayst be ready to lay down thy life for his sake! May thy soul continually overflow with love, swallowing up every unkind and unholy temper, till he calleth thee up into the region of love, there to reign with him for ever and ever! (*WW*, 1:509)

Wesley's frame of reference is the vision of the ultimate establishment of God's eternal kingdom of peace, righteousness, and happiness. Essential to his vision is the integration of the ideas of salvation and creation. Consequently, his theology keeps creation and salvation together. Salvation implies the re-creation of the entire cosmos, including the created nature and human society, as well as the person. Any individualistic interpretation of his soteriology will be reductionist because the person always is rooted in the world; his "individualism" is evenly balanced by the social context of the person and the challenge to discipleship. The concept of salvation basic to his soteriology is cosmic rather than individualistic, however, it does not exclude the idea of personal salvation.

The Merciful (5:7) Compared

Luther and Wesley alike identify mercifulness as "an outstanding fruit of faith" (*LW*, 21:29; cf. *WW*, 1:509). They equally affirm ethical implications of the relationship through faith and characterize this mercy as an indication of holiness. The difference in interpretation is related to differences in their basic hermeneutics: Luther declares that all persons have a righteousness on their own to be lived out within the limits of the secular kingdom. This righteousness has nothing to do with Christ, but it works independently on the basis of inherent human capacities. Wesley anticipates that the merciful will apply their faith to the widest possible context. Their mercy is not inherent but results of God's mercy and love imparted in the believers' lives.

Both Luther and Wesley relate their interpretations to creation. Luther's presupposition is that God's creating and sustaining activity is expressed through the orders and stations of the secular kingdom, which implies that God's creating will is tied to a certain social structure. Wesley's concept of creation is rather tied to a dynamic vision of the historical realization of peace. It is, first, realized in the life of the believer, and thereafter, in human society. Contrary to Luther, he has no preset pattern for the conception of God's creative and sustaining work. He rather seeks the fulfillment of the basic principles of peace in an innovative mind. His theology of creation has therefore a more dynamic character than Lu-

ther's. It is also directly related to soteriology. The goal of creation
is salvation and the goal of salvation is the new creation. God's
activity in the world is, to a considerable degree, performed
through regenerated believers. In Luther's system, the instruments
of God are the civil stations and the holders of office, who may or
may not be Christians. Whether they are Christians or heathens is
an irrelevant issue.

Luther and Wesley agree that the fruits of faith have their function within God's creative and sustaining work. It follows from
their theologies of soteriology as well as creation that while Luther
tends to restrict the application of the fruits of faith to a limited
spectrum of life only, namely for the sustenance of the structured
civil stations and offices, Wesley widens the spectrum so that it
comprehends the totality of life, spiritual and secular (a distinction
he basically disputes and rejects), natural, social, and personal.

The Pure in Heart (5:8)

To Wesley, the purity of heart is "the fulfilling of the law" interpreted as the unconditional love of God and the neighbor. The
source of love is God, and its ethical expressions are fruits of
faith. The pure in heart is totally sanctified by the grace of God,
received through faith.

It is important at this point to understand the relationship between faith and love in Wesley. He restricts faith to be the foundation of the soteriological process. It is a means for salvation, too,
as the ultimate goal is not faith but love. Faith is instrumental to
love, "the handmaid of love ... it has no value in itself" (*WW*,
2:38). The theological reason is, faith is not in itself *imago dei* but
leads to it. Love is *imago dei*.

The sanctified Christian is "purified through faith" and empowered by God's grace "so that they now love the Lord their God
with all their heart, and with all their soul, and mind, and strength"
(*WW*, 1:510-511). Though God has the initiative in the process of
salvation, an active response is required by the person. The assurance of being in the state of grace leads to renewed attitudes and
ethical actions. Consequently, Wesley connects this beatitude with

the second antithesis, on adultery (Mt. 5:27-32), however, without joining the long tradition of interpreters making purity the opposite of sexuality in particular. Though he comments that marriage must not "be used as a pretence for giving a loose to our desires" (*WW*, 1:512),[17] this is hardly an indication of antagonism to sexuality as such. He affirms that it is possible to unite family life and sexuality with a pure heart.

Though Wesley's intention is to interpret the antithesis on marriage, adultery, and divorce in an absolutist way, he—overlooking the more restrictive synoptic and Pauline passages on the issue (Mk. 10:11-12; 1 Cor. 7:10-11)—follows the moderating version of Matthew. He therefore actually supports a moderate interpretation over against an absolutist. One reason may be an ongoing discussion of the issue within Anglicanism, and he may have been supporting the liberals.[18] Wesley accepts adultery as the only exception for divorce and remarriage.

To the promise that the pure in heart "shall see God." Wesley's point is that the fully sanctified person has the most intimate relationship with God. Consequently, she or he experiences God in everything, in nature, in everyday life, and in the ordained means of grace. When non-sanctified persons experience material and social realities, sanctified persons experience a divine reality. This probably indicates that sanctification to him implies that the natural reality is experienced as being filled by God's Spirit.

The promise of seeing God is actually fulfilled in a few only, namely those who are perfected in holiness. At this point Wesley seems to restrict his universal vision of salvation to a minor "remnant." It is not the universal promise for salvation which is restricted, he rather expresses a realistic expectation of the number of people who will receive this promise.

From a psychological point of view, purity of heart, sanctification, or "Christian perfection," implies the transformation of human values and motivations. It is the total identification of the believer's personality and being with the world of God. To become like God means that "The glory of God penetrating our inmost substance ... that sight will transform us into the same likeness" (*NT-Notes*, 910). This comment offers a key to his theology of sanctification. The aim of sanctification is the restoration of the sinner to the likeness of God, thus healing the effects of the Fall. The agent behind this transformation is God's spirit penetrating the "inmost substance" of human nature with God's glory. The process of it may be described as a radiation of God's glory, effecting an actual change of the sinner.[19]

This insight leads Wesley to relate the antithesis against swearing to this beatitude. To swear upon God indicates that God is distinguished from the world of the swearer and a sign of "practical atheism" that is incompatible with full sanctification. Contrary to this he affirms that

> God is in all things, and that we are to see the Creator in the glass of every creature; that we should use and look upon nothing as separate from God, which indeed is a kind of practical atheism; but with a true magnificence of thought survey heaven and earth and all that is therein as contained by God in the hollow of his hand, who by his intimate presence holds them all in being, who pervades and actuates the whole created frame, and is in a true sense the soul of the universe. (*WW*, 1:516-517)

Wesley assures that God has created everything, all belongs to God, and God "is in all things." To deny this is "practical atheism." He implies a more intimate relationship between the Creator and creation than commonly accepted in the Western theological tradition. A more Eastern orientation is emphasized by the use of the Platonic and Stoic notion *anima mundi*, "the soul of the universe."

Wesley's practical pan*en*theism—no pantheism is implied!— probably serves as a safeguard against the deist doctrine of creation, implying that God after creation withdrew from it. It is a positive affirmation to the theological tradition from the Pre-Nicean and Eastern Fathers. The phrase "we are to see the Creator in the glass of every creature" comes very close to the Orthodox belief that God is revealed through icons; the idea is that the picture of a holy person is transparent, so that through meditation of an object from the created world the divine reality is made the created world the divine reality is made manifest to the person, who experiences divinization by participation in God.[20]

The meaning of salvation is not different from the meaning of creation. The ethical conduct implied in salvation as the fruits of faith and grace is always in harmony with God's will for creation.

The Pure in Heart (5:8) Compared

To Luther, the pure in heart is a person who keeps the pure word of God by (1) giving up all merits and clinging to God's word of consolation by justification by faith alone, and (2) doing one's duty in the stations. The structure of his soteriology is bifocal with the doctrine of justification by faith and the doctrine of the two kingdoms as its foci. His soteriology has a highly cognitive orientation, the reception of salvation is to some degree dependant on abstractions and knowledge.

Faith is a key word to Wesley, too. Different from Luther he uses an instrumental conception of faith which end is love: "Faith is the handmaid of love" (*WW*, 2:38). The pure in heart is perfected in heart. She or he is a believer who is transformed through faith by grace into the likeness to God. Thus being conformed with Christ, the fullness of God's love is brought out into the world. He at this point indicates that the antitheses serve as a pattern for practical Christian life for the regenerated believer.

Both Luther and Wesley on commenting this beatitude, speak of Christian perfection. Their notions of perfection are, however, different. To Luther, the nature of perfection differs with the two kingdoms. In the spiritual kingdom, the Christian's perfection is faith. By faith the merits of Christ are imputed to the Christian. Perfection is a purely religious and not a moral concept. For that reason, the perfection of faith is not contradicted by the believer's actual sinfulness. On the other hand, in the secular kingdom, perfection is the same as perfect obedience in one's station. But this obedience gives no merits toward God.

Wesley understands Christian perfection as the perfection of the heart after its purification by God, emptying of sin, and filled with divine love or the mind which was in Christ. This does not mean that a dichotomy is implied between a perfection of heart and a perfection of life, which is the case for the perfection of the spiritual kingdom according to Luther. On the contrary, he takes care to indicate that the perfection of the heart is basic to the perfection of life. The purifying agent is not the merits of the believer's "holy" works, but God's grace and spirit. On this point, Luther and Wesley share a common concern. Another shared emphasis is how purity of heart leads to love of the neighbor.

The notion of perfection and its function in the anthropologies of Luther and Wesley are basically different. Luther insists that no inherent righteousness or perfection of the believer is implied in the spiritual kingdom. But any human person has in the secular kingdom a different kind of righteousness, which is his or her own. Wesley's starting point is the same as Luther's, that the righteousness of the Christian actually is the imputed righteousness of Christ. But contrary to Luther he insists that this righteousness is imparted to the believer so that it becomes the actual righteousness and perfection of the Christian. For that reason, it is not necessary for him to speak of two kinds of righteousness.

Though Wesley emphasizes that the promise of perfection is universal, he does not expect the majority of Christians to experience the pure and perfected heart. At this point Luther's more modest set of goals for the Christian life does not cause the problems evolving from Wesley's theology of sanctification. Particularly in the area of ethics, Luther's theory is, with its basis in the doctrine of creation, universal in its application, while Wesley's theory of ethics presupposes perfection and is consequently restricted to the perfected believers.

The Peacemakers (5:9)

With this beatitude Wesley comes to a new turning point on the way of salvation. So far the way has dealt with the holiness of heart, but now the holiness of life is in the focus. Christian holiness and ethics are formed in the dynamic tension between the being and doing of the Christian: "Thus far our Lord has been more directly employed in teaching the religion of the heart. He

has shown what Christians are to be. He now proceeds to show
what they are to do.

Wesley relates peacemaking to every aspect of life. Holiness is
an actual transformation of the believer due to the gracious work
of God, and he now spells out the social consequences of this religion of the heart. Starting from "the Greek word for peace,
eirene," and St. Paul's greeting "grace and peace," he affirms that
all spiritual and temporal blessings come upon the sanctified
Christian "as a fruit of the free, undeserved love and favour of
God" (*WW*, 1:517). His interpretation of who a peacemaker is
comes out of the biblical concept of peace. It basically deals with
the point that a believer who is "filled with the love of God and of
all mankind" cannot restrict works or love to her or his family or
friends only, "but steps over these narrow bounds that he may do
good to every man; that he may some way or other manifest his
love to neighbors and strangers, friends and enemies. He doth
good to them all as he hath opportunity, that is, on every possible
occasion" (*WW*, 1:518-519).[21]

Peacemaking is, to Wesley, border-crossing activities completely independent of formal relationships to the persons involved. The only motive is to perform God's will and be an ex-
tended instrument of his redeeming love. On discussing the practical implications of peacemaking, he turns to activities described in
Mt. 25:31ff, dealing bread with the hungry, covering the naked,
visiting the sick and those in prison, etc. When it comes to social
work he identifies with the biblical roles, in preaching as well as in
personal activities.[22]

The Peacemakers (5:9) Compared

Luther and Wesley continue to develop their interpretations logically on the basis of their general hermeneutics. Luther emphasizes that the roles in peace-making of the Christian as person
and as the holder of office are different, while Wesley has
reached the step on the way of salvation where the holiness of
life is focused. Luther's frame of reference is the empirical, political, and social world. Wesley rather relates his interpretation

to the Hebrew and Christian ideas of peace and love, which he adapts to the world as he experiences it. The peacemaker consequently acts in the world according to the Messianic era of peace. His concept of peace is more utopian, at least as it is evaluated from the standpoint of Luther. While Luther emphasizes peace as freedom from war, Wesley has a stronger emphasis on human justice in general.

Those Who Are Persecuted for Righteousness' Sake (5:10-12)

Wesley comments on the paradox that the sanctified Christian really "should be the darling of mankind" (*WW*, 1:520), and yet Christ concludes the beatitudes with warnings against persecution. *Who*, *why* and *how* are they persecuted, and *how should they behave* in such situations?

(1) Who are persecuted? They are the holy people of God whom Wesley describes by referring to the virtues implied in the beatitudes (*WW*, 1:521).

(2) Why are they persecuted? The cause is the righteousness the Christians have from God: "because they 'will live godly in Christ Jesus'; because they 'are not of the world.' Whatever may be pretended, this is the real cause" (*WW*, 1:521), Wesley affirms. In using the scheme of the beatitudes, he describes the reasons for persecution in detail. He shows that each beatitude represents a specific stage on the way of salvation as well as a characteristic aspect of the Christian life in its fullness. A sanctified Christian is not only pure in heart but also poor in spirit, mourning, meek, hungering and thirsting after righteousness, merciful, and, not least, peacemaking as well. Because the divine life is so well integrated with the life of the Christian, persecution appears as a natural consequence.

(3) Who are they that persecute them? "The spirit which is in the world is directly opposite to the Spirit which is of God ... Therefore ... all the servants of the devil will persecute the children of God" (*WW*, 1:523). Like Luther, Wesley identifies the perse-

cutors with the diabolic powers in the world. In this supposition they both are in line with old exegetic traditions.[23]

(4) How are they persecuted? Wesley suggests that because persecution takes place for righteousness' sake, God does not prevent persecution but makes it tolerable and for the ultimate good of God's children, for God "will tend most to his children's growth in grace and the enlargement of his own kingdom" (*WW*, 1:523). The reasons for God's allowance of persecution may differ. The persecutions of the primitive Church primarily, but also those of the heroes of the English Reformation, had their backgrounds in the need to testify to the strength of true Christian faith. He comments that "*he [God]* suffered this with regard to the apostles" (*WW*, 1:524), thus implying God's personal suffering along with God's children. There were other reasons for the persecutions of the 2nd and 3rd-century. God then used persecution to punish the Church in order to direct its way, "because of the monstrous corruptions which even then reigned in the church; these God chastised, and at the same time strove to heal" (*WW*, 1:524).

Probably these ideas came to Wesley through his studies of the Church Fathers[24] as well as of later church history and his personal experiences of persecution. Before his assurance of faith experience of May 24, 1738, he regards persecution as a criterion for being in a state of grace, mainly based on the words of Ignatius:[25] "When he [the Christian] is hated by the world, he is beloved of God" (*ANF*, 1:74). He realized the truth of Ignatius's statement on experiencing persecution directed to himself as the leader of the Holy Club in Oxford. At that time he knew no other holiness than that which he created through his own disciplined life. When this kind of life leads to persecution, he regards it as proof of his being in the state of salvation. This view he develops in his letter to his father as a defence for not coming to Epworth as a parish chaplain.[26] He here states that persecution "is the badge of his discipleship, the stamp of his profession, the constant seal of his calling; insomuch that though a man may be despised without being saved, yet he cannot be saved without being despised" (*WW*, 25:407). In his Sermon on the Mount discourse he sharpens his view: "it [persecution] is the very badge of our discipleship; it is one of the seals of our calling. It is a sure portion entailed on all the children of God; if we have it not we are bastards and not sons" (*WW*, 1:525-526).

(5) How are the Christians to behave with regard to persecution? Wesley develops four main rules for conduct in times of persecution. His primary rule is to avoid persecution, if possible, according to Mt. 10:23, etc. That does not mean, however, that persecution can be avoided completely, for, "If you escape the persecution you escape the blessing" (*WW*, 1:527). The second rule is: Do not seek persecution, but when it comes, "Rejoice and be exceeding glad ... because by this mark also ye know unto whom ye belong" (*WW*, 1:527).

Wesley's letters and journals contain many accounts on persecution, which cover the 1730s through the 1780s. The peak is in the 1740s, when the persecution of the revival movement was on its highest. After 1738 he does not seek persecution, rather he attempts to avoid it when possible. "But though I do not *desire* persecution, I *expect* it" (*WW*, 11:485), he comments as late as 1762. The main reason for his change of attitude has probably to do with his experience of assurance of faith, that made the assurance of *syllogismus practicus*[27] less significant. The "outward witness" now was replaced by the "inner witness."[28] In this discourse he still interprets persecution in harmony with the principle of *syllogismus practicus*.

Wesley's third rule is: "Let no persecution turn you out of the way of lowliness and meekness, of love and beneficence" (*WW*, 1:528). He introduces the antithesis on retaliation (Mt. 5:38-42) as a model of Christian conduct in the face of persecution. Evil should not be met with counter-evil but with love. His view on Mt. 5:42 has an absolutist and a restrictive tenor at the same time:

> (1). Take care to owe no man nothing. For what thou owest is not thy own, but another man's. (2) Provide for those of thine own household. ... Then, (3), give or lend all that remains from day to day, or from year to year: only first, seeing thou canst not give or lend to all, remember the household of faith. (*WW*, 1:528)

These rules are not the same as Wesley's general rules of Christian economic stewardship of "earning, saving and giving" money away.[29] At this point the issue is how Christ's prescript of Mt. 5:42 is related to situations of persecution. The first two rules mentioned indicate that persecution does not excuse anybody from taking care of everyday responsibilities. The giving away should not be so excessive that a personal debt becomes the result.

Wesley as a fourth rule for conduct facing persecution points to the last antithesis of Mt. 5:43-48 on love for enemies. His goal for this meek and loving conduct in persecution situations is to demonstrate the kind of Christian perfection which may win the enemy for Christ.

Those Who Are Persecuted for Righteousness' Sake (5:10-12) Compared

Christian perfection implies, according to Luther, to live properly and decently in general, to suffer, and to administer one's duties in the offices and stations. Perfection is related to the proper righteousness of the believer and not to his or her alien righteousness that is imputed by God. To Wesley, perfection is a matter of being transformed in grace to God's likeness. It is, therefore, a function of the imputed and imparted righteousness of God.

According to both Luther and Wesley perfection may lead to persecution and suffering. They agree that diabolic powers frequently stir persecution. Wesley is less consistent in his explanations of persecution than is Luther. Wesley sometimes implies that God is the cause of suffering, thus presupposing an image of God more Calvinistic than what is the case elsewhere in his writings. They offer, therefore, similar interpretations of the cause of persecution for Christ's sake, which they both define as perfection. The dissimilarity is implied in their interpretation of the character and function of perfection.

The Salt and Light of the Earth (5:13-16)

To Wesley, the twin parable of Mt. 5:13-16 reveals the responsive life of any Christian who is united with Christ, into whom the image of God has become engraved:

> *Ye*—Not the apostles, not the ministers only; but all ye who are thus holy, *are the salt of the earth*—are to season others. (*NT-Notes*, 30)
> The beauty of holiness, of that inward man of the heart which is renewed after the image of God ... they [the people of the world] cannot but perceive how desirable a thing it is to be thus [by the blessings of the Holy Spirit through the Beatitudes] transformed into the likeness of him that created us. (*WW*, 1:531)

Wesley then addresses the problem that Christians insist that the Christian life should remain hidden. They

> have advised us "to cease from all outward actions"; wholly to withdraw from the world; to leave the body behind us; to abstract ourselves from sensible things—to have no concern at all about outward religion, but to "work all virtues of the will," as the far more excellent way, more perfective of the soul, as well as more acceptable to God. (*WW*, 1:532)

The point, "to cease from all outward actions," is directed toward the Moravian quietism[30] as it was represented by Philip Molther, the German leader of the Fetter Lane Society.[31] The point "to work all virtues of the will" is directed toward "will-mystics" like Thomas a Kempis, Count Zinzendorf, William Law, and others, who emphasize the surrender of the human will to God.[32]

Wesley knows "will-mysticism" through his extensive studies of Jeremy Taylor, Thomas a Kempis, William Law, De Renty, Gregory Lopez, Lorenzo Scupoli, William Lester, Robert Mohan, and others. He accepts their emphasis on the surrender to God's will, but when it is combined with quietism and antinomianism, he calls it a "masterpiece of the wisdom from beneath, this fairest of all the devices wherewith Satan hath ever perverted the right of the Lord!" (*WW*, 1:532).[33] In the parable of salt and light Christ "defends, in the clearest and strongest manner, the active, patient religion he had just described" (*WW*, 1:533). The blessings of the beatitudes may be experienced by a person, but they are certainly not individualistic in character:

> In order fully to explain and enforce these important words I shall endeavour to show, first, that Christianity is essentially a social religion, and that to turn it into a solitary one is to destroy it; secondly, that to conceal this religion is impossible, as well as utterly contrary to the design of its author. I shall, thirdly, answer some objections; and conclude the whole with a practical application. (*WW*, 1:533)

Wesley's "social religion" must not be confused with a "social gospel" or interpreted in light of our popular understanding of "social," as this concept had another meaning in his time. It should be interpreted in its etymological sense as a religion that "cannot subsist at all without society" (*WW*, 1:534), as an expression of the necessity of *communio sanctorum*. Personal devotion is necessary, but if this daily withdrawal swallows up all time, "this would be to destroy, not advance, true religion" (*WW*, 1:534).

This "social religion" is dependent on fellowship in three directions. The basis is the incarnated God. This religion is dependent on the fellowship with other believers, but "social religion" is also "intercourse with the world." Speaking of the beatitudes, he affirms that "the most essential branches thereof," cannot be alive without communication with the world. For instance, to turn meekness "into a solitary virtue is to destroy it from the face of the earth" (*WW*, 1:534), and peacemaking "cannot possibly subsist without society (*WW*, 1:535).

Wesley answers the objection that Christians should not interfere with the non-Christian world. They should not be isolated to social "ghettos," nor should they "separate wholly, even from wicked men," and if they did, they could not continue to be Christians: "Much more the words of our Lord, who is so far from directing us to break off all commerce with the world that without it, according to his account of Christianity, we cannot be Christians at all" (*WW*, 1:536). Nor is it possible to experience the blessings of the beatitudes and the active faith working through love performed through the antitheses because it is contradictory to the very character of being a Christian:

> Indeed, were we wholly to separate ourselves from sinners, how could we possibly answer that character which our Lord gives us. ... It is your nature to season whatever is around you. It is the nature of the divine saviour which is in you to spread to whatsoever you touch; to diffuse itself on every side, to all those among whom you are. This is the great reason why the providence of God has so mingled you together with other men, that whatever grace you have received of God may through you be communicated to others; that every holy temper, and word, and work of yours, may have an influence on them also. (*WW*, 1:536-537)

To Wesley, a genuine relation to God will by necessity lead to a renewed relationship to the neighbor, society, and created nature. If religion is not "social," it cannot be the religion of Christ, that aims at the restoration of creation to its original shape and purpose.

Backsliding into sin does not happen by meeting the world, but by hiding instead of using the grace which is received: "Our Lord proceeds to show the desperate state of those who do not impart the religion they have received" (*WW*, 1:537). To be a partaker of the divine love and then keep it to oneself is to "crucify to themselves the Son of God afresh, and put him to an open shame" (*WW*, 1:538). Wesley encourages the Christian to live according to the new life in Christ and bring it into the world. Though satanic powers are in the world, God is at work also, and God equips the believers with the power of the Spirit.[34] In case of backsliding his emphasis is on the possibility of forgiveness and restoration: "A believer may fall, and not fall away. He may fall and rise again" (*WW*, 1:538). He disagrees with the Puritans and the Pietists who think communion with the world is dangerous. The reality is the other way round. To conceal religion will lead to backsliding. Wesley's emphasis on going into the world is highly eschatological. He points to the salt and the light as a prelude to the twin parable at the end of the Sermon on the Mount (Mt. 7:24-27) with its focus on orthopraxis. He shows that the parable of the salt and the light has its basis in the new life given to the believer through faith and grace, and its message is to live this new life in the world. The created and human nature has need for salt as well as for light, and Christians have a certain responsibility in the eschatological fulfillment of *shalom* by preserving the world and society from corruption.

Another emphasis is Wesley's interpretation of the salt in Mt. 5:13 within the framework of the Old Testament practice of salting the burnt-offerings (cf. Num. 18:19; Lev. 2:13; Ezek. 16:4, 43:24; cf. Rom. 12:1-2):

> [Mk. 9:] 49. ... *salted with fire*—Preserved, not consumed, thereby: whereas *every* acceptable *sacrifice shall be salted with* another kind of salt—even that of divine grace, which purifies the soul ... and preserves it from corruption.
>
> [Mk. 9:] 50. ... every one who, denying himself and taking up his cross, offers up himself as a living sacrifice to God, shall be seasoned with grace; which, like salt, will make him savory, and preserve him from destruction for ever.
>
> As salt is good for preserving meats, and making them savoury, so it is good that ye be seasoned with grace, for the purifying your hearts and lives, and for spreading the saviour of My knowledge, both in your own souls and wherever ye go. (*NT-Notes*, 172)

The notion of the believers' sacrifice of themselves to God's service at the Lord's Table is at the core of the Wesleyan understanding of the sacrament.[35] His emphasis on the Eucharist as the place for God's regenerative activity with the believer moves the ontological issue from the elements to the communicants. By the reception of the elements in faith, the communicants are imparted in an ontological reality that includes the renewal of the entire cosmos as well the sinner (Runyon 1985:11). Thus being in harmony with the new creation, the sanctified believer may go into the world to perform God's will there.

To conceal Christianity is impossible because love makes Christians visible to the world: "Love cannot be hid any more than light; and least of all when it shines forth in action, when ye exercise yourselves in the labour of love, in beneficence of every kind" (*WW*, 1:539). The holiness of the Christians is not visible *per se*, but their outward expressions are, their "labour of love," the "*active* lover of God and man." "Whatever religion can be concealed," Wesley concludes, it "cannot be the religion of Jesus Christ," because "it is the design of God that every Christian should be in an open point of view; that he may give light to all around; that he may visibly express the religion of Jesus Christ" (*WW*, 1:540). We should not follow the words of Christ only, but his example also. Wesley's personal life is replete with examples showing that he patterned his life after biblical models (cf. Källstad 1974:283-310).

Wesley now answers objections of his interpretation of this parable by Lutherans and the mystics. He affirms

> that religion does not lie in outward things but in the heart ... that outside religion is nothing worth ...
>
> I answer, it is most true that the root of religion lies in the heart, in the inmost soul; that this is the union of the soul with God, the life of God in the soul of man. But if this root be really in the heart it cannot but put forth branches. As these are the several instances of outward obedience, which partake of the same nature with the root, and consequently are not only marks or signs, but substantial parts of religion. (*WW*, 1:541-542)

In his interpretation of this scripture, Luther puts the priority on faith, indicating the lower value of works. Wesley holds that outward works are essential because they are "of the same nature" and "substantial parts of religion." He agrees that faith is primary in terms of mediating salvation. But works, too, as fruits of salvation, belong to the essence of religion, making proper expressions of salvation ethical rather than doctrinal.

The second objection Wesley meets is the antinomian view that love is "the fulfilling of the law" and "the end of the commandment." He agrees that without love religion

> profits us nothing. But it does not follow that love is all (in all) in such a sense as to supersede either faith or good works. It is "the fulfilling of the law," not by releasing us from but by constraining us to obey it. It is "the end of every commandment" as every commandment leads to and centres in it [love]. (*WW*, 1:542)

Wesley's position is closely related to his general view of the law. To him, love and works do not nullify each other but they work together.

The third objection is that God is supposed to be worshipped "in spirit and in truth" (*WW*, 1:543). In Wesley's understanding, "to worship in spirit and in truth" is worship relating to the nature of God, who is love:

> It is to love him, to delight in him, to desire him, with all our heart and mind and soul and strength; to imitate him we love by purifying ourselves, even as he is pure; and to obey him whom we love, and in whom we believe, both in thought and word and work. Consequently one branch of the worshipping God in spirit and in truth is the keeping his outward commandments. (*WW*, 1:544)

There is no contradiction between contemplation and loving, imitating, and obeying God. They are significant expressions of the Christian religion according to Wesley.

The fourth issue is the disappointment when people object, "Our light did shine; we used outward things many years; and yet they profited nothing. We attended on all the ordinances; but we were not better for it" (*WW*, 1:545). Wesley's answer is significant in light of his theology of works as well as the means of grace. He implies that a common abuse of the ordinances has taken place, "mistaking the means for the end, supposing that the doing these or some other outward works either was the religion of Jesus Christ or would be accepted in the place of it. But let the abuse be taken away and let the use remain" (*WW*, 1:545). It does not follow from this that the means are bad as such. To replace abuse with proper use is a frequently used aphorism by him.

Some of Wesley's opponents extend this objection further, affirming, "Experience ... shows that the trying to do good is but lost labour" (*WW*, 1:545), pearls should not be cast before swine (Mt. 7:6). He completely rejects this objection by answering,

> (1), whether they will finally be lost or saved, you are expressly commanded to feed the hungry and clothe the naked. If you can and do not, whatever becomes of them, you shall go away into everlasting fire. (2). Though it is God only changes hearts, yet he generally doth it by man. It is our part to do all that in us lies as diligently as if we could change them ourselves, and then leave the event to him. (3). God ... builds up his children by each other in every good gift, nourishing and strengthening the whole "body by that which every joint supplieth." ... Lastly, how are you assured that the persons before you are dogs or swine? Judge them not until you have tried. (*WW*, 1:546)

Still further it may be objected that "We have laboured to reform sinners," but with no lasting effect, so "Therefore we had better have kept our religion to ourselves." Wesley still refuses to give up the labor: "You are not accountable for this: leave it to him who orders all things well ... this is no reason for disobeying God" (*WW*, 1:546-547). His point is: The works of God are not to be performed for the sake of human success, but for the fulfillment of God's will. The believer is a major instrument in God's work, or, an agent of God's love, and must submit to it.

To Wesley, the issue is not how to live a life of casuistic ethics, but how to "let your words be the genuine picture of your heart" (*WW*, 1:548). Words and works should be united expressions of the renewed nature according to the image of God. His last admonishments characterizes his personal piety by works, modesty, and discipline:

> Let the light which is in your heart shine [1] in all good works.
> ... And in order to enlarge your ability of doing good, [2] re-
> nounce all superfluities. Cut off all unnecessary expense, in
> food, in furniture, in apparel. Be a good steward of every gift of
> God. ... [3] Cut off all unnecessary expense of time, all needless
> or useless employment. ... In a word, be thou full of faith and
> love; do good; suffer evil. (*WW*, 1:548-549)

Wesley in describing the holiness of heart uses the terminology
of the mystics. He combines the holiness of heart with the holiness of life, which he understands socially and ethically. His idea
of divinization is not to be understood in the context of neo-
Platonic idealism, but as a motive for sanctification and religious
development. He shares the mystics' concern for the religious
experience and inward holiness. His emphasis, however, is in the
communio, the fellowship between the believer and God and not
in the *unio* with God. His emphasis is not that of a bride mysticism, but that of dedication and discipleship.

The Salt and Light of the Earth (5:13-16) Compared

A most significant variation between Luther and Wesley is that,
Luther is primarily occupied with doctrinal religion, while
Wesley's emphasis is on experimental and ethical religion.

Luther's general interpretation of the salt and the light is that
they are metaphors for the preaching of the pure gospel performed
by preachers who are properly called. His hermeneutics is governed by the bifocal structure of his soteriology, the doctrine of
justification by faith and the doctrine of the two kingdoms. The
salt is the criticism of false doctrine and the light is the preaching
of orthodoxy. Both are performed by properly called holders of the
preaching office. He addresses this part of the Sermon on the
Mount to preachers who are properly called to their office. These
parables are not addressed to Christians in general. The forensic
character of salvation is underscored by his emphasis on the accompanying doctrine of the Christian as *simul iustus et peccator*,

thus implying the change of formal status of the sinner before God but with no actual change implied.

Wesley's focus is on the actual change of the sinner, the transformation of the human being due to the recovery of God's image in the heart of the redeemed believer. His interest in sanctification is not based on a pelagian soteriology. The basis is faith and grace alone. God renews the creation and sanctifies the believer, making her or him a steward of God's love. To this eschatological perspective another emphasis is added, that of the believer's sacrifice of oneself for ministry in response to God's loving sacrifice in Christ.

In this discourse, Wesley affirms strongly the social character of the Christian religion. To individualize religion or to conceal it, is to distort it. Religion should be personal, but that must not be confused with subjectivism or individualism. In his theology, religion is personal and social at the same time. Contrary to Luther's imitation of the application of the parable of salt and light to the properly called holders of the preaching office, Wesley affirms that every Christian is supposed to be God's salt and God's light to the world. He admonishes the Christian to enter the world in the power of God's Spirit without fear of backsliding. There is no indication of anxiety for the world in his theology. On the contrary, the believer is saved for the sake of the salvation of the world. He or she is to bring God's love to the neighbor.

An illustration may indicate the differences between Luther and Wesley at this point. When comparing the role of the neighbor in their theological systems with the pelagian soteriology, the differences in function are striking. In pelagian soteriology, the neighbor is instrumental in the believer's search for merits. The end is the salvation of the believer, reducing the neighbor to a means for another person's salvation. In Wesley's theology the neighbor has an opposite position. The end of his soteriology is the salvation of the believer's neighbor, but through the believer. To conceal religion is therefore to stop the process of God's salvation in a selfish way that inevitably will result the believer's falling out of grace. In Luther's soteriology, the neighbor has no role at all. Faith alone is valid in the believer's relation to God. To take one's neighbor in account in terms of salvation will lead to a concern for works which threatens to destroy the Lutheran soteriology. According to the doctrine of the two kingdoms, however, the neighbor has a role in the secular kingdom. But Luther is here speaking of sustaining God's creation, and not of salvation. He also strongly affirms good works as fruits of faith. When he affirms that the Christian should be a Christ to his or her neighbor, he speaks of the effect of salvation. In Wesley's soteriology, however, the purpose of salvation transcends the individualistic level as it is directed to the neighbor of the believer. Evangelistic and diaconal motives are, therefore, included as basic to his soteriology.

The Law (5:17-20)

Wesley defines more closely what part of the law is fulfilled by Christ, and what is not. He follows the Anglican article of religion no. 6 in its distinction between the ceremonial law

> which related to the old sacrifices and service of the temple, [and which] our Lord indeed come to destroy, to dissolve and utterly abolish, [and] the moral law,[36] contained in the Ten Commandments, and enforced by the prophets, he did not take away. It was not the design of his coming to revoke any part of this. (*WW*, 1:551)

Wesley has a positive view of the law in general.[37] After the Fall, the religious and ethical values of the law remain "upon all mankind, and in all ages; as not depending upon time or place, or any other circumstances liable to change, but on the nature of God and the nature of man, and their unchangeable relation to each other" (*WW*, 1:551-552).

In his explanation of Christ's meaning with the fulfillment of the law, Wesley avoids the Augustinian option which also was rejected by Luther, namely, that the deficiencies of the law are supplemented (cf. *LW*, 21:69). Unlike Luther, he rejects that Christ fulfills the Law on behalf of humanity. On the contrary, Christ has "come to establish it in its fullness" (*WW*, 1:552).

At this point Wesley repeats a statement which he made in the beginning of this discourse, that this is in no way a "new religion." He roots the religion of Christ in the creation, or the beginning of this history. The close connection between soteriology and creation in his theology is confirmed:

> He [Christ] has not introduced a new religion into the world, but the same which was from the beginning: a religion the substance of which is ... "as old as the creation;" being coeval with man, and having proceeded from God at the very time when "man became a living soul." (*WW*, 1:552)

In contrast to Luther's devaluation of the message of Matthew (*LW*, 21:65, cf. 293), Wesley considers the Sermon on the Mount to be a genuine breakthrough in the history of revelation; not since Adam's days has God ever spoken so clearly to any human person as God does here. By "all the essential branches" he refers to the beatitudes and to the antitheses.

Wesley's exegesis affirms that *an panta*, which he translates "*all things*," does not refer to the fulfillment of the law, but to the universe. He rejects explicitly the popular theology that is represented also by Luther, that the dispensation of the Gospel first came after Christ's fulfillment of the law on behalf of humanity (*WW*, 1:553-554). The law therefore is significant in the economy of salvation. Its function is not to be an agent for corruption to be replaced by the Gospel of grace and faith, but to be a part of the constructive restoration of God's original will for creation. This insight on the function of the law he applies to the believer's attitudes to the law:

> there is no contrariety at all between the law and the gospel; ... there is no need for the law to pass away in order to the establishing of the gospel. Indeed neither of them supersedes the other, but they agree perfectly well together. Yea, the very same words ... are parts both of the law and of the gospel. If they are considered as commandments, they are parts of the law: if as promises, of the gospel. Thus, "Thou shalt love the Lord thy God with all thy heart," when considered as a commandment, is

a branch of the law; when regarded as a promise, is an essential part of the gospel—the gospel being no other than the commandments of the law proposed by way of promises. ...

There is therefore the closest connection that can be conceived between the law and the gospel. On the one hand the law continually makes way for and points us to the gospel. On the other the gospel leads us to a more exact fulfilling of the law. The law, for instance, requires us to love God, to love our neighbour, to be meek, humble, or holy. We feel that we are not sufficient for these things, yea, "with man this is impossible." But we see a promise of God to give us that love, and to make us humble, meek and holy. We lay hold of this gospel, of these glad tidings: it is done unto us according to our faith, and "the righteousness of the law is fulfilled in us" through faith which is in Christ Jesus.

... every command in Holy Writ is only a covered promise. (*WW*, 1:554-555)

This quote contains some of the key principles of Wesley's interpretation of the Sermon on the Mount:

(1) There is no contrariety between law and gospel: Wesley admits that there is a dialectical relationship between the two, but there is no dichotomy in which law and gospel are opponents.

(2) In the history of salvation the law is a revelation of God's loving nature as well as of the covenant of grace. The law is an instrument of God and it will last as long as this world lasts. The law and the gospel belong to the same dispensations; God has offered salvation through grace since the fall of Adam, a fact that is revealed through Christ's atoning sacrifice.

(3) The same scripture may belong both to the law and to the gospel,[38] depending on the context of interpretation. Taken as commandment, it is part of the law, taken as promise, it is part of the gospel. The principle that each commandment is a covered promise is "a prime rule for Wesley's hermeneutics" (*WW*, 1:554, note 18).[39]

(4) The most challenging commandment in the law, the commandment to love, may be fulfilled in the life of the believer who regards it to be a promise. First, the promise of love is experienced

by the believer who accepts the gift in faith; secondly, love is expressed to the neighbor not as the accomplishment of the believer, but even the believer's acting as an instrument or channel for God's love to the world. Wesley comments: "Believe, and thence love and obey" (*NT-Notes*, 94). Faith, love, and obedience form a characteristic pattern in his theology. Through faith the sinner is given salvation by grace and transformed into God's image, working love as a fruit of this faith. By her or his obedient conformation to the will of God, love is directed to its end, which is the neighbor in need. The order is not coincidental, "Believe, and thence. ..."

(5) Wesley's framework for the discussion of law and gospel is the eschatological promise of peace and love in the present world as a foretaste of its consummation. He describes the fulfillment of the prophetic vision, "This is the covenant I will make after those days, saith the Lord; I will put my laws in your minds, and write them in your hearts," stressing that the eschatological event is *now*; "God hath engaged to give whatsoever he commands. Does he command ...? It is enough. He will work in us this very thing.[40] It shall be unto us according to his word" (*WW*, 1:555), for "Christianity ... is designed by God to be the last of all his dispensations ... This is to endure till the consummation of all things" (*WW*, 1:555).

By viewing the commandments of the law as evangelical promises and stressing at the same time that the fulfillment will be done by God through faith and grace, Wesley avoids the threat of antinomianism. Conceiving the law as a means of general grace because of its function of being both precept and promise, he also avoids a soteriology based on human merits through works.

Christ requires a total surrender of the complete life of a person. Backsliding tends to become total in a similar way. The open offender of God's commands "soon commences an advocate for sin. ... He excuses sin which he will not leave, and thus directly teaches every sin which he commits" (*WW*, 1:557). This person has no part in the kingdom, no part in the blessings of the kingdom, and as a natural result, transgresses God's holy law which is an expression of the principles of peace.

Wesley affirms that "we must all declare, 'By grace ye are saved through faith: not of works'" (*WW*, 1:559). To be "saved by faith" means to be "delivered from the power as well as the guilt of sin" as well as "believe and thou shalt be holy," for the proper faith is "that 'which worketh by love.'" The faith in Christ implies that "thou shalt have peace and power together. Thou shalt have power from him in whom thou believest to trample sin under thy feet; power to love the Lord thy God with all thy heart, and to serve him with all thy strength" (*WW*, 1:560). Justification is to be saved from the guilt of sin, or, to be restored to the *favor Dei*. But this is only the door to salvation. The merits of Christ bases a salvation that includes being saved from the power of sin as well, and to be restored to the *imago Dei*. Both aspects of salvation are wrought by faith. If the faith that works these effects does not bring forth good works at the same time, it cannot be the faith of which the bible speaks, for any person who is given the new life of the kingdom of God will live according to this new life. It is not accidental that Gal. 5:6 probably is the most frequently quoted scripture by Wesley (cf. Meistad 1985).

Wesley rejects that "faith supplying the place of holiness," for there is no contradiction between them. He is talking about a holiness which is imparted to the believer by faith and God's grace, but he is not talking of a merited holiness of works. Over and over again he insists that we are sanctified by faith in the same way that we are justified by faith; for instance, he affirms that faith is the means that the Holy spirit uses to convey God's grace to persons (*WW*, 2:163). Where there is no holiness, faith has not been given opportunities to grow in grace.

Wesley was concerned to avoid "cheap grace" (cf. Bonhoeffer 1963:45-47). Recent research emphasizes that the covenant structure of the Methodist movement offers a methodical search for opportunities to make the believers accountable to God (Watson 1985:144-145).

In the end Wesley deals with the character of the Pharisees. He finds them to be a most remarkable religious people, and he probably aims to restore their reputation among Christians. Their work and zeal for God's law is emphasized as is their learning, piety, and general esteem for holiness. They thus form an example to be imitated: "Be as tenacious of inward holiness as any mystic, and of outward as any Pharisee" (*WW*, 3:507).

The Christian righteousness should exceed that of the Pharisees in three ways: in extent, in using God's ordinances, or the means of grace, and in doing good. But, Wesley admonishes, "rest not here. ... Thou can do all things through Christ strengthening thee, though without him thou canst do nothing. ... Let thy religion be the religion of the heart. ... Be thou a lover of God and of all mankind" (*WW*, 1:570-571). He gives here the standards of the Christian life of discipleship in a sum, which is to love God and all of the neighbors from the heart, out of the power which is wrought by Christ. Such a Christian will be invincible.

The Law (5:17-20) Compared

Luther's concern regarding the law is doctrinal and not ethical. His basis is that a fulfillment of the commands of the law is impossible for a human person. The only hope is the perfect fulfillment of Christ as our substitute. Luther's Sermon on the Mount discourses put the emphasis on the human nature of Christ. The atonement corresponding to this christology is focused on human guilt, however, the atoning sacrifice of Christ is replaced by his atoning fulfillment of the law. Consequently, the soteriology of Luther is separated from the ethical efforts of the sinner, while a strong emphasis on faith in Christ is the sole foundation for the reception of God's grace. For that reason, the law has no meaning in the religious life of the Christian, except that it may cause persons to realize their need for repentance.

In the secular kingdom, however, the law remains as a model for behavior. The Christian is guided by the law in performing the duties and obligations of the stations. "The law" here means the natural or the imperial law, and not necessarily the Mosaic law. But the Mosaic law is full of references to the natural law, and for that reason it is interesting. The commandments of the second table of the Decalogue, which deal with secular affairs, are also significant. Therefore, though Luther does not identify the Mosaic and the natural law, he finds evidence for the natural law in the Mosaic law.

To Wesley, the moral law reveals the nature of God. The regenerated believer whose life is restored to the image of God, will therefore live according to the law. His theology of law has soteriological significance as a model for Christian life and discipleship. This does not mean that a sinner can be saved by observing the law, because the basis for salvation is the atonement of Christ and nothing less. But a person who has been given the new life in Christ by grace will observe the law joyfully in a dynamic and not a mechanical way. He therefore anticipates that sanctified Christians who are liberated from the power of sin and empowered with the divine grace will be able to fulfil the law. The fulfillment of the law results from God's restoration of creation in a person.

The Wesleyan dialectics of commandments and promises are basic to the understanding of the law as a pattern for discipleship. The emphasis in this dialectics is on the promise of grace. His concern is to value the fulfillment of the law of the Christian as an expression of the new nature re-created in the Christian's life.

The Antitheses (5:21-48)

Wesley's interpretations of the antitheses are found as scattered comments, particularly among those on the beatitudes. He thus implies that the antitheses are normative for the life imputed and imparted by the blessings of beatitudes. To him, the antitheses have to be interpreted as eschatological gifts pronounced in the beatitudes, the implications being that the antitheses are viewed as the proper attitude or conduct as a response to the beatitude. Further, his idea is that the gifts of the beatitudes, as well as the obligation of the antitheses, are essential to Christian life wherever it is to be expressed. There is to him no distinction between private and public.

Wesley's basic interpretation of the antitheses is that they materialize the perfect fulfilling of the law that ought to be natural to all sanctified Christians. He rejects that the works of the Sermon on the Mount have meriting value. They are fruits of the faith based upon justification in Christ. Faith and works are therefore held in dynamic tension with the works viewed as the human response to God's grace. The commandments of the antitheses must be understood in light of the beatitudes.

The Antitheses (5:21-48) Compared

In Luther's comments on the antitheses, the doctrine of the two kingdoms is fully elaborated. His hermeneutical problem is that the antitheses should be interpreted literally from an exegetic point of view. If the precepts of the Sermon on the Mount are observed in an absolutist way in all spheres of life, they would not be practicable in situations where responsibility to persons other than oneself is implied. He solves this problem by distinguishing between a spiritual and a secular sphere of life on the one hand, and the Christian as a person and a citizen on the other. Because the Sermon on the Mount is understood Christologically, it deals with salvation and the Christian's relation toward God, and with the life in the world. Therefore, any righteousness merited by works is out of the question. Consequently, the Sermon on the Mount has to be related to the spiritual kingdom and to the Christian "in-person."

When meeting situations "in person," the Christian turns the other cheek to the evil-doer and loves the enemy. In situations where the Christian has responsibilities for other persons, however, they are to be met with a different set of norms. When being "in office" the Christian is representing the authority of God's created order with obligations to obey superiors or to rule subjects, and to punish the evil-doer.

The two kingdoms have two common characteristics. First, they are both ordered by God, but ruled according to different principles. In the spiritual kingdom God rules by the gospel, in the secular kingdom by the law and "the sword." Secondly, Christian conduct is regulated by the Sermon on the Mount in the spiritual kingdom but by the law in the secular. In both kingdoms, however, the love to God and the neighbor has to be expressed.

To Wesley, the beatitudes function as promises of undeserved grace, and the antitheses function as patterns of discipleship. The antitheses should therefore be interpreted as examples of how the fruits of faith may be expressed rather than as a new law to be observed. The beatitudes represent the divine grace, the antitheses the human response to this grace, however, after the sinner's renewal in the image of God. In contrast to Luther, who regards the antitheses to be dangerous to the social order if observed in the civil society, he affirms the antitheses as a pattern to be imitated in the social relationship between persons and nations. It should be kept in mind, however, that he does not understand the antitheses as casuistic moral codes. They are only examples of how love may be materialized in certain situations. Love is what should be imitated, therefore, and not precepts of a code which are limited to a specific historical and cultural situation.

Luther and Wesley alike insist that love is the ultimate ethical norm for Christians at all times. But their concerns are yet not the same, as love has a different role in their theological systems. To Luther, love is the attitude of the believing heart. To Wesley, love is a transforming power. The divine love changes sinners to the image of God, and the love of sanctified sinners changes neighbors and societies according to God's peace.

In contrast to Luther, Wesley is concerned to hold God's creating and saving work systematically united. Instead of separating the two and placing them in separate spheres of life, he envisages creation leading via the fall to salvation in Christ, and salvation to the new creation. The ultimate purpose of salvation being the renewal of the sinner is therefore the entire humanity understood universally (as well as cosmologically) and not the sinner "in-person." The idea of the antitheses is to demonstrate the effects of salvation on humanity and the renewal of the human society (as well as nature), too. He explains:

We ought to do them [the people of the world, enemies included] all the good that is in our power, all they are willing to receive from us; following herein the example of the universal Friend, our Father which is in heaven, who, till they will condescend to receive greater blessings gives them such as they are willing to accept. (*WW*, 3:131)

The little word "till" gives a clue to the understanding of the strong goal-orientation of Wesley's theological system; the aim of salvation is not to be understood individually but socially.[41]

On Anger (5:21-26)

Wesley first makes observations that are similar to Luther's. He establishes that "We ought not for any cause to be angry with the person of the sinner, but at his sin only" (*NT-Notes*, 31). He regards *eike* in Mt. 5:22 to be an insertion,[42] arguing for the omission of the word because "this is utterly foreign to the whole scope and tenor of our Lord's discourse" (*NT-Notes*, 31). Additionally, "if *anger at persons* be a temper contrary to love, how can there be a cause, a sufficient cause for it?" (*WW*, 1:491). One kind of anger he allows, and that is anger at sin.

Wesley's textual criticism is based on his general interpretation of what he supposes to be Christ's intentions. The hermeneutical key is love; the anger that may lead to murder is contrary to love, a supposition which restricts anger to sin only, and not to any person. The example for this practice he finds in Christ himself.

On Anger (5:21-26) Compared

In spite of a number of similarities with Luther, the general tone of Wesley's interpretation is different from Luther's. To Luther, the first antithesis has to be interpreted within the context of the doctrine of the two kingdoms, the implications being a split between the Christian "in person" and the Christian "in office" with contrary rules for conduct. It must now be concluded definitely that this doctrine is the basic hermeneutical key used by him for the interpretation of the Sermon on the Mount.

To Wesley, the antithesis has to be interpreted within the context of the eschatological blessings pronounced in the beatitudes, the implications being that the antitheses are viewed as the proper attitude or conduct as a response to the beatitudes. Further, his idea is that the gifts of the beatitudes, as well as the obligations of the antitheses, are essential to Christian life wherever it is to be expressed. There is to him no distinction between private and public.

On Adultery and Divorce (5:27-32)

Wesley has an absolutist interpretation of the first part of this antithesis. This literalism is not based in hostility against sexuality, as the point rather be that the needs of the neighbor must come before those of the Christian. His frame of reference is love, respect, and responsibility toward others. If sexual desires threaten to harm other persons, it is better to sacrifice physical organs in order to protect the neighbor.

The same rigorist attitude is revealed in Wesley's discourse on the purity of heart: "God admits no excuse for retaining anything which is an occasion of impurity" (*WW*, 1:511). His theological problem is the lack of love and not the issue of "sexual impurity;" he relates the "lusting after women" to the "hurting your brother." A short review of his other works on marriage indicates the same conclusion, for instance, his tract *Thoughts on a Single Life*. He here insists that marriage is no hindrance for perfection: "Nor can it be doubted but persons may be as holy in married as in a single state" (*WW-J*, 11:457). Though "it is good for a man not to touch a woman," yet this is not a universal rule. A Christian may be married "without any impeachment of our love to God" (*WW-J*, 11:459), "since perfection does not consist in any outward state whatever, but in an absolute devotion of all our heart and all our life to God" (*WW-J*, 11:463). He does not picture marriage as a secondary or imperfect Christian. The following verse by Charles Wesley is illustrating John's view well in its emphasis of the woman as the equal cooperator with man: "Not from his head was woman took, So made her husband to o'look'; Not from his feet, as one designed The footstool of the stronger kind;' But fashioned for himself, a bride, An equal, taken from his side" (cited after Conn 1979:35). Nevertheless, the tone of the tract is ascetic. It is directed "to this happy few ... "who is able to 'receive this saying'—to abstain from marriage, and yet not burn, however, that happens only after the reception of a specific spiritual gift for celibacy" (*WW-J*, 11:458). Celibacy is a gift because,

> You may "attend upon the Lord without distraction. ..." You enjoy a blessed liberty from the "trouble in the flesh. ..." You are exempt from numberless occasions of sorrow and anxiety. ...
>
> Above all, you are at liberty from the greatest of all entanglements, the loving one creature above all others. It is possible to do this without sin, without any impeachment of our love to God. But how inconceivably difficult! to give God our whole heart, while a creature has so large a share of it! (*WW-J*, 11:458-459)

Basically, to be married is of no hindrance for loving God unto perfection, however, there are practical problems like attending "upon the Lord without distraction," "numberless occasions of sorrow and anxiety," and, above all, the problem of the single heart, or, to be entirely focused on God. Wesley's main concern for a single life is that nothing should compete with the love of God, and a spouse and children will do just that. Though he never explicitly underestimates marriage, the general impression of his preference to the single life is undeniable. His comment is probably a good summary of his views on marriage and single life:[43]

> [Mt. 19:12] *There are eunuchs, who have made themselves eunuchs for the kingdom of heaven's sake*—Happy they who have abstained from marriage (though without condemning or despising it) that they might walk more closely with God! *He that is able to receive it, let him receive it*—This gracious command ... is not designed for all men; but only for those few who are "able to receive it". Oh, let these receive it joyfully! (*NT-Notes*, 93)

Wesley's attitude corresponds well with his frequent advice that his preachers be careful in their relationships with women.[44] His attitude regarding divorce and remarriage generally follows

Clemens of Alexandria's interpretation of the moderating insertion of "except for the cause for fornication".[45]

On Adultery and Divorce (5:27-32) Compared

Though Wesley generally is more positive regarding the single life than is Luther, they basically agree in affirming marriage as legitimate for Christians. Without denying that married Christians may be as perfect as single Christians, Wesley suggests that perfection is easier to experience by single persons because they do not need to worry about spouses and children. His reasons for the preference of a singular life is pragmatically and not religiously founded.

Luther comes to the opposite conclusion, affirming marriage for two reasons. First, it protects the married person against sinful desires because of the sexual content in marriage. Secondly (and less emphasized in this specific antithesis), is the obligation to fulfil God's vocation in the secular kingdom by being a family member and by participating in God's creating activity. The pragmatic motive is dominant in the first reason given. In the second, a religious motive is implied as well. He at this point has a stronger theological argument for marriage than has Wesley. The exegetic problem of castration is solved by Luther by using it as a support of the doctrine of the two kingdoms, while Wesley points to the sacrifices that may be required for the sake of neighborly love.

That Luther's theological position is complex is highlighted in the issue of marriage. According to his ideas marriage is a divine ordinance but regulated by secular law. Family life is one of the three basic orders of creation.

Luther's and Wesley's exegetic positions on Christ's teaching about divorce are compatible. They both affirm a rather absolutist interpretation. But Luther's basis in the doctrine of the two kingdoms makes a difference when it comes to the actual act of divorce. To him, issues of marriage and divorce are not exegetical problems only. First and foremost, they are issues for the secular kingdom. For that reason, he may suggest an absolutist exegesis and be willing to accept a liberal practice of divorce at the same time, provided that this practice is founded in the civil law. This is an example where the imperial law is above the commandments of the Sermon on the Mount.

On Oaths (5:33-37)

As observed earlier, Wesley connects this antithesis with the beatitude of the purity in heart. The reason is that Christ in Mt. 5:33 refers to the promise "of seeing God in all things." He relaxes his previous absolutist interpretation and does not take this antithesis to be a general prohibition against oath: "What He [Christ] forbids is, the swearing at all (1) by any creature, and (2) in our daily conversation" (*NT-Notes*, 33). He does not explain his comment on swearing by creatures, but the meaning is probably that the Creator is violated by that kind of swearing.

On Oaths (5:33-37) Compared

In their interpretations of the antithesis on oaths, Luther and Wesley probably demonstrate a more extensive agreement than on other parts of the Sermon on the Mount. They both reject excessive swearing but affirm the necessity of oaths when required by civil courts. The difference between them appears in their basic hermeneutics. To Luther, this antithesis reinforces his doctrine of the two kingdoms. To Wesley, the interpretation is related to his doctrine of perfection.

To the understanding of Luther's doctrine of the two kingdoms, a few additional observations should be made. First and foremost the requirements of the secular and the spiritual kingdoms may be contradictory. A Christian-in-office must punish and kill when required by civil law in situations when a Christian-in-person is expected not to punish. The immediate relation of the Christian to other people is what determines which set of regulations is to be observed. When one is in office, the commandments of the Sermon on the Mount should not be taken into account. The implication is, secondly, a principled and practical autonomy of the civil institutions and authorities over against the laws of the spiritual kingdom, to which the Sermon on the Mount belongs. Thirdly, the commandments of the Sermon on the Mount are not supposed to be observed literally, either in the secular kingdom or in the spiritual. To act in love is superior to any casuistic commandment. At this point he admits a situational ethics based upon love over against a deontological ethics.

Wesley, too, is more concerned about the actual acting in love than of a casuistic fulfillment of the law.

On Retaliation (5:38-42)
On Violence (5:38-41)

Wesley interprets the fourth antithesis as a realization of the third beatitude of the meek (*WW* 1:691, 696-697; *NT-Notes*, 33), the seventh beatitude as a realization of the peacemakers (*WW* 1:518), and the eighth beatitude as a realization of those who are persecuted for righteousness' sake (*WW* 1:528). The combination with the last beatitude serves as the key to his understanding of this antithesis as presented in *Explanatory Notes upon the New Testament*; the key being social holiness or holiness of life:

> 39. But I say unto you, That ye resist not the evil man.[46] ... If a man smite thee on the right cheek—Return not evil for evil.
>
> 40-41. Where the damage is not great, choose rather to suffer it ... than to demand "an eye for an eye." ... The meaning of the whole passage seems to be, rather than return evil for evil, when the wrong is purely personal, submit to one bodily wrong after another; give up one part of your goods after another. That the words are not literally to be understood appears from the behaviour of our Lord Himself (John 18:22-23).
>
> 42. Thus much for your behaviour towards the violent. As for those who use milder methods, Give the one that asketh thee—Give and lend to any so far ... as is consistent with thy engagements to thy creditors, thy family, and the household of faith. (NT-Notes, 34)

To interpret this antithesis, Wesley uses the method of reading the text in light of scriptural parallels. He points to the incident from the trial of Christ when Christ was slapped in his face without turning the other cheek to the officer. When this method is used in the history of the interpretation of the Sermon on the Mount, the aim usually is to weaken its radical precepts (McArthur, 1960), however, his motive is rather the opposite. His intention is to confirm the radical character of Christ's words as related to the persecution of the sanctified Christian.

By the comment, "When the wrong is purely personal," Wesley does not indicate a distinction between the Christian as a private and a civil person, he relates it to various kinds of persecution. To understand this distinction I have investigated how he used to meet persecution by mobs in his career as an evangelist.[47] The mysterious "Where the damage is not great," then becomes clear; he distinguishes between persecution directed against individual Christians on the one hand and groups of Christians, societies, or churches on the other. In both cases Christ's commandment of meeting violence with patience and meekness should be observed. Under no circumstance is violence to be met with counterviolence. Here lies the distinction between individuals and groups. He actually develops a strategy for meeting riots and persecution in each of these two contexts, according to the patterns described in Mt. 5 and Mt. 10, especially:

1. When individuals are attacked, persecution ought to be avoided; if not possible, it ought to be endured and suffered;[48] the distinction is between individuals and social groups and not between persons and offices, nor between spiritual and secular regulations. To Wesley, the precepts of the Sermon on the Mount are functional ethical norms for individuals as well as for groups of believers. The goal is always the same, to win the persecutors for the Gospel.[49]

2. After the formation of a group or society, the issue is different; a certain kind of resistance is now accepted as long as it can promote the kind of acts of love which may win the opponents to Christ. A society of Christians cannot easily flee to another town, neither should it, because that would be to give up the basic civil right of freedom of religion. Therefore they have to stay in order to fight against the evil with the means of love. If necessary, Wesley advises the societies to seek protection by help of the local police or judicial authorities.[50]

3. Wesley interprets Christ's words as precepts for the inclusion of those who persecute Christians, too, in the active evangelism of people.[51]

On Violence (5:38-41) Compared

The comparison of Luther's and Wesley's interpretations of the antithesis on retaliation indicates that they equally affirm that love, understood as the fruits of faith, provides the basic ethical norm for Christian conduct. When Luther puts the imperial law before the commandments of the Sermon on the Mount, love still is the superior ethical norm. Their concerns, however, are different. To Luther, the issue is to clarify when counter-violence is a proper reaction to violence, and who is in authority to use counter-violence. Wesley's concern is what kind of reaction to violence will serve as the best strategy to convert violent persecutors. While Luther's interpretation of this antithesis has genuine social and political implications, Wesley's exegesis is more directed to evangelism.

This difference is a logical consequence when taking their historical and theological situations into consideration. Luther's problem is to separate state and church politically and still affirm the divine origin of the state. On the one hand, his concern is to restrict the actual possibility of the Roman Catholic church and the Baptists to exercise temporal power. On the other hand, his concern is to defend the autonomy of the civil administration. He does so on the basis of a theological consideration rather than a political. The doctrine of the two kingdoms presupposes that the secular kingdom is ordered by God, a fact that gives the secular orders the legitimacy necessary as the basis for autonomy. When a secular ruler is subject to criticism by political reasons, he is still theologically authorized by God. Luther therefore approves police, courts, and armies as valid instruments in God's hands for the sake of restricting and punishing evil powers.

Wesley's problem is different. He insists that police and judges are appointed to protect his civil rights. In one sense, he can build on the historical contribution of Luther in this respect. Though he does not view the secular authorities as divine instruments in the world in the way Luther does, he accepts police forces and courts on pragmatic grounds. If his thought on this issue ever changed, it probably did so in the opposite direction of that of Luther. Wesley's critical attitude toward the civil administration increased rather than decreased. His more pragmatic position is politically significant as well, because a pragmatic orientation necessarily will be more flexible than Luther's orders and stations ever can be, though they are founded theologically.

When it comes to the issue of pacifism and the use of violent means in conflict-solving, Luther changed from a pacifist view to a military position before he delivered his discourses on the Sermon on the Mount. Wesley remains a pacifist. This follows from his sayings on how to handle situations of persecution, his disgust concerning "Christian armies," and the general tenor of his theology.

To Luther, the use of armed force easily can be reconciled with his teachings of love, expressed in terms of the doctrine of the two kingdoms. To Wesley, love is irreconcilable to violence of any kind. On discussing the implications of original sin, he refers to war as a proof of the existence of original sin, concluding: "Now, who can reconcile war, I will not say to religion, but to any degree of reason or common sense?" (*WW-J*, 9:221). Neither reason and common sense nor religion can justify war; "wherever war breaks out, God is forgotten, if he be not set at open defiance" (*WL*, 6:151). In general he supports non-resistance as the more reasonable means of defense (Semmel 1974:54, 66).

Luther attempts to distinguish between the kingdoms without separating them. He demonstrates how they are different and yet related, and dependent on each other. He makes the pure and loving heart the ideal basis for the life in both kingdoms. On the one hand, he indicates that in the secular kingdom the Christian has nothing more than the heathen, both being governed by reason and human law. On the other hand, only pious Christians have love which comes out of their relationships with God through faith. My understanding is that the paradox here discussed should not be mediated too much. If the two kingdoms are successfully harmonized, the genuine tension between the kingdoms disappears and the genius of his doctrine of the two kingdoms is lost.

In discussing persecution, Wesley's distinction between Christian persons and groups looks similar to Luther's contrast between individuals and groups. Their distinctions are nevertheless different. Luther distinguishes between the Christian-in-person and the Christian-in-relation, permitting the latter only to resist evil provided the Christian is properly commissioned in an office for that purpose. His purpose is to protect the orders of society from chaos. Any notion of social change is excluded. Wesley's distinction is between persecution of preachers or individual Christians, and persecution of societies or congregations. His general advice is to avoid persecution of individuals or suffer, but also to seek the protection of groups of Christians who are unable to flee to another place. For both situations the ultimate goal is to win the persons persecuting, for Christ.

On Economy (5:42)

Affirming that the Christian is obliged to give and lend to anybody without limitation to person, Wesley limits the obligation to give and lend to the person who asks for alms by giving it a second priority after the social responsibilities of the believer to family, creditors, "and the household of faith," are taken care of. The principles of the sermon "The Use of Money" (*WW*, 2:263-280) are developed in his discourse on Mt. 6:19-23. The background of "The Use of Money" is the problems that occurred as the Methodists prospered. His most radical points are "the rejection of surplus accumulation" (*WW*, 2:265), and his insistence on a redistribution of money that includes the poor. His concern for a just economy has a social as well as a theological basis. First, he is afraid that wealth should lead to a spiritual decline of the revival movement. Secondly, he worries about the widened contrast between the rich and the poor in 18th-century England. Thirdly, his theological foundation in peace and love requires a just distribution of privileges of every kind.

The scripture of the sermon "The Use of Money" is Lk. 16:9. Wesley understands Christ's words as addressed to Christians. He is not willing to admit that money is bad as such; the problem does not lie in the money as such, but in the ways it is used, for they also open up the possibility of doing good:

> in the present state of mankind it [money] is an excellent gift of God, answering the noblest ends. In the hands of his children it is food for the hungry, drink for the thirsty, raiment for the na-ked. It gives to the traveller and the stranger where to lay his head. By it we may supply the place of an husband to the widow, and of a father to the fatherless; we may be a defence for the oppressed, a means of health to the sick, of ease to them that are in pain. It may be as eyes to the blind, as feet to the lame; yea, a lifter up from the gates of death. (*WW*, 2:268)

The economy of the Jerusalem church was based on distribution according to actual needs, and Wesley intends to imitate it. He therefore begins to develop his economic ethics with its three basic rules: (1) *Gain all you can*, but not at the expense of your life, be it health, or soul, nor at the expense of your neighbor. (2) *Save all you can*, but not for the desires of the flesh, pride or vanity. He is especially worried if money is saved for the benefit of one's children in the future; in particular, inherited wealth may cause severe problems for many people. (3) *Give all you can* to people with more basic needs than yourself: "do good unto all men.' In so doing, you *give all you can*; nay, in a sound sense, all you have" (*WW*, 2:277). He reminds us that God is the real owner of things. A person is never more than a steward in God's place, whose first duty is to provide things needful for himself, secondly, for his family, and thirdly, for other people in need.

The aim of gaining and saving money is a just distribution of money. According to Wesley's definition of (properly) "saving" the aim is not the accumulation of money, but first taking care of personal basic needs, then giving to people with deeper needs. "Giving" is a genuine religious act because it is to give back to God what God has given to the believer.

The ends for the Christian's earning and saving is the giving to the poor and to guarantee a just distribution of money, not the accumulation of private fortunes. Wesley in examining the causes of poverty never regards the beggars with suspicion or accuses the poor of laziness.[52] He rather investigates the nature of poverty because he realizes that he can best help the poor if he contributes in removing the causes of poverty. Contrary to Luther's wish to establish a system that prevents the receiving alms of rascals, he institutes actions for the removal of poverty. He does so in many ways, for instance by establishing home industries and a cooperative selling of the products, to reduce the effects of unemployment, by working for the improvement of health conditions in order to reduce poverty caused by sickness, by establishing schools to eliminate illiteracy, and by founding a system of "stewards," who from their local Methodist societies and classes visited poor people regularly and took care of the needs of the whole families. It is a historical fact, too, that the Methodist societies were organized to make the collection of money for the poor more effective.

Wesley's passion for the poor is obvious.[53] His views cannot be misunderstood: Christians must give according to their power. If they have plenty, they should give plenty. To include the poor in the distribution of money within a society is a major concern to him:

> Be ye "ready to distribute" to everyone according to his necessity. Disperse abroad, give to the poor: deal your bread to the hungry. Cover the naked with a garment, entertain the stranger, carry or send relief to them that are in prison. Heal the sick; not by miracle, but through the blessing of God upon your seasonable support. Let the blessing of him that was ready to perish through want come upon thee. Defend the oppressed, plead the cause of the fatherless, and make the widow's heart sing for joy.
> ... Be a steward, a faithful and wise steward, of God and of the poor; differing from them in these two circumstances only, that your wants are first supplied out of the portion of your Lord's goods which are first supplied out of the portion of your Lord's goods which remains in your hands, and that you have the blessedness of giving. (*WW*, 1:630)

A comparison of Wesley's interpretations of "Happy *are* the poor in spirit" (Mt. 5:3) with "Happy *are* ye poor" / "But woe to you that are rich!" (Lk. 6:20/24) is enlightening. According to him, these beatitudes are the beginnings of two different sermons given by Christ (*NT-Notes*, 223) and, consequently, Christ probably addresses himself to different groups. The poverty of the spirit is interpreted spiritually as having a penitent mind, being "deeply sensible of their sinfulness, guiltiness, helpless-ness" (*NT-Notes*, 28). The poverty of Lk. 6:20 he interprets liter-ally. The poor hinted to are not the kind of people who are de-prived of social benefits, however, they have deliberately chosen their poverty, because they "have left all for Me" (*NT-Notes*, 223). He is not here speaking of the voluntary poverty of monks but of persons who have redistributed their money to the poor as a fruit of their sanctification. The rich person, on the other side, can be neither satisfied nor happy.

A problem is Wesley's open mind toward poor people on the one hand and the fact that he interprets 5:42 within the context of persecution on the other. The exegetic reason is the scriptural context, the verse follows immediately after 5:38-41. But there may be a religious reason as well. To him, suffering for the sake of Christ is considered in positive terms. It is an indication of the Christian's holiness of heart, and it follows that his valuation of persecution is highly positive. He has, therefore, no problem in combining the happy giving of alms with the notion of persecu-tion, since he considers both to be affirming signs of his relation-ship with God.

On Economy (5:42) Compared

Both Luther and Wesley interpret Mt. 5:42 in the light of its tex-tual context. Luther characterizes this context as suffering, Wesley as persecution. A common trait is their statements about the Christian's right to seek protection by the secular law, though their reasons for this differ. Both interpret the teaching of Christ in a semi-absolutist way. Their comments seem to be absolute, but limitations are introduced. The absolute part of the interpretation is that the Christian ought to give to everybody who asks for alms or loans. The common limitation is that the Christian is not commanded to give away money which is needed for the care of family and similar responsibilities. There are, however, a variety of differences in interpretation as well.[54]

Luther's interpretation of this text, as well as all texts dealing with the Christian in the world, is related to his doctrine of the two kingdoms. For a secular person the accumulation of treasures is required. When a prince accumulates money, he does so as part of his responsibilities for his country and his people, "as a universal father of his entire land" (*LW*, 21:171) and not for himself. In the same way a family father has to take care of those for whom he is responsible. Luther and Wesley agree until this point, though the doctrine of the two kingdoms is not supported by Wesley. But he would agree with the following comment by Luther: "Everyone should earn enough to support himself without being a burden on other people, and to be able to help others as well. Thus one should contribute to others in time of need" (*LW*, 21:171-172). Luther and Wesley would probably depart, however, when coming to the implications of the first sentence of the quotation. Wesley is willing to go further than Luther in his openness for a more active (but not forced?) distribution of the wealth of the nation, for example by creating work for unemployed and use taxes and other regulations to govern the social economy. An example is his concern for the scarcity of provisions during the winter 1772-73, caused by the war and a bad harvest. December 9, 1772, he wrote to *Lloyd Evening Post* about the problem. December, 31, he devoted his prayer for the poor in particular: "Being greatly embarrassed by the necessities of the poor, we spread all our wants before God in solemn prayer" (*WW*, 22:357). January, 20, 1773, he expanded the newspaper letter and published it as a pamphlet, *The Present Scarcity of Provisions* (*WW-J*, 11:53-59). Formally, this is not a theological piece of work, except for his unmentioned but basic concern for the poor as the small sisters and brothers of Christ according to Mt. 25:31ff. His intention is to provide an overall analysis of the problem based on social-economic reasoning.

Wesley begins by referring to the ongoing debate concerning the scarcity of provisions. He states that the writers until then in general have been occupied with just a few reasons. He now will take all the reasons into account and discuss every single cause, affecting the prices. The pamphlet has two main parts. The first is the analysis of the problems. He finds that the basic reason for poverty is that a vicious circle is established by unemployment combined with a decrease of commerce because people have no money to buy commodities for. The food prices are too high because "such immense quantities of corn are continually consumed by distilling ... little less than half the wheat produced in the kingdom is every year consumed," and the oats are used for the luxury use of horses. The shortage of beef and mutton is caused by increased breeding of horses. Pork, poultry, and eggs are expensive because of the monopolizing of farms. The luxury of the nobility and the gentry is even a grand cause for poverty because it leads to scarcity. Other causes are the rent on farming land and the enormous taxes, which again are caused by a heavy national debt. It is interesting to observe that though he is not an economist, he attempts to describe the relationships between the various problems.

In the second part, Wesley describes the kind of remedies he will recommend: Provide work and stimulate trade. Prohibit the distilling of alcohol. Reduce the number of horses used for luxury by "laying a tax of ten pounds of every horse exported to France," laying tax on gentlemen's carriages and five pounds yearly upon every horse used for luxury. Increase the breed of sheep and horned cattle. Put a limit on the rent on farms, restrain luxury "which is the grand and general source of want," save 2 mill pounds a year by discharging half the national debt and, not least, "By abolishing all useless pensions, as fast as those who now enjoy them die: Especially those ridiculous ones given to some hundreds of idle men, as Governors of forts or castles; which forts have answered no end for above these hundred years, unless to shelter jackdaws and crows."

To Wesley, the basic scarcity of provisions is due to the lack of true religion. His general remedy is the conversion of the sinner into a holy life, however, he acknowledges the necessity of Parliament regulations, too, like laws and regulations. If the social problems be fought effectively, structural evils will be removed by the use of political and economic means.[55]

Wesley would also agree with Luther in his supposition that great fortunes only rarely are "accumulated in a God-pleasing manner" (*LW*, 21:174). But there are differences as well. Luther holds that the consequences of these financial efforts are a dead end, because "Moths and rust shall come over it and consume it, and it shall be stolen. Thus no one succeeds if he is greedy and grabs everything for himself this way" (*LW*, 21:172). Wesley is more radical in his warnings. Greedy persons will not lose their fortunes alone, but their souls as well.

There is no trace at all of Luther's two-kingdom doctrine in Wesley's entire biblical exegesis. On the contrary, he encourages his followers to appeal to the police or the judges in cases where the laws for securing religious freedom are violated. Though he does not seek suffering, he holds positive attitudes to persecution in general, and he does not seem motivated by a wish to remove suffering as such. What he attempts by seeking support is never to protect himself as an individual, but to defend the freedom of faith and his societies. Luther's important motive for the protection of the family has no dominant place for him. It is referred to but not expounded. His advice to seek protection of the civil authorities is related to a different situation than was the case for Luther. He is not concerned with personal security and property, but with the rights securing the freedom to believe. He therefore resists any kind of persecution against organized Methodist groups by reference to the legal rights of the Methodists as English citizens.

It might seem that Wesley in more general terms has more positive attitudes to the poor than does Luther, particularly if their Sermon on the Mount exegeses are compared out of context. A glance into their personal priorities, however, indicates that this is a too hasty conclusion. Catherine Luther was more than once upset because her husband gave away money and food to the poor out of their limited provisions.

In conclusion, both Luther[56] and Wesley have an open mind to their poor neighbor. Consequently, their general interpretation of the commandment of Christ is rather absolute, however, their theological motivations are different. Luther's basis is the community of the believers as a "loaf" which is spread out for the benefit of the world, like Christ gave his own body. Wesley's basis is the concept of God as the prime owner of everything in the world and the human person as God's steward. They differ in their poor relief, too. Luther's concern for the poor comes from his conception of the Church as a corporate body, while Wesley's basis is the notion of God as the owner of all things and the model of Mt. 25:35-36.

So, in spite of a common starting-point, the effects are not the same. While Luther's practical problem is how to limit the giving of alms to worthy beggars, Wesley's is the opposite, namely, how to get enough money to cover all the needs. The protective attitude of Luther and the social active design of Wesley should, however, be understood historically. Each of them interprets the Sermon on the Mount not as a literal response to the words of Christ but as a responsible answer to the challenges from their different historical, social, economic, and religious situations. In Luther's mind the mendicant orders and the Baptists are his opponents because of their dissolution of the social and economic structures, and he sought support from the rich. To Wesley, the opponents are the rich who increase the sufferings of the poor by accumulating their fortunes for their own luxurious needs, and he makes the poor his partners in the struggle against poverty.

The basic disagreement between Luther and Wesley revolves around Luther's two-kingdoms doctrine. Wesley hardly can imagine that such a separation of the spiritual life from the world is based on the scriptures.

On Love For Enemies (5:43-48)

Wesley comments: *"Bless them that curse you*—Speak all the good you can to and of them who speak all evil to and of you. Repay love in thought, word, and deed to those who hate you, and show it both in word and deed" (*NT-Notes*, 34). He points to the crucified Christ's example in forgiving his murderers (Lk. 23:34), this indicating that he does not follow the explicit precepts of Christ only, but Christ's example as well. It is important to realize the significance of scriptural models to understand the norms of the Wesleyan ethics. He looks to the scriptures for examples to imitate no less than commands to observe.

Wesley's introduction to Mt. 6 states that Christ in Mt. 5 "described the nature of inward holiness" (*NT-Notes*, 35), a statement that is expressed in the comment on the conclusion of this first chapter on the Sermon on the Mount:

> *Therefore ye shall be perfect, as your Father who is in heaven is perfect*—So the original runs, referring to all that holiness which is described in the foregoing verses, which our Lord in the beginning of the chapter recommends as happiness, and in the close of it as perfection. (*NT-Notes*, 35)

Wesley interprets Mt. 5 as a closed unity under the heading "the nature of inward holiness." The phrase "In the beginning of the chapter" relates to the beatitudes (Mt. 5:3-12) described by Christ as a state of happiness, of which the believers share as a result of the graceful blessings of God. The parables of the salt and the light (Mt. 5:13-16) illustrate that this inward holiness of heart must have outward consequences in the life of the Christian. The antitheses (Mt. 5:21-48) provide examples of how this divine life functions in concrete and everyday situations in the lives of the believers, where they are ruled by the love of God and of their neighbors.

Wesley ends his comments on the antitheses underlining the fact that the moral commandments are accompanied by an offer of the grace of God. No human being can fulfil the precepts of God by her- or himself. But filled by the power of God it is possible.

The moral commandments lose their character of being claims, and they turn out to be the actualization of the life in grace, a consequence of the undeserved love of God and an act of divine grace in the midst of human life. He explains his thoughts more fully in his fifth discourse on Mt. 5:17-20. The law leads the sinner to Christ and the reborn and regenerated sinner is led back to the law, not to merit justification, but on the basis of the justification that is imputed because of Christ's atonement. By adding the notion of the commandments as "covered promises" he manages to keep the doctrine of justification by faith alone without losing the law as the model for the Christian life.

In Wesley's interpretation of Mt. 5:48 the issue of natural law is raised. He quotes from Jer. 31:33, however, this does not indicate that the natural human being may know the will of God and have the capacity to discriminate between good and evil. Another verse, which is much quoted on this issue, is Rom. 1:19, interpreted by him like this: "*For what is to be known of God*—those great principles which are indispensably necessary to be known. *Is manifest in them*—By the light which enlightens every man that cometh into the world" (*NT-Notes* 520). That the latter part of the comment does not imply that the knowledge of God is enlightened to human beings from birth is apparent from other comments, for instance, of Jn. 1:9: "*Who lighteth every man*—By what is vulgarly termed natural conscience, pointing out at least the general lines of good and evil. And this light, if man did not hinder, would shine more and more to the perfect day" (*NT-Notes*, 303).

Obviously, Wesley accepts that God has laid something manifest into the soul of human beings that may be developed to salvation if not "hindered." The problem is persons will effectively hinder salvation by the corrupted will, making salvation impossible because of the original sin, cf. his note to Jn. 1:5 "*And the light shineth in darkness*—Shines even on fallen man. *But the darkness*—Dark, sinful man, *perceiveth it not*" (*NT-Notes*, 303). The problem is that the sinner does not properly use the light he or she has, and therefore the incarnation of Christ is necessary.

Wesley rejects the belief in the natural capacities of humanity. His valuation of "natural conscience" is utterly negative. He does not approve the concept at all but replaces natural law with the doctrine of prevenient grace. The concept "natural conscience" is a "vulgar term" (*WW*, 3:207) because it does not give credit to God who really is at work through prevenient grace. As far as I can see, he gives no room for any "natural religion" either in his theology or in his anthropology.

On Love For Enemies (5:43-48) Compared

Luther reinforces his hermeneutics by holding that a proper interpretation is meaningless unless a distinction is made between the two kingdoms. To love enemies is obliged in the spiritual kingdom but dangerous in the secular kingdom. The obligation is here to punish the evil-doer in order to protect the social order. Wesley's interpretation is absolutist and affirms the opposite, the commandment to love is to be observed without limit.

Luther solves the conflict between love according to Christ's commandments in the Sermon on the Mount and the need for punishment of the evil according to the imperial laws for the protection of social order, by insisting that the Christian-in-person never is to show hatred and revenge, only non-resistance and love. The Christian-in-office, however, never is to show forgiveness, only punishment. The love and forgiveness of the Christian's heart is supposed to remain hidden and not to show forth in the way an office is administered. In the secular world, the evil-doer is not to be forgiven, but punished. The difference is, the Christian-in-office is acting not from hatred and revenge but from love, though also in obedience and loyalty to the secular authorities.

The dichotomy of Christian ethics implied in the doctrine of the two kingdoms is here brought to its extreme. The very same act of violence may lead to opposite reactions, depending on which kingdom is involved. If the object of violence is a Christian-in-person, this situation should be met by the Christian according to Christ's teaching in the Sermon on the Mount, with forgiveness and love. If the Christian is in office, however, he or she has to express Christian love by protecting those for whom he or she is responsible, also when the result is the killing of the evil-doer. In both situations and kingdoms, Christian love is decisive, but the ways of expression are opposite and incompatible.

On interpreting the perfection of Mt. 5:48 Luther distinguishes the perfection of doctrine and the perfection of the secular office. In the spiritual kingdom an actual perfection of the believer is out of question. But in the secular kingdom he anticipates the possibility of actual righteousness of the human holder of office, thanks be to reason and faithful observance of the civil law. At this point Wesley recognizes one perfection only, the perfection of God imputed to the believer through faith by grace, and imparted to the totality of life as the believer is transformed to the image of God.

Contrary to Luther, Wesley explicitly denies that there is a perfection based upon a natural recognition of God's will. He replaces natural law with his doctrine of prevenient grace and emphasizes that the human will freely becomes open for God's regenerating grace. The basis for this is his soteriology. He rejects the notion of natural law on the basis of the fall. At the same time his emphasis on the corruption after the fall is connected to an optimism of grace which partly is expressed as God's universal grace, offering salvation to humankind and partly as God's transforming grace, offering new life to the sinner, even unto perfection.

The Three "Works" (6:1-18)

There is a shift in the outline of the Sermon on the Mount between the 5th and the 6th chapters of Matthew. Wesley understands the 6th chapter to deal with "right intention" (*WW*, 1:474, 650-651). To him, "inward religion" is the same as "inward holiness" (*NT-Notes*, 35).

The Three "Works" (6:1-18) Compared

While Luther distinguishes between the 5th and the 6th chapters for doctrinal purposes, Wesley makes the distinction of inward and outward religion, supposing that both are parts of the same religious experience. By the emphasis on the significance of intention,[57] the outward actions are related to the Christian experience as well. Luther has some basic criticisms against the works of almsgiving, prayer, and fasting. If they become institutionalized, as they are in the Roman Catholic Church, they will be exterminated for devotional or other kinds of religious value. Therefore, these works must remain voluntary and "left to the discretion of every individual" (*LW*, 21:162). If they continue to be public acts, they will be emptied of their religious meaning, for the Christian life has to be lived in a secret way, "the whole of the Christian life has to be hidden and remain hidden" (*LW*, 21:163-164). But where is the Christian life to be hidden? He answers, in the heart, adding that the power of the Christian life is to fill the life in the stations of the secular kingdom, and show up as love expressed in obedience to the authorities. He is convinced that God has organized the order of life in two kingdoms to remain separate without confusion. The Christian virtues have to be "intended," but not put into action. God will take care of the changes in the world without help from Christians, who are to be concerned about their salvation and nothing more. The human instruments that God has appointed for the purpose of changing the world are the civil authorities. It follows that his ethics is primarily an ethic of intention or one of disposition (cf. Gustafson 1968:125, 129).

A dividing line between Luther and Wesley is their views of what kind of change takes place in the Christian. Luther focuses partly on a forensic, partly on an epistemological change. In principle, the sinner's situation before God is different after justification. The sinner may acknowledge this change but no actual change takes place in the nature of the person. Christ's righteousness is imputed to the sinner. This righteousness is not imputed in a renewed nature of the believer, however, it remains the believer's alien righteousness. The proper Christian existence is, consequently, characterized by the notion of *simul iustus et peccator*.

Wesley focuses on the actual change of the person. As demonstrated in his exegesis of the *basileia theou* (the kingdom of God) of the Lord's Prayer in particular, his position is that the sinner is regenerated after the image of God.

Logan (1985a:364) illustrates Wesley's soteriology and eschatology within the framework of creation in a way which is fully confirmed by my observations of Wesley's interpretations of the Sermon on the Mount. He demonstrates how the starting point of Wesley's soteriology is the first creation, and that its ending point is the new creation. In every part of his soteriology, the human change results from divine grace. No human merits are implied.

Alms-giving (6:1-4)

The concept of "righteousness" in Mt. 6:1 directs Wesley's understanding of the three "works": Mt. 6:1-4, on alms-giving, describes the righteousness in relation to our neighbor; 6:5-15, on prayer, the righteousness in relation to God; and 6:16-18, on fasting, righteousness in relation to ourselves.[58] He exemplifies the works of mercy by referring to Mt. 25:35-38. Practices already developed by the Methodist revival movement are included as well.

More important than the secret doing of good is the actual doing of good. Wesley's fear of antinomianism is here coming to the surface. He is afraid that Christ's "proverbial expression" may be understood as an excuse for not doing good at all.

Alms-giving (6:1-4) Compared

Both Luther and Wesley distinguish between alms-giving on the one hand as a "work of mercy" and prayer and fasting on the other hand as "works of piety" (*LW*, 21:131; *WW*, 1:573). Wesley suggests this outline for Mt. 6:

> [Mt. 6:1] This chapter contains four parts: (1) the right intention and manner in giving alms (verses 1-4); (2) the right intention, manner, form, and prerequisites of prayer (verses 5-15); (3) the right intention and manner of fasting (verses 16-8); (4) the necessity of a pure intention in all things, unmixed either with the desire of riches, or worldly care and fear of want (verses 19-34). (*NT-Notes*, 35)

Wesley further emphasizes that "Our Lord does not enjoin either fasting, almsdeeds, or prayer; all these being duties which were before fully established in the Church of God" (*NT-Notes*, 39; comment to Mt. 6:16). These three works represent a continual practice from the Old Testament times into the New.[59]

The teachings of Luther and Wesley at this point are generally the same. What makes alms-giving a good work is the intention of the Christian. Wesley has, however, a stronger emphasis on actually doing works of mercy because of a soteriological focus on regeneration. The works are signs of the kingdom of God present in the midst of human existence. Luther on this point stresses the significance of "motivation" (*LW*, 21:123) in a way parallel to Wesley's "intention."[60]

Prayer (i) (6:5-15)

Wesley insists that we need to pray as much as possible. Long prayers should be avoided because they are regularly "without meaning" (*WW*, 1:577). There is no reason to believe that prayer has to do with magic. An important psychological effect is its function as self-instruction:[61]

> So that the end of our praying is not to inform God ... but rather to inform yourselves, to fix the sense of those wants more deeply in your hearts, and the sense of your continual dependence of him who only is able to supply all your wants. It is not so much to move God—who is always more ready to give than you to ask—as to move yourselves, that you may be willing and ready to receive the good things he has prepared for you. (*WW*, 1:577)

According to Wesley, The Lord's Prayer is "the model and standard of all our prayers" (*WW*, 1:577); it includes everything, contains all we can desire as well as "all our duty to God and man." Implied in the request directed to "Our *Father*" is, first, the revelation of the specific image of God as a loving and caring father. The father-image is not connected to judgment and punishment but to the granting of salvation because of grace; secondly, the revelation of a holistic image of God, being savior as well as creator and sustainer:

> "Our *Father*"—our Creator, the Author of our being; he who raised us from the dust of the earth, who breathed into us the breath of life, and we became living souls. (*NT-Notes*, 37)
>
> "Our *Father*"—our Preserver, who day by day sustains the life he has given; of whose continuing love we now and every moment receive life and breath and all things. ... Above all, the Father of our Lord Jesus Christ, and of all that believe in him; who justifies us "freely by his grace. ..." We pray, because we love. And "we love him, because he first loved us". (*WW*, 1:579)

In this introductory comment Wesley evolves his creation soteriology. His soteriology has its beginning in the first creation ("our Creator ... who breathed into us the breath of life"), its continuation in justification ("freely by his grace, through the redemption that is in Jesus"), and its end in sanctification or the transformation of the sinner as the new creation ("who hath begotten us ... of incorruptible seed, and created us anew in Christ Jesus") wrought by the establishment of the kingdom of God, that is in function in this world already by love. Jim Logan (1985a:364) illustrates Wesley's soteriology within the context of creation in the following way (here slightly modified by me):

GOD'S ACTION	HUMAN SELF
CREATION	
Divine Law	Imago Dei
Liberty	
Human Rights	
Social Structures	
FALL	
	Guilt
	Loss of Moral Image
CHRIST'S SALVATION	
Prevenient Grace	Knowledge of the Law
	(convincing, convicting)
Justifying Grace	Freedom from Guilt
	Formal Change
New Birth	Conversion
	(act of the will)
Sanctifying Grace	Empowerment
	Actual change
	Restoration of Image
	Entry into Kingdom
	Conformity with the Law
Perfection	
NEW CREATION	

Next, Wesley comments that God is "'*Our* Father'—not *mine* only who now cry unto him; but *ours*. ... Therefore with him there is no respect of persons. He loveth all that he hath made. ... But 'if God so loved us, we ought also to love one another'" (*WW*, 1:579). God is the source of caring and neighborly love, God is "not *my* Father only, who now cry unto Thee, but the Father of the universe, of angels and men" (*NT-Notes*, 37). The caring for neighbors is based in the universality of God.

Wesley is critical of the translation of *ap aionos* in Acts 15:18 to "from the beginning of the world," it ought rather to be translated "from all eternity, from everlasting to everlasting" (*WW*, 1:580). This eschatological aspect comes to a climax in his exegetical commentary to Mt. 6:10:[62]

May Thy kingdom of grace come quickly, and swallow up all the kingdoms of the earth! May all mankind, receiving Thee, O Christ, for their King, truly believing in Thy name, be filled with righteousness and peace and joy, with holiness and happiness, till they are removed hence into Thy kingdom of glory, to reign with Thee for ever and ever. (*NT-Notes*, 37)

"Righteousness and peace and joy" is Wesley's favorite phrase for the preliminary experience of peace in this world as a foretaste of the full experience of peace in the eternal world. He affirms the eschatological character of the conversion of a sinner:

This kingdom comes to a particular person when he "repents and believes the gospel"; when he is taught of God not only to know himself but to know Jesus Christ and him crucified. As "this is life eternal, to know the only true God, and Jesus Christ whom he hath sent," so it is the kingdom of God begun below, set up in the believer's heart. (*WW*, 1:581)

The quotation from Jn. 17:3 signifies that Wesley is influenced by the eschatology of St. John. He comments to this scripture that eternal life, "is both the way to, and the essence of, everlasting happiness" (*NT-Notes*, 374). The evangelical dispensation is to him the same as the eschatological dispensation, the time for the divine promises of restoration to be fulfilled by the coming of Christ, God's personal entry into human history. The comment to Jn. 17:3 makes the human entry into the divine world dependent on the knowledge of Christ, a knowledge that he defines as experimental rather than doctrinal; it is the "kingdom of God begun below set up in the believer's heart."

That Wesley's eschatology is not individualistic is demonstrated as he continues. The universal restoration of peace has effects on the natural as well as the social world. It begins in this world and is completed in heaven:

We pray for the coming of his everlasting kingdom, the kingdom of glory in heaven, which is the continuation and perfection of the kingdom of grace on earth ... the final restoration of all things by God's putting to an end all misery and sin, to infirmity and death, taking all things into his own hands, and setting up the kingdom which endureth throughout all ages. (*WW*, 1:582)

The petition to do God's will is not a prayer of passive resignation but one of "active conformity to the will of God" (*WW*, 1:583). The idea of the meritorious surrender of the will has now disappeared in Wesley. He expects God to transform the believer on the basis of the atonement and God's covenant of grace and prays that

> all the inhabitants of the earth, even the whole race of mankind, may do the will of their Father which is in heaven as *willingly* as the holy angels; that these may do it *continually*, even as they, without any interruption of their willing service. Yea, and that they may do it *perfectly*; that "the God of peace, through the blood of the everlasting covenant, may make them perfect in every good work to do his will, and work in them all which is well-pleasing in his sight." (*WW*, 1:584)

Wesley does not advocate a passive resignation to God's will as a predestined fate, he rather pleads for an active conformation with the will of God thus making an actual change of life and society possible, because the believer is acting according to the will of God.

With the petition for daily bread of Mt. 6:11, Wesley comes to the next main part of the prayer. The first part is universal in character, the last is particular. The context of God's giving out of free grace is underlined, "for we claim nothing of right, but only of free mercy. ... All our desert, we own, is hell. But God loves us freely. Therefore we ask him to *give* what we can no more *procure* for ourselves than we can *merit* it at his hands" (*WW*, 1:585).

The meaning of the Greek word *epiousios* has been debated by the exegetes from the Church Fathers until this day. Wesley's view is that the bread petitioned for in the Lord's prayer is the bread for today, understood both as the sacramental as well as the natural bread, both being necessary "for our souls" and "bodies."

Basic to Wesley's interpretation of forgiveness is the idea of an overwhelming human debt: "We are utterly insolvent; we have nothing to pay; we have wasted all our substance" (*WW*, 1:586). This debt is understood legally as well as existentially; "substance" may refer to Lk. 15:13 where this word is interpreted as "all the grace he had received" (*NT-Notes*, 261). The catastrophe of the fall implies a judicial as well as a dramatic change of the ontological basis of human existence as a consequence of the loss of grace. This disaster is caused by the human misuse of free will. For this reason the reception of the grace through Christ has ontological significance as it leads a person back to God's original purpose with humanity. His focus is precisely here, as the Greek word for "forgive" has its primary meaning in the loosing of a chain. To be a new person in Christ therefore means to be in the *favor dei* as well as in the *imago dei*. He is possibly polemical against the Lutheran exclusive emphasis on the *favor dei* part only: "if our debts are forgiven, the chains fall off our hands. ... Sin has lost its power; it has no dominion over those who "are under grace," that is, in favour with God" (*WW*, 1:586). To him, *dynamis* or power rather than that of substance or metaphysical speculation is the basic quality of God's enabling grace (cf. Borgen 1972:212).

Prayer (i) (6:5-15) Compared

Luther and Wesley in their interpretations of the Lord's Prayer have differences of emphasis more than of substance. Wesley does not delimit himself as clearly from possible Pelagian implications as does Luther. His admonition to forgive the neighbor is stronger. This nuance of emphasis is significant in its focusing the stronger doctrinal interest of Luther on the one side, and the stronger ethical interest of Wesley on the other. A similar interest is that on prayer as self-instruction, but this aspect of prayer is probably not the basic one neither to Luther nor to Wesley.

Wesley's exegetic commentary of the concluding doxology[63] has the same universal emphasis as observed above. In addition, he interprets the text within a trinitarian perspective:

[Mt. 6:13:] *For thine is the kingdom*—The sovereign right of all things that are or ever were created. *The power*—The executive power, whereby Thou governest all things in Thy everlasting kingdom. *And the glory*—The praise due from every creature, for Thy power, and all Thy wondrous works, and the mightiness of Thy kingdom, which endureth through all ages, even *for ever and ever.* It is observable, that though the doxology, as well as the petitions, of this prayer is threefold, and is directed to the Father, Son, and Holy Ghost distinctly, yet it is the whole fully applicable both to every Person, and to the ever-blessed and undivided Trinity. (*NT-Notes*, 38)

Wesley's concept of the kingdom is universal and not reserved for a specific part of life. It comprehends everything. The interpretation of God's power focuses its active and dynamic character. Taken together, he draws an image of God which is very close to that of the Mosaic Jahveh (Ex. 3) who enters the human world and history, takes an active part of it, and changes it according to God's ends. On this point there is another substantial difference from Luther in his emphasis on God's working an actual change of the believing human being.

In his comments on the Lord's Prayer, Luther clarifies his theology of perfection in a way which makes a comparison to Wesley's position easy. He emphasizes that Christian perfection is a perfection of faith and forgiveness. Perfection is a state which a person has or has not, there are no degrees of perfection. Christian perfection is also the same as being *simul iustus et peccator*. He would probably reject completely Wesley's idea of any actual change of the sinner.

Like Luther, Wesley emphasizes the obligation to forgive as a condition for a life in forgiving grace:

God forgives us *if* we forgive others. ... Secondly, God forgives us *as* we forgive others. So ... if we do not ... fully ... forgive all men their trespasses, we far cut short the forgiveness of our own. ... Now ... by his grace, forgive as you would be forgiven! Now have compassion on thy fellow-servant, as God hath had and will have pity on thee! (*WW*, 1:587)

A substantial difference between Luther and Wesley is the contexts of interpretation. The theological framework, to Luther, is still the doctrine of the two kingdoms. To Wesley, the kingdom of God is conceived as a unity with no distinctions between spiritual and secular implied.

Fasting (6:16-18)

Wesley devotes an entire discourse to the issue of fasting (*WW*, 1:592-611).[64] His introduction resembles his general interpretation of all the "tree works" in discussion: "It has been the endeavour of Satan from the beginning of the world to put asunder what God had joined together; to separate inward from outward religion." (*WW*, 21:592)

The main issue is the proper relationship between faith and works. Wesley wishes to avoid the extremes. He is also concerned about the exchange of means for the ends concerning the means of grace, "neglecting meantime the end of all these, the love of God and their neighbor" (*WW*, 1:593). Fasting is a good example of such exchange, it is neither an end in itself nor has it meriting effects on salvation. It is a means of grace.

Wesley proceeds to show "the grounds, the reasons, and the ends of fasting" (*WW*, 1:597). After having referred to a number of occasions when fasting comes "naturally" as a response to specific situations or emotional conditions, he argues for the practices, such as to remove the food of lust and sensuality, to withdraw the incentives of foolish and hurtful desires, and of vile and vain affections. These are, to some degree, similar to Luther's reasons. But Wesley's primary reason for fasting is, "that it is an help to prayer" (*WW*, 1:600). He continually repeats that fasting and prayer are to be held together in accordance with the practice of the apostles, because God has linked his "great gospel promise" thereto (*WW*, 1:603). In the end he does not really care what reasons may be given for fasting. Whatever reason may be found, fasting is a clear commandment by Christ which has to be observed in light of its attachment to evangelical promises.[65]

After having met objections against fasting, Wesley adds some remarks on in "what manner we are to fast":

> first, let it be done *unto the Lord*, with our eye singly fixed on him. Let our intention herein be ... to glorify our Father, ... to express our sorrow and shame for our manifold transgressions of his holy law; to wait for an increase of purifying grace.
>
> ... Fasting is only a way which God hath ordained wherein we wait for his *unmerited* mercy; and wherein ... he hath promised *freely* to give us his blessing. (*WW*, 1:608-609)

Wesley is concerned to prevent the idea of fasting as a meriting work. Fasting is nothing else than a means of grace that God uses. As he closes his discourse on fasting, he refers to the true fast prescribed in Is 58:6-11. The unmerited grace given by God is here converted to love to the neighbor as a result of the realization of peace. We should be zealous in "works of mercy, after our power, both to the bodies and souls of men," like "to undo the heavy burdens, to let the oppressed go free ... to deal thy bread to the hungry, and that thou bring the poor that are cast out to thy house" (*WW*, 1:610-611). Mt. 25 offers the model.

Fasting (6:16-18) Compared

Luther and Wesley agree on fasting as a means of grace. Luther's polemics toward Roman Catholic piety led him to emphasize fasting more as a means for constraining and disciplining the body than as a means with religious significance. He fears that the practice of fasting may confuse people to think it has meriting value. For that reason, fasting is a highly problematic means of grace that he usually does not recommend to the church members.

Wesley does not face Luther's polemical situation and holds more positive attitudes to fasting, which, according to his view, should be regarded as a commandment if viewed in light of the promises of the gospel. The larger theological context for Wesley's interpretation is his vision of peace. Fasting therefore ought to lead to works of love and not be restricted to the spiritual nourishment of the individual in an exclusive way. He here takes the same position as in the issue of withdrawal from society in order to pray; it is a good activity, but if it takes all time without leading into social activity, it is a hindrance to true religion (cf. *WW*, 1:534).

Wesley aims to prove that Christian holiness imparted to the believer must show up in everyday life no less than in religious life. By his emphasis he more than Luther unites everyday life and spiritual life rather than distinguishing between them.

The change implied by Wesley in the outline starting with Mt. 6:19 has no substantial meaning. It is a change from "action" to "intention." The truly big change in the Sermon on the Mount is that between Mt. 5:16 and Mt. 5:17. What is regarded as an introduction by Luther, provides for him the theological foundation for the interpretation of the entire the Sermon on the Mount, namely, the beatitudes.

Wesley is concerned that the person with a single eye on God is a holy person and a partaker of the kingdom of God. Such a person is liberated from the fear of the daily needs in order to concentrate the efforts on taking care of the neighbor in need. The basis for this caring is not charity but the struggle for the justice and peace that belong to God's peace. On this point, his concept "social holiness" is directly connected with social justice. Any individualistic-pietist interpretation of his theology fails to focus the basic concern he has for his entire theological system, that salvation is for the world and that the role of the individual believer is to contribute to this goal through ministry.

Treasures upon Earth, in Heaven, and Anxiety (6:19-34)

Wesley observes a change in the outline of the Sermon on the Mount Mt. 6:18 and 6:19. The three works of 6:1-18 he describes as "religious actions ... which are real branches of true religion where they spring from a pure and holy intention" (*WW*, 1:612). From this background "our Lord proceeds to the actions of 'common life' and shows that the same purity of intention is as indispensably required in our ordinary business as in giving alms, or fasting, or prayer" (*WW*, 1:612).

Treasures upon Earth, in Heaven, and Anxiety (6:19-34) Compared

Comparing Luther and Wesley on the issue of treasures upon earth and in heaven, it is not the practical implications which are different so much as their theological bases. They equally affirm that to be rich is no sin by itself, the target of Christ's attack is the desire for riches. Likewise, they are concerned that accumulation of private fortunes hardly is possible without losing one's soul. They agree that the only accumulation of capital which can be accepted is for the benefit of the common people. But while Luther leaves the responsibility of doing so to the princes and the government, Wesley urges the sanctified Christian to work for a lasting change of the structures of society by the removal of social evils. Supposing that they are authorized by God, Luther trusts the officials of the secular kingdom to change evil systems as their reason becomes enlightened and their Christian consciousness is expressed. Wesley rather trusts the transforming power of God's grace in individual persons as well as in the created nature and human society.

Eschatological ideas are predominant in Luther as well as in Wesley, but in opposite ways. As a general rule Luther really doubts that the governors of this world ever will leave their sinful way, and he is waiting for the future breakthrough of the Parousia for the reestablishment of God's heavenly city. Wesley has a stronger emphasis on the presence of the eschatological events without the exclusion of the future aspects at the same time as the final fulfillment of God's plans. He also replaces Luther's admonition to the Christian of a daily conversion (from sin) with the notion of a daily reception of grace (on the way toward holiness).

Mt. 6:19 introduces the second of the two main parts of the Sermon on the Mount. The first and main part (Mt. 5:21-6:18) deals with orthodoxy, the second part (Mt. 6:19-7:27) with orthopraxis. The first part on orthodoxy is providing the ethical principles for his orthopraxis.

The hermeneutical key for Luther's interpretation of Mt. 6:19-34 is his doctrine of the two kingdoms. There is no need to have anxiety for the daily needs, because God has ordered the offices of the secular kingdom to take care of them. As the head of a household cares for the family, a prince like a universal father fulfills the needs of his people. The effects of the spiritual kingdom in the secular life are to demarcate the borders around the authority and responsibility of an office, and also to fill the offices with Christian love.

While the "eye" is Wesley's main metaphor of the Christian's intentions, Luther uses the "heart" as his main metaphor. If the heart is right, God is served when the lords of this world are served. Though God is governor of one world, God rules it by use of two kingdoms, each with its own righteousness. To "see" the kingdom of God does not therefore imply to leave this world but to have faith in God and to be an obedient servant of God in the stations and offices of the secular kingdom. The kingdom of God does not effect an ontological change of the person, but an epistemological change takes place. The believer may experience being a child of God more cognitively than affectionally. At this point a continual progress of doctrinal illumination is admitted.

In the secular kingdom Luther speaks of an actual human righteousness that is dependent on reason and the fulfilling of the civil law. It is not clear how these two kinds of righteousnesses are related. In general he very strongly affirms that they have nothing to do with each other, they are completely different. But if he admits a growth of Christian understanding and expects the true Christian to enter the obligations of the secular kingdom, an indirect connection must be implied, after all.

Treasures upon Earth and in Heaven (6:19-23)

Wesley interprets "the eye" as "the intention: what the eye is to the body, the intention is to the soul" (*WW*, 1:613). The "single" eye describes the focused look at one thing only, leaving out any

other design or desire "but to 'know God, and Jesus Christ'...
loving him ... to serve God (as we love him) ... and to enjoy God
in all and above all things" (*NT-Notes*, 39). He thus makes clear
that Christian perfection is to be actual in the whole life of the
Christian.[66] He does not teach this in a mood of self-sacrifice and
suffering, his emphasis is the joy in loving and serving God.
Christian perfection is, after all, an experience of God's peace
affecting the entire existence of the Christian. In the midst of
suffering the basic experience is peace and joy. "Thy whole
body" signifies

> all that is guided by the intention, as the body is the eye. All
> thou art, all thou dost: thy desires, tempers, affections; thy
> thoughts and words and actions. The whole of these "shall be
> full of light"; full of true, divine knowledge. ... He shall en-
> lighten the eyes of thy understanding. ... His Spirit shall reveal
> unto thee the deep things of God. (*WW*, 1:613)

Wesley's holistic understanding of the Christian is evident. The
quotation highlights his epistemology, as well, as indicated by
his interpretation of light as the illuminated reason. The eye directed to God will be illuminated through the knowledge of
God's nature and will as a result of God's grace along the way of
salvation, prevenient, justifying as well as sanctifying grace.[67]
With John Locke he insists that the illumination of reason may
be experienced.

Wesley's second interpretation of "light" is that it is the same
as holiness:

> While thou seekest God in all things thou shalt find him in all,
> the fountain of all holiness, continually filling thee with his own
> likeness, with justice, mercy, and truth. ... Thy soul shall be re-
> newed day by day after the image of him that created it ... then
> as thou beholdest the glory of the Lord thou shalt be
> "transformed into the same image, from glory to glory, by the
> Spirit of the Lord."
> ... as long as it is steadily fixed thereon, on God in Christ,
> reconciling the world into himself, we are more and more filled

with love of God and man, with meekness, gentleness, long-
suffering; with all the fruits of holiness, which are, through
Christ Jesus, to the glory of God the Father. (*WW*, 1:614)

This last quotation summarizes significant elements of Wesley's
theology of holiness: (1) An active human response is a condition for the experience of God's saving grace. That activity implies no more than to turn to God and seek God, no merits are
implied. (2) "thou shalt find him in all" resembles his interpretation of the pure in heart as the fully sanctified Christian, why
"The pure in heart see all things full of God" (*WW*, 1:513). This
definition implies a full awareness of God, and one's frame of
reference will interpret the reality experienced by the believer in
light of the kingdom of God. (3) Sanctification is, no less than
justification, wrought by grace through faith. (4) Sanctification is
a consequence of the single eye fixed on God. (5) An effect of
sanctification is the transformation of the human person to the
image of God, creating power over sin as a secondary effect, and
a perfect experience and expression of love. (6) God's agent is
the Holy Spirit. (7) The goal is the renewal of human existence
"after the image of him that created it," that is, the restoration of
God's original purpose for creation, peace, love, and holiness.

The third interpretation of "light" is "happiness" (*WW*, 1:615),
which comes naturally to the person "whose eye is single." The
content of this promise is the preliminary fulfillment of peace in
this world with experiences of consolation, comfort, peace, joy,
and hope for the final fulfillment of the promises of God.

The eye is good or evil dependent on its direction. If it is directed to God, it is good, but it is evil "if we seek anything else"
(*WW*, 1:615). Wesley now leads the attention to the warning of the
text, which he translates: "Therefore 'lay not up for yourselves
treasures upon earth'" (*WW*, 1:616; *NT-Notes*, 39). His translation
of the Greek *humin* (2nd pers. pl. dat.) clarifies that the problem is
not to lay up treasures as such, but to do it for personal interest. He
again attacks the usual way of calling the European nations
"Christian," this time applied to the issue of economy. The
"heathens of Africa or America" is put before Europeans as an

example to be imitated. His romanticism is expressed as a similar admiration for the simple, natural life as that shown by his contemporary in France, Jean-Jacques Rousseau, in his formulating the slogan "Return to Nature."[68] As a matter of fact, early romantic elements exist in the literal descriptions of nature and human emotions written by John and Charles Wesley.[69]

A more significant observation for this study is what the quotation above reveals of Wesley's economic philosophy. He is no advocate of capitalism, which he declares to be worse than heathen. There is no reason to include him among the spokesmen of "the Protestant ethic of Calvinism," as Max Weber does.[70] But there is good reason to suspect that the average Methodist leans to the capitalistic ethics. Wesley observes with uneasiness the growing prosperity of the members of the revival movement. His anxiety as he watches the increasing number of affluent Methodists is not without reason. In his *Thoughts upon Methodism* (1786) his despair is apparent. After having stated that, "The essence of it [Methodism] is holiness of heart and life" (*WW-J* 13:260), he concludes with reference to Mt. 6:20:

> I fear, wherever riches have increased (exceeding few are the exceptions), the essence of religion, the mind that was in Christ, has decreased in the same proportion. Therefore do I not see how it is possible, in the nature of things, for any revival of true religion to continue long. For religion must necessarily produce both industry and frugality; and these cannot but produce riches. But as riches increase, so will pride, anger, and love of the world in all its branches.
>
> How, then, is it possible that Methodism ... should continue in this state? For the Methodists in every place grow diligent and frugal; consequently, they increase in goods. Hence they proportionably increase in ... the pride of life. So, although the form of religion remains, the spirit is swiftly vanishing away.
>
> Is there no way to prevent this? ... We ought not to forbid people to be diligent and frugal: We must exhort all Christians to gain all they can, and to save all they can; that is, in effect, to grow rich! What way, then,(I ask again), can we take, that our money may not sink us to the nethermost hell? There is no way,

and there is no other under heaven. If those who "gain all they can," and "save all they can," will likewise "give all they can;" then, the more they gain, the more they will grow in grace, and the more treasure they will lay up in heaven. (*WW-J*, 13:260-261)

Unlike the Calvinist writers who focus the attention on richness and welfare as a proof of God's grace, Wesley emphasizes an inherent paradox of the Christian religion: The reborn sinner will work harder and become richer because of God's grace, which in its turn will lead to a decline of religion because of an increased love in riches. There are no temptations that may destroy God's work as "the deceitfulness of riches," says he (*WW*, 2:560), and, "As money increases, so does the love of it—and always will, without a miracle of grace" (*WW*, 2:468).[71]

At the end of his sermon "The Mystery of Iniquity", in which Wesley lays out his philosophy of history, he pictures the new world by referring to typical *shalom* texts, Is. 60:18, 21, et al. His main points are: Few Christians exist in the world; corruption has spread to an astonishing degree; the economy of his country is entirely corrupt; and Christians must be on watch so they do not partake in these sins of the world. The last part is devoted to the remnant,

those who have escaped the corruption that is in the world ... the time is at hand when righteousness shall be as universal as un-righteousness is now. ... God will arise and maintain his own cause. And the whole creation shall then be delivered both from moral and natural corruption ... holiness and happiness will cover the earth. (*WW*, 2:469-470)

Wesley observes with astonishment how a great number of Christians who will not dream of robbing and stealing in tradi-tional ways, still lay up treasures on earth. But they are deceiving themselves, for they are robbers but in socially accepted and honored ways. The accumulation of money is to him a robbery because it is contrary to the vision of peace, which requires a just distribution of economic and natural resources and privileges:

"they are not only robbing God continually, ... but also robbing the poor, the hungry, the naked, wronging the widow and the fatherless" (*WW*, 1:628).

Wesley's interpretation of economy in direct relation to the peace concept has to do with his views of the Jerusalem church as the ideal church. He admires the first Christians' extensive use of the means of grace as well as their equal distribution of money (Acts 2:44-45; 4:32-35). The members of the primitive church in Jerusalem were "of that union of heart" which proves that, and "So long as that truly Christian love continued, they could not but *have all things common*" (*NT-Notes*, 408-409). He concludes:

> *The church*—This is the first time it is mentioned. And here is a native specimen of a New Testament church; which is, a company of men, called by the gospel, grafted into Christ by baptism, animated by love, united by all kind of fellowship, and disciplined by the death of Ananias and Sapphira. (*NT-Notes*, 411)

By organizing his Select Societies, Wesley aimed to restore the primitive church within the Methodist movement, as is proven by their rules: "Every member, till we can have all things common, will bring once a week, *bona fide*, all he can spare towards a common stock" (Outler 1964:144). His purpose was to use these select societies for the encouragement of the movement, establishing a goal and a hope at the same time: "and whom I could propose to all their brethren as a pattern of love, of holiness, and of good works" (*WW*, 9:270). His concern for a covenant community sharing property is based on his eschatological ideas and not on absolutist and legalistic interpretations of the Sermon on the Mount. As in a number of other issues, he is in harmony with the tradition of the Baptists to a larger degree than what is generally acknowledged.[72]

Wesley observes, first, that it is not forbidden to "provide things honest in the sight of all men," "whatsoever they can justly demand of us," without owing "no man anything"[73] (*WW*, 1:618-19); the condition being that any accumulation of money or property should take place in a way which is just for everybody. No good end can justify economic exploitation of anyone.

Secondly, we may provide "for ourselves such things as are needful for the body; a sufficiency of plain, wholesome food to eat, and clean raiment to put on. Yea, it is our duty, so far as God puts it into our power, to provide these thing also ... and be 'burdensome to no man'" (*WW*, 1:619).

It is important to keep in mind his personal habits were utterly modest and not at all comparable with that which people today reckon as "needful for the body." He recognizes that it is not in the power of some people to provide for themselves. He never accuses poor people in general for idleness, for instance, but explains their sad condition as a result of sickness or unjust economic and social circumstances, such as unemployment, the taxation system, unjust prices on food, etc. (Hynson 1985:377).

Thirdly, we may "provide for our children and for those of our own household." Wesley repeats that this must be done in modesty; twice in a short paragraph he uses the phrase "the plain necessaries of life" and he adds for explanation, "—not delicacies, not superfluities—and that by their *diligent labour*" (*WW*, 1:619). His thinking is closely connected to neighborly love in general and must be understood on the basis of his inaugurated eschatology.

Fourthly, "we are not forbidden in these words to lay up from time to time what is needful for the carrying on our worldly business in such a measure and degree as is sufficient to answer the foregoing purposes" (*WW*, 1:619). This affirmation includes saving money for possible future economic crises, for instance, if the salary earner of the family dies.

What is forbidden by Christ? Wesley's answer is, "the designedly procuring more of this world's goods than will answer the foregoing purposes" (*WW*, 1:619). The distinction between what is accepted and what is forbidden is, "We may observe with what exact propriety our Lord places purity of intention between worldly desires and worldly cares, either of which directly tend to destroy it" (*NT-Notes*, 39).

If a person collects silver and gold for other purposes than what is accepted by God, "he lives in an open habitual denial of the

Lord that hath bought him. He hath practically 'denied the faith, and is worse than an' African or American 'infidel'" (*WW*, 1:620). This comment includes at least three aspects: He contrasts laying up treasures with Christ's commandment, he contrasts works with faith, indicating that the works of laying up treasures are incompatible with the Christian faith, and he contrasts the lack of faith in God, viewed as low trust, with the fact of atonement,[74] implying that God who gave his only Son for humanity is fully capable and trustworthy of taking care of our daily, bodily needs as well. The religious effect of the excessive laying up of treasures is, therefore, disastrous:

> You have murdered your own soul. ... You are a living man, but a dead Christian. ... You have gained riches, and hell-fire. ... O ye rich, how can ye escape the damnation of hell? (*WW*, 1:620-621)
> They [the riches] put out the eyes, harden the heart, steal away the life of God; fill the soul with pride, anger, love of the world: make men enemies to the cross of Christ; and all the while are eagerly desired, and vehemently pursued, even by those who believe there is a God! (*NT-Notes*, 70)

The core of the problem is "the *desire of riches*" (*WW*, 1:621). This desire is contrary to the zeal for love that God wants the believers to have: "*Lay not up for yourselves*—Our Lord here ... warns us of another snare, the love of money, which is inconsistent with purity of intention as the love of praise" (*NT-Notes*, 39). With Luther, Wesley emphasizes the problem of greed as self-contradictory to true piety.

Just as love is the source of all good, money is "the root of all evil" (*WW*, 1:621). "The *desire of riches*" represent a change of covenant in the life of a person. The covenant of grace[75] makes it possible to be saved by grace only, presupposing an exclusive trust in God. Once treasures are laid up on earth for one's own sake, a transition takes place in the basic trust of a person, and "these enter into a covenant with death and hell; and their covenant shall stand" (*WW*, 1:621-622). A Christian is "a man who hath overcome the world, who desires nothing but God" (*WW*, 1:622), that is, any man and woman whose entire life zeal is for God in every respect, and who trusts in God for everything, spiritually as well as temporally.

God does not esteem us for riches nor for anything else but our faith. Wesley admonishes, "estimate thyself only in the measure of faith and love which God hath given thee" (*WW*, 1:622). A Christian who measures him- or herself according to God's love has a completely different basis for self-respect compared with those who are captured in love for temporal value. Because self-esteem is based on God's love and forgiveness, no sin nor temporal change of life can disturb the peace and joy in God.

Wesley interprets Christ's "Lay not up for thyself treasures upon earth" in an absolutist way for eschatological reasons. He regards it as "a flat, positive command, full as clear as 'Thou shalt not commit adultery.'" It is not possible for a rich person to grow richer without denying God, and no person who has already the necessaries of life and who aim at more, is without guilt. On the other hand, an absolutist observation of this command will lead to the behavior being in harmony with the will of God. He states, with Luther, that to be rich is no evil as such, and he also shares Luther's serious doubt that the practical reality is not that easy. Rich people are in general inclined to be sinners because their riches have corrupted them; he affirms that it is not sinful to be rich in itself but "dangerous beyond expression" (*WW*, 4:11).

There are many ways in which money may be wasted and misused. The two worst are "the laying them up for your posterity or the laying them out upon yourselves in folly and superfluity" (*WW*, 1:627). The serious issue is, however, that riches do not destroy the spiritual life of the rich person only, an accumulation of money for the building up of fortunes is also a social and economic crime:

A vast majority of them [the rich] are under ... the peculiar curse of God; inasmuch as in the general tenor of their lives they are not only robbing God continually, embezzling and wasting their Lord's goods, and by that very means corrupting their own souls; but also robbing the poor, the hungry, the naked, wronging the widow and the fatherless, and making themselves accountable for all the want, affliction, and distress which they may but do not remove. Yea, doth not the blood of all those who perish for want of what they either lay up or lay out needlessly, cry against them from the earth? (*WW*, 1:628-629)

To Wesley, it is a pity that persons destroy their life either on riches or other sins. But much worse is the violation that large fortunes represent to the poor neighbor and to God as the sovereign proprietor of the world. By clinging to their wealth, rich people are robbing the resources that God created for the benefit of the entire humanity, and not for a certain group of privileged people alone. By accumulating money they in the most effective way destroy the just distribution of money for everybody's good. The rich become personally responsible for the distress of the poor in that way.

Wesley refers to Mt. 25:40 as the model for giving to the poor: "Give to the poor with a single eye, with an upright heart, and write, 'So much given to God'" (*WW*, 1:629). To give to the poor is to give to God, because it is the fulfillment of God's will and purpose of establishing the eschatological state of peace and social justice, everybody living in perfect harmony with one another because they live according to God's ultimate goal, their hearts and lives being conformed to the image and likeness of God. If this sanctified Christian happens to be rich, Wesley has a concluding admonition for him or her:

We "charge you," therefore, "who are rich in this world," as having authority from our great Lord and Master, *agadoergein*—"to be habitually doing good," to live in a course of good works. "Be ye merciful as your Father which is in heaven is merciful," who doth good and ceaseth not. "Be ye merciful"— "How far?" *After your power*, with all the ability which God giveth ... We charge you "be rich in good works;" as you have much, to *give plenteously*. Freely ye have received; freely give; so as to lay up no treasure but in heaven. Be ye "ready to distribute" to everyone according to his necessity. Disperse bread, give to the poor: deal out your bread to the hungry. Cover the naked with a garment, entertain the stranger, carry or send relief to them that are in prison. Heal the sick; not by miracle, but through the blessing of God upon your seasonable support. Let the blessing of him that was ready to perish through pining want come upon thee. Defend the oppressed, plead the cause of the fatherless, and make the widow's heart sing for joy. (*WW*, 1:630)

Wesley's words "Heal the sick; not by miracle but through the blessing of God upon your seasonable support" indicate that there is no easy way for humanity to solve social problems. The only way is through the loving and active caring for the neighbor in need. Then the basic motive of the philanthropy of the Methodist revival movement is not charity for the purpose of showing up piety, but the vision of God's peace and kingdom realized in the world through the transformation of human beings and societies by grace. Observe the inclusion of the idea of a just distribution in the quotation above, the ideal of the original Christian church, and the likewise dual responsibility toward God and the poor. The existence of oppression and poverty is by itself a sign of a corrupt world that God requests Christians to fight on God's behalf.

The foundation of the blessing "is the Lord Jesus Christ, his righteousness and blood, what he hath done, and what he hath suffered for us." A third time in this discourse Wesley refers to the atonement as the basis for the establishment of God's kingdom. He indicates that rather than giving reason to rest, Christ's merits should encourage Christians for work according to the eschatological parable in Mt. 25:31-46, from which he quotes.

Treasures upon Earth and in Heaven (6:19-23) Compared
Luther insists that this scripture should be interpreted according to his doctrine of the two kingdoms. A Christian-in-person should not gather treasures upon earth. In that case money will turn into a diabolic power threatening to the spiritual life. Those who are superiors in office, however, are obliged to gather treas-

ures moderately, or to secure a sufficient economic basis of their subjects.

Wesley's primary concern is to establish a divine command for a just distribution of money to the poor. With Luther he affirms that it is not contrary to the will of God to be rich. He also agrees that a father should earn and save money to take care of the needs of his family. Different from Luther he maintains that every Christian has the responsibility to level social and economic differences. All Christians are obliged to take care of themselves and earn extra, too, making distribution of money possible.

Luther and Wesley equally are concerned to distribute money to persons in need. Using the family as a model for the entire society, Luther is depending on the hierarchical social structure to cover the needs of the poor. Wesley trusts any sanctified Christian to be an agent in God's care for persons.

Care and Anxiety (6:24-34)

Wesley preached on Mt. 6:22-23 as early as 1736 (*WW*, 4:371-377). The original sermon has two parts only, the first is focused on right intention, and the second on the application of the single eye within the setting of "your religious exercise" (*WW*, 4:374). He affirms that "To love God, and to be beloved by him, is enough." There is no hint here of the social awareness so characteristic of him all his life. His habitual reference to "peace, and joy, and love!" (*WW*, 4:377) is present, but probably conceived more from an individual experience. The change from an individual to a social perspective came after he started his work in Kingswood, April 1739. The proper context of peace is now social justice. His philanthropy before this time has a Pelagian basis, its aim being the salvation of the merciful Christian. After 1739 its aim is the realization of the kingdom of God among sinners; this is a necessary fruit of the new life in Christ.

In the Sermon on the Mount discourse Wesley expounds the meaning of serving God and serving mammon. To serve God requires belief and trust in God as the foundation. Without faith it is not possible to serve God at all. Secondly, it means to love God and "desire God for his own sake." Thirdly, to serve God is "to resemble or imitate him" (*WW*, 1:634-635). Fourthly, to serve God is "the obeying him" (*WW*, 1:636). To serve mammon is likewise described in four points, the first being "the *trusting* in riches, in money, or the things purchasable thereby" (*WW*, 1:636); the second, "loving the world"; the third, "to be conformed to the world," and, "lastly, to obey the world, by outwardly conforming to its maxims and customs." In conclusion, it is not possible for anybody to serve both God and mammon. To try that is a vain delusion and contradictory to the essence of religion. Only a person who is under the law but not under saving grace tries that:

> He has religion enough to make him miserable, but not enough to make him happy: his religion will not let him enjoy the world, and the world will not let him enjoy God. So that by halting between both he loses both, and he has no peace either in God or the world. (*WW*, 1:637-638)

This person described is under the influence of God's prevenient grace and acknowledges her or his state as a sinner, but the love of the money in the world is a hindrance to the full submittance to God's pardoning and renewing grace. Wesley implies this is true for most rich people.

Christ does not forbid to care for oneself and for one's household, but "he here condemns ... the anxious, uneasy care; the care that hath torment" (*WW*, 1:640-641).

> Before ye give place to any other thought or care let it be your concern that the God and Father of our Lord Jesus Christ, who "gave his only-begotten Son ... may reign in your heart, may manifest himself in your soul, and dwell and rule there. ... Let God have the sole dominion over you. Let him reign without a rival. Let him possess all your heart, and rule alone. Let him be your one desire, your joy, your love; so that all that is within you may continually cry out, "The Lord God omnipotent reigneth." (*WW*, 1:642)

Wesley's conception of the kingdom of God is here entirely eschatological by nature and yet entirely viewed within the frame of the present dispensation. The fulfillment of the promises of God are expected in the lives of the believers here and now already, in anticipation of the ultimate fulfillment in the heavenly world. Discussing "his righteousness," the same frame of reference determines the interpretation; love is imparted righteousness, or, holiness:

> what is righteousness but love? The love of God and of all mankind, flowing from faith in Jesus Christ, and producing humbleness of mind, meekness, gentleness, long-suffering, patience, deadness to the world; and every right disposition of heart toward God and toward man. And by these it produces all holy actions, whatsoever are lovely or of good report; whatsoever works of faith and labour of love are acceptable to God and profitable to man.
>
> "His righteousness." This is all *his* righteousness still: it is his own free *gift* to us, for the sake of Jesus Christ the righteous, through whom alone it is purchased for us. And it is his *work*; it is he alone that worketh it in us by the inspiration of his Holy Spirit. (*WW*, 1:642-643; cf. *NT-Notes*, 41)

Wesley affirms that the Christian's righteousness is inherent, but he avoids Pelagianism by insisting that it is God's righteousness wrought in the human life by the Spirit.

The anxious caring for the future is problematic because it is essentially rooted in lack of faith. Wesley discusses various kinds of concerns. The fear of temptation is illustrative for his understanding of the dialectics of promise and grace; the Christian will get grace for the present day only:

> "take no thought" for the temptations of tomorrow. ... Think not, "When such a temptation comes, what shall I do, how shall I stand? I feel I have not power to resist: I am not able to conquer that enemy." Most true: You are not able at *this time* to conquer that enemy; and at *this time* he does not assault you. With the grace you have now you could not withstand the temptations

which you have not. But when the temptation comes the grace will come. In greater trials you will have greater strength. ... So that in every situation the grace of God will be sufficient for you. (*WW*, 1:647)

At the end of his sermon, Wesley anticipates the existentialist orientation of Søren Kierkegaard: "Live thou today. Be it thy earnest care to improve the present hour. This is your own, and it is your all. ... Therefore live today. ... Now is thy turn upon earth. ... Enjoy the very, very now" (*WW*, 1:647-648).[76] It will, however, be a misunderstanding to take his existentialism in the philosophical sense in which it has been developed during the present century. His concern for the moment has its origin in his zeal of evangelism, which again is rooted in his eschatology: *Now* "the time is fulfilled, and the kingdom of God is at hand: repent ye, and believe the gospel" (*NT-Notes*, 143).[77]

Care and Anxiety (6:24-34) Compared
Luther suggests that seeking the kingdom of God is a primary motive for Christ's preaching of the Sermon on the Mount. This kingdom has its own righteousness that is entirely different from that of the world. The righteousness of the kingdom is basically Christ's righteousness that is imputed upon the Christian, and that therefore becomes her or his foreign righteousness. But in the secular kingdom the Christian has his or her own righteousness.

Wesley affirms that the Christian righteousness is inherent, imputed by faith but also imparted. To serve mammon indicates that a person may have the form of religion, but not its life, which is love.

Religious Duties (7:1-12)
To Wesley, the matters of judging others, prayer, and the ethos of the golden rule all are expressions of a Christian orthopraxis. A sanctified Christian is living according to these norms because

these works are coming forth naturally, as fruits of faith, and not as works that are merely observed as commands.

Religious Duties (7:1-12) Compared

Comparing Luther's and Wesley's interpretations of the first part of Mt. 7, it is obvious that their concerns are different. Luther is primarily preoccupied with the issue of orthodoxy, or Wesley with orthopraxis. I do not imply that Luther is uninterested in orthopraxis, or Wesley in Christian doctrine. On the contrary, this part of the Sermon on the Mount actually deals with issues of orthopraxis, according to Luther. It is their emphases that are different. Luther's concern is how to judge right doctrine, as observed from his founding of the office of the preacher as the proper doctrinal judge and from his discussion of the relations between natural and special revelation or recognition of God's will. Wesley's concern is how to imitate the love of God in a way that creates justice among people in the world as God's peace is materialized.

Contrary to Wesley's emphasis on the actual transformation of the created humanity and society according to the image of God, Luther distinguishes between God's creating and saving work. The consequences are distinctions between spiritual and secular, between law and grace, and between revealed and natural recognition of ethics.

Judging Others (7:1-6)

Wesley first reviews the outline of the Sermon on the Mount. Christ's "main design" is now finished by, first, the delivery of "the sum of true religion ... those dispositions of soul which constitute real Christianity"[78] (the fifth chapter), and secondly, the rules for right intention for outward action (the sixth chapter). What remains in the seventh chapter is to present "the main hindrances of this religion" or "holiness" (*WW*, 1:650-651).

The first "common and most fatal" hindrance "is judging." "Occasions of judging can never be wanting. And the temptations to it are innumerable" (*WW*, 1:651). Wesley applies the text, first, on Christians who

> spend their time in finding out their neighbor's faults, instead of amending their own. They are so busied about others going out of the way, that themselves never come into it at all; at least, never get forward, never go beyond a poor dead form of godliness without power. (*WW*, 1:652)

The habit of judging demonstrates the lack of the power of religion; sanctified Christians do not judge. A Christian who judges others, Wesley affirms, will not mature and make progress. A condition for spiritual development is the second repentance, or, the feeling of absolute dependence of God, that is leading to the desire for a deepened grace from God. As long as the primary concern is to detect other people who are worse than oneself, this occupation removes the need of further personal improvement.

Another condition is that the grace must be used, or given away, in order to be renewed. The ongoing criticism of the neighbor will limit the experience of need for works of love, and thereby the spiritual life will die out. For Wesley, the basis for acceptance of Christ's teaching from this specific point of view is the idea of spiritual growth.

This specific scripture Wesley believes is applicable to everybody, believers or not. He observes a tendency of people of the world to notice the mote in the eyes of Christians as an effective way of avoiding the problem of the first repentance. As long as the repenting sinner is "as good as" or even "better" than any Christian, why then become a Christian? But this is a self-delusion. A realistic self-assessment with a full apprehension of one's own corrupted state as a natural human being would rather be:

> Know and feel that thou art a poor, vile, guilty worm, quivering over the great gulf! What art thou? A sinner born to die; a leaf driven before the wind; a vapour ready to vanish away, just ap-

pearing, and then scattered into air, to be no more seen! See this. "And then shalt thou see clearly to cast out the mote of thy brother's eye." (*WW*, 1:654)

It is not better, however, when the pulling out motes from the eyes of other persons is covered behind a godly mask, when making "a show of zeal for the cause of God, when in truth thou neither lovest nor fearest him!" To these persons Wesley can only say: "Cast out the beam of impenitence. Know thyself. See and feel thyself a sinner" (*WW*, 1:653).

In his interpretation Wesley paraphrases Pascal, whom he admires: "Only *use* the world, but *enjoy* God."[79] He probably paraphrases Pascal because of Pascal's theology of "heart religion." Inward holiness will eliminate judging in the most effective way.

Wesley asks what kind of judging is here forbidden by Christ. It cannot be "Evil-speaking" in general, "although it is frequently joined therewith, nor "*thinking* evil of another" (*WW*, 1:654). First and foremost, it is the transgression of the commandment of love: "The thinking of another in a manner that is contrary to love is that judging which is here condemned; and this may be of various kinds" (*WW*, 1:654). All the examples of judging given by him are basically examples which reveal unloving attitudes to the neighbor.

In his comment on Mt. 7:1 Wesley emphasizes that no judgment ought to be performed "without full, clear, certain knowledge" (*NT-Notes*, 41). This is a use of a moderating hermeneutics because of its implication: based upon full knowledge, judgment may be acceptable. But his point is rather that no judgment should be passed on the basis of rumors. A "full knowledge" will probably create sympathy for the unhappy person, too, and for that reason eliminate the impulse of judgment. Not least, a "full knowledge" of the neighbor's mote will reveal the beams of the Christians as well.

Wesley implies that the effect of the Christians' judgment is that they themselves become separated from salvation. God is the only judge, and by taking the role of the judge Christians put themselves between the others and God, thereby separating them from salvation. "But at the same time, we put *them* between God and us and separate ourselves from his love" (Minor 1988:3). There is a way of judging which is driven by love, however, and this is not condemned by Christ. It is the constructive judging which essentially aims to guide the neighbor back to the right way, if she or he has left it. Wesley supports a strategy for cases like these. The model is clearly taken from Mt. 18:15-17.[80] Judging is acceptable only when its aim is to restore a state of grace. It is properly done when used as a means in God's redeeming and re-creating work.

To understand the full meaning of Wesley's advice on judging, the system of accountability which he built up through the class system ought to be kept in mind. The members helped each other through testifying, confessing, advising, and praying for one another. They depended mutually on each other in a manner that released their capacities in the most optimal way, spiritually, personally, and socially.[81]

On coming to Mt. 7:6, Wesley warns against calling persons "dogs" (*WW*, 1:656) or "swine" (*WW*, 1:658).[82] He encourages to hope for redemption of the worst sinner. There are persons, however, for whom the holiest Christian can do nothing. In those cases Christ has given "this needful caution" in order "to prevent this spending our strength in vain." He is unwilling to withdraw the preaching from any person, however, and he gives practical advice for how to approach enemies of the Gospel with its message. He probably implies that there are other ways to show them the way of salvation, if a direct verbal proclamation is rejected. To present the gospel is essentially a demonstration of love. Therefore, these people should be met with love, not condemnation.

Judging Others (7:1-6) Compared

Comparing Luther and Wesley on judging, basic differences are revealed. To Luther, this pericope offers the scriptural basis for laying doctrinal judgments to the office of the preacher. By doing that, he reinforces the significance of orthodoxy without removing it from orthopraxis. He indicates that the ordering of offices in the secular kingdom is necessary for spiritual matters, too, and he authorizes the office of the preacher with the power of doctrinal judging. He reaffirms the cognitive character of the gospel supposing that a religious belief may be true or false according to preset formulations of orthodoxy. The Lutheran churches logically are confessional bodies. In light of this doctrinal basis, Mt. 7:6 is interpreted as a scriptural admonishment for church discipline, particularly when it comes to the exclusion of non-orthodox persons from communion. Consequently, the Lord's Supper is a confirming sacrament. It should be kept in mind, though, that the ultimate proof of un-orthodoxy to him is not mere heretic opinions, which give reason for exclusion by themselves, but even more the evil fruits of faith. When bad fruits show forth from Christians whose doctrines seem to be pure on the surface, the proof of un-orthodoxy is still final.

Wesley has another attitude than Luther in this matter. Streiff's analysis of the ecumenical spirit of early Methodism concludes that though Wesley is open-minded to other opinions than his own, this attitude does not imply theological indifferentism (Streiff 1985:69).[83] Ravindratas (1987:7-12) likewise analyzes Wesley's various uses of the concept "opinion." He concludes that Wesley regards with suspicion doctrinal formulations that aim at orthodoxy, stating that "Orthodoxy, or right opinions, is, at best, but a very slender part of religion, if it can be allowed to be any part of it at all" (*WW*, 9:254-255), and, "Even right opinion is as distant from religion as the east is from west" (*WW*, 2:374).

Outler, too, deals with Wesley's ecumenical attitudes, emphasizing that Wesley's distinction between

> essentials ... [and] opinions ... points to the basic difference in Wesley's mind between the fact of faith and all the conceptualizations of faith. ... Religious reality lies deeper than religious conceptuality. ... The important thing is that reflection upon reality not be confused with reality itself. (Outler 1964, 92)

Wesley did believe that there was an "essential core of Christian truth" that required an absolute loyalty, "But he never supposed that this core ever had been or even could be captured in a single form of words" (Outler 1964:92). He regarded much of the theological discussion as arguments over words without really affecting the object (*WW*, 2:79).[84]

Wesley is concerned about the relationship between judging and loving. Doctrinal discussions are, in general, disputes about words, and he consequently allows a wide variety of "opinions" on the Christian religion to exist within the Christian community. Judging is acceptable only when the motive is a loving concern of helping a sinner back to the way of salvation. Apart from that, he has a rather absolutist interpretation of the text.

A comparison between Luther and Wesley on this point clarifies that they represent different theological paradigms. The analysis of their exegeses does not reveal significant differences in their word-to-word-interpretations, apart from the fact that the notion of the judging office in doctrinal matters is completely foreign to Wesley. The basic difference is not one of exegetic details but one of context, or rather, of emphasis. While Luther emphasizes doctrine, Wesley emphasizes a love that is functional in daily life.

Prayer (ii) (7:7-11)

Wesley's main comment on this text is that the lack of prayer is a "grand hindrance of holiness. Still we 'have not, because we ask not.' ... 'Knock': continue in prayer, and in every other way of the Lord" (*WW*, 1:659). Prayer is one among several means of grace, and a prominent one, which ultimate goal is holiness. The issue is not to perfect the outward life of the Christian, providing a better economy and a higher social position, but to find "the love and the image of God" (*WW*, 1:659). What can be prayed for is not everything pleasing to the Christian as a person, but "what is agreeable to God's will" (comment to Mt. 7:8; *NT-Notes*, 42).

Prayer (ii) (7:7-11) Compared

The last time Luther interprets Christ's teaching of prayer (Mt. 6:5-15), he emphasizes prayer as self-instruction. The idea is that the believer in prayer does not inform God, but rather that in prayer the will of God is made known to the believer. This time he adds another aspect: Prayer is a means of grace empowering the Christian to the life in the world and to the struggle against the devil. Without prayer, the Christian is lost, for by obeying the commandment of prayer the promise of the gospel is given to the believer. His emphasis is, therefore, on the believer's active response to God's grace. That this response is necessary is evident from the conflicts experienced from the life in between the three kingdoms in discussion, the two kingdoms of God and the kingdom of the devil.

To Wesley, prayer is necessary to life on the way of salvation or, more explicitly, to grow in sanctification. The theological frame is therefore the transformation of the believer into the image of God.

Luther and Wesley agree that prayer is a means of grace necessary to the promotion of holiness. But the different implications indicate that their agreement does not have the same basis. Luther's presupposition is that prayer is needed to overcome the conflicts of the Christian life caused by the split between the kingdoms. Wesley is working within the categories of a new nature against the desire to increase material privileges, a task which is one of the duties of the secular kingdom, according to Luther.

The Golden Rule (7:12)

Wesley ties the golden rule to the foregoing admonition of prayer, making neighborly love a condition of receiving blessings from God: "nor can you expect to receive a blessing from God while you have not charity towards your neighbour. Therefore let this hindrance [to holiness] be removed without delay. ... Love them, not in word only, but in deed and truth" (*WW*,

1:660). The theological context is his image of the Christian as an instrument of God's work and a channel for God's grace in the world. In the moment a person is blessed by God and keeps the blessing for him- or herself, the world, which is the ultimate goal of God's salvation, is not reached. He continually insists that the salvation has the purpose of doing God's will in relation to the neighbor in need in the midst of the world.

Mt. 7:12 is "that royal law, that golden rule of mercy as well as justice" (*WW*, 1:660). Mercy cannot be demanded, but justice can. The golden rule is only partly a word of admonition of mercy to Christians. Yet more it is a reminder of the fact that people suffer need and distress because of unjust and evil conditions, which it is the bounden duty of Christians to fight against in solidarity with the least of Christ's brethren. By his remark Wesley moves the golden rule from a mercy which is motivated by selfishness, to the sphere of human justice and social rights. The reason is, the goal in the first case is merely to bring praise to the "merciful" as well as the using of neighbors in need as instruments for personal interest. The goal of salvation is not to create nice Christian people but to create an army of God for the restoration of peace and love, which includes an active struggle on behalf of deprived and marginalized people. All the visions of the prophets and the law of grace are included in "this short direction. And this, rightly understood, comprises the whole of that religion which our Lord came to establish upon earth" (*WW*, 1:661). Christ aims at more than simple kindness among human beings. He works to establish the kingdom of God on earth.

Wesley summarizes his interpretation of the golden rule: "The whole is comprised in one word—Imitate the God of love" (*NT-Notes*, 42). After this principle he orders his theological system and organizes the Methodist revival movement.[85]

At the end of this discourse, Wesley states: "This is pure and genuine morality. This do, and thou shalt live" (*WW*, 1:662). This does not imply any legalistic religion based on merits of works. On the contrary, he describes that kind of life which contemporary scholars of the Hebrew bible affirm as typical to the people of the eschatological remnant. Because of their experience of God's glorious grace and their participation in the new reality of God's transformation of the world, they place themselves on God's side and on the side of those who are oppressed. This participation necessarily leads to the life of God experienced in the midst of doing God's work:

> ... none can love his neighbour as himself, unless he first love God. And none can love God unless he believe in Christ, unless he have redemption through his blood, and the Spirit of God bearing witness with his spirit that he is a child of God. Faith therefore still is the root of all, of present as well as future salvation. Still we must say to every sinner, Believe in the Lord Jesus Christ, and thou shalt be saved. Thou shalt be saved now, that thou mayst be saved for ever; saved on earth, that thou mayst be saved in heaven. Believe in him, and thy faith will work by love. Thou wilt love the Lord thy God because he hath loved thee; thou wilt love thy neighbour as thyself. (*WW*, 1:662-663)

The way to heaven is here described by help of evolutionary concepts. Wesley conceives this way as a growth in grace and holiness, which means growth in love to God and the neighbor. The insistence on human response is also on a firm Christological basis. He suggests an "evangelical synergism" (Snyder 1980:47) in contrast to a semi-pelagian synergism (C. Williams 1962:72). With Luther, he fights against synergism as a basis for salvation. At the same time he affirms the believer to be God's cooperator (Hildebrandt 1951:124). His "synergism" is therefore related to the discipleship following justification and rebirth as a response to God's grace.

In a letter Wesley summarizes the doctrines of Methodism by referring to the double commandment of love and the golden rule, thus affirming their significance for his theology:

> The sum of our doctrine with regard to inward religion ... is comprised in two points: the loving God with all our hearts, and the loving our neighbour as ourselves. And with regard to outward religion, in two more: the doing all to the glory of God,

and the doing to all what we would desire in like circumstances should be done to us. (*WW*, 26:475)

The golden rule here serves as a model for the social actions of the Methodist movement. It is deduced from the double commandment of love, thus making the golden rule a fruit of experienced religion or the religion of heart.

In his exegetic comment on Mt. 7:12, Wesley states that the golden rule is the end of the doctrinal part of the Sermon on the Mount. In the next verse "the exhortation to practise it" (*NT-Notes*, 43) begins. He identifies the conclusion of the doctrinal teaching of the Sermon on the Mount as love. At the beginning of his exegesis he makes Mt. 5:17-7:12 the corpus part of the sermon, framed by the phrase "the law and the prophets." That makes the sum of the Sermon on the Mount to be "holiness" (*NT-Notes*, 28) or love, which to him is one and the same thing. His hermeneutics is determined by these two concepts.[86]

The Golden Rule (7:12) Compared

Summarizing Luther's and Wesley's interpretations of the golden rule, Luther's concern is to show that the golden rule of Mt. 7:12 is a genuine expression of the natural law.[87] In the daily life there is no reason to ask for the law of Christ revealed in the scriptures in order to be informed about actual ethical expectations, for every human being learns to know them from the civil law and reason. Consequently, Luther in principle separates faith from ethics.

While Luther's hermeneutical context is the natural recognition of morals and the life in the secular kingdom, Wesley's context is the eschatological expectations of peace that God will fulfil in the renewed believers in the midst of the present dispensation. His notion is not individualistic. His hope for this kingdom of God is basically focused on a world without social injustice and oppression. The calling to every Christian is to work for that kind of society not driven by human reason but by the power of God's will and love.

If the hermeneutics of the Sermon on the Mount of the Lutheran Orthodoxy may be termed "Pauline," it is as justifiable to characterize Wesley's interpretation as "Pauline". He however, finds his inspiration in different parts of Paul's theology than the Orthodox theologians do. They base their understanding on Paul's negative comments on the law as an enemy to the gospel, for instance, Rom. 3:19-21, cf. Rom. 7. His basis is rather the references of Paul to the new life in Christ expressed in the categories of obedient discipleship (for instance, Rom. 6, 8) and even in love as the fulfilling of the law (Rom. 13:8-10). His theological argumentation is similar to Paul's affirmation of love as the fulfilling of the Decalogue. From an exegetic point of view, Rom 13:8-10 must be understood as Paul's counterpart to the antitheses of the Sermon on the Mount. He, too, may be termed "Pauline" when making (holiness and) love the key word for his interpretation of the Sermon on the Mount.

Exhortations (7:13-27)

Wesley in the concluding part of the Sermon on the Mount establishes Christian discipleship as a way to holiness. This way is characterized by salvation as a free gift of grace, and discipleship as fruits coming out of salvation.

Exhortations (7:13-27) Compared

By the end of Luther's and Wesley's interpretations of the Sermon on the Mount the structures of their theologies are fully exposed. To Luther, the basic concern is orthodoxy which is equally focused on the doctrines of justification by faith and the two kingdoms. To Wesley, a triad is drawn with God, the believer, and the world as its angles. According to his system, God is setting the goals in creation. Salvation is the same as new creation. The salvation of the world is wrought through sanctified Christians who do not restrict their experiences of God's grace to themselves, but proclaim the good news in words and works.

The Narrow Gate and the Narrow Way (7:13-14)

Christ's sermon still deals with hindrances of true religion. Previously, he has dealt with hindrances from within, now he deals with hindrances from without (*WW*, 1:664). The doctrinal part of the Sermon on the Mount ends with Mt. 7:12, and the exhortation to practice its message begins with Mt. 7:13.

First, Wesley explains what "the way to hell" looks like; "sin is the gate of hell, and wickedness the way to destruction" (*WW*, 1:666). This has been the situation of humanity since the Fall of Adam and Eve. The delusion of naming people, cities, and countries "Christian," is an example of the degree of corruption: "We call ourselves Christians; yea, and that of the purest sort; we are Protestants, reformed Christians! But alas! who shall carry on the reformation of our opinions into our hearts and lives?" (*WW*, 1:666).

What then about the way to life? The gate to heaven is "The Holiness described in the foregoing chapters" (*NT-Notes*, 43). This gate is so strait "that nothing unclean, nothing unholy, can enter. No sinner can pass through that gate until he is saved from all his sins. Not only from outward sins ... but inwardly changed, thoroughly renewed in the spirit of his mind" (*WW*, 1:668). The way is truly narrow, for who can boast of freedom from sins? He anticipates that as a possibility only as a result of God's transforming and renewing work of the sinner to God's own image only. All is wrought by grace and faith.

Describing attitudes characteristic of the narrow way or "universal holiness," Wesley uses the beatitudes and the fourth antithesis as examples (*WW*, 1:668-669). According to his consideration, very few are on this way. He fears nominal Christians who have the form of religion without having its power more than the open enemies of God. They are "all who have not a firm trust in God, a sure reliance both in his power and love" (*WW*, 1:670).

Some preachers are easily tempted to gain cheap success by criticizing obvious sins of weak and marginalized people, for instance, the poor, street people, alcoholics, prostitutes, etc. Not so with Wesley. He rather defends their positive opportunities. It is easy to understand why his message was so well received by the poor and unemployed. Through his thoughts and actions they were given outlet for their frustrations at the same time as they were given hope. He helped the underprivileged classes to dispute the lifestyle of the rich, religiously, socially, and economically. On dealing with riches, he asks: "How then is it possible for a rich man to grow richer without denying the Lord that bought him?" (*WW*, 1:626-627). He assumes that "Many rich are likewise in the broad way" (*WW*, 1:671). The renunciation of the glory of this world which is necessary for those who want to stay on the narrow way, is the main reason why so few are there.

The last part of Wesley's sermon is an admonition, of "Enter ye in at the strait gate," or, better, "Strive to enter in" (*WW*, 1:672). He reminds us of Christ's words in Lk. 13:24 that many will try to enter the kingdom of God without being able to do so possibly because "barely seeking will not avail" (*NT-Notes*, 255). Some persons will not seek God in the right way. But more frequently the problem is "their delaying to seek at all, rather than the manner of seeking, was the reason why they were not able to enter in. But it comes in effect to the same thing" (*WW*, 1:672).

How is it possible to know on which way one is traveling? Wesley suggests that if "many wise, many rich, many mighty or noble travelling with you in the same way" (*WW*, 1:672), it is probably the way to hell. The background for Wesley's critique of rich people has already been given above. He basically rejects the accumulation of fortunes because they distort the just distribution of money. Nor can the rich possibly "be singular." This is one of his favorite expressions,[88] and it denotes the holy life from youth and providing the basis of his concluding admonition:

> "Strive to enter in at the strait gate," ... by walking with all thy strength in all the ways of God, the way of innocence, of piety, and of mercy. Abstain from all appearance of evil; do all possible good to all men; deny thyself, thy own will, in all things, and take up thy cross daily. Be ready to cut off thy right hand, to

pluck out thy right eye and cast it from thee; to suffer the loss of goods, friends, health, all things on earth, so thou mayst enter into the kingdom of heaven. (*WW*, 1:673-674)

Wesley's literal understanding of Christ's interpretation of the commandments in the antitheses probably means: If the sacrifice of a part of the physical body is necessary for salvation, then do it. But more important is his insistence that a person ought to start acting according to her or his faith. Genuine trust in God is to pray for a blessing, and then start practicing it immediately, as if the blessing was received already. There is no reason to postpone a Christian life until the experience expected of assurance of faith is given. "Strive to enter in at the strait gate," and then act as if you were there!

This aspect of Wesleyan piety characterized the discipline of the classes designed for persons who desired to be Christians and who acted according to it. The bands, on the other hand, consisted of persons who had the experience of faith and had already matured as Christians to some degree, and who desired to go on to perfection. Wesley admonished his people to "wait for the Lord," however, he never implied a quietist waiting for religious experiences. His idea of waiting was dynamic and included works of piety (the means of grace) and works of mercy (doing good to the neighbor) (cf. *WW*, 1:384, note 47). It was as he said: If you have hope, then live as if your hopes were fulfilled!

The Narrow Gate and the Narrow Way (7:13-14) Compared

Luther and Wesley emphasize that Christians must be willing to sacrifice social privileges and other kinds of worldly satisfaction in favor of salvation. Luther warns against conformity to the world. Wesley repeats his earlier statements that rich people habitually are on the way to hell; his concern for marginalized people is apparent.

A significant emphasis of Wesley for Methodist ethos is his understanding of how Christians ought to live in the hope for God: The waiting for the fulfillment of God's promises does not imply passivity but a dynamic expectancy including works of piety and works of mercy and love, that is, to seek God in the means of grace and to act as if the hopes were fulfilled already. He understands "the way that leadeth to life" to be "the way of universal holiness" (*WW*, 1:668), thus emphasizing the universal and transforming character of grace at one and the same time.

False Prophets (7:15-20)

Wesley begins his interpretation of Mt. 7:15-20 by reminding his audience about the significant role the prophets have played through the generations by exhorting "all men not to be conformed to this world." The problem arises when these "watchmen themselves fall into the snare against which they should warn others," which happens when the prophets do not "teach men the way to heaven" but "in fact teach them the way to hell." A caution is therefore "of the utmost importance" (*WW*, 1:675).

The "false prophets" are those "who teach a false way to heaven." "Every broad way is infallibly a false one." But "to be more particular," Wesley says, "The only true way is that pointed out in the preceding sermon. Therefore they are false prophets who do not teach men to walk in *this way*" (*WW*, 1:677), defined more detailed in the following way:

> Now the way to heaven ... is the way of lowliness, mourning, meekness, and holy desire, love of God and of our neighbour, doing good, and suffering evil for Christ's sake. They are therefore false prophets who teach as the way to heaven any other way than *this*.
>
> It matters not what they call that other way. They may call it "faith," or "good works;" or "faith and works;" or "repentance;" or "repentance, faith, and new obedience." All these are good words. But if under these, or any other terms whatever, they teach men any way distinct from *this*, they are properly false prophets. (*WW*, 1:677)

To Wesley, the Sermon on the Mount is the revelation of the only way to heaven. Its message contains the essence of the Gospel. In the citation above he first sketches the way to heaven as described in his comments of Mt. 5, starting with the sinner's knowledge of his or her corrupt state, repentance, justification, and sanctification. All these concepts are related to God's transformation of human beings into his image.

These false prophets, whom Wesley accuses of being "traitors both to God and man" (*WW*, 1:678), are wolves "in sheep's clothing; that is, with an appearance of harmlessness". They may look mild and inoffensive in their behavior, with an appearance of usefulness or of religion. But "above all," says he, "they come with an appearance of love. They take all these pains only for *your* good," and, therefore, "they advise you to keep still in the plain middle way" (*WW*, 1:679. The reference to the "middle way" is probably an implicit polemical utterance against Anglicans who persecute the Methodists.[89]

The next issue is how to disclose the false prophets. The criterion given by Christ is the check of their fruits, and Wesley asks what effect the gospel has had on their lives as well as their hearts: Are they holy, do they have the mind of Christ, do they love God, and are they "zealous of good works"? If not, "if they do not effectually teach either themselves or others to love and serve God, it is a manifest proof that they are false prophets; that God hath not sent them" (*WW*, 1:680). Holiness of heart and life in the "prophets" as well as their followers, or lack of holiness of heart and life, is the good or bad fruit that infallibly proves to which category they belong.

Though Wesley admonishes his people to "beware of these false prophets" (*WW*, 1:681), he does not draw the conclusion that false prophets should be isolated completely. He clarifies that Christ warns against false prophets, but he does not "forbid them to hear even these." The false prophets he is speaking of are apparently the impious clergy of the Anglican Church, for they are also administering the sacraments. The Methodists should receive the sacraments from these priests regardless of their spiritual condition, for "the validity of the ordinance doth not depend on the goodness of him that administers, but on the faithfulness of him that ordained it; who will and doth meet us in his appointed ways" (*WW*, 1:682-683).

Wesley revives the discussion from the Donatist struggle on the issue of the worthiness of ministers related to the administration of the sacraments, which split the African church for more than one hundred years.[90] He faces two problems here, first, the secularization of large parts of the Anglican clergy.[91] Secondly, the fact that Methodists frequently suffered persecution initiated by hostile Anglican priests did not encourage them to attend the Anglican services. In addition to the problem of the open hostility of the clergy, the Anglican preaching in general was so rationalistic that Methodists hardly recognized the gospel in it. He all his life insisted that the Methodists should remain within the Church of England. At least he expects the Methodists to celebrate the Lord's Supper in the parish churches.[92] He warns them at the same time to "receive nothing untried" (*WW*, 1:683) and to "Believe nothing they say unless it is clearly confirmed by plain passages of Holy Writ" (*WW*, 1:683-684). But in general this sermon is an example of his decision to keep Methodism as a revival movement within the Church of England.

Wesley warns against these "false prophets," "ye blind leaders of the blind!" affirming that they are personally responsible for the damnation of the souls they are commissioned to shepherd: "They shall perish in their iniquity; but their blood will God require at *your* hands!" (*WW*, 1:684); "Do not persist to damn yourselves and them that hear you!" (*WW*, 1:685), etc. The last part of the discourse is dedicated to his address to these "false prophets." His admonition has not the character of an anathema, however, it is rather the offering of grace through Christ.

False Prophets (7:15-20) Compared

In this chapter, Luther offers the full expression of what orthodoxy is. It implies an equal emphasis on the doctrine of justification by faith alone and the doctrine of the two kingdoms. The structure of his theological system has these two foci, and anyone who teaches one of them only with the neglect of the other, is a false teacher or prophet. The proper fruit of this orthodoxy is to live faithfully in the stations. Sin is here defined as transgressing the borders between the stations. Luther may say so because he identifies the structure of social order with God's created will and order. Good works and good fruit are therefore always conceived within the context of the stations. This position is perhaps expressed more clearly in his interpretation of this scripture than elsewhere in his Sermon on the Mount discourses.

Wesley's criterion for detecting false prophets is whether or not the effect of their preaching is to promote holiness in their adherents. With Luther, he takes sides in the Donatist controversy, holding that God's ordinances are not dependent on the administrator. Like Luther, he points to the fact that good and right theological concepts by themselves are no guarantee for a good theology. The issue is their context and how they are interrelated. It is possible to use the key concepts in the Sermon on the Mount and yet use them in a way that distorts "the way to heaven."

This does not mean that Luther and Wesley agree on the structure of these concepts. They both speak of repentance, justification, faith, and good works, even "Christian perfection" is used by both. But the basic concept of justification is interpreted slightly differently, as it to Luther has a more comprehensive meaning than to Wesley, who distinguishes between justification, the new birth, and sanctification. Luther in general understands sanctification as identical with justification. The works coming out of faith as fruits he places in the civil stations. The structure of the stations and offices is ordered by God, and that which requires loyalty and obedience is the social structure by itself. Wesley emphasizes sanctification as an actual transformation of the believer as he or she is made a part of God's eschatological new reality. This transformation will affect social structures ("a new creation") as much as personal lives ("a new being").

The common trait of Luther and Wesley is that both insist that a good tree carries good fruit, or, a genuine Christian will produce works which answer to the nature of the gospel. In defining what these good works are, however, they depart. Luther canalizes the fruits of the gospel to the works preset by the social structure of stations and offices. Wesley emphasizes holiness of heart and life and implies an actual transformation of the Christian's entire life to the image of God.

The Two Foundations (7:21-27)

Opening his last discourse on the Sermon on the Mount, Wesley returns to his comments on the authority of Christ as the preacher of the Sermon on the Mount. At the beginning as well as at the end of the sermon he emphasizes the uniqueness of Christ's teaching. He is here referring to Christ as "Our divine Teacher" who has "declared the whole counsel of God with regard to the way of salvation" (*WW*, 1:687). By emphasizing Christ as a teacher, he does not imply a Christology that is essentially ebionitic, as this teacher is also the redeemer of the world. The teachings of Christ are a divine revelation and not a humanistic-moralistic philosophy.[93] For this reason he conceives the Sermon on the Mount as "the whole counsel of God with regard to the way of salvation," or, "the noblest compendium of religion" (*WW*, 22:293).

Wesley then considers "the case of him who builds his house upon sand." He first explains the exegetic method he will use: "By comparing spiritual things with spiritual, we may show the meaning of the oracles of God" (*WW*, 1:688). He does not here talk of the method of allegorical interpretation, which is utterly foreign to him. His intention is to make use of the hermeneutical rule called *analogia fidei*, one of his basic methods of interpretation.[94]

Wesley is positive that "all good words, all verbal religion" is characteristic of the man who builds on sand (*WW*, 1:688), neither does his religion "imply doing no harm," nor the lack of "good works" (*WW*, 1:689). Nevertheless,

> he is a stranger to the whole religion of Jesus Christ; and in particular to that perfect portraiture thereof which he has set before

us in this discourse. For how far short is all this of that righteousness and true holiness which he has described therein! How
widely distant from that inward kingdom of heaven which is
now opened in the believing soul!

... your heart was not right toward God. Ye were not yourselves meek and lowly; ye were not lovers of God and mankind;
ye were not renewed in the image of God. Ye were not holy as I
am holy. (*WW*, 1:690)

This group of believers have the form of religion, but its power
they have not. Their religion is neither a religion of heart, nor a
religion expressed by faith working through love. The saying
"Lord, Lord" symbolizes a false hope for heaven, resting on
"verbal religion" with a mechanical reading of prayers and litur-
gies. Basically, this religion depends on human merits and not on
the atonement of Christ.

In his presentation of the man who builds his house on the
rock, Wesley's conclusion is that he is the one "whose 'righteousness exceeds the righteousness of the scribes and Pharisees.'" He draws a picture of a person in whom the beatitudes are
in actual function. By doing that, he repeats the hermeneutical
method observed in the analysis of his interpretation of the beatitudes, when he connects them with various antitheses.

Wesley first describes the person who "is poor in spirit;
knowing himself even also he is known." This is the "first repentance" (cf. Mt. 5:3). This person knows him- or herself as a
sinner but without despair, because of the experience that "he is
known", which means the same as the assurance of God's grace.
At the same time the poor in spirit acknowledges his or her "utter
inability to help himself till he is filled with peace and joy in the
Holy Ghost." This is the "second repentance". The necessity of
"the atoning blood" is included as a condition in the process surrounding the experiences of guilt and sin, and the experience of
peace at the same time. So in one moment he sketches the basic
structure of his theology. On the one hand, God is the gracious
creator and savior who atones for the sin of humanity and transforms it according to the new ontological reality, described as

"peace and joy in the Holy Ghost," or peace. On the other hand, the sinner is by nature corrupt and in the state of guilt, but is restored to the image of God by faith and grace. Salvation is not separated from creation and eschatology, but they are all related.

Coming to the meek (cf. Mt. 5:5), Wesley essentially describes the implications of God's saving work for human beings, for, the meek person is

> gentle, patient toward all men, never "returning evil for evil, or railing for railing, but contrariwise blessing," till he overcomes evil with good. ... He loves the Lord his God with all his heart, and with all his mind and soul and strength. He alone shall enter into the kingdom of heaven who in this spirit doth good unto all men; and who, being for this cause despised and rejected of men, being hated, reproached, and persecuted. (*WW*, 1:691-692)

Wesley here describes the "second meekness." The "first meekness" implies the end of struggle against sin. Any person who is meek in this meaning of the word is sanctified, the love of God and the neighbor being the two foci of life. Because of this, the meek suffers persecution. These two beatitudes are now connected with the fourth antithesis, the meek person does not return evil for evil. The theological significance is that the meek person so totally is surrendered to God's will, that he or she has identified him- or herself completely with the methods of God's dealing with human beings, the ultimate goal being the overcoming evil with good. This is the strategy God uses in approaching humanity, and this is the strategy used by those who imitate God in their conformity to his image. What we can say about this person is that

> He knows himself: an everlasting spirit[95] which came forth from God ... to do ... the will of him that sent him. He knows the world: the place in which he is to pass a few days or years ... as a stranger and sojourner in his way to the everlasting habitations; and accordingly he uses the world, not abusing it, and as knowing the fashion of it passes away. He knows God: his Father and his friend, the parent of all good, the center of the spirits of all

flesh, the sole happiness of all intelligent beings ... with equal clearness he sees the means to that end, to the enjoyment of God in glory; even now to know, to love, to imitate God, and to believe in Jesus Christ whom he hath sent. (*WW*, 1:692)

Wesley here sketches a triad of God, the world, and humanity. They are all related in his vision of the new world, when Cosmos in its totality will be restored to its original glory. The nature, the society, and the individual human being will be parts of it. The sanctified Christian "buildeth on Christ by faith and love; therefore he shall not be cast down" (*WW*, 1:693). Faith is the foundation, and love is the life bursting out from the fountain of faith.

The application of the parable forms the end of Wesley's discourses on the Sermon on the Mount. He admonishes his people "Diligently to examine on what foundation" they build, "whether on rock or on the sand," and, "to inquire, What is the foundation of *my* hope?" It is certainly not orthodoxy in the form of the theological confession:

> Upon *orthodoxy* or right opinions (which by a gross abuse of words I have called *faith*); upon my having a set of notions—suppose more rational or scriptural than many others have? Alas! What madness is this? Surely this is building on the sand; or rather, on the froth of the sea! (*WW*, 1:694)

To Wesley, the most excellent and orthodox doctrine cannot secure the salvation of anyone, he rather regards the notion of "right opinion" as "a gross abuse of words." Luther would certainly disagree on this point. Wesley's concern is that religion is not a matter of cognitive abstractions but it has to be settled in the heart and life of the believer as an experience of God's transforming grace. If one takes care to use all the established means of grace and does good works, this is not enough. Religion is not a matter of outward form but of faith active in works of love:

> That faith which hath not works, which doth not produce both inward and outward holiness, which does not stamp the whole image of God on the heart, and purify us as he is pure; that faith

which does not produce whole of the religion described in the foregoing chapters, is not the faith of the gospel. (*WW*, 1:695-696)

Though a believer may have all the formal elements of religion, right doctrines, the use of the means of grace, and good works, Wesley yet expects the wholeness of faith active in love that is wrought by the Spirit of God. Summarizing the meaning of the beatitudes he makes one last attempt to describe this wholeness:

> By the grace of God, know thyself. Know and feel that thou wast shapen in wickedness ...
>
> Now, weep for your sins, and mourn after God till he turns your heaviness into joy. And even then weep with them that weep; and for them that weep not for themselves. Mourn for the sins and miseries of mankind ...
>
> Now add to your seriousness, meekness of wisdom. ... Be mild to the good; be gentle toward all men, but especially toward the evil and the unthankful. ... Be angry at sin ...
>
> Now do thou hunger and thirst. ... Trample under foot the world and the things of the world—all these riches, honours, pleasures. ... Let nothing satisfy thee but the power of godliness, but a religion that is spirit and life; the dwelling in God and God in thee ...
>
> ... Be merciful as thy Father in heaven is merciful. Love your neighbour as thyself. Love friends and enemies as thy own soul. And let your love be *long-suffering*, and patient towards all men ...
>
> Now be thou pure in heart: purified through faith from every unholy affection, "cleansing thyself from all filthiness of flesh and spirit, and perfecting holiness in the fear of God" ...
>
> In a word: let thy religion be the religion of the heart. Let it lie deep in thy inmost soul. ... Be thou a lover of God and of all mankind. In this spirit do and suffer all things. Thus show thy faith by thy works. (*WW*, 1:696-698)

Wesley has concluded his comments on the Sermon on the Mount. He has exposed his view of the true Christian religion. This religion of the heart is a social religion at the same time, in which the beatitudes and the antitheses form the model of Christian experience of grace and the life of love.

The patterns of Wesley's combining beatitudes and antitheses are not quite consistent. In his last discourse on the Sermon on the Mount he presents a pattern that is different from the pattern of his three first discourses on the Beatitudes:

Beatitudes	Antithesis in the first three discourses	Antithesis in the last discourse
5:3: Poor in Spirit		
5:4: Mourning		
5:5: Meek	5:21-26: On anger	5:38-42: On retaliation 5:21-26: On anger
5:6: Hunger and thirst after righteousness		
5:7: Merciful	5:27-32: On adultery and divorce 5:33-37: On oaths	5:43-48: On love for enemies
5:8: Pure in heart		
5:9: Peacemaking		
5:10: Persecuted for righteousness' sake	5:38-42: On retaliation 5:43-48: On love for enemies	5:38-42: On retaliation

Wesley combines beatitudes and antitheses[96] only when the believer is in the state of grace, otherwise the antitheses may be abused in a legalistic way. The antitheses are commandments but only in light of grace and the promises of God. The schemes of combinations are different. This second time he attaches other antitheses to the beatitudes then the first time. That very fact suggests that he does not see these combinations in a static but in a dynamic way. The specific pattern of conduct to be adopted by a Christian is conditioned by external situations, needs of the neighbor, etc. He here implies an element of situational ethics; however, God is always the center of the situation. The life as a

Christian is always driven by love on the foundation of God's grace, and its practical application is dynamically adapted to its historical context.

The Two Foundations (7:21-27) Compared

Luther and Wesley both summarize their general understanding of the Sermon on the Mount but each in his own way. At the same time, they point to the basic structures of their theologies. They also offer their exegeses of the parable as conclusions of their general interpretations of the Sermon on the Mount.

Luther repeats his dual emphasis on the doctrines of justification by faith and the two kingdoms as the core of the Christian religion. The person building on rock is the truly orthodox Christian who is justified by faith alone without works, performing the works of the stations in the secular kingdom faithfully. He identifies belief in Christ with being in a calling and in a secular station. The true miracles are the ones performed as ordinary works in the offices. The dynamism of God's work is expressed right here. It does not matter if the holder of the office is good or bad as long as the office and its works are good. It is the office and not the holder of office that is the instrument of God.

Wesley pictures the Christian on the way to heaven. The Christian has the form and the power of religion, who knows him- or herself as well as God and the neighbor. For that reason, the experience of unmerited grace (the beatitudes) is expressed through love in everyday life (the antitheses). His interpretation is conditioned by the basic presupposition that the faithful Christian is transformed to the image of God. Thus being sanctified, the experience of dependence on God leads to social expressions of faith in the power of God.

Hermeneutics

The starting point of Wesley's exegesis is the issue of how the antitheses can serve as a model for Christians' lives. Like Luther, he is a pessimist with regard to the human capacity for fulfilling the law, and he is equally concerned about avoiding Pelagian soteriology. But his analysis of the text of the Sermon on the Mount leads to other conclusions with respect to the fulfilling of the law than those of Luther. The reason is primarily one of theological and exegetic method, since he finds the gospel in the Sermon on the Mount. Therefore, it is unnecessary for him to go outside the Sermon on the Mount in order to find its hermeneutical key.

As a matter of fact, Wesley holds the Sermon on the Mount to be the expression of the gospel in sum, the Sermon on the Mount is

> the whole plan of his [Christ's] religion, ... a full prospect of Christianity, ... a general view of the whole. Nay, we have nothing else of this kind in all the Bible. (*WW*, 1:473)
>
> Yet was it [the Christian religion] never so fully explained nor so thoroughly understood till the great Author of it himself condescended to give mankind this authentic comment on all the essential branches of it. (*WW*, 1:553)

Wesley also speaks of the beatitudes as a summary of the Sermon on the Mount or of the Christian religion as "the sum of all true religion in eight particulars" (*WW*, 1:475); and (possibly about Mt. 5) "the sum of true religion" (*WW*, 1:650).

According to Wesley's exegesis, the beatitudes describe nothing but the way of salvation by grace. They give the account of the work of God restoring the sinner from being totally corrupt after the fall, to God's likeness in Christian perfection. A person who is saved is actually transformed by faith through grace after the image of God, which means that the person is completely filled with love and dedication to the will of God. Therefore, he does not speak of holiness of heart only but of life as well (cf., for instance, *WW*, 3:75). Schematically, he interprets each beatitude as a step on the way to heaven, each representing a specific work of grace.[97] Lindström (1961:109-120) suggests a scheme for the understanding of Wesley's ideas of the way of salvation. Though it is too mechanical to include the flexible dynamics of Wesley's ideas of grace working the salvation of human persons, it does illustrate how the beatitudes are related to the way of salvation according to Wesley (Lindström's scheme is here modified by me):

Wesley's Interpretation of the Beatitudes As the Way of Salvation		
BEATITUDE	GRACE	THE WAY OF SALVATION
The Natural Condition		
(Lk. 6:32)	Prevenient	The sinner is in a state of condemnation, sins on purpose but without guilt, fear or love of God.
Under the Law		
Poor in spirit	Prevenient	The sinner is convinced of his or her utter guilt and sinfulness and repents. She or he fights against sin but without victory, and is stricken by fear of God.
Mourning	Prevenient	As above; the sinner mourns his or her sins.
Under grace (personally: "Holiness of life")		
Meek	Justifying	Pardon is experienced as well as the new birth; the justified believer is in a state of *favor dei*, loves and fears God, and combats sin with victories as well as losses.
Hungering and thirsting for righteousness	Sanctifying	The reborn believer longs for the mind which was in Christ and for holiness. The sanctified believer loves God, combats sin, and wins victory; the power of sin is broken.
Merciful	Sanctifying	Faith is at work through love (Gal. 5:6). The sanctified believer is in the state of *imago dei*, loves the neighbor as him- or

Wesley's Interpretation of the Beatitudes As the Way of Salvation		
BEATITUDE	GRACE	THE WAY OF SALVATION
		herself, and does not sin intentionally.
Pure in heart	Sancti-fying	The sanctified believer is in a state of "Christian perfection" or completely filled with love to God and to the neighbor, rests in the peace of God, and the heart is always in accordance with God's will.
Under grace (socially: "Holiness of life")		
Peacemaking	Sancti-fying	The outward holiness of the sanctified believer, who does all possible good to all persons out of love to God, reveals God's atoning love to the world and society.
Persecuted for Christ's sake	Sancti-fying	The sanctified believer is not of this world, loves enemies, and suffers perse-cution because of actual righteousness and holiness.

It is important to note that, to Wesley, the natural condition of the sinner is a state that only exists in principle and not as an actual experience. In his exposition of Mt. 5-7 he affirms that no person is completely isolated from the (prevenient) grace of God, unless this is a deliberate choice.

The interpretation of the beatitudes as the way of salvation[98] provides Wesley with the hermeneutical key to his interpretation of the rest of the Sermon on the Mount. Other scriptures are understood as illustrations or admonitions on how the regenerated life of a Christian ought to be patterned (Mt. 5), teaching right intentions (Mt. 6), and admonitions to avoid hindrances for holiness (Mt. 7). The key words are, to him, holiness and love. He does not depend on scriptures outside the Sermon on the Mount to defend the conclusions of his exegesis, though he frequently refers to other scriptures for further support and exemplification.

Wesley, in maintaining the radical application of the antithe-ses for the total life of the Christian, actually develops further

Luther's insights in soteriology. The new law given by Jesus at the mount is not a series of commandments necessary to merit justification. It rather is conceived as implications or fruits of the new relation between God and human beings based on grace and faith. God is the acting and giving part, the believer is the acting but receiving part. This is, according to him, the real meaning of Christ's words in Mt. 5:17 regarding the fulfillment of the law. He has not fulfilled the law in a way that makes God's law irrelevant to the life of the Christian, as the Moravians affirmed. On the contrary, God regenerates the believer and gives him or her the power to fulfil the law, not to merit salvation, but on the basis of the imputed and imparted righteousness.

Four distinctive hermeneutical methods may be deduced from Wesley's interpretation of the Sermon on the Mount:

(1) Wesley advises a literal interpretation of the Bible text.[99] If the result is obscure, he goes to scripture parallels or other texts to let less obscure texts illuminate the interpretation.[100] Like Luther, he allows the Bible be its own interpreter.[101]

(2) The faithfulness to certain scripture passages does not imply isolation of the text from its context. Wesley gives a number of examples of contextual exegesis. Like Luther, he interprets the scriptures according to the analogy of faith, biblically as well as systematically, however, his lists of doctrines applicable to this method do not include Luther's doctrine of the two kingdoms.[102]

(3) Wesley's solution to Luther's problem of the different character of gospel and law is to view any scripture from the dual perspectives of command and promise. He understands the typical commandments of the law in light of the promise of divine power to fulfil them, thus making the fulfilling of the law a matter of fruits of faith and not merits for salvation. The typical promises of the gospel may very well be experienced as a command for service. In this emphasis, he is as "Pauline" as Luther, who emphasizes Paul's negative attitudes to the law when it comes to meriting salvation, but who at the same time neglects Paul's positive attitudes to the law as a pattern for Christian life.[103]

(4) Wesley's hermeneutics is a "hermeneutics of holiness" or a "hermeneutics of love." These concepts are decisive to all his exegesis.[104]

The primary hermeneutical principle that Wesley uses when interpreting the Sermon on the Mount is to regard the beatitudes as proclamations of God's undeserved grace. The sinner is accepted and restored by God through faith. The ethical challenges of the Sermon on the Mount have to be viewed in this light. The antitheses are applicable as models for the Christian life. In this way he combines the second and the third use of the law (according to Lutheran nomenclature) in his interpretation of the Sermon on the Mount. The law leads the sinner to Christ (the second use), and Christ leads the reborn believer back to the law, making it a model for the Christian life in the world (the third use). But the third use of the law is interpreted dynamically and not legalistically.

Hermeneutics Compared

Luther and Wesley both hold that any interpretation of the Holy Scripture has to consider that the scriptures are texts revealing salvation. Both attempt to see the biblical message as a totality with Christ as its center. But while Luther emphasizes the role of faith because of his polemics against the Pelagian soteriology of the Medieval Roman church, Wesley emphasizes the role of love because of his polemics against the antinomianism of certain Lutheran pietists.

The difference between them at this point is striking when it comes to the issue of law and gospel. According to Luther, the law is perfectly fulfilled by Christ and therefore put out of order. To Wesley, salvation creates a new nature in the reborn sinner providing the power of the actual fulfilling of the law, not as a command meriting salvation, but as an evangelical promise of dominion over sin.

Technically, Luther's and Wesley's exegetic methods are basically the same. Their different conclusions have to do partly with their different choices of material from the biblical context, partly with the way they are facing different historical contexts. Under the pressure of polemics, Luther is far more doctrinally oriented than Wesley is. The doctrines of justification by faith alone and the two kingdoms are imposed on the text of the Sermon on the Mount as its hermeneutical key, thus giving his interpretation a stronger doctrinal character. Wesley finds his hermeneutical key within the text itself, thus giving his interpretation a stronger exegetical character.

Basic to Wesley's understanding of the Sermon on the Mount is his interpretation of the beatitudes. First of all, their message is the gospel of free grace. As strongly as Luther, he maintains the doctrine of justification by faith alone as the foundation of his soteriology. But contrary to Luther, whose concept of justification mainly is a forensic one, he stresses justification as a part of a longer process of salvation. It is the gate of "the way to heaven" or "the royal way which leads to the kingdom" (for instance, *WW*, 1:470). Previous to justification, too, the sinner is included in and surrounded by God's prevenient grace, working repentance and making the sinner seek redemption in Christ.[105] After the forensic act of justification comes God's regeneration of the person. By faith the believer is reborn and sanctified after the image of God which was lost in the Fall, working personal as well as social holiness. He implies that the antitheses are actually the model of the everyday life for sanctified Christians. On the other side the works of the antitheses do not merit salvation, they are merely fruits of faith.

It is evident from their hermeneutics that Luther's system of theology is built on the basis of doctrines, while Wesley's system is built on biblical models to be imitated for experience and life. Luther of course implies religious experience and a Christian life as well, however, he is inclined to describe religion by abstractions. If his basic doctrines for his interpretation of the Sermon on the Mount are compared with Wesley's hermeneutical keys, it is easily observed that they correspond with each other:

The Basic Hermeneutical Tools of Luther and Wesley Compared		
	Luther	**Wesley**
PROMISE	The Doctrine of Justification by Faith Alone	The Beatitudes
RESPONSE	The Doctrine of the Two Kingdoms	The Antitheses

Equally characteristic for Luther and Wesley are their emphases on interpreting the scripture in close relation to their contemporary situations. They equally aim at an understanding which is the prophetic word of God to their contemporaries. Both offer an elaborated "system" for a Christian understanding of the Sermon on the Mount as a theology for the life in the world. The distinctions in their conclusions are probably largely a result of the differences in their historical settings due to the 200-250 years of development between Luther and Wesley, and of the different structures of their theologies, too. The differences in their hermeneutical methods, taken by themselves, are probably less significant.

Though to a lesser degree than Luther, Wesley's interpretation to some degree is developed under the pressure of polemics. His opponents are not Roman Catholics but (Lutheran) quietists and antinomians. On the one hand, against the spiritualism and the quietism of the Moravians, he maintains the necessity of using the means of grace. God is always willing to offer grace, and the reception of God's grace has to be sought through the ordained means. On the other hand, he rejects the notion that Christ has fulfilled the law on our behalf, in a way that makes the human fulfilling of the law unnecessary. A person who is sanctified and regenerated after the image of God will naturally want to do God's will, and has the power to do it as a fruit of faith and by the grace of God. If the law is not fulfilled in the life of the Christian, it is like a bad tree which carries bad fruit.

The different theological paradigms of Luther and Wesley can not be explained by different methods of hermeneutics, nor by their different historical contexts. Basically, the differences of exegesis are consequences of different structures of theology. These differences of structure become evident when their suggested outlines of the Sermon on the Mount are compared. Luther's outline focuses on the doctrines of justification by faith and the two kingdoms, while Wesley's outline is based upon his theology of holiness.

NOTES

[1] From the beginning of the revival, Wesley personally was the owner of the Methodist chapels. They were handed over to the revival movement by *The Model Deed* of 1763, that aimed to secure Methodist unity after his death. The standard of doctrine to be preached in the chapels was legally defined by reference to his *Explanatory Notes upon the New Testament* and to his four volumes of Standard Sermons (*EWM*, 646, 698). Consequently, his comments on the Sermon on the Mount were made a significant part of the doctrinal standards of the Methodist revival.

[2] Moltmann (1985:176) is positive that Luther's doctrine of the two kingdoms originated from his experience of the radical side of the reformation, particularly Thomas Müntzer.

[3] Outler identifies a practical monophysitism (*WW*, 1:470, note f) in Wesley. He repeats this assumption several times in his editorial comments but nowhere with a definite proof; probably he relies on Deschner's (1960) conclusions on Wesley's christology (Duling 1979:154). Borgen (1972:64-68) more accurately makes the point that Wesley's christology should not be separated from his trinitarian doctrine; in the revelation of Christ the whole trinity is present and acting.

[4] This is contrary to the supposition commonly made by Wesleyan scholars, that he never designed to write a systematic theology. See for instance, Bett 1937:129; Cannon 1946:7; Tuttle 1978:69-70; Holifield 1986:xiii; Cragg in, *WW*, 11:8; Joy 1985:299; Logan 1985:361a.

[5] "The kingdom of God" is experienced here and now because "it is the immediate fruit of God's reigning in the soul" or, "heaven is opened in the soul" (*WW*, 1:224). Borgen (1972:45, 90, 92, 219, 234, 240, 268) describes this aspect of Wesley's realized soteriology as an "Eternal Now."

[6.] Wesley points to his commentary of Ex. 3:14, where the Greek translation uses *ho on* (*OT-Notes*, 1:204-205). Interpreting the Lord's Prayer in
light of *ho on* he is in harmony with Augustine, who concludes that "I
am" refers to the essence of God and not God's substance (*NPNF*, 3:111).
[7.] The *Imitatio Dei* motif is found in Augustine's commentaries:
"assuredly the perfection of love is proposed to us in our being asked to
imitate God the Father Himself, when in the following words it is said:
Love your enemies, do good to them that hate you, and pray for them that
persecute you" (Augustine, 76). The parallel indicates that Augustine
served as the model for Wesley's notes rather than Bengel. Augustine, like
Wesley, stresses holiness as a gift of grace and as love (*NT-Notes*, 29).
[8.] Wesleyan theologians, who do their systematic reflections within a
revivalist context, would affirm that God's prevenient grace is the first
step on the way of salvation. It is not hard to find support in many of
Wesley's writings for this position. In his Sermon on the Mount exegesis,
however, prevenient grace is more thought of as God's universal grace, by
which God embraces the world in love and sustains all that is created.
[9.] The "second" repentance is defined as "a continued sense of thy total
dependence of him [God] for every good thought and work, and of thy
utter inability to all good unless he 'water thee every moment'" (*WW*,
1:696). The concept is treated more thoroughly in the sermon "The Repentance of Believers" (*WW*, 1:335-353). The second repentance creates
an awareness of complete dependence on the grace of God for every
aspect of human life.
[10.] Calvin as well as Luther supported the doctrine of Predestination; cf.
The Bondage of the Will (*LW*, 33:3-295). On Wesley's doctrine of sin, cf.
Borgen (1972:172, note 213).
[11.] Wesley translates "blessed" in the first edition of *Explanatory Notes*
(1755), but he alters his translation to "happy" in the 1770s (Dr. Frank
Baker's information). Of the 50 times *makarios* is used in the New Testament he translates "happy" in 45 of these cases and "blessed" in the five
(Mt. 13:16; Lk. 10:23; 11:27-28; 14:14-15). His choices of "happy" or
"blessed" are by no means accidental but intentionally emphasizing nu-
ances of theological significance. For instance, in Lk. 14:14-15 he translates *makarios* in v. 14 as "blessed" and in v. 15 as "happy"; "happy"
resembles the positive attitudes to the law expressed in the Hebrew tradition of piety, for instance, in the Psalms. The prophets predict the restoration of the law as one of the major blessings in the dispensation of *shalom*,

which is the decisive concept ruling his choice of translations, cf. his comment to Is. 54:10; (*OT-Notes*, 3:2089).

[12.] The concept "realized eschatology" is formulated by Dodd (1961:159). Quoting Wesley's poem *"Everlasting life is won, / Glory is on earth begun"* (*WW*, 1:224), Logan (1985a:363) more accurately concludes that his understanding should be conceived as an inaugurated eschatology.

[13.] This early in his career Wesley uses the Protestant technical term of the imputation of Christ's righteousness to the sinner. He later changes this use, regarding it an "ambiguous, unscriptural phrase, which is so liable to be misinterpreted." After having used the phrase for 34 years, partly to please Lutherans and Calvinists, he finds that "it has had the contrary effect," and "I will use it no more" (*WW-J*, 10:388). As a matter of fact, he restricts the use of imputation to his discussion of justification, while impartation is essential to sanctification.

[14.] The issue of self-control was essential to Wesley partly because of the accusations of "enthusiasm." His early readings of Taylor, Kempis, and Law made him emphasize self-control as a means for salvation (cf. Källstad 1974:57). From 1725 his life was one of rigid self control. In 1738-1739 he learned that self-control cannot merit salvation, however, it remained as a fruit of God's saving grace. On this basis only, God's salvation of the Christian, he affirmed the dedication of one's total life to the service of God and doing God's will: "The soul and the body make a man; the spirit and discipline make a Christian" (*WL*, 6:324).

[15.] For a parallel in Luther's writings, see *The Disputation Concerning Justification* (1536; *LW*, 34:145-196).

[16.] Cf. the sermon "On Zeal" (*WW*, 3:308-321), no. 2.11, and the comment on 1 Tim. 6:11: *"love*, the glorious spring of all inward and outward holiness" (*NT-Notes*, 785). Lindström (1961:172) concludes that love was for Wesley the essence of sanctification, implying that persons are formed to Christ's likeness because God is love.

[17.] Cf. Meistad 1983:53-54. Contrary to Luther who views marriage as essentially remedial for the containment of sexual desires, Wesley emphasizes more the social nature of marriage as a partnership between the spouses.

[18.] For a survey of the 18th-century discussion, cf. *WW*, 1:512-513, note 18. The conservative wing aimed at preventing remarriage after divorce for any reason, the liberals accepted remarriage of the "innocent" part.

[19.] Wesley sees God's love as the transforming power: "In the society God did indeed sit upon His people as a refiner's fire. He darted into all (I believe hardly one expected) the melting flame of love" (*WW*, 20:21). Other places the Spirit is the agent (for instance, comment to 1 Th. 5:23; *NT-Notes*, 763).

[20.] After careful studies of Wesley's theological sources, several scholars have found that he drank deep of the Eastern Byzantine tradition; cf. particularly Outler (1964:9, note 26), Campbell (1984, 1991), Maddox (1990, 1994), and McCormick (1991).

[21.] Bengel (1859:165) restricts peacemaking to the mediator's role in conflict negotiations.

[22.] A historical documentation is easy. "Thus the old Foundry in London, for instance, became a veritable melting pot of projects—'a house of mercy for widows, a school for boys, a dispensary for the sick, a work shop and employment bureau, a loan office and savings bank, a book-room, and a church'" (Madron 1981:113; cf. Woodward 1983, 22-32; an overview of the philanthropic aspects of the Wesleyan movement is also given by Marquardt 1977). Examples directly referring to Wesley's social welfare activities are, for instance:

✓ Collection of clothes and employment of women (*WW*, 19:173, 193-194; cf. Warner 1930:214-218).

✓ Stewards for poor relief (*WW*, 3:300-301; cf. Outler 1964:146).

✓ The lending stock (*WW*, 20:204).

✓ The educational program (cf. Prince 1926; Warner 1930:225-236; Ives 1970; Marquardt 1977:54-78).

✓ Strangers' Friends Society (*WJ*, 8:49; cf. Madron 1981:114; Warner 1930:221).

✓ Prison visitations (Warner 1930:236-239; Marquardt 1977:90-101).

✓ Visitations of sick (*WW*, 19:193).

✓ Dispensary (*WW* 20:150-151, 177, 204).

✓ Electro-therapy clinics (*WW*, 21:81).

✓ *Primitive Physic: Or An Easy and Natural Method of Curing Most Diseases*, published 1747 with at least 22 more editions in Wesley's own life-time (Heitzenrater 1984, 1:137).

[23.] For instance, Tertullian wrote: "peace among you [Christians] is battle with him [the devil]" (*ANF*, 3:693).

[24.] Tertullian states that "Therefore God suffers that we thus suffer. ... The oftener we are mown down by you, the more in number we grow; the blood of Christians is seed" (*ANF*, 3:55). In spite of the Pelagian tendencies implied, Wesley was beyond doubt impressed by the notion of the sacrifices of the martyrs.

224 Luther and Wesley on the Sermon on the Mount

25. That Wesley studied Ignatius is evident from his publication of *The Epistles of the Apostolical Fathers, St. Clement, St. Ignatius, St. Polycarp; and the Martyrdoms of St. Ignatius and St. Polycarp* (preface in *WW-J*, 14:223-227). In the forward of his publication of *Fox's Acts and Monuments of the Christian Martyrs* he refers to Ignatius: "Here we see that true and amiable religion evidently set forth before our eyes; assaulted, indeed, by all the powers of earth and hell, but more than conqueror over all" (*WW-J*, 14:227-228). He studied Ignatius as a cheque of Luther's *Comment on the Epistle to the Galatians* (*WW*, 19:200-201); he quotes Ignatius for support of his inclusive policy in terms of society membership (*WW*, 19:313); and he leans to Ignatius for support of his doctrine of assurance (*WW*, 26:575).

26. Wesley's process of decision-making is described in Källstad (1974:104-107). A historical assessment is made by Heitzenrater (1972:295-297).

27. From Calvin, *syllogismus practicus* has played a significant role as an assurance of faith in Reformed piety, making good works not a means for salvation but a sign of election. To Calvin, assurance of faith does not remove the anxiety of eternal condemnation but it makes the Christian take refuge in God without doubt that God is ready to help (*Institutes*, 2:863). Nevertheless assurance is a criterion of true faith (*Institutes*, 1:562). The concept *syllogismus practicus* points back to the Heidelberg Catechism's dealing with good works as the fruits of faith; precisely because they are fruits they serve as a practical proof of a personal state of grace (cf. *Creeds*, 3:338).

28. Samuel Wesley's greeting to his son (*WW*, 26:289).

29. These rules are fully developed in the sermon "The Use of Money" (*WW*, 2:263-280). In the Sermon on the Mount discourses they are only hinted at (*WW*, 1:628-631).

30. Wesley expresses admiration as well as doubts about the Moravians (*WW*, 25:567). The main ideas of the antinomians against whom he engages in polemics are the same that he accounts as Zinzendorf's position (Outler 1964:367-372); "I found it absolutely necessary openly and explicitly to warn all that feared God of the German wolves (falsely called Moravians), and keep close to the great Shepherd of their souls" (*WW*, 20:364).

31. Charles and John Wesley were among the founding members of the religious society in Fetter Lane, May 1, 1738 (*WW*, 18:236-237). It was formed as an Anglican religious society but Moravian influence is appar-

ent in its rules. When John Wesley 1739 went to Bristol to take over the open field-preaching ministry of George Whitfield, he did more or less function as a missionary for this society. Shortly after the foundation the tensions between the Wesleys and the society increased. Its leader, Philip Molther, represented a quietism that was accepted by the members of the society in general but rejected by the Wesleys (*WW*, 19:131-134). After the break with the Wesleys the society developed into the first Moravian congregation in London, 1742.

32. The surrender of the human will to God was a vital concern for the Puritans of the 1600s. They insisted that liberty of conscience meant submission to God, not to self, and that it had nothing to do with personal autonomy (David 1992:516).

33. Wesley fights against mysticism in two variations, namely, the mysticism of the Moravian quietists who neglect the means of grace because of their emphasis upon forensic grace ("alone"), and the rationalistic mysticism of William Law, who neglect the significance of Christian community. His controversy with the Moravians is actually a dispute with the forensic doctrine of sanctification of the Lutheran Orthodoxy and the quietist form of Pietism that resulted from it. Runyon (1981:38-44) concludes that as the Moravians look to heaven and Law look to the inner light, both fail to see that the existence in faith is social and must therefore issue in action.

34. Wesley affirms the work of God's prevenient grace in the world, thus maintaining that no place and no situation is excluded from God's domain (*WW*, 3:130). No human being is completely without God, who is working among inhabitants of the world in the Holy Spirit through prevenient grace. His connecting prevenient grace with free will is apparently inspired by Arminius: "It is grace which operates the mind, the affections, and the will; which infuses good thoughts into the mind, inspires good desires into the affections, and bends the will to carry into execution good thoughts and good desires. This [prevenient] grace goes before, accompanies, and follows; it excites, assists, operates that we will, and cooperates lest we will in vain" (Arminius, 2:700).

35. Cf. Charles Wesley's frequent references to the sacrifice of the believers and their equipping for ministry (for example: *The Richest Legacy*, nos. 93-113) and the sacrificial language in the eucharist liturgy of the United Methodist Church (*The United Methodist Hymnal*, nos. 830, 832); cf. Borgen (1972:252ff, etc.)

[36.] "Although the Law given from God by Moses, as touching Ceremonies and Rites, do not bind Christian men nor the civil precepts [...] no Christian man whatsoever is free from the obedience of the Commandments which are called Moral" (*EWM*, 1:148). This distinction is an example of Calvinistic influence upon the English Reformation. Contrary to this theory orthodox Lutherans in general view this distinction as uninteresting or even misleading. Neither the ceremonial nor the moral law are valid divine commandment for Christian life (Prenter 1979:115).

[37.] Wesley regards Moses as "the greatest Prophet that ever lived" (*WW*, 4:76). He is positive that God's name is revealed through Moses (*WW*, 1:202-203). But he does not draw the parallel with Christ as far as do Bengel and Beijer (both Lutherans!) in their observations of the parallels in the Sermon on the Mount with Moses' giving the Decalogue in Sinai, for though Moses is a genuine prophet, Christ only is savior. He relates, however, the number of the disciples to the number of "the twelve patriarchs and the twelve tribes of Israel" (*NT-Notes*, 52). The relation to the covenant of grace, for which the law is a significant expression, is more basic than the relation to the law.

[38.] Similar thoughts are found in Zwingli (cf. Locher 1981:197, 199, and note 255).

[39.] Thomas Aquinas distinguishes between the new and old law, too, maintaining that the new law is granting what the old is claiming. The basic difference between Thomas and Wesley is, to Thomas grace is primarily related to the human metaphysical nature (*NTU*, 2:1303-1304), while to Wesley, grace is an eschatological gift, offered by God but never imparted contrary to the human will. Both speak of the necessity of *sola gratia*, but while Thomas emphasizes its sacramental and physical transmittance and its character of being supra-nature, Wesley, without neglecting the means of grace, emphasizes more strongly the experience and spiritual power of grace.

[40.] Wesley's understanding resembles Augustine's prayer in his *Confessions*: "give me what Thou commandest, and command what Thou wilt" (*NPNF*, 1:153); cf. his Covenant service liturgy.

[41.] Cf. Bockmuehl's (1979:32-33) polemical analysis (against Luther) of the systematic implications of the New Testament word *hina* (for instance, 2 Cor. 5:15; Rom. 6:4; Tit. 2;14); it is essential to the message of the New Testament that a renewal of human life is the goal of salvation. Paul's soteriology always implies an ethical aspect, cf. Eph. 2:8-10.

[42.] Wesley's opinion is contrary Bengel (1859:174) and Doddridge (1810:207).

[43.] Hall (1988a:44) argues convincingly for the thesis that Wesley's personal problems in marriage partly was due to his traditional understanding of sexuality, and partly to his self-understanding as a radical disciple and evangelical prophet. I will add to this that Susanna's upbringing probably influenced her son's attitudes in this issue as well as in others.

[44.] *"To the 'Assistants'*: Touch no woman. Be as loving as you will but hold your hands off 'em. Custom is nothing to us" (Outler 1964:145). *"To the 'Helpers'*: 'Converse sparingly and cautiously with women; particularly, with young women.'" "Take no step toward marriage, without first consulting with your brethren" (*WW-J*, 8:309). "But on this and every other occasion avoid all familiarity with women. This is deadly poison both to them and you. You cannot be too wary in this respect; therefore begin from this hour" (*WL*, 5:133).

[45.] "Now that the scripture counsels marriage, and allows no release from the union, is expressly contained in the law, 'Thou shalt not put away thy wife, except for the cause of fornication;' and it regards as fornication, the marriage of those separated while the other is alive" (*ANF*, 2:379).

[46.] Against the King James use of neuter, Wesley (with Doddridge 1810:214) translates *to ponero* in masculine, "the evil *man*", or: The man who is persecuting the Christian.

[47.] I have studied all entries where *mobs, riots*, and *persecution* are referred to in Wesley's journal and letters (Meistad 1983:140-146). His accounts of persecution are numerous; in vol. 3 of his journal alone (covering the time from May 1742 till November 1751), there are at least 74 references to riots and persecution related to himself personally, to lay preachers or to other Methodists. In 1744 he comments on England's war against Spain: "The war against the Methodists ... was fought with more spirit than THAT against the Spanish!" (*WW*, 20:40).

[48.] Wesley's strategy for avoiding persecution, or, for behaving if persecution is not to be avoided, is as follows: (1) According to Mt. 10:23: Do not provoke persecution by arranging meetings at unexpected times and places, or, by traveling on to the next place (*WL*, 8:23, 25). In places with frequent riots Wesley could give up preaching for a period of time in order to calm down the emotions (cf. *WL*, 8:26, note 1). (2) According to Mt. 10:28: If mobs are not successfully avoided, stay calm and make no resistance (*WW*, 26:324). (3) According to Mt. 5:39: When being in the midst of a riot, meet the leaders openly, face to face. Greet them friendly by hand and present your message to them (cf. *WW*, 20:179). (4) According to Mt. 10:19-20, 27: Make the mob quiet, and preach to the people (*WW*, 20:309). (5) According to Mt. 5:41: If it is not possible to calm the riot, try to escape (*WW*, 19:328, 21:263) or suggest a visit to the nearest magistrate or police authority (*WW*, 19:344-349). (6) According to Mt. 5:10; 2 Tim. 1:7: If interrupted in the midst of a sermon, always finish what you have to say (*WW*, 19:297).

[49.] Cf. Wesley's exegetic comment on Rom. 12:21: "Conquer your enemy by kindness and patience" (*NT-Notes*, 571); cf. his comment on 1 Cor. 4:12: "We do not return revilings, persecution, defemination; nothing but blessing" (*NT-Notes*, 597).

[50.] The strategy described above is only used when riots are directed against preachers. As soon as a society is established, however, Wesley's strategy is different (*WL*, 8:25-26). Consequently: (1) According to Mt. 5:39: Suffer persecution without provoking anybody by help of fasting with prayer (*WL*, 6:228). (2) According to Mt. 5:44: Return evil with good, and love your enemies. His primary attitude to persecution must not be understood as a passive resignation and suffering, it rather is an active and consciously planned method for the conquest of the enemies by the means of love; cf. his comments to Rom. 12:21; 1 Cor. 4:12; (*NT-Notes*, 571, 597). (3) If persecution does not come to an end by the help of fasting, prayer, and acts of love, constitutional rights should be claimed according to the civil law with reference to freedom of conscience and religion in particular (*WL*, 7:269-270). The basis for doing this is to claim protection of basic civil rights such as liberties of religion and of conscience (*WW*, 26:475; cf. Semmel 1974:172-173).

[51.] To put an end to riots and persecution was secondary only to the primary goal, which was to win the persecutors for Christ (cf. *WW*, 20:344, note 13).

[52.] "Absent in Wesley's economic reflection is any suggestion that their distresses are due to the laziness of the poor. They would work if work were to be found. Bound up in all of this analysis is the gradual shift from an agrarian to an industrialized society. Wesley perceived the process from the side of agrarian dislocation. While some economists have downplayed the enclosure movement with its consequent disruption of the lives of many simple people, and have lauded the larger process which lead to economic growth, Wesley assumed a posture of commitment to the poor" (Hynson 1985:377).

[53.] "*Monday* the 8th [January 1787] and the four following days I went a-begging for the poor. I hoped to be able to provide food and raiment for those of the society who were in pressing want, yet had no weekly allowance. These were about two hundred. But I was much disappointed. Six or seven, indeed, of our brethren gave ten pounds apiece. If forty of fifty had done this, I could have carried my design into execution. However, much good was done with two hundred pounds, and many sorrowful hearts made glad" (*WJ*, 7:235-236). The basic problem is, in becoming rich many Methodists had lost their former willingness to "Give all that you can." The Methodist societies had become a mirror of the gap between the classes of the nation.

[54.] See, for instance, *LW*, 21:115; *NT-Notes*, 34. Wesley adds the duties to take care of one's creditors and "the household of faith," thus indicating a new historical and economic situation in a twofold way: The society had become more dependent on monetary transactions and there had developed a need for offerings to the revival movement.

[55.] Wesley repeated some of his concerns mentioned here to the recently elected Prime Minister William Pitt in a letter September 6, 1784. He was still occupied with tax and other regulations to improve the social situation, in particular to prevent the distilling industries (*WL*, 7:234-236).

[56.] Luther's thesis no. 43 of October 31, 1517, recommends alms-giving and lending to the poor as more favorable than buying indulgences. Obviously, Luther is referring to Mt. 5:42: "Christians should be taught that he who gives to the poor or lends to the needy has done better than by buying indulgences" (Meyer 1963:11; cf. *LW*, 31:202).

[57.] The concept "intention" was basic to the will-mysticism of which Wesley was much occupied the years 1725-1738. That he was concerned about disciplining his intentions already in 1725, can be seen in the "General Rules" which he designed for his personal life in Oxford by devoting a special chapter to "General Rules as to Intention" *(WJ*, 1:48). These rules are taken from Jeremy Taylor's *Holy Living*.

[58.] Against Luther's and the King James rendering *eleemosunen* (works of mercy) in Mt. 6:1, Wesley follows Bengel and Doddridge in arguing for *dikaiosunen* (righteousness).

[59.] This point is apparently contradictory to Wesley's distinction between the moral law which is fulfilled by Christ, and the ceremonial law which is abolished. According to him, however, fasting is a part of the sacrifice of ourselves to God (Borgen 1972:120). He finds support for his view in Bengel (1859:195) who explicitly states that fasting is excluded from the ceremonial law. Possibly, this idea comes from Calvin, who rejects the idea that fasting "is an external ceremony which [...] ended in Christ. No, it is an excellent aid for believers today" (*Institutes*, 2:1244), and, actually, "one sent from heaven" (*Institutes*, 2:1246).

[60.] Luther and Wesley join an old hermeneutical tradition, going back to Augustine at least, which states that "The right intention is all-important" (Augustine, 131). Outler comments that this is the central theme even of the "holy living tradition" (*WW*, 1:573, note 2) in which Thomas a Kempis is an outstanding representative. With regard to praise from humans beings or from God, Thomas affirms: "Man looks at the outside, but God looks at the heart; man weighs actions, but God probes intentions" (Kempis 1963, 92).

Wesley is frequently speaking of the necessity of "the single heart" or "the single eye" (for instance, in sermon no. 12, "The Witness of Our Own Spirit"; *WW*, 1:299-313; cf. no. 10, 1:306-307). This is the main concept of Augustine's interpretation of Mt. 6:1-4: "Those who do this, that is, who simulate goodness, have duplicity in their hearts. The heart of simplicity, that is the clean heart, belongs only to him who lives beyond human praise and in his right living looks only to Him and strives to please only Him who alone reads the conscience" (Augustine, 92-93). In the sermon mentioned, Wesley affirms that "what the eye is to the body, that the intention is to all the words and actions," a notion going back to Macarius's *Spiritual Homilies*, Homily 4 (*WW*, 1:306, note 36). See also discussion of Wesley's sermons no. 125, "On a Single Eye" on Mt. 6:22-23 (1789; *WW*, 4:120-130); and no. 148, "A Single Intention."

[61.] Wesley's studies of Catholic and Anglican devotional literature taught him that prayer is a means for the spiritual disciplining of the Christian. Prayer serves the end of total surrender and imitation of Christ (Källstad 1974:89).

[62.] Wesley here follows the translation of Wyclif with emphasis on the third petition. In his sermon "Public Diversions Denounced" (*WW*, 4:318-328) he follows Tyndale and Cranmer with a parity of the first three petitions (*WW*, 4:320, note 8).

[63.] Wesley must have been aware of the textual problem of Mt. 6:13 where the Greek manuscripts offer a number of variations. In general he uses *Textus Receptus* as the basis for his translation of the New Testament, and *TR* has left out the doxology. He has here, probably for liturgical or theological reasons, followed other texts, for instance, Tyndale's, cf. Tyndale's homily (1964:264-265), which gives him reason to include the trinitarian statement of the comment. Outler suggests that he may not have known the Latin Mass, in which the Lord's Prayer ends with *Libera nos a malo* (*WW*, 1:588, note 116). There is more reason to believe that Luther is polemical at this point, for he knew the Latin mass very well. He includes the doxology in his scripture (*LW*, 21:141) as well as in his discourse, where he has indications of polemical comments against the Roman concept of authority (*LW*, 21:147-148).

[64.] On Wesley's attitudes to and practices of fasting, see *WW*, 4:85-96; 19:88; 21:130; 22:395; 25:158, 343, 513; *WL*, 5:145, 7:256, 8:243, cf. Heitzenrater 1984, 1:214, 2:23, 39, 42; Tyerman 1880, 1:81, 3:164, 287.

[65.] Ole E. Borgen observes that Wesley does not always include fasting when he mentions the means of grace. Wesley lists two or more of the means of grace in 68 places: Prayer 61 times, Communion 59 times, the Word (read, heard, preached, meditated upon) 54 times, Fasting 29 times, and "Christian conference" (church, assembling together) 28 times. "Wesley basically follows the list of Acts 2:42, with two exceptions: that verse does not at all list fasting, while Wesley generally includes it. It appears, however, that he did not always consider fasting a means of grace" (Borgen 1972:106).

[66.] The Greek *haplous* is frequently translated "healthy" or "sound," however, Wesley affirms that a primary meaning is "whole"; the eye can be healthy only when it is whole, or simple (*NT-Notes*, 39).

[67.] Outler notices that Wesley's thoughts on the eye, body, and intention, have their source in Macarius, Homily IV, *Spiritual Homilies* (1721:118-119), and that he probably was inspired by Flavel and Poole as well (*WW*, 1:306, note 36).

[68.] Cf. Frisch 1962, 4:58. Wesley was no pure empiricist. Philosophically, he emphasized the cognitive life in its fullness by adding the importance of emotional experiences to the rational capacities. Rousseau had a similar role in the philosophical milieu in France: "Where the philosophers of Enlightenment focused too much on emphasized reason, Rousseau emphasizes emotions. Where the philosophers of Enlightenment applaud the interests of the individual, Rousseau praises social values and the general good (*la volonte generale*). Where the philosophers of Enlightenment speak of progress, Rousseau's message is a "Return to Nature" (Skirbekk 1985, 1:308).

In spite of the many differences in opinion between Rousseau and Wesley, Rousseau's non-Christian view on nature included, significant similarities exist between them. They emphasize equally new values of life; the right of private property is a root of many social evils, why a more just distribution of property is necessary; Rousseau advocates the monarchy as the best system of government of a nation; they agree to some extent on human freedom, and both are optimistic with regard to education; they both reject materialism as absurd and believes in God and the immortality of the soul. In spite of similarities, however, Wesley's attitudes to Rousseau are rather negative. He apparently regards Rousseau to be a representative of French atheistic philosophy; cf. his *A Thought on the Manner of Educating Children*, 1783 (*WW-J*, 13:474) and other comments *WW*, 4:60-71, 69; 22:214-215, 411-412).

[69.] The Chinese scholar, Jerome Ch'en, on investigating the roots of the European civilization brought to China in the 1800s, emphasizes equally Rousseau's and Wesley's contributions to "the romanticization of Christianity" (Ch'en 1979:23). It is true that Charles and John Wesley were early representatives of the Romantic era in English literature. Gills emphasizes the significance of their literary contributions for the rise of the English novel as well as in the emergence of biographical and psychological literature, they "played a part in the development of the clear style and emotional climate of the Romantic period" (Gills 1954:12). Though the Wesleyan Methodism was not the only influential factor in the development of Romantic literature in England, it did not share the prejudice against art common among Puritans and Calvinistic Methodists, and its ideas corresponded well with the ideals of the Romantics. Gills concludes: "The case for Methodism, therefore, in its relation to the English Romantic movement, appears particularly strong. No just estimate of the Romantic awakening can afford to ignore it. Whether direct or oblique, its influence was profound. Not only did it provide moral earnestness and ethical sincerity, which were soon reflected in the new forms of literature, but, what was even more important, new imaginative passion and liberated emotion. Methodism gave rise to new forms of self-expression. It contributed also its quota to the new forms of speech, the new images of Nature, and the new conceptions of personality" (Gills 1954:16-17; cf. Bett 1937:169-199).

[70.] Weber (1976:125, 175; cf. 139-143) discusses Wesley in his *The Protestant Ethic and the Spirit of Capitalism*. Madron (1981:109) argues that Wesley represents an exception to the general ethic of Calvinism. Wogaman's (1976:207) concern is that Wesley is understood in favor of a *laissez faire* capitalism, however, a distortion of his economic rule had to take place first; the "give all you can" has to be replaced by an un-

Wesleyan "accumulate all you can." Outler remarks, "Wesley's economic radicalism on this point has been ignored, not only by most Methodists, but by economic historians as well (*WW*, 3:228).
[71.] Writing his sermon "The Use of Money" (1760, *WW*, 2:263-280), Wesley still hopes that the Methodists will follow his admonition of giving away the money they do not need for themselves. Twenty years later he uses much stronger words on this issue, as his sermon "The Danger of Riches" (1780, *WW*, 3:226-246) is addressed to affluent Methodists: "O ye Methodists ... O ye lovers of money" (*WW*, 2:240). His sermon "On Riches" (1788, *WW*, 3:518-528) exhorts Mt. 19:24: "It is ... absolutely impossible, unless by that power to which all things are possible, that a rich man should be a Christian—to have the mind that was in Christ, and to walk as Christ walked" (*WW*, 3:520). The sermon "On God's Vineyard" (1787; *WW*, 3:502-517) reviews the Methodist revival, honoring its theology and its discipline. But in its midst wild grapes are brought forth, the rich Methodists! He writes his last sermon on the subject a few months before his death, "The Danger of Increasing Riches" (*WW*, 4:177-186). In Outler's assessment "his tone is almost despairing. ... He has no new arguments to offer" (*WW*, 4:177). In this sermon he admonishes his people: "After having served you between sixty and seventy years; with dim eyes, shaking hands, and tottering feet, I give you one more advice before I sink into dust" (*WW*, 4:185).

The deceitfulness of riches is focused by Wesley in a number of sermons, for instance, "The Sermon on the Mount, X (*WW*, 1:662); "The Good Steward" (*WW*, 2:281-298); "The Mystery of Iniquity," describes "the love of money" as "the great plague in all generations" (*WW*, 2:456); "The Wisdom of God's Counsels" (*WW*, 2:555, 560-561); "The More Excellent Way" (*WW*, 3:274-277); "Dives and Lazarus" (*WW*, 4:11-12); "Causes of the Inefficacy of Christianity" (*WW*, 4:95); "On the Single Eye" (*WW*, 4:120-130); "On Worldly Folly" (*WW*, 4:134).
[72.] Cf. Snyder (1980). From the beginning, the community of goods was a characteristic trait for the Baptist movement. The rigorist interpretation of the Sermon on the Mount of Felix Manz (ca. 1498-1527), "the first 'Protestant' martyr at the hands of Protestants" (G.H. Williams 1962:146), is probably representative. Certain groups, like the Familists, denied their ministers the right of private property (G.H. Williams 1962:481).
[73.] In the *General Rules of the United Societies* Wesley includes the prohibiting clauses against "laying up treasures upon earth; borrowing with-

out a probability of paying; or taking up goods without a probability of paying for them" (*WW-J*, 8:270).

[74.] The notion of *commercium admirabile* is implied. Wesley repeats the thought of Christ's buying the sinner from the devil (*WW*, 1:627). He affirms the ransom theory of atonement but not in exclusion from other classical theories (Duling 1979:54).

[75.] Cf. Wesley's comments to, for instance, Gen. 17 (*OT-Notes*, 1:67-72) and Rom. 9:4: "The covenant was given long before the law. It is termed *covenants*, in the plural, because it was so often and so variously repeated, and because there were two dispensations of it (Gal. 4:24), frequently called two covenants; the one promising, the other exhibiting the promise" (*NT-Notes*, 555). He does not identify the "old" covenant with the covenant of works and the "new" covenant with the covenant of grace. The sacrifice of Christ initiates a "new" covenant, but the "old" and the "new" covenants are both parts of the covenant of grace; cf. the relationships between the covenant of faith and the covenant of works as explained in his sermon "The Law Established through Faith, I" (*WW*, 2:27). After his fall Adam, too, was under the covenant of grace. His comments on the fall in Gen. 3 illuminates the significance of grace in his theology (*OT-Notes*, 1:16).

[76.] Similar but not identical concepts are found in *The Confessions of St. Augustine* (*WW*, 1:648, note 105). Outler also refers to John Byron's poem "Time Past, Future, and Present": "Time present only is within thy pow'r: Now, now improve, then whilst thou can'st, the hour!"

[77.] Mk. 1:15 is the most frequently used sermon text recorded by John Wesley (Outler 1975:12-13).

[78.] "Dispositions of soul" are not constitutive of Christianity. The affections Wesley is talking about are secondary and qualified by the primary religious experience of the encounter with God. They are created "when flowing from their proper fountain, from a living faith in God, through Jesus Christ" (*WW*, 1:651). The relationship between affections and theology in Wesley is investigated by Greg Clapper, who concludes that "Wesley placed true religion in the kingdom of the affections, but to correctly understand what he means by this is to see that the grammar of the religious affections bursts open the self in two different ways. At their genesis, the affections are formed by attending to the work of Christ, which is not something self-generated but is something which comes to us as proclamation. After grace has thus led us to faith, we are naturally led to do the 'works of mercy' by the love of God and neighbor which has grown within us. Thus the affections have not only their genesis outside of the self, but their telos as well" (Clapper 1985a, 211).

[79.] Wesley rightly attributes the sentence to Pascal (*WW*, 25:270). He read Pascal's *Pensees* in the English translation (*WW*, 20:441 + note 56), after which he abridged it and published it as vol. 23 in his *Christian Library* (*WW*, 25:270, note 6; cf. *WW*, 1:653, note 20; *WL*, 6:205). He refers to Pascal as one of the great champions for "the religion of the heart; the religion which Kempis, Pascal, Fenelon enjoyed: that life of God in the soul of man, the walking with God and having fellowship with the Father and the Son" (*WL*, 8:218).

[80.] Wesley's comment to Mt. 18:15 lays the emphasis of the scripture as a model to be imitated: "He [Christ] lay down a sure method of avoiding all offences" (*NT-Notes*, 89).

[81.] Watson concludes: "God's grace ... moved through their lives and made a distinctive impact on their social context; but only because they were first of all obedient in their discipleship, the occasion and the dynamic of which was the relationship with God which they sought to maintain through mutual accountability of their weekly meetings ... *The signifi-cance of the class meeting is not to be found in its efficacy for Methodism as movement or church, nor yet in its impact on society as instrument or obstacle of reform. It was a prudential means of grace whereby Christians in witness to the world could sustain one another in their distinctive tasks assigned by God at a particular time and place in human history*" (Watson 1985:144-145).

[82.] A long exegetic tradition interprets this scripture as related to the means of grace. The issue raised here was actualized to Wesley in his relations with the Moravians who held that nobody ought to receive communion until they had the experience of assurance of faith. In Herrnhut nobody was accepted for Communion until after having a conversation with one of the elders for an assessment of "the state of his soul" (*WJ*, 2:51). He questions this praxis by defining communion as a means of grace, and it is not logical to deny communion to persons who seek grace. Consequently, he "exhorted the [Methodist] society [in Bristol] to wait upon God in all his ordinances" (*WW*, 19:122). He based also this admonition on Christian tradition: "in the ancient Church, every one who was baptized communi-cated daily. ... But in the latter times many have affirmed that the Lord's Supper is not a converting, but a confirming ordinance" (*WW*, 19:158). His theological argument is that communion is a converting means of grace and not confirming only. The Reformation and confessional churches commonly took communion to be a confirming rite and a token of the good doctrinal standing of the communicants (cf. G.H. Williams 1962:166). Contrary to this, he maintains that the only condition required for communicants ought to be their recognition of being sinners in need of God: "I showed at large: (1) That the Lord's supper was ordained by God to be a means of conveying to men either preventing, or justifying, or sanctifying grace, according to their several necessities. (2) That the persons for whom it was ordained are all those who know and feel that they want the grace of God, either restrain them from sin, or to show their sins forgiven, or to renew their souls in the image of God. (3) That inasmuch as we come to His table, not to give Him anything, but to receive whatsoever He sees best for us, there is no previous preparation necessary, but a desire to receive whatsoever He pleases to give. And (4) That no fitness is required at the time of communicating, but a sense of our state, of our utter sinfulness and helplessness, every one who knows he is fit for hell being just fit to come to Christ in this as well as other ways of His appointment" (*WW*, 19:159).

　　Wesley's main point is that all the means of grace are functional at any time and for any step on the way to salvation. His sacramental theology is dynamic in its actual conveying of God's grace (Borgen 1972:198-199). Therefore, however the primary function of the Lord's Supper is to convey sanctifying grace to persons being believers already, it conveys prevenient and converting grace to persons who are not experiencing salvation (Borgen 1972:202). In Borgen's estimation, he at this point "differs basically from the Reformers' views" (Borgen 1972:281).

[83.] Streiff particularly analyzes Wesley's works *Letter to a Roman Catholic* (*WL*, 3:7-14), the sermon "Catholic Spirit" (1749; *WW*, 2:79-95), and *The Character of a Methodist* (*WW*, 9:32-46).

[84.] Weber comments: "John Wesley emphasizes the fact that everywhere, among Quakers, Presbyterians, and High Churchmen, one must believe in dogmas, except in Methodism" (Weber 1976:251-252, note 163). According to my opinion the origin of Wesley's doctrinal tolerance comes from the Baptists. Though Karlstadt, Müntzer, and the revolutionary wing of the Baptist movement could be intolerant, tolerance was far more typical for the movement in general. An example is Sebastian Franck who wanted to get rid of religious hatred (Hygen 1971:158).

　　A problem with Wesley's doctrinal openness is that the non-confessional character of the Methodist movement opens up for a doctrinal pluralism. This is actually implied as a principle in the *Book of*

Discipline; for instance, no. 69: "we recognize under the guidance of our doctrinal standards and guidelines (nos. 67-68) the presence of theological pluralism," and, "No single creed or doctrinal summary can adequately serve the needs and intentions of United Methodists in confessing their faith or in celebrating their Christian experience" (*Discipline* 1984, 72, 83). This principle has been heavily discussed (cf. Walls 1986), and led to a major debate at the General Conference of the United Methodist Church in 1988.

[85.] Wesley's "stewards" embody the visiting ministry of social care and other philanthropic aspects of the Methodist movement. Some of the rules for their work are designed after inspiration from his contextual interpretation of the golden rule: "Put yourself in the place of every poor man, and deal with him as you would God should deal with you" (*WW*, 20:177). The formation of the Social Creed of Methodism is inspired by the Golden Rule, too: "The Methodists called on Christians to recognize the golden rule and the mind of Christ 'as the supreme law of society'" (Holifield 1986:52-53).

[86.] "Love is the controlling principle in all his theological activity. Wesley sought to understand all of life from the perspective that God is love," and, further, "Love is central to his hermeneutics" (Cubie 1985:123, 137).

[87.] According to Luther, God at creation engraved the natural law in the hearts of all human beings. After the fall the natural recognition of God's will is unreliable. Because of the distortion of the human capacities of ethical recognition, God explained the natural law through Moses and The Old Testament. The Mosaic law and its summary in the form of the Ten Commandments in particular are, therefore, identical with the natural law. He defines the golden rule as another summary of the natural law. From a Lutheran point of view, the Sermon on the Mount is the proclamation of an essential revelation and absolutist ethics as well as an ethic which has its basis in the natural law (Aukrust 1965:56, 92), the first being applicable to Christians-in-person, the other to Christians-in-relation.

[88.] Cf. the broad list of references given by Outler (for instance, *WW*, 1:339, note 35; 1:562, note 80) and the two additional sermons by Wesley on Mt. 6:22-23, "On a Single Eye" (*WW*, 4:120-130), and "A Single Intention" (*WW*, 4:372-377).

[89.] Anglican theology was from the beginning described as a "*via media* between Rome and Geneva*" (Hägglund 1963:268; cf. Watson 1985:20, 39). Wesley's rejection of the "middle way" is parallel to his denunciation of indifferent or lukewarm (Rev. 3:16) Christians. In other places he advocates the "middle way," but he then uses the concept in another meaning, as avoiding the extremes of religious doctrine or behavior (*WW*, 1:593-594; 2:588, 600; 3:171, 374).

[90.] Kelly 1978:410. The Donatists claimed that the holiness of the church does not depend on God but on the sanctity of its members, and on the fullness of the Spirit in the bishop in particular. Consequently, they required rebaptism from persons who joined their part of the church if they had been baptized previously in non-Donatist congregations. Donatist issues were on the agenda in the Reformation period, too, a fact that is traced in a number of confessions, Lutheran (*Creeds*, 3:12-13; cf. *LW*, 21:276-280 as well as Reformed (*Creeds*, 3:883-884). In Wesley's revision of the 39 Anglican Articles of Religion this article was not included in the 25 Methodist Articles of Religion, however, he agrees with its content (*EWM*, 2:153; cf. Borgen 1972: 80, 164, note 179).

[91.] This valuation is done by Anglicans (cf. Lean 1964:75ff) and historians alike: "bishops became first and foremost politicians, and politicians are rarely men of spirit" (Plumb 1963:43).

[92.] Wesley instructed his preachers, "Exhort all our people to keep close to the Church [of England] and sacrament" (*WW-J*, 8:320). He became, however, more ambiguous with the passing years (*WW-J*, 13:244-245).

[93.] In this respect, Wesley anticipates Kierkegaard (1977:12-16, 58) in his descriptions of Christ as the "Teacher."

[94.] In his exegetic comment to *ten analogian tes pisteos* (Rom. 12:6), Wesley explains his basic hermeneutical principle: "St. Peter expresses it, 'as the oracles of God'; according to the general tenor of them; according to that grand scheme of doctrine which is delivered therein, touching original sin, justification by faith, and present, inward salvation. There is a wonderful analogy between all these; and a close and intimate connexion between the chief heads of that faith 'which was once delivered to the saints.' Every article, therefore, concerning which there is any question should be determined by this rule; every doubtful scripture interpreted according to the grand truths which run through the whole" (*NT-Notes*, 569-570). In his Preface to the *Explanatory Notes upon the Old Testament*, he gives advice for Bible reading: "Have a constant eye to the *analogy of faith*; the connexion and harmony there is between those grand, fundamental doctrines, Original Sin, Justification by Faith, the New Birth, Inward and Outward Holiness" (*OT-Notes*, 1:ix). In the introduction to the Sermon on the Mount, he writes: "All the parts of this discourse are to be applied to men in general or no part; seeing they are all connected together, all joined as the stones in an arch, of which you cannot take one away without destroying the whole fabric." Outler takes this statement as "A crucial example of Wesley's twin principles of hermeneutics. This first is that scripture is scripture's own best interpreter; thus, 'the analogy of faith' (i.e., one's sense of the whole) should govern one's exegesis of each part. ... The second is that one begins, always, with a literal translation and holds to it unless it should lead into a palpable absurdity; in which case, analogy and even allegory become allowable options" (*WW*, 1:473, cf. note 27). Personally, I am reluctant to accept Outler's view on Wesley's use of the allegorical method.

[95.] Wesley firmly believes in the immortality of the human soul, however, this doctrine is hardly scriptural. In the Hebrew bible the theory of life after death is related to the belief in God's regenerative power. In the Christian bible immortality in a more explicit way is connected to the Kingdom of God; through salvation the believer participates in the new life in Christ. When Paul in 1 Cor. 15:53-55 speaks of immortality no immanent capacities of the human soul are implied but rather a transformation wrought by a divine initiative, cf. Eph. 6:24; Heb. 7:16; which in the present life already grants a foretaste of the life of resurrection, cf. 1 Pet. 1:4. 23; 3:4; Jn. 17:2. Some of the Apologetes (Justin, et al.) moderated the Christian message at this point in contrast to Greek ideas (*NTU*, 2:362-363). At this point Wesley seems to be more influenced by Greek philosophy than by the scriptural message.

[96.] The only parallel I have found to Wesley's combining of beatitudes and antitheses is in a work by Bligh, who suggests similar interpretations (cf. Bligh 1975:47, 53, 55; see in particular p. 60, where the system is fully developed).

[97.] Charles Wesley is using the same hermeneutical principle (Albin and Beckerlegge, 1987:55, 7ff).

[98.] Wesley offers a number of descriptions of "the way to heaven" or "the way of salvation," and the scheme referred to above is actually a combination of them (a good survey is given by Lindström 1961:109-120), for instance, *WW*, 1:153-169, 214-421, 248-266; *NT-Notes*, 541-542).

[99.] Wesley's hermeneutics has a Pietist and an Anglican emphasis: "Wesley's specific method of biblical interpretation stressed the Reformation principles that one should look for the plain, literal sense of a passage and that 'Scripture interprets Scripture.' But he had a higher estimation of human reason than Luther's, and he criticized Luther and the mystics on this very point. His Pietist inclination is reflected in his belief that the result of interpretation should be 'plain truth for plain people,' free from 'all nice and philosophical speculations; from all perplexed and intricate reasonings.' Wesley also differed from the Reformation thinkers in being somewhat more concerned with maintaining Christian orthodoxy. Drawing on his Anglican background, he believed that scripture should be interpreted in relation to tradition" (Duling 1979:153).

[100.] "Wesley did compare scripture with scripture, even in an evaluative sense. For example, in identifying the law which Paul says is good (1 Tim. 1:8), he made a sharp distinction between 'the Mosaic dispensation,' 'that imperfect and shadowy dispensation' and the New Law in Christ. The comparison being made is not between the texts of the Old and New Testament so much as between dispensations, between that written on stone and that written upon the heart (Sermon: 'The Original, Nature, Property, and Use of the Law,' no. 1.5 (1749); *WW*, 2:7-8). Nevertheless, a comparison between the Old and New Testament is implied. He also compared the lawgiver Moses and 'the great Author of it himself' (sermon 25, 'Sermon on the Mount: Discourse V', no. 1.4; *WW*, 1:553). It is the 'authentic comment on all the branches of (the law)' by the Great Law-giver, that the Sermon on the Mount and other teachings of Jesus surpass all other passages of scripture" (Cubie 1985:137).

[101.] An example is Wesley's way of solving the problem as to whom Christ addresses the Sermon on the Mount. He comes to the same conclusion as Luther, namely, that all people are addressed and not certain groups only, for instance, apostles or ministers. The ways leading to the same conclusion are, however, quite different. Without any explicit exegetic consideration, Luther, from his polemical position, immediately attacks the Catholic doctrine of the Sermon on the Mount as "evangelical counsels" designed for perfected Christians only (*LW*, 21:3-4). Wesley performs an exegetic analysis of the Greek concepts *hoi mathetai autou* compared to *hoi ochloi*. He concludes that Christ addresses the sermon to the people actually present at the mountain, as well as to "all the children of men, the whole race of mankind, the children that are yet unborn—all the generations to come." Then, after the completion of his exegesis, he expresses a polemics similar to that mentioned above (*WW*, 1:471-472).

[102.] Commenting on Rom. 12:6, Wesley emphasizes that *analogia fidei*, according to his understanding, primarily comprehends "that grand scheme of doctrine which is delivered therein, touching original sin, justification by faith, and present, inward salvation. ... Every article, therefore, concerning which there is any question should be determined by this rule; every doubtful scripture interpreted according to the grand truths which run through the whole" (*NT-Notes*, 569-570). This list of doctrines is not completely settled in Wesley's mind; in his advice for scriptural reading he states: "Have a constant eye to the *analogy of faith*; the connexion and harmony there is between those grand, fundamental doctrines, Original Sin, Justification by Faith, the New Birth, Inward and Outward Holiness" (*OT-Notes*, 1:ix).

[103.] Stendahl (1977:79) suggests that Luther, because of the religious concerns of his own as well as of his contemporaries, misinterpreted Paul on the issue of the law. According to Stendahl, Western culture has been so preoccupied with the problem of guilt and the experience of the burdened conscience, that Luther in a very effective way answered that problem. He illuminated a "problem of late medieval piety and theology. ... but this formula *simul iustus et peccator* cannot be substantiated as the center of Paul's conscious attitude towards this personal sins" (Stendahl 1977:82). From a strictly exegetic point of view, Stendahl is thus critical of Luther's general interpretation of Paul.

[104.] "Love is central to his hermeneutic" (Cubie 1985:137). "That love is his coordinating principle in exegesis can also be seen by examining several of his sermons. An investigation of Wesley's thirteen discourses, 'Upon Our Lord's Sermon on the Mount,' reveals that all of these are constantly ordered by the theme of love" (Cubie 1985:138-140). Analyzing the hermeneutics of the Wesleyan Holiness Movement in America, Hynson concludes: "Scripture questions are developed less in terms of its full authority than by the hermeneutics of holiness. ... (As Luther developed a hermeneutic of justification, the Holiness people developed a hermeneutic of holiness)" (Hynson 1985a:20).

[105.] "Poverty of spirit, and mourning ... are the gate of Christian blessedness" (*WW*, 19:98).

The Theologies of Luther and Wesley Compared

After having analyzed Luther's and Wesley's exegeses of the Sermon on the Mount, my intention is to describe the theological emphases coming out of their exegeses, and compare them.

In comparing the theologies of Luther and Wesley I restrict my analysis to the data coming out of their interpretations of the Sermon on the Mount. I have no intention to offer a comprehensive presentation of Luther's nor of Wesley's theology. Most contemporary research on Luther as well as on Wesley emphasizes that their theology changed significantly during their lifetimes, and my research primarily covers a short period only of their theological development.

Discussing their different attitudes to the society in particular, it is necessary to realize that Luther and Wesley developed their attitudes in different directions, thus making the comparison more complicated. The young Luther was quite radical, however, the Peasants' War (1524-1525+) indicated to him that spiritual liberation might lead to an undesired political liberation as well. From a political point of view, he therefore became rather conservative. Because he gave his discourses on the Sermon on the Mount

(1530-1532), after this war, his concern for the protection of the social structure was predominant. For this reason as well as others, a number of contemporary Lutheran scholars prefer to emphasize the writings of the young Luther.

Wesley's development was the opposite. On his ordination as a priest in the Anglican church his political views were conservative. Almost 25 years later, however, when he formulated his homiletic and exegetic interpretations of the Sermon on the Mount, he as an itinerant evangelist had observed that poverty was an effect of an unjust distribution of economic and social resources. At that time he believed this problem could be corrected by encouraging Christians to give their surplus to the poor, and thus secure a just redistribution of money. But as the time passed and this program failed, his ideas were more radicalized. From 1770 at least he realized that it would be necessary to change the structure of society by means of legislation, regulations, and taxation.[1]

The ethical models recommended by Luther and Wesley illustrate how their attitudes are different. They both affirm love as the basic ethical attitude of the Christians. In all situations Christians should be governed by love. The crucial issue is, however, how do they recommend love to be transformed to actual ethical conduct? Luther points to the hierarchical structure of the society, strongly advising Christians to support it by loyal observations of the norms of their offices; superiors should take responsibility for their subjects, and subjects should obey their superiors. A most important norm is to remain loyal in one's station; he does not approve that persons have ambitions of being elevated to other social classes than they have been born into.

Wesley recommended other ethical models than did Luther. When it comes to Christian works, he particularly points to the imitation of Christ; the most important example he finds in Christ's sermon in the synagogue of Nazareth (Lk. 4:16-21), in which Christ presents his program by reading from the prophetic visions of the Messianic age (Is. 61:1-2), declaring their fulfillment in him. This program he implements to the Methodist movement as well. The poor is put in the center of his concern, and he expects the Methodists to engage in activities that remove the roots of poverty. Contrary to Luther, he is positive that changed people will change the social structure in reforming the nation.

The differences between Luther and Wesley explained above illustrate the problem of comparing the two. Is it evident that Wesley would have become more radical if he had lived in Luther's time, or that Luther would have been more conservative if he had lived in 18th-century England? Or, how certain is it that they would have recommended different ethical models if they had faced the same historical challenges, and simultaneously? It is not possible to answer such questions. Luther and Wesley may have reacted similarly to some issues, and perhaps have been more distant from each other on other issues. If they had lived in the same historical situation, some basic differences may have prevailed between them. A first and most basic observation is that Luther is, culturally, a German, while Wesley is an Englishman. Besides, and probably more basic, is the fact that though Luther is informed by Irenaeus, he builds his theology on the Western Christian tradition as developed by Tertullian and Augustine. Wesley is dependent on both Christian traditions, too, but he more substantially builds his theology on the tradition from Irenaeus and the Eastern antiquity. For these reasons I expect that identity in historical context would not eliminate substantial differences in their theologies.

Luther and Wesley, in interpreting the Sermon on the Mount, intend to answer specific historical challenges that are important in their time. In doing so, they both interpret the scripture on the basis of specific theological paradigms that function as hermeneutical frames of reference. For this reason a comparison of their interpretations will highlight characteristic distinctives in their theologies.

Another complicating problem is that Luther and Wesley both founded movements which developed opposite traditions in their attitudes toward theological confessions. Most Lutheran churches have declared the manuscripts published in the *Book of Concord* as their confession; some Lutheran churches hold only a few of them as their confession. The Scandinavian Lutheran churches in particular are positive that their confession expresses the authoritative and final presentation of the pure Christian religion. This position creates uncritical attitudes to Luther's exegesis as well. For instance, Paul Althaus is positive that Luther has contributed substantially by his exegesis of the Sermon on the Mount. He is confident that, "There is no doubt that Luther has interpreted Jesus' statement as the Master himself understood it" (Althaus 1978:66). It is hard to value the work of other theologians with such an attitude.

Rather than founding a confessional church Wesley established a movement that was essentially conciliar in character. The theological discussions of the Methodist conferences were informed by the biblical scriptures, the traditions of the Christian church, and a rational analysis of experiences. Consequently, an openness to a contextual analysis was built into the system. From a confessional point of view, such a theology is less structured. The result is that comparisons between them are hard to perform on an equal basis.

Luther and Wesley in Light of the History of Christian Theological Traditions

Wesley has often been interpreted as a theological heir of Luther. He comes out of the Anglican tradition, which is one of the reformation traditions of the 1500s. Besides, German Lutherans were instrumental in his journey to the experience of salvation by faith alone. It is true that he was profoundly influenced by the Moravian interpretation of justification. To imply that he is informed basically by the Lutheran tradition, however, is a too hasty conclusion. It is as relevant to relate his exegetic interpretations to the Eastern tradition, particularly to the Ante-Nicene fathers.

My conclusions are at this point in harmony with Justo González's (1989) analysis of the Christian theological traditions. Reflecting on the differences between theological paradigms, he observes that traditional polarities like that of Roman Catholic vs. Protestant, and liberal vs. fundamentalist, are insufficient as descriptions of theological distinctives. As an alternative he suggests to define Christian traditions according to their roots in a wider cultural, philosophical, and historical context. He concludes that three basic types of theology are the result of the enculturation of Christianity in different cultural contexts:

Type A originated in the Western part of the Mediterranean area. In Rome and Carthage the theological reflection was dominated by issues as well as philosophical tools provided by Roman law and Stoic philosophy. The father of this tradition, Tertullian, was a trained lawyer. Consequently, issues like the natural law and morality became important, law was made a main category, the theological vocabulary was taken from the legal system, and the Christian message was interpreted accordingly. God was conceived as a lawgiver and a judge, sin as the breaking of the law, and salvation as forgiveness. The description of this paradigm as "forensic" is right to the point. The meaning of the incarnated God was Christ's satisfaction of God's wrath by his atoning death.

From González's point of view, the Roman Catholic, Lutheran, and Calvinistic traditions all belong to the same type of theology, coming out of the forensic interpretation of the gospel. Their basic theological issue is compatible, how to be saved from sin understood as human transgressions of the law. Of course their theological solutions are different, but paradigms of theology should be distinguished according to their questions rather than their answers.

Type B was developed in Alexandria in a time when the Hellenistic culture was at its zenith, and Christianity had to face the challenges of Platonic and neo-Platonic philosophy. Father of the Alexandrine theology was Origen, a teacher of biblical exegesis and "Christian philosophy," who interpreted the Christian message with truth as the primary category. Such truth was immutable and transcendent. Accordingly, the relations between God and the world were conceived in the context of the Platonic distinction between the spiritual and the material world. God is conceived as distant from this world. Salvation implies the purification of human persons, and its goal is in another, immaterial world.

The purpose of Irenaeus, the father of the **type C** theology, was the opposite of Origen's, namely, to demonstrate that God does relate directly to the world. This theological paradigm had its roots in Antioch, where Hebrew religious traditions were therefore strong. God interacted with the world by creating the world and leading the history, and the incarnation was given meaning because it demonstrated how closely God related to nature, humanity, and society. The incarnation was not necessary because of sin, as held by the Western theology, but because of God's love for the creation, which was only the beginning of God's interaction with the world. The image of God is that of a parent, shepherd, or physician, and salvation is conceived as liberation or healing.

González's **type A** theology has become the basis of the Western tradition, and it consequently was the framework for Luther's works. When referring to the Eastern tradition I combine González's **types B** and **C**. I suggest that Wesley's theology should be interpreted as a place where the Western and Eastern traditions meet and merge.

Eschatology

Luther

All his life, Luther had a vivid expectation of an immediate *parousia*. This apocalyptical awareness he shared with most of his contemporaries, but he never based his eschatological expectations on speculative exegesis. The chiliastic background of his exegesis is revealed already in his comment on the first beatitude. In his criticism of voluntary poverty and the Baptist hope for a Christian communal economy he argues: "All this is intended to say that while we live here, we should use all temporal goods and physical necessities, the way a guest does in a strange place, where he stays overnight and leaves in the morning" (*LW*, 21:13).

Consequently, Luther's exegesis has obvious eschatological presuppositions. In the first place, he states that the contents of the Sermon on the Mount reveal his soteriology, and this soteriology is rooted in eschatology. A metaphysical struggle is fought between God and the devil. Through salvation in this world God liberates the imprisoned sinner from the devil in a preliminary way. The final salvation is to be won in the new *aeon* following Christ's *parousia*. Until then, liberation from sin is a matter of principle, understood in a forensic way as freedom of the guilt of sin. The justified sinner is not liberated from the power of sin until the heavenly world is a fact. In this world, salvation is limited to the assurance of God's acceptance of the sinner for the sake of Christ's atoning death. Salvation in the present world is, therefore, essentially hope for the next world to come.

The promises of the Sermon on the Mount are interpreted by Luther in accordance with this understanding of eschatology. Christ's purpose is to console the Christian who experiences the afflictions of this world, a view Luther in particular emphasizes in his postscript:

> These [passages about reward and merit] are simply intended to comfort Christians. (*LW*, 21:290)
> You see, these passages are correctly interpreted when they are applied ... to the consolation of Christians and believers. ...
> In this sense we concede that Christians have merit and a reward with God, but not in the order to make them children of God and heirs of eternal life. Rather it is to console believers who already have this, to let them know that He will not leave unrewarded what they suffer here for Christ's sake, but that if they suffer much and labor much, He will adorn them specially on the Last Day. ...
> [Referring to Mt. 5:11-12: ...] He is not teaching me where to build the foundation of my salvation, but giving me a promise that is to console me in my suffering and in my Christian life. (*LW*, 21:292-293; cf. *LW*, 21:206-207)

As demonstrated, Luther's hermeneutics is strongly founded in an eschatology that is oriented toward the future fulfillment of the promises of God. In this world salvation offers, first and foremost, hopes for a better world. The Christian existence in the world is one of tension between the present and the coming *aeon*, sin and righteousness, flesh and spirit, as indicated by his favorite concept *simul iustus et peccator*; Christians are totally justified and totally sinners at one and the same time. Salvation is worked on the sinner *"senkrecht von oben."* The tension of the Christian life is a tension of eternal struggle between God and the devil until God wins the final victory at the *parousia* and the final judgment. Forell (1964:166-167) suggests that similar interpretations, derived from Luther's studies of the epistles of Peter, indicate that he actually was not much concerned about the development of Christian ethics, particularly not an ethic which focused upon social reform. Christians should consider themselves as pilgrims on this earth, and they should live as guests in a foreign land. Because Christ's second coming was so soon to be expected, ethics was given a second priority compared to the issue of salvation, and the Christians should not bother with problems like the reorganization of the social order.

I do not think it is possible to find support for Forell's thesis in Luther's interpretation of the Sermon on the Mount. It is true that Luther has an essential future eschatology, and he advises against any reorganization of the social structure. But he continuously affirms that love and obedient service in the secular stations have to be expected as fruits of faith. I doubt that his concern for the social order has anything to do with his eschatology. He rather indicates that issues of social order—as well as social change (in cases of evil princes, for instance)—should be handed over to the civil authorities. According to his view, the Sermon on the Mount is not concerned about these matters. The social order has to do with God's creation, not salvation.

Wesley

Like Luther, Wesley has a strong eschatological background for his exegesis. His notion of the history of salvation is likewise characterized by a metaphysical struggle between God and the devil. But he does not expect an immediate *parousia*, nor is he oriented toward the future fulfillment of salvation as much as is Luther. Although his theological orientation is teleological, the emphasis of his soteriology is on the present.

Wesley's eschatology is formed by the prophetic vision of the realization of *shalom* in the Messianic age. This concept points toward the future, but its affirmation of God as the active defender of justice in the present world is equally significant. Its idea is that the goals to be perfectly fulfilled in the future are beginning to be realized in the present. *Shalom* is a gift and a task at one and the same time (Brueggeman 1987:85); the fact that the visions have utopian character makes them a historical challenge. It is typical of his piety that he acts in the present according to the grace he hopes for in the future, because he expects the fulfillment in the very same moment that he acts upon God's promise (see, for instance, *WW*, 1:647). To him, the establishment of divine love in the human soul is the definite proof that the Messianic age is present. A person who is a being, a new creation, will live according to this new nature.

This expectation of the immediate blessings of God emphasizes salvation as a present reality. To Wesley, the meaning of salvation is not explained in its fullness merely by referring to a forensic declaration or to its future consolation. Salvation is more than hopes for the future, it is to be actually included in the operational field of the Holy Spirit. The point is that the joy and peace of salvation is to be experienced in its fullness here and now, in this world. It is not only the hope for victory over sin in the future, but power over sin today.

In Wesley's soteriology, therefore, the fulfillment of the divine promises is in the process of being actualized all the time. What is to come after the *parousia* is the final victory over the evil powers and the full restoration of the cosmos. The restoration begins in this dispensation, however, and for this reason the future experiences of the wholeness of salvation are inaugurated in the present. He affirms that God's grace re-creates the sinner and that "Christian Perfection" is an actual possibility. But, until the *parousia*, this perfection is possible only within the limits of the brokenness of this world. This saving and re-creating work is entirely based upon the merits of God and is worked through grace by faith, but it is at the same time dependent on human response for its fulfillment. The sanctified Christian functions as a channel for

God's love to the world, thus contributing to God's ongoing re-creation of humanity, society, and the created nature.

Comparison

Luther's eschatology is oriented from the present to the future, and Wesley's eschatology from the future to the present. Both positions are in harmony with the biblical scriptures. The tension between these two kinds of eschatology is found in the bible itself. The question is, does Luther restrict the present aspect too much? Or, does Wesley take the presence of the evil of this world too little into consideration?

Luther recognizes the present aspect of eschatology, but in one respect only. His acknowledgment of salvation as a present reality is restricted to its spiritual sense. From a Wesleyan perspective this eschatology implies that the Christian religion is restricted to a basically forensic principle. Consequently, it will have limited significance for life in the world. A further problem is how to understand the role of the secular kingdom with its orders, offices, and stations, in relation to this eschatology. It could be deduced that this kingdom is not included in his future eschatology; the secular kingdom has no need of redemption. It is perfect as it is by itself, because its orders are created and authorized by God. The only eschatological role of the secular kingdom is to keep and strengthen the created orders against attacks from evil; however, this is a metaphysical function which does not necessarily imply an eschatological change concerning human and social life.

Wesley's eschatology includes the totality of the cosmos, nature, humanity, and social structures. More strongly than Luther he emphasizes that social systems, too, are subject to the judgment of God. On the other hand, he is optimistic when it comes to the eschatological transformation of the structures of this world. His eschatology is penetrated by his optimism of grace. There is literally no part of the human, social, and natural world which is excluded from the redeeming power of God. Seen through the eyes of Luther, Wesley is a utopian. But the difference between Wesley's vision of *utopia* and that of political utopians, for example, is that Wesley's *utopia* is identical with his vision of God's love and peace prevalent in the world. For that reason, divine promises undergird his vision.

In conclusion, both Luther and Wesley have a strong eschatological basis for their theologies. Therefore their interpretations of the Sermon on the Mount have an obvious eschatological emphasis. Luther's theology has its emphasis on the future fulfilling of God's promises. The transformation of the natural and human world is to take place after the *parousia*. Until then the issue is how to protect the created world against the devil. Wesley's eschatology has its emphasis on the realized or inaugurated fulfilling of God's promises in this world already. He therefore anticipates an actual transformation of the sinner in this life to the image of God, and the transformation of society according to the vision of *shalom*, understood as God's love present among us.

Creation and Salvation, Law and Gospel

Luther

For Luther, it is crucial to distinguish sharply between God as savior and God as creator. This distinction probably provides the most significant premise of his theology. Most aspects in his theology depend on it, as, for instance, his soteriology, sociopolitical theory, and ethics. Because salvation and creation are performed by God as the activities of God's two hands, Luther may insist on a theological monism, however, this monism leads to a practical dualism between the spiritual and secular.

Luther has no explicit discussion of the relationship between creation and salvation in his discourses on the Sermon on the Mount; however, he discusses frequently the distinction between law and gospel and that between the secular and spiritual kingdoms. Basic to both these differences is a distinction between the creating and saving works of God. To him, God's creating activity continues in the secular kingdom. To live in the civil stations and offices is not only significant in social terms, such as bonds of duties and loyalties toward superiors and subjects; it also implies to be God's co-operator. God's creating work in society is understood dynamically, but the dynamics is restricted to each station and office. The focus of Luther's interest is the office itself. As a consequence, there is no need to imply that the Christian is re-created as a person. God's sustenance of creation is in part taken care of by the Christian's responsible and obedient work in the office. By supporting the order of society through faithful life in the stations, in Luther's view, the creative dynamics is understood primarily as an ongoing struggle against chaos. His model presupposes a hierarchical society ordered by God with various levels of authority evenly balanced. The primary practical goal is to keep that balance.

Another consequence of Luther's separation of creation and salvation is the sharp distinctions between law and gospel on the one side, and between the secular and spiritual kingdoms on the other. Each pair of opposites has its own set of righteousness. In the secular kingdom, a person has his or her proper righteousness along with the rational capacity to fulfil the demands of the natural and the civil laws. The concept of sin is purely religious. His forensic understanding of grace puts the focus on the removal of the guilt of sin, and requires, for that reason, an alien righteousness. It is God's righteousness, which is accounted to the sinner. His aim is to explain the oneness of God's activity. The result, however, comes close to a practical dualism.

God's sustenance of creation presupposes an eternal struggle with the satanic powers, which are as universal as God's law. They continually threaten to destroy the created order. All life depends on God's preservation of creation. In his Sermon on the Mount discourses Luther repeatedly demonstrates the significant role of the civil stations and orders in this work of God. From an eschatological point of view, therefore, his system is unchangeable until the coming of the new heaven and the new earth. From a theological point of view, however, it may be described as dynamic, provided the dynamics is conceived to be a metaphysical fight expressed through God's daily re-creation of the cosmos. The aim is to keep the created order unchanged, however, and the means are the offices and stations.

Most significantly, the universalism implied in Luther's theology of creation provides a basis for solidarity between people (Wingren 1971:117). This aspect is clearly demonstrated in his discourses. The idea behind the creation of hierarchical levels in the secular kingdom is to take care of everybody. The obvious responsibility of the offices bestowed with authority is to take care of their subjects and protect them from evil. The dynamics of works in the secular kingdom is focused on the needs of the neighbor.

This focus on universal human solidarity does not answer the problem of the dualism created between God and the evil forces in the world. The result is a dichotomy between the spiritual and the secular which threatens to alienate either the spiritual from the secular, or the secular from the spiritual. In affirming the universalist aspect as basically a part of creation, the soteriological issue is turned into individualism. This problem is clearly demonstrated in Luther's discourses on the Sermon on the Mount. By definition, the issues of universalism and individualism constitute the Christian's fundamental criterion for distinguishing between the two kingdoms. In the secular kingdom, the Christian is related to family and society. In the spiritual kingdom, however, the Christian is always conceived as "individual" (see, for instance, *LW*, 21:23-24, 99, 106, 123, 170).

From a strictly soteriological point of view, therefore, the person in Luther's theology is alienated from the social context. His constant expectancy of works of love for the neighbor as a fruit of faith in the spiritual kingdom, does not provide a basis for Christian solidarity as this is commonly understood today. The social issues are left to the secular kingdom, to which Christ in the Sermon on the Mount has nothing substantial to add. The gospel is not troubled with these matters, Luther affirms (for instance, *LW*, 21:108). For this reason, he removes the larger part of human existence from the sphere of salvation. I doubt that his distinction between faith and experience is biblically and theologically valid at this point. It is also an open question whether or not his anthropology has gained by this distinction, in particular, his secular anthropology from being separated from the spiritual kingdom.

Law and gospel are valued from Luther's theology of creation as "God's two hands," by which God takes care of the secular business through sustaining the created world with the one hand, and the salvation of humanity with the other. Apart from their soteriological functions, Luther does not anticipate any contrariety between the two activities. Both law and gospel lead to the Christian's service of the neighbor, but with different dynamics. The gospel takes the justified believer to the neighbor in order to materialize love, the law in order to eliminate the possible *hubris* of the believer. From a soteriological point of view, law and gospel have complementary functions. The law reveals the destruction and death of the carnal nature, the gospel grants life through redemption and resurrection. Luther views these effects of the gospel to be relevant to the spiritual kingdom only and not to the secular kingdom.

Luther's discussion of law and gospel is basic to the understanding of his soteriology and ethics (Gustafson 1968:121). Two issues on gospel and law are actualized by Luther's interpretation of the Sermon on the Mount. First, he deals with the problem of the imperfect fulfilling of the law by humanity. He presupposes that from a soteriological point of view, a perfect fulfillment of the law is an absolute requirement for salvation. He solves this problem by implying that Christ in a perfect and substituting way has fulfilled the law on behalf of sinful humanity. Basic to his soteriology is, therefore, a demand for merits compensating for human sin. Salvation is secured by the imputation of Christ's righteousness, which is conceived as a righteousness resulting from his perfect fulfillment of the law. By grace through faith, Christ's righteousness is accounted to the sinner. Christ's merits alone are taken into account. The only effect of the works of the law is, from this point of view, to emphasize the extremity of human sin, proving that damnation is the outcome of the law, were it not for Christ's intervention.

The role of the law in the economy of salvation is explained by
Luther particularly in his comments on Mt. 5:17-20. Fundamentally, no human being is capable of fulfilling the law:

> we must always creep to Christ. He has fulfilled it all purely and
> perfectly, and He gives Himself to us, together with His fulfill-
> ment. Through Him we can take our stand before God, and the
> Law cannot incriminate or condemn us. So it is true that all must
> be accomplished and fulfilled even to the smallest dot, but only
> through this one Man. About this we have said enough else-
> where. (*LW*, 21:72-73)

The law, then, is a constant reminder of human incapacity to satisfy God's demands; this function is often called the second use of
the law. Its only contribution to salvation is to lead the sinner to
Christ's perfect fulfillment of it. Salvation of the individual sinner
is essentially that the merits of Christ's fulfilling of the law are
accounted to him or her. In other works, Luther affirms Christ's
atoning death at the cross as the basis for salvation. In his Sermon
on the Mount discourses, however, his emphasis is on Christ's
atoning fulfillment of the law. In both cases, the dynamics of salvation are the same, namely, the imputation of Christ's righteousness to the sinner by faith and grace alone.

Luther's exegesis of the law emphasizes the "most important
doctrine, the righteousness of faith through Christ" (*LW*, 21:70).
This emphasis is indeed characteristic to the whole tenor of his
Sermon on the Mount discourses, with their strong focus on orthodoxy. Is this the reason why he possibly admits ways of fulfilling
the law for the Christian after all?

> He [Christ] does indeed go beyond Law and doctrine when He
> gives His grace and Spirit to enable us to do and keep the Law's
> demands, but that is not "supplementing" the Law. And so He is
> not talking about that here, but about that fulfilling which takes
> place through teaching. (*LW*, 21:69)

At this point, Luther probably recognizes the possibility of fulfilling the demands of the law, because the Christian is empowered to

do so by God's grace and the Spirit. This is the only reference I have found in his discourses indicating such an attitude to the law. I doubt, however, that a third use of the law, or, making the law applicable to the Christian life, is what Luther has in mind. The last part of the quotation indicates that the law may be fulfilled "through teaching," namely, of the right understanding of law and doctrine. In similar ways the doctrinal and cognitive aspects of Luther's theology are emphasized throughout his interpretation of the Sermon on the Mount. It is no wonder that doctrinal preaching and catechisms became important characteristics of the Lutheran churches, while the emphasis of the Wesleyan churches were more on the Christian ethos. According to Luther, the fulfillment of the commandments of the law is of no relevance to the Christian's relation to God. Christ has fulfilled the law in a perfect way and has substituted the Christian's fulfilling of it.

Secondly, there is the issue of the universal character of the law, or, its first use. Wingren (1971:116) rightly observes that, in Luther's theology, the gospel is personal but the law is universal, because it has to do with the created order. In the light of soteriology, the law and the gospel are in almost hostile opposition to each other, because the gospel gives freely what the law demands. This dialectic governs Luther's hermeneutics throughout his Sermon on the Mount exegesis. In light of ethics, however, the natural law is basic because of its universal character.

To Luther, "The law commands that we should have love and that we should have Christ, but the gospel offers and presents both to us" (after Forde 1983:242). Forde affirms that "Luther was driven to distinguish between God's activity as judge and lawgiver and God's saving activity in Jesus Christ. The distinction between law and gospel is the solution to the problem of the anxious conscience" (Forde 1983:242-243). Forde suggests that Luther's sharp distinction between law and gospel has a psychological basis and ought to be found in the history of his religious development. Other scholars have similar views, for instance, Stendahl (1977) in his analysis of Luther's exegesis of Paul. Their insights do not diminish the theological significance of his systematics; his distinction between law and gospel has had a tremendous impact on later exegesis and theology.

In his Sermon on the Mount discourses, Luther operates with two uses of the law, the civil or political use (*usus civilis* or *usus politicus*), and the spiritual or educational use (*usus theologicus* or *usus pedagogicus*). He affirms the constructive role of the law in the secular kingdom. In the spiritual kingdom, the law has the restricted and negative function of stimulating the recognition of sin. There is no evidence of a third use of the law in Luther's exegesis of Mt. 5-7. The Christian-in-person has no use for the law, because he or she is driven by Christ. If the law is made compulsory for Christians, his system will be distorted. The unconditional acceptance of the sinner will be displaced by an ethos based on legalism and morality. Worse still, the soteriology may be confused by moving the attention from Christ's fulfilling of the law to human merits.[2]

Wesley

Wesley's theology is monistic in its presuppositions as well as in its implications. To him, salvation and creation are two aspects of the very same activity, whose end is the establishment of love and peace, and not two different activities that must be separated. Salvation is essentially a new creation, or the renewal of creation.

In Holifield's understanding, Wesley's doctrine of creation is fundamental to his theology and ethics:

> Wesley's doctrine of creation ... was an attempt to discern the moral and religious implications of the assertion that men and women were created in the image of God and to understand the "universal restoration" when God would create "a new heaven and a new earth." Thus his doctrine of creation functioned not so much to explain the distant past as to provide a normative depiction of appropriate behavior in the present and to chart the end toward which the whole creation was groaning and travailing in its present pain. The doctrine that men and women were created in the image of God suggested ethical norms for a social order.

... Implicit in Wesley's depiction of the image of God was an ethic which prohibited the suppression of understanding, the shackling of choice, the subversion of proper dominion, and the denial of love.

The doctrine of creation thus functioned as an axiomatic foundation for ethical judgment. It elaborated the presuppositions implicit in moral demands that were binding upon every man and woman, whether Christian or not. Every ethical claim presupposes a set of dogmatic beliefs, which are usually unstated. Wesley's doctrine of creation provided a way for him to be explicit about the dogmatic beliefs underlying his own ethical judgments.

His doctrine of creation provided not only a normative depiction of the image of God but also a broader conceptual background for ethical decision. The harmony and order of the original creation offered a pattern for 'a far nobler state of things,' a 'new creation' which would restore a natural order without pain, without destruction, without cruelty and fierceness, without wasting and violence, without sickness and death. Indeed, he thought that the new creation would offer 'an unmixed state of holiness and happiness, far superior to that which Adam enjoyed in paradise.' But the old creation foreshadowed the new, so the description of the original created harmony offered a mythic image of the goal toward which the whole world moved. To act in accord with created human nature was also to act in anticipation of the new creation.

... The doctrine of sanctification became Wesley's way of asserting that the Christian life brought about a real change in the believer, a reorientation of character and conduct. The process had ethical implications: external deeds of mercy became means by which God engendered love. (Holifield 1986:110-111, 112-113)

In my assessment, Holifield is right in emphasizing Wesley's theology of creation. His observation has been neglected by Wesleyan scholars for too long. For a general understanding of his theology and ethics his Christology and his pneumatology should be equally emphasized along with the significance of creation. His theology and ethics are trinitarian in their well-balanced emphases on all three persons in the Godhead.

In conclusion, the goal of Wesley's ethics is simply to materialize the *shalom* of the Messianic age that was introduced with Christ's first coming. The goals implied in this vision are the goals of ethics in the world. The power of ethics is the love of the creating and saving God, filling the heart of the Christian. The model is Christ. The essence of Christian ethics is to make oneself accountable to God's will for the world, being an instrument of God's love. The fulfilling of God's promises is anticipated in the present. His genius is that he manages to make discipleship a response to God's grace and not a striving for virtue (Watson 1985:87), while still preserving discipleship within a context of accountability.[3]

Wesley nowhere indicates that a contradiction exists between law and gospel. In general, his attitudes to the role of the law in the life of the Christian is more positive than Luther's, for instance, by speaking of a "law of love" (*WW*, 2:40). His theological presuppositions are more fully revealed in his three sermons on the law following the 13 discourses on the Sermon on the Mount in his Standard Sermons. These sermons must be valued in light of his interpretation of the message of the Sermon on the Mount. They are, "The Original, Nature, Properties, and Use of the Law [Rom. 7:12]," and "The Law Established through Faith, I-II [Rom. 3:31]" (*WW*, 2:1-43). He is more influenced by the puritan tradition on the law (*WW*, 2:2) than by the Lutheran tradition. For instance, he affirms the three uses of the law to be: (1) to convict the sinner of sin, (2) to convert, and (3) to keep the believer alive in God (*WW*, 2:15-19).

Contrary to his usual habit, Wesley in these sermons has a quite polemical style. Primarily, the object of his polemics is the Lutheran view of the law. He rejects the following ideas of the law, which all may be traced back to Luther:

Luther's position as interpreted by Wesley	Wesley's answer to the Lutheran position
The law is a corrupting power.	The law is a constructive power used by God for nurturing the Christian (*WW*, 2:18).
Persons are saved from the guilt but not from the power of sin.	The law of God is written anew in the heart of the sanctified Christian (*WW*, 2:19), who is released from the power of sin.
Faith supersedes the necessity of holiness, which implies to put the law aside.	Warning against the notion of cheap grace (*WW*, 2:26); faith should lead to holiness.
In the present dispensation the covenant of grace has displaced the covenant of works, "and therefore we are no longer under the necessity of performing works of the law."	Adam was created with a perfect image of God. He was before the fall under the covenant of works, which required perfect, universal obedience. All other persons were and are under the covenant of grace; the free grace of God, through the merits of Christ, offers pardon to those that believe (*WW*, 2:27). Adam was the only person with capacities to fulfil the law. From the moment he sinned, God established the covenant of grace for him and his successors. This covenant replaced the covenant of works in the moment of the fall and not in the moment of Christ's atonement.
Christ's righteousness is imputed to the Christian but not imparted.	"We are justified by faith without the works of the law" as any previous condition of justification. But the works of the law are an immediate fruit of that faith whereby we are justified. ... This ... is indeed the main pillar of antinomianism. ... The Apostle ... does teach that there is no righteousness *before* faith; but where does he teach that there is none *after* it? He does assert holiness cannot *precede* justification; but not that it need not follow it". (*WW*, 2:27-28)
Faith is the heart of Christian piety.	Faith "is only the handmaid of love" (*WW*, 2:38); love is the heart of Christian piety.

Wesley warns against "those who magnify faith beyond all proportion" (*WW*, 2:39). He affirms that love existed from the moment of their creation, and that "Faith then was originally designed of God to re-establish the law of love. ... It is the grand means of restoring that holy love wherein man was originally created" (*WW*, 2:40). To live in love is the same as living according to the commandments of the law.

All these polemical statements are based on a theology that establishes the law at the center of Christian piety but in a different way than in the Reformed tradition. Though justification is given by faith, this initial phase of salvation is not what Wesley is most concerned about. His focus is on what follows after justification, namely, the restoration of the image of God. In these parts of the way of salvation, to live according to the law becomes the natural way of Christian life, transformed to God's grace. Unlike Calvin and many Lutheran pietists he does not want to introduce a new legalism under the cover of the gospel. The law is rather established in a new way, from the perspective of the evangelical promise (*WW*, 1:554-555).

Wesley does not view the Christian's fulfilling of the law within the context of meriting salvation but for the full unfolding of it. There is probably reason to conclude that to him, a life according to the law is necessary for the sustenance of salvation. Fundamental to his theology of the law is, however, his interpretation of it in light of the establishment of love. The restoration of the law is a part of the eschatological blessings of God's love and peace.

The issue of the natural law is a critical point of difference between Luther and Wesley and needs therefore to be discussed. With "natural law" I mean, in this context, all the ethical demands that the human person is able to recognize logically with the help of reason, independent from the Hebrew-Christian revelation. Contrary to this moral law are all the ethical demands that only Christians are able to recognize as a function of their faith. What is discussed, therefore, is the basis of Christian ethics with specific reference to the relationship between natural reason and revelation.

Wesley does not discuss the issue of natural law in his discourses on the Sermon on the Mount, however, his views are implied in his exegesis. A great number of Wesleyan scholars rightly maintain that he completely rejects the concept of the natural law. Almost all of his comments concerning the natural law are utterly negative, for instance:

> it [salvation] will include all that is wrought in the soul what is frequently termed "natural conscience", but more properly, "preventing grace;" all the "drawings" of "the Father," the desires after God, which, if we yield to them, increase more and more; all that "light" wherewith the Son of God "enlighteneth everyone that cometh into the world". (*WW*, 2:156-157)
>
> For allowing that all souls of men are dead in sin by nature, this excuses none, seeing there is no man that is in a state of mere *nature*; there is no man, unless he has quenched the Spirit, that is wholly void of the Grace of God. No man living is entirely destitute of what is vulgarly called *natural conscience*. But this is not natural: It is more properly termed, *preventing grace.* ... So that no man sins because he has not grace, but because he does not use the grace which he hath. (*WW*, 3:207)
>
> For though in one sense it ["natural conscience"] may be termed "natural," because it is found in all men, yet properly speaking it is not *natural*; but a supernatural gift of God, above all his natural endowments. No, it is not nature but the Son of God that is "the true light." (*WW*, 3:482)

Wesley disputes the traditional understanding that the natural law belongs to the sphere of creation over against salvation. Contrary to the traditional Western position, he affirms that the created nature is totally corrupt with no capacity by itself ever to recognize God nor ethical demands (*WW*, 4:163). It is the saving activity of God alone that enlightens the human mind. Logan concludes that "Wesley did not maintain that the natural law of God is fully accessible to everyone. Only through prevenient grace does one know anything of that law, and then no doubt not perfectly" (Logan 1985a:364-365). This view is particularly true in his interpretation of the first beatitude (*WW*, 1:477; cf. *WW*, 1:526).

The natural law is therefore, in Wesley's theology, replaced by the notion of universal grace expressed through the doctrine of prevenient grace (cf. Hendricks 1983). In his discussion on the issues of predestination and free grace[4] he summarizes the opposing views in the following way (cf. Borgen 1972:279):

Arminians	Calvinists
Conditional predestination: He who believes shall be saved; he who does not believe shall be condemned.	Absolute predestination.
Generally, any person may resist God's grace.	Irresistible saving grace.
Any Christian may fail, and perish eternally.	The believer cannot fall from God's grace.

Wesley's doctrine gives no basis for natural revelation, which he regards as a contradiction in terms. It rather opens up for a general revelation, allowing a universal activity of God (Dunning 1985:53). Consequently, (1) in soteriology he avoids the doctrine of predestination by insisting on a human response to God's grace. This response is made possible because the human will is empowered to accept the grace of God by God's Spirit. Persons are made "capable of God" which is a gracious and not a natural capacity (Dunning 1985:54). (2) In ethics he provides a trinitarian foundation. At the same time he avoids ethical exclusiveness by insisting that God through the Spirit illumines all human minds in a sufficient way to make ethical choices possible. This illumination is a work of the Spirit. Logan rightly states that, "Precisely at this point Wesley's theology offers us one of the greatest of his contributions to ethical discourse and a continuing debate in contemporary Christian ethics" (Logan 1985a:365).[5] This seems especially relevant in light of the renewed interest by contemporary Wesleyan ethicists in natural law as a basis for Christian ethics (Logan 1985a:369-370). A revival of Wesley's emphasis on revelation is a healthy corrective to the development which has taken place within Methodist theology "from revelation to reason" (Chiles 1983:76-114).

Wesley is critical of Luther's tendency to identify the civil law ("the law of the Emperor") with God's law. His sarcasms on "Christian nations" (*WW*, 1:508) and "a Christian country" (*WW*, 1:666) indicate that. He explicitly rejects positions like that of Luther. In his *Thoughts upon Slavery* (*WW-J*, 11:59-79) he characterizes civil laws as merely human regulations:

> The grand plea is, "They [slavery and the slave trade] are authorized by law." But can law, human law, change the nature of things? Can it turn darkness into light, or evil into good? By no means. Notwithstanding ten thousand laws, right is right, and wrong is wrong still. There must still remain an essential difference between justice and injustice, cruelty and mercy. So I still ask, Who can reconcile this treatment of the Negroes, first and last, with either mercy or justice? (*WW-J*, 11:70)

Wesley goes back to his ultimate source of ethical judgment at this point, namely God's law and justice. The Messianic age requires that secular laws are evaluated critically according to the visions of God's society. Therefore, "I absolutely deny all slaveholding to be consistent with any degree of natural justice" (*WW-J*, 11:70). He refers to God's original will for creation and humanity, and not to examples of human depravity caused by the fall. Consequently, he finds liberty to be a human right based in the divine will: "Liberty is the right of every human creature, as soon as he breathes the vital air; and no human law can deprive him of that right which he derives from the law of nature" (*WW-J*, 1:79). "The law of nature" is conceived as the universal creating and saving will of God and not as the natural law as suggested by the philosophers of the Enlightenment. His point is, this law of nature is not natural, but it is essentially the will of God.

Introducing his discourses on the Sermon on the Mount, Wesley asks some basic questions which focus on the character of the preacher of the Sermon on the Mount: Who is actually speaking? What is he speaking? To whom? And, how? (*WW*, 1:470-474). He implies that the interpretation will take place within this larger context. At the same time he suggests a general frame of reference within which the interpretation may take place. "The way of salvation" is "the way to heaven," or, "to the kingdom" (*WW*, 1:472). The preacher is the creating, loving, and redeeming God, whose aim it is to restore the original purpose of creation. The way of salvation is at the same time "the path to calm, joyous peace, to heaven below and heaven above!" (*WW*, 1:474). The theological frame for his interpretation of the Sermon on the Mount is, therefore, a combination of its soteriology with its emphasis on regeneration, and eschatology with the emphasis on realized fulfillment of God's promises.

Integral to Wesley's soteriology are his theologies of creation and eschatology. His theology of creation provides, on the one hand, the basis for his interpretation that humanity is to be created in the image of God. On the other hand, it expresses the goal of his theology and ethics, namely, the transformation to the image of God. His theology of creation forms a general model for the Christian's life, the *telos* of his soteriology. At the same time, his eschatology focuses on the dynamics of soteriology in the actual transformation of the human mind and world by the activity of the trinitarian God, fatherly love, Christ's atonement, and the empowerment by the Spirit. Very few scholars have taken into full consideration the aspects of creation and eschatology in his theology. The result is that the holistic nature of his thought disintegrates. Those who make a holistic approach, however, like Holifield (1986), for instance, are able to describe his theology in a broader perspective.

Wesley summarizes the characteristics of his own "system of Christian perfection" in this way:

> This is to be "a perfect man," to be "sanctified throughout," [1] "created anew in Jesus Christ", even [2] "to have a heart so all-flaming with the love of God" ... "as [3] continually to offer up every thought, word, and work, as a spiritual sacrifice, acceptable unto God through Christ." (*WW*, 11:340)

The first point describes the soteriological basis, the effect of salvation, and the ethical model implied. Salvation in Christ by faith through grace establishes a new creation (2 Cor. 5:17), and the former sinner is made a disciple of Christ. The second point describes divine love as the spiritual energy filling the Christian completely. The third point defines the goal of salvation which is the conformity of the believer's entire life and person to God's purposes. Basic to this description is Wesley's vision of God's *shalom* inaugurated by Christ and realized in the world. This love and peace continue in the transformation of the sinner, and the engraving of the mind which was in Christ in the heart of the believer. The salvation is perfected in the future at the final restoration after the *parousia*.

Comparison

It is easy to observe that Luther and Wesley have contradictory views on the significance of the law within the life of the Christian. Luther's intention is to distinguish as sharply as possible between creation and salvation, while Wesley's intention is to unite them. According to Wesley, salvation is the fulfilling of God's intentions for creation. For this reason it is not possible to separate between them. To Luther, however, Wesley is confusing creation with salvation, which is the same as to put at risk the purity of the Christian religion.

Luther affirms without reservation the role of the law within the secular kingdom. In the salvation of the spiritual kingdom, he establishes one function of the law only, namely, its continuous disclosure of sin. Regarding the ethos of the spiritual kingdom, however, it is more complicated to characterize his position. From one point of view, he is more of a spiritualist than a legalist. He anticipates that conduct in the spiritual kingdom is governed by the love of God and the neighbor in a general way according to the inspiration of the bible and the Spirit (*LW*, 21:260). This life in love he explains in general terms, for instance, in his comments to the last antithesis (Mt. 5:43-48): "But 'to love' means to be good-hearted and to wish the best, to have a heart that is friendly, kind and sweet toward everyone, not one that makes fun over misery or misfortune" (*LW*, 21:122). He seems to argue for an ethics of disposition in which works "is purely a gift, bestowed from heaven and brought to me by Christ" (*LW*, 21:290).

On the other hand, Luther affirms that Christ in the Sermon on the Mount instructs "how individual Christians should behave in their everyday life" (*LW*, 21:99). On giving examples to imitate, he explicitly refers to Christ's teaching of the law, or, the antitheses. At this point his view is coming close to the third use of the law of Lutheran orthodoxy, making the law a model to be imitated in the Christian life. But his emphasis is less casuistic than that of the orthodoxy. He is more concerned to emphasize that Christ by using the antitheses teaches "Christians ... the kind of people they should be" (*LW*, 21:107). From this point of view his ethics in the spiritual kingdom is a kind of disposition ethics. Apart from its general commandment of love, the specific contents of the law have minor value.

Wesley, too, affirms love as the essence of the law. He, however, emphasizes the significance of the law as a whole more than Luther. One reason is that he has less problems than Luther with the law within the life of the Christian. On the contrary, by regarding its commandments as hidden promises of grace, he makes the law an important instrument in the religious growth of a person. This concern may, however, be another reason why Luther neglects the law; he is not interested in religious growth other than doctrinal insights.

Wesley's positive attitudes toward the law must not be confused with the traditional understanding of the third use of the law as conceived in the Lutheran and Reformed confessions based on Calvin's theology. His idea is not that Christ has brought a new law to be observed by Christians. Nor has Christ offered a perfect revelation of the Mosaic law. Wesley is not interested in Luther's notion of Christ as the perfect fulfiller of the law. He has no need for it. Though he agrees fully with Luther that no human observation of the law can merit salvation because of sin, he never regards the law as an enemy of the gospel. The law rather reveals the true nature of God. Consequently, if the law is removed, the revelation of God is not complete. When a sinner is born again and regenerated to God's image, the new life in God will be established as a life in the fulfillment of the law. The character of this fulfillment is not, however, conceived as any formal adaptation to nor as any observation of its casuistic commandments, but as a life in God which is expressed in love (Rom. 13:8-10). Sanctification is nothing but being a partaker of the divine nature (2 Pet. 1:4), which is love.

Both Luther and Wesley affirm the role of the law in the economy of salvation. But while Luther maintains the human incapacity to fulfil the law and projects the fulfillment to the office of Christ understood as the perfect human person, Wesley maintains the capacity of the sanctified Christian to fulfil the law on the basis of God's transforming and empowering grace (cf. Wilson 1977:57-58). According to Luther, the merits of the law are fundamental in the economy of salvation, though after Christ's perfect fulfillment of the law human beings are saved through his merits and not by their own. To Wesley, the law is basic for the understanding of the divine as well as the human nature. To destroy the law would be to destroy the relations between God and humanity.

In Wesley's theology, law and gospel are complementary and not irreconcilable. He views love and law theocentrically and in correlation. They are theocentric because both are expressions of God's nature and righteousness. This theocentricity is exactly what helps him not to fall into pelagianism.

In the Lutheran and Calvinistic discussions of the third use of the law, the marrow of the law is still conceived as commandments, precepts, and demands. Wesley's approach is different, because he emphasizes that the heart of the law is the evangelical promise of the transformation into God's likeness and having the mind that was in Christ. The center of his theology of the law is not that the sinner is empowered to fulfil the demands of the law after all, but rather that the law is the perfect expression of the life in God:

> Now although a believer is "not without law to God, under the law to Christ," yet from the moment he believes he is not "under the law" in any of the preceding senses. On the contrary, he is "under grace". ... And he now performs (which while "under the

law" he could not do) a willing and universal obedience. He obeys, not from the motive of slavish fear, but on a nobler principle, namely, the grace of God ruling in his heart, and causing all his works to be wrought in love.

What then? Shall this evangelical principle of action be less powerful than the legal? Shall we be less obedient to God from filial love than we were from servile fear? (*WW*, 2:29-30)

In conclusion, Wesley displaces Luther's dichotomy of the law and gospel with a dialectical relationship in which the gospel promises what the law demands as a general pattern for life in Christ more than casuistics. The obedience of the law which is demonstrated by the person who is in Christ, is a "universal obedience" worked by the love which is filling the heart and life of the Christian. The following table indicates the positions of Luther and Wesley:

THEOLOGIES OF THE LAW COMPARED	
Luther	**Wesley**
Presupposition: The law is necessary because of the human sin. *The covenant of works.*	*Presupposition:* The law is necessary to reveal God's nature. *The covenant of grace.*
Theological issues and conclusions: - Violation of God's holy law. - Fulfillment of law required as *the basis of salvation.* Christ substitutes the fulfillment of the law on behalf of humanity because of sin.	*Issues:* - Loss of God's image. - Fulfillment of the law is *the fruit of salvation*, following after the renewal of God's image.
1. use: Usus politicus / civilis The law reveals Gods grace to the world, but it is not a means of grace. The function of the natural law is to sustain creation and to model the life in the secular world.	*1. use: Usus elenchticus / pedagogicus* The law brings forth recognition of sin and leads the sinner to Christ for forgiveness (*prevenient grace*).

THEOLOGIES OF THE LAW COMPARED	
Luther	**Wesley**
2. use: Usus elenchticus / pedagogicus The law brings forth recognition of sin and leads the sinner to Christ for forgiveness.	*2. use: Bringing the sinner to conversion* The law destroys human righteousness and thereby contributes in bringing the sinner to life in Christ (*justifying grace*).
3. use: Usus didacicus / normativus (Not Luther but Melanchton and the Lutheran Orthodoxy.)	*3. use: Keeping the believer alive in God* Actual but no formal observance of the law; works are fruits of the new life in God, who is love. The law links commands and promises of God's blessings (*sanctifying grace*).
Similarities:	
Salvation is acquired apart from law merits by grace through faith. Works are fruit of the life in God.	
Dissimilarities:	
The law constitutes the basis for the doctrine of justification by faith alone. Emphasis on the 2. use of the law (in the spiritual kingdom as a basis for the doctrine of justification.	The revelation of God's promises; the eschatological transformation of the person to the image of God. The law is conceived in light of eschatological promises and the restoration of the image of God in the person.

Fundamental to the exegeses of Luther and Wesley are their theologies of law and the relationship between the grace of the gospel and the law. Some similarities are apparent: They equally affirm that the law revives a recognition of sin in the human heart. They also agree that the Christian's "observance" of the law must not be understood as casuistics, but as a disposition of love which leads to works for the neighbor. Luther will not speak, of course, of any actual observance of the law at all. But in his interpretation of the antitheses, he opens up for a general fulfillment of the law in the spiritual kingdom as the fruit of faith. A third similarity is that they both reject the third use of the law in the way understood by Calvinism and Lutheran orthodoxy.

The differences are, however, more fundamental. In the first place, Wesley's emphasis on the law in the life of the Christian has no counterpart in Lutheran piety and ethos. Luther's general position is to regard the law as an enemy of the gospel. This is true when he discusses the basis of salvation, but his fear of pelagianism makes him affirm that there is also no need to fulfil the law because of Christ's perfect and substitutionary fulfilling of it.

Wesley criticizes Luther for opening the doors to antinomianism. Luther has often been understood as an antinomian, but his discourses on the Sermon on the Mount give evidence that the opposite is closer to the truth. At this point, Luther's distinction between salvation and creation needs to be examined for a just assessment of his position. It is in regard to salvation only that the law cannot help. In ethics, however, he affirms strongly the unity of the natural law and the law of God. And, as a matter of fact, Christ's teachings in the Sermon on the Mount, which is his interpretation of the right observance of the law, are applicable to the Christian-in-person. Luther's point is that Christ's teaching of the law is for the spiritual kingdom only, not for the secular. The natural law is unnecessary in the spiritual kingdom. But faith in Christ definitely leads to works of love in the spiritual kingdom and faithful obedience in the offices of the secular kingdom. Wesley's criticism of Luther is at this point based on prejudices created by his indirect acquaintance with his theology through the Moravians.

From a Wesleyan point of view, a more serious objection to Luther is his neglect of the positive values of the law in the Christian life. The result of Luther's theology on the law causes a restriction of the full experience of salvation in this world, and becomes an example of theological reductionism.

Another Wesleyan objection has to do with Luther's insistence on the role of human reason as a natural source for ethics, over against the revelation of God. Wesley rejects that such "natural" capacities ever existed after the fall. They are all totally corrupted. Does Luther's doctrine of natural law and his general ethics imply that the secular person is not affected by the fall, or partly affected only? This seems to be the basis of his distinction between the two kinds of righteousness, between the secular and the spiritual kingdom, and between law and gospel. If so, the theological bases of Luther and Wesley are fundamentally different. According to Wesley, the corruption of humanity at the fall was total. The corruption affected the entire cosmos, nature, society, and humanity included. For this reason, salvation initiates a healing process in the corrupted world. In Wesley's soteriology, gospel and law cooperate in the work of restoration; they are not enemies. Their relationship is one of dialectical cooperation by their offering grace and the divine standards for the life in salvation at one and the same time.

In Luther's point of view, theologies like that of Wesley confuse law and gospel in a most dangerous way. As a result, human efforts threaten to displace the divine grace. The problem is, however, that their paradigms are different. Their common concern of both is to affirm the primacy of grace in salvation, but their implications are not the same. Luther's system presupposes a future fulfillment of salvation, and it is logically established for this end. He starts his soteriology with the fall and ends in the *parousia*, while he is struggling to maintain the social order in the meantime. Wesley's system requires different theological conclusions for this world because his emphasis is on the present actualization of salvation in and for this world, thus implying that salvation works social changes no less than human.

Both Luther and Wesley hold salvation and creation in a dialectical relationship to each other, however, in a contradictory way. Luther's distinction between salvation and creation leads to a dialectic that threatens to separate the spiritual from the secular. The consequences are a relationship of disunity between law and gospel which makes possible a split between the believer's experience of salvation and his or her ethical behavior in the world. Wesley's distinction between salvation and creation is less real than formal, because he expects the effects of salvation to be a new creation to be realized in the created, human, and social world. Therefore, his dialectics implies a dynamic tension between salvation and creation leading to a bifocal system with the two doctrines of justification and the two kingdoms closely interrelated. The consequences are an integrated view of law and gospel, the believer's experience of salvation, and the ethical life in the world as the effects of salvation.

Ethical and Religious Recognition

Luther

In the secular kingdom, Luther emphasizes human reason as the instrument for ethical recognition. When it comes to knowledge about God and salvation, however, reason is of no use. The special revelation in Christ is then necessary. He distinguishes logically between ethical and religious recognition in the same way that he distinguishes between secular and spiritual, law and gospel.

Luther presupposes that the ethical demands of God's law have been known since creation and they may be known after the fall, too. God's will was expressed long before the Mosaic law was given, and Christian ethics is basically identical with the natural law. The content of the moral law is therefore identical with the mosaic law and the moral admonitions of the gospel, and the biblical code has nothing substantial to add in terms of ethical norms (cf. Wingren 1971:118). The decalogue was given by God through Moses as an interpretation and clarification of the natural law written in the human hearts (*WA* 39[1]:454, 458). Nor was Christ a lawgiver (*WA* 39[1]:387). The golden rule of Mt. 7:12, for instance, is the nucleus of the natural law:

> It was certainly clever of Christ to state it this way. The only example He sets up is ourselves, and He makes this as intimate and possible by applying it to our heart, our body and life, and all our members. No one has to travel far to get it, or devote much trouble or expense to it. The book is laid into your own bosom, and it is so clear that you do not need glasses to understand Moses and the Law. Thus you are your own bible, your own teacher, your own theologian, and your own preacher. The way

He directs you, you only need one look at them to find out how the book pervades all your works and words and thoughts, your heart and body and soul. Just guide yourself by this, and you will be more wise and learned than all the skill and all the books of the lawyers. (*LW*, 21:236-237)

Get used to looking at this saying once in a while and practicing it on yourself. Thus in your whole existence, you have a daily sermon in your heart. From it you can easily learn to understand all the commandments and the whole Law, how to control and conduct yourself personally and socially. On this basis you can decide what is right and wrong in the world. (*LW*, 21:239)

It is evident that Luther's emphasis is on creation over against revelation when it comes to the source for ethical recognition. He is not, however, unaware of the problems connected to this view. In the first place, the biblical clarification of the natural law is necessary because of the distorted human rational capacities after the fall. Luther admits that the natural recognition of God's will is sometimes complicated because it is distorted by human sin.[6]

A basic tension in Luther's theology is at this point revealed as a distinction between soteriology and ethics. The ethical demands are to be recognized by reason and logic because they belong to the sphere of creation. When it comes to soteriological issues, however, reason can not inform the human mind at all. Therefore, the revelation of Christ is necessary for soteriological reasons, but not for ethical. By making this distinction, Luther protects his soteriology from the danger of being confused with works and merits, but at the expense of placing ethics outside of the sphere of soteriology. Luther's solution of this dilemma is his doctrine of the two kingdoms, which affirms obedience to God by faith in the spiritual kingdom, and obedience to God by the works of the stations in the secular kingdom.

Wesley

Wesley rejects the idea that ethical recognition ever is "natural." He replaces the notion of natural law with his doctrine of prevenient grace. By grace, God illuminates the corrupted human mind and gives the human being power to receive God's salvation as well as to recognize God's will in ethical issues. A sinner who is yet not reborn and a sanctified Christian is both dependent on God's grace and the illumination of the Spirit in their ethical and religious recognition. His doctrine of prevenient grace is an epistemological principle of his theology; by grace every person is able to recognize the will of God.[7]

Comparison

Because of Luther's distinction between creation and salvation he is forced to introduce the idea of two different sources of moral and religious recognition. The Christian is informed about salvation by God's spirit. In the secular world the human reason and civil laws are the sources for moral reflection.

To Wesley, there is no distinction between spiritual and secular. Salvation is received as an unmerited gift by grace through faith, but he in contrast to Luther presumes that Christ's righteousness is not only imputed but imparted as well. He thereby displaces Luther's doctrine of *simul iustus et peccator* and its double set of sources for religious and moral recognition, with his doctrine of sanctification, which implies the actual regeneration of the sinful human being to the image of God.

Basic Structures of Theological Systematics

It is generally agreed among the scholars that neither Luther nor Wesley aimed at creating a new theological system. This does not at all imply that their theologies lacked systematic structures. On the contrary, they both suggested alternatives to the classical scholastic theology with their own ways of doing theology.

Luther

Luther formed his own theology on the basis of his experiences as a monk working on his salvation. His failure gave him the idea that the works as ordered by the Roman Catholic church could not merit salvation. His exegetic studies taught him that salvation could only be bestowed upon a person by God's grace on the function of Christ's atoning sacrifice. He therefore offered new answers to old questions; however, his theology never revolted against the Western paradigm. Furthermore, he accepted its deductive methods. As he replaced the pelagian soteriology of the church with his own evangelical orthodoxy, he neither disputed fundamentally the basic issues nor the methods of Western theology.

Luther's basic theological issue is how to be saved from the guilt of sin. His theology therefore starts with the human fall in sin. Within the limits of this world, salvation is the same as forgiveness, the remission of sin for Christ's sake. For the purpose of fighting against sin God ordered the two kingdoms, the secular kingdom to avoid social chaos, and the spiritual kingdom to offer the grace of the gospel. The salvation cannot be unfolded as a full reality until the next world. For this reason, the gospel is given for comfort in the time of waiting for Christ's *parousia*, the final judgment, and the final salvation. In the present, salvation is forgiveness and hope for a future redemption. Salvation is restricted to God's imputing the blessings of Christ's atoning death to the sinner in justification. The sinner remains a sinner, though a forgiven sinner (*simul iustus et peccator*), as long as she or he lives. God's work *for* the sinner is the focus.

Consequently, Luther's system of theology was established around two doctrines as its foci, the doctrine of justification by faith alone and the doctrine of the two kingdoms. My aim in this chapter is not to enter the discussion of Luther's theological doctrines. I will restrict my presentation to observations made on their implications in his Sermon on the Mount discourses.

Luther's interpretation of the gospel is determined by the doctrine of justification by faith alone. The precepts of the Sermon on the Mount are compatible with this interpretation only if the doctrine of the two kingdoms is inserted as an additional hermeneutical key. If not, he faces two problems, one soteriological (the risk that the works of the Sermon on the Mount may be taken as meriting), and one practical-sociological (the risk that the meekness prescribed will turn the order of the social establishment into chaos). The doctrine of the two kingdoms provides a theological understanding of the problem of the double righteousness of the Christian, thus making an actual righteousness in the secular society possible without threatening the soteriological system. For that reason, a distinction between the two kingdoms is as necessary as the distinction between law and gospel. These two distinctions actually depend on each other, because both are related to Luther's dual image of God, God as creator and God as savior. Without the doctrine of the two kingdoms, the structure of Luther's theology will fall to pieces.[8]

It is indeed significant that Luther makes the doctrine of the two kingdoms a criterion of doctrinal orthodoxy, which is evident from his exegesis of the false prophets of Mt. 7:15-20 (*LW*, 21:255-256). The consequence is that the doctrine of the two kingdoms has basic functions in Luther's soteriology. It indicates how fruits of faith may be expressed without being confused with merits for salvation.

(1) Justification by Faith Alone

The doctrine of justification by faith alone is the chief article of faith with which the Christian church stands or falls, Luther affirms, it is not simply one doctrine among others (Althaus 1981:224). He establishes this doctrine directly related to Paul's discussion on justification (Rom. 1:4 ff.), conceiving justification as God's act imputing the righteousness of Christ to the sinner. God sees the sinner as one with Christ, and his righteousness is therefore imputed to the sinner. The basis is entirely God's grace, the human person is completely passive in this process; this concern he stresses to the point of admitting the predestination of the justified sinner. Justification is received as God grants faith to the sinner, in which Christ makes himself present to the person.

It is basic to Luther that the incarnation of Christ comes as a result of the human fall in sin, and that is an act of eschatological significance. He conceives Christ as the perfect man, the beginning of the new creation. The justified sinner will always remain a sinner, however a forgiven sinner restored to the favor of God. She or he will until the next world be daily judged by God and be in daily need of God's gracious forgiveness, and is therefore conceived as a person who is *simul iustus et peccator*. A battle between divine and diabolic forces will be fought in the mind of the Christian; to Luther, Paul's conflict-ridden person in Rom. 7:14ff. is an accurate description of the normal Christian.

Though Luther insists that the human will is in bondage and not at all free, he also points out that justification is a process of liberation. The Christian is completely free, and this freedom should be understood as a freedom for ministry.

(2) The Two Kingdoms

A number of scholars agree with Spitz in his statement: "Luther's teaching concerning the two kingdoms,[9] church and state, is certainly one of the most discussed aspects of his theology" (Spitz 1985:126; cf. Bornkamm 1966:1). Because this doctrine is so fundamental to his Sermon on the Mount hermeneutics, I will summarize some observations as follows:

(a) *The doctrine of the two kingdoms is necessary for Luther's conception of the world and society in light of the gospel.* The doctrine of the two kingdoms provides theological legitimacy to the civil society and to the life in the secular kingdom. The secular is not inferior to the spiritual, for it has its independent authority. For that reason, an office is good because it is instituted by God and belongs to God. On the other hand, his eschatological basis of the doctrine of the two kingdoms as presented in his discourses on the Sermon on the Mount has such an future orientation, that his ethical responsibility of the Christian to society almost disappears. He affirms:

> For here [in the Sermon on the Mount] and in all His sermons He [Christ] is not talking about the way a secular person should work and live, but about the way you should live uprightly before God as a Christian, as one who does not have to be bothered

about the world, but who should direct his thoughts exclusively to another life. (*LW*, 21:171)

(b) The doctrine of the two kingdoms is not a social-ethical program to Luther but rather a hermeneutical model for a theological interpretation of human existence. The doctrine of the two kingdoms is a basic hermeneutical model for the Christian life towards God, on the one hand, and toward the world, on the other. The goal of the doctrine is to explain the two sets of relationships within which the Christian has to live. He has clearly established the doctrine of the two kingdoms as a decisive element of his concept of orthodoxy.

The Christian life in the world, consequently, is a life toward God. Nowhere in his Sermon on the Mount discourses does Luther describe explicitly the life of the offices and stations as a calling, but this idea is presupposed (*LW*, 21:209, 269). It is evident, for instance, in his exegesis of purity of heart (Mt. 5:8), in which he rejects the outward holiness of monasticism because the purity of heart is to live a holy life in the midst of the world (*LW*, 21:32). In doing this, the spiritual kingdom is brought into the secular sphere of existence by the faithful life in the stations. To serve God and do one's duty in the stations are the same (*LW*, 21:188).

(c) *The concept of the two kingdoms is relational and not institutional.* The division between the two kingdoms runs through the midst of the Christian life (*LW*, 21:23-24). The kingdoms should not be identified with any outward institutions of the kingdoms. For instance, the Church is not the same as the spiritual kingdom, and the state is not the same as the secular kingdom. As a social institution the Church belongs to the secular kingdom, too. And the state serves the spiritual kingdom when it protects the pure preaching of the word and the right administration of the sacraments. Luther's concept of the two kingdoms is therefore primarily relational and not institutional. It is the spiritual, personal, and social relations of the Christian that determine whether the spiritual or the secular kingdom is at work. When the Christian as a person is related to God and God alone, the spiritual kingdom is in function (*LW*, 21:45, 113). When the Christian is related to social structures in some way, such as to superiors or to subjects, the secular kingdom is in function. A Christian prince, therefore, "must not rule as a Christian ... his princedom does not involve his Christianity," Luther insists (*LW*, 21:170). It is the relations of the prince which determine which set of regulations is involved:

> Insofar as he is a Christian, the Gospel teaches him not to do injury to anyone and to put up with any injury or injustice that may be done him. That, I say, is the Christian's duty. But it would not make for a good administration if you were to preach that sort of thing to the prince. This is what he has to say: "The status as a Christian is something between God and myself. It has its own directions about how I should live in relation to Him. But above and beyond this I have another status or office in the world: I am a prince. The relation here is not one between God and this person, but between me and my land and people. "The issue here is not how you should live in relation to God, what you should do and what you should tolerate for yourself. That applies to you as a Christian person who is not involved with land and people. But this is not the business of your princely person, which should not do any of these things but should think about the administration of the government, the maintenance and protection of justice and peace, and the punishment of the wicked. (*LW*, 21:170)

Luther distinguishes between the Christian as a person or individual, and her or his office (*LW*, 21:83, 99, 106-108, 109-110, 278). The result is, "every human being on earth has two persons: one person for himself, with obligations to no one except to God; and in addition a secular person, according to which he has obligations to other people" (*LW*, 21:171).

(d) *The spiritual and secular kingdoms have each their own set of norms and regulations.* A crucial point to Luther is that the Sermon on the Mount is not to be taken as a law for the secular kingdom, it is entirely designed for the spiritual kingdom. In general, the commandments of the Sermon on the Mount are to be considered as revealed precepts for pious Christians only. For these reasons the morality of the Sermon on the Mount cannot be applied to the secular world, because the society is populated by non-Christians and bad Christians as well as pious Christians.

In the secular kingdom the norms are not given by a special revelation but by the natural law, the human reason and conscience, and the civil law or "the law of the emperor." Because of human sin, these laws are protected by the use of punishment, "the sword." There are, however, examples of natural law in the Sermon on the Mount, too. Luther refers to the Golden Rule (Mt. 7:12) in particular as a significant expression of the natural law (*LW*, 21:236-237, 239). That the civil law may be formulated in ways contrary to God's will is not anticipated by him, however, he conceives ungodly and unjust rulers to be a possibility. He affirms, "everything that the government orders is right, and God confirms it ... when they keep within the limits of their office and do what the law demands, this is all God's business" (*LW*, 21:277-278). The ethical codes to which the Christians are subject, are, therefore, not only different, they are also contradictory:

> So you see that each status or office is properly distinguished from the other; and yet they are combined in one person and, so to speak, are contradictory. At one and the same time, the same person is supposed to tolerate everything and not to tolerate it, but in such a way that what is distinctive about each office is applied to it. That is, as have been said above: If it involves me as a Christian, I should tolerate it; but if it involves me as a secular person—an obligation not between God and me, but between me and my land and people, whom I am commanded to help and protect with the sword that has been placed in my hand for that purpose—then my duty is not to tolerate it, but the opposite. Thus every human being on earth has two persons: one person for himself, with obligations to no one except to God; and in addition a secular person, according to which he has obligations to other people. (*LW*, 21:170-171)

The practical effect is that the social and political life is withdrawn from the authority of God's special revelation in Christ.[10]

(e) *The doctrine of the two kingdoms presupposes a third kingdom, namely, the evil kingdom of the devil.* The two kingdoms are established by God as instruments in God's metaphysical struggle against the devil (cf. Moltmann 1985:177). The secular kingdom exists for the preservation of the created nature and the order of human society, the spiritual kingdom exists for the salvation of humanity. From time to time Luther as another hermeneutical presupposition of his Sermon of the Mount discourses describes the kingdom of the devil also. The kingdom of the devil is actually implied all the way through his exegesis. On interpreting the Lord's prayer, he admonishes to pray for protection "against all the power of the devil and his kingdom" (*LW*, 21:146). The same is basic to other of his works. In *Temporal Authority: To What Extent It Should Be Obeyed* he states: "Christians are always a minority in the midst of non-Christians. ... The world is un-Christian" (*LW*, 45:92), and, "The world is God's enemy" (*LW*, 45:113). In these passages he refers to the world as the kingdom of the devil and not as the secular kingdom of God. The use of harsh means for the protection of the world against the devil is essentially good. The kingdom of the devil threatens to make chaos in God's created order. Luther therefore attempts to avoid everything that may lead to social confusion and chaos (*LW*, 21:171, 185-186). This results in dominant values of social stability and immobility. To remain in one's station is a primary ethical virtue to a Christian (*LW*, 21:274), and to transgress the limits of the stations is explicitly condemned by Luther (*LW*, 21:267).

(f) *Luther's acceptance of the use of violence to protect society is in harmony with the intentions of the law of retaliation.* The actual effect of his teaching is that the permit to use violence is limited to certain offices with public recognition. Persons who are offended should not defend their rights, but leave the punishment to the civil offices established and authorized for this. The tenor of Luther's exegesis is, therefore, in harmony with the mosaic law of retaliation (Ex. 21:24). The point of the Mosaic law is not to accept murder, but to limit the use of vendetta. The law of retaliation basically restricts the spiral of violence. It is significant at this point, that he continuously admonishes the Christian civil servants to execute the power of the sword without hatred and revenge in their hearts (*LW*, 21:113) but with love and meekness (*LW*, 21:30).

(g) *The doctrine of the two kingdoms should not be understood as two separate rooms of existence but as two modes of God's governing activity.* The activation of one kingdom does not exclude the actual significance of the other, especially when the secular kingdom is dominating. The two kingdoms are interrelated (*LW*, 21:138). In his exegesis of judging (Mt. 7:1-6), Luther affirms the judging in discussion as belonging to the secular kingdom, however, "What we are discussing here is another kingdom, one which in no way weakens or annuls the other, namely, the spiritual existence among Christians" (*LW*, 21:211). In situations when the conduct of the Christian is regulated by civil law, he still expects the Christian to act as a Christian, namely, with love, and without hatred and revenge in the heart. From a practical-ethical point of view, the concept of love is crucial as the concept binding the two kingdoms together. Any situation in the secular kingdom should be met in the spirit of Christian love, including situations that require violence from certain authorities and stations (such as, for instance, judges, hang-men, soldiers, and fathers).[11] It ought to be noted, however, that love, to him, is not a part of the divine revelation. It is primarily a part of the natural law (cf. above), for even "nature teaches—as does love—that I should do as I would be done by (Lk. 6:31 [Mt. 7:12]). ... Love and nature law may always prevail" (*LW*, 45:128).

Though the two kingdoms are distinguished because their duties are different, they should be conceived as modes for ministries rather than power structures. In *Temporal Authority: To What Extent It Should Be Obeyed*, Luther affirms: "Their government [the princes' and the bishops'] is not a matter of authority or power, but a service and an office, for they are neither higher nor better than other Christians" (*LW*, 45:117).

(h) *The holder of office is the visible image of the invisible God.* Luther's exegesis of the Sermon on the Mount reveals that all holders of office are the representatives of God. By stating that the secular prince is God's representative in the world (*LW*, 21:148, 171-172), he follows the tradition of Origen. Moltmann's description is, "the one almighty emperor is to a pre-eminent degree *the visible image* of the invisible God. His 'glory' reflects God's glory. His rule represents God's rule. Hence the one God is venerated in him. He is not merely regent; he is the actual lord and possessor of the imperium" (Moltmann 1981:195).

(i) *The doctrine of the two kingdoms excludes antinomian interpretations of the Christian faith because of its emphasis on works in the secular society as necessary fruits of faith.* If a Christian does not perform good works, that person cannot be a good Christian according to Luther's Sermon on the Mount discourses. There are sayings by him indicating that if a person is justified by faith, that person is a good Christian and cannot be a bad one. From a strictly soteriological position, however, one may come to the opposite conclusion, that all human works are sinful.[12] In his interpretation of the Sermon on the Mount he clearly excludes the possibility of antinomianism in full harmony with his *Against the Antinomians* (1539; *LW*, 47:99-119). A characteristic pattern is that he states that the fruits of faith are to be exercised within the limits of the secular stations and offices. A connection between the doctrine of justification by faith and the doctrine of the two kingdoms is implied at this point. If faith is right, it will create fruits, which are "doing good works, [and] fulfilling your station of office diligently and faithfully" (*LW*, 21:205; cf. 232). Fruits in the secular kingdom is actually a proof of doctrinal orthodoxy (*LW*, 21:226, 254, 255-256).

(j) *The vocations and stations in the secular kingdom provide the normal expressions of a Christian's fruits of faith.* A good Christian, who is justified by faith, will carry fruit. Over and over again, Luther affirms that the primary fruit is love. Faith forms love, and love directs the Christian's attitudes to the world. To him, the Christian life is hidden in the world behind the various masks of the stations (*LW*, 21:170-171). The difference between the Christian and the non-Christian is not the actual outward behavior or office, but the attitudes of love motivating the life in the world. In his understanding, the fruits of faith can be expressed in no better way than through the civil offices and stations. The Christian calling is, par excellence, to fulfil the civil obligations with loyalty and fidelity (*LW*, 21:26, 257, 260-263).

Luther's interpretation of the meaning of the parable of salt and light is an example in this respect. He understands the salt and the light as metaphors for the preaching of the pure gospel performed by preachers who are properly called. His hermeneutics is governed by the bifocal structure of his soteriology, the doctrine of justification by faith and the doctrine of the two kingdoms. The salt is the criticism of false doctrine and the light is the preaching of orthodoxy.

Wesley

Wesley's soteriology is based in creation; it starts with creation and ends in the new creation. This does by no means imply that he overlooks the reality of sin. On the contrary, he insists on an entire corruption of humanity following the fall. However, he also establishes that God's immediate reaction on the fall is to meet humanity with grace. For this reason he regards human history from the fall to the consummation to be covered by God's covenant of grace.

While Wesley generally accepts the Calvinist view of human depravity, he does not give up the free will. By replacing the Calvinist doctrines of predestination and irresistible grace with the doctrine of prevenient grace,[13] he unites the doctrines of total corruption and free will. His solution of the dilemma of total corruption presupposes that the concept "natural man" (after the fall but before the grace of God) is a theological construction, however not an actual reality. There is no person who is completely left without the grace of God unless having rejected God consciously, for all human beings are under the influence of God's grace. This is the theological basis on which he interprets the Sermon on the Mount as the way of salvation, making human response to God's grace possible.[14] Implied in his theology of salvation is, therefore, an expectation of human response to God's grace (for instance, *WW*, 1:614, 662-663).

As observed in the exegetic discussions of the Sermon on the Mount, Wesley does not limit his understanding of sin to the personal, individualistic level. He also brings social, natural, and cosmological perspectives into the concept of sin. Because Wesleyan scholars traditionally have emphasized the legalistic aspect of sin as transgression of the law, they have failed to acknowledge that in his insistence on the corruption of the totality of human nature there is a natural, a personal as well as a social aspect. The total human life is distorted after the fall and not only the relation between God and humanity. Consequently, a personal and individualistic concept of salvation is too limited.

To Wesley, then, the nature of salvation is to be a re-creating work of God that is not limited to the daily sustaining of creation but the actual transformation of the corrupted human, social, and natural world after the ends for which they were created from the beginning. Salvation is no formal matter limited to a change of relationship between God and the believer. It implies also an actual change of the believer as well as a change in the believer's attitudes to the world. In Watson's words: "Rather than a preoccupation with sin, the emphasis was on a growth in grace. Rather than a probing for hidden faults, the openness of fellowship was a means of mutual guidance toward a perfection of love, in which, as he put it, "the chains were broken ... and sin had no more dominion over them" (Watson 1985:119).

Wesley in his sermon on Mt. 5:17-20 expounds the relations between law and gospel as a relation of commandment and promise (for instance, *WW*, 1:554). On this basis, he sent the people of the Methodist revival into the society as ambassadors for Christ. The new relationship to God causes a new relationship to the neighbor as well as to the human society and the created world. As creator as well as savior of the world God authorizes Christians to be stewards. The believer who is reborn is a new creation according to 2 Cor. 5:17. In Wesley's view, Paul here combines the creating and the saving work of God:

> [2 Cor. 5:]*17.* [translated:] Therefore if any one *be* in Christ, *there is* a new creation: the old things are passed away; behold, all things are become new. [Commented:] *There is a new creation*—Only the Power that makes a world can make a Christian. ... *All things are become new*—He has new life, new senses, new

faculties, new affections, new appetites, new ideas and conceptions. His whole tenor of action and conversation is new, and he
lives, as it were, in a new world. God, men, the whole creation,
heaven, earth, and all therein, appear in a new light, and stand
related to him in a new manner, since he was created anew in
Christ Jesus. (*NT-Notes*, 657)

It is obviously invalid to separate Wesley's ethics from his soteriology. A distinction can be made only for theoretical reasons.
But the dynamic of his systematics overshadows this abstract distinction. The dynamic is indicated by these movements:

The Dynamic Movements of Wesley's Systematics			
	Starting-point	**via**	**Goal**
Soteriology	Creation	Salvation	New creation / *shalom*
Salvation	The sinner	Imputed and imparted right-eousness	Sanctified to the image of God
Discipleship	Command	Promise	Imitation of Christ

Wesley's concept of soteriology as a theology of the way from
creation to the new creation is basic to his understanding of how
salvation is experienced in this world and of discipleship. A sinner
experiences justification as the imputation of Christ's righteousness and the impartion of it as well, as she or he is sanctified to the
image of God by the Spirit of God. The Wesleyan ethics is conceived as a dialectics between the commandment of the law and
the promise of the gospel, leading to the imitation of Christ empowered by the Spirit.

Comparison
While Luther in the Western tradition conceived a new doctrinal
structure in order to overcome the theological confusion of his
time, Wesley is more in harmony with the Eastern tradition conceived as a way, the way of salvation, beginning in creation and

ending in the creation. For that reason his starting-point becomes different. To him, the end of the way determines where to begin. Because the end is the restoration of cosmos in a new heaven and a new earth, the beginning is not in the fall in sin (as indicated by the Western paradigm of theology) but in God's goals for creation (as indicated by the Eastern paradigm of theology). In his view, salvation conceived as a way comprehends an inaugurated fulfillment of God's eschatological promises of redemption of nature, persons, and social structures. To turn to God and accept salvation in Christ therefore implies a divine work that is not restricted to justification but that imparts fresh divine life in the human life as well. Without neglecting what God works *for* the person his focus is on God's work *in* the person, who thereby becomes a new creation, the first fruit of the consummation. Sanctification actually implies the participation in God's life that is made concrete as love fills heart and life.

Illustrating differences of theological emphases, it could be said that Luther is primarily preoccupied with the issue of orthodoxy, and Wesley with orthopraxis. But this does not imply that Luther is uninterested in orthopraxis, nor Wesley in Christian doctrine. Their emphases are, however, different. Luther's main concern in his Sermon on the Mount discourses is how to judge about right doctrine, as observed from his founding of the office of the preacher as the proper doctrinal judge and from his discussion of the relations between natural and special revelation or recognition of God's will. His aim is to reestablish pure doctrine, from which ethics may be deduced. Wesley's concern is how to imitate the love of God in a way that creates justice among people in the world as God's love and peace is materialized. His aim is more to establish theology by use of inductive method on the basis of experience.

Wesley combines a deep pessimism of human capacities with an optimism of grace. The fall caused a total corruption, and no human being is able to work one's own salvation. But there are no limits for the transformation of a sinner who is open to the grace of God. Basic to his soteriological considerations is his anthropology which differs from Luther's in particular by a more pessimistic valuation of the natural condition of humanity after the fall. While Luther distinguishes between the foreign righteousness and the proper righteousness of the person, presupposing that the fall affected the spiritual kingdom only, Wesley declares the corruption to be complete, naturally, morally, and spiritually as well as politically.[15]

The basic presuppositions for the theological paradigms of Luther and Wesley, causing most of the differences which are observed, is that they conceive the relationship between creation and salvation differently. They both have a soteriological focus on their interpretations. But this difference in method makes them establish almost opposite systematic approaches to the biblical scriptures. Luther's "reformatory discovery" of salvation by faith on the basis of Christs's merits and not on human works creates the need of another doctrine to take care of the significance of works. The doctrine of the two kingdoms with its distinctions between spiritual and secular is meeting this need. Basic to this distinction is another between salvation and creation. A consequence is that the Christian "in person" and the Christian "in office" must relate to contrary rules for conduct. Wesley, who starts with the experience of God's grace in the midst of human life, has no need to distinguish between salvation and creation. On the contrary, his interest is to demonstrate how salvation is experienced right in the middle of the total human existence.

The nominalist theology, in which Luther was trained, indicates that God changes the names of things, however, leaving the things themselves untouched (Jennings 1990:142). This philosophical basis makes his doctrine of the two kingdoms and his *simul iustus et peccator* anthropology possible. Wesley does not accept this kind of nominalist theology. He insists that God really does transform things, too. To him, Luther's concept of a Christian as totally a justified person and totally a sinner at the same time, implies a phantom grace. It is like saying that a resurrection leaves the dead in their graves. God is saving the whole person and not in principle only, as God's salvation is implemented in secular life no less than in spiritual life. He does not reject that sin prevails in the justified nor in the sanctified Christian, but he rejects that sin is in power.

Peder Borgen (1981a:102-103) suggests that Luther at this point reduces the authority of the scriptures to personal and individual spheres of life. This position is illustrative of a Wesleyan response to Luther's doctrine of the two kingdoms. According to this tradition, salvation applies to the entire human and social life, making life an integrated whole. From this point of view Luther's theology focuses on the fall as well as the forgiving part of Christ's work, however, without taking the fullness of Christ's recapitulation of humanity completely into consideration. It therefore leaves the sinner in the tension between sin and forgiveness. In addition the Christians are two persons in one, a "Christian-in-person" (spiritually) and a "Christian-in-office (secularly), who are ruled by norms that quite often are contradictory. Consequently, it opens up to a disintegrated life.

Salvation As Experienced in This World

It is evident that to Luther no less than to Wesley, their soteriologies are determining the structure of their theological systems. To both, the basic issue of theology is salvation. The meaning of salvation, however, they conceive differently, particularly when present salvation is discussed.

Luther

Luther in his Sermon on the Mount discourses defines soteriology as a set of doctrines. Salvation is particularly dependent on a pure doctrine of justification by faith. If this is not right, and a person confuses God's grace with human merits, salvation is distorted. The Christian religion is essentially hidden in the heart of the Christian; for this reason ethics is—in principle—distinguished from soteriology. Christian ethics belongs to the secular kingdom and is informed by the natural law as revealed in the human conscience and in the laws of the emperor.

It is important to clarify Luther's exact meaning of his paradigm, *simul iustus et peccator*, which is his "nutshell description of the Christian believer's state as a redeemed man" (Hall 1963a:182). According to Hall (1963a:176), this notion is both ambiguous, paradoxical, and contradictory. Augustine imagines that the two realities of righteousness and sinfulness may exist side by side in the Christian, who is *both* righteous *and* sinner, or, *partly* righteous and *partly* sinner. Luther does not accept this understanding but sharpens the paradox by making the Christian *totally* righteous and *totally* sinner. To make this paradox workable, he has to declare that while sin is an empirical fact, the righteousness of which he is here speaking is a reality of a different sort. It is a righteousness which actually is not the human's own, but the foreign righteousness given by God's grace.[16]

Luther's frequent references in the Sermon on the Mount discourses to the imputed righteousness of Christ as the alien righteousness of the believer indicate that salvation within the limits of this world is conceived in a principled way only. It is obvious that the doctrine of predestination is a fundamental presupposition to his exegesis and to his theology. His terminology used for descriptions of salvation points to the same conclusion. Predestination is a logical consequence of his non-pelagian soteriology. More clearly than in his Sermon on the Mount discourses, this idea is expressed in *The Bondage of the Will*, which he himself regarded to be his most important work (*LV*, 4:116). He here postulates that grace and free will are irreconcilable. There is a logical development from the doctrine of original sin to the doctrine of predestination: "Grace is preached, therefore free choice is abolished; the help of grace is commended, therefore free choice is destroyed" (*LW*, 33:244). This is a logical conclusion of the Augustinian tradition. In the following statement he confirms how deeply rooted he is in this tradition:

> I will not here elaborate the very strong arguments that can be drawn from the purpose of grace, the promise of God, the meaning of the law, original sin, or divine election, any one of which would be sufficient by itself to do away completely with

free choice. For if grace comes from the purpose or predestination of God, it comes by necessity and not by our own effort or endeavour, as we have shown above. (*LW*, 33:272)

Luther's doctrine of justification by faith is crucial to his understanding of the Sermon on the Mount. Without it, the soteriology of the Sermon on the Mount would be "hopelessly heretical" and useless for Luther's purposes (Windisch 1951:6).

Wesley

As a consequence of Wesley's inaugurated eschatology it is essential to establish salvation as a present reality. Grace is conceived as a transforming power and as an offer of actual change. Salvation is free, full, and present, implying the experience in the world of "heaven below" (*WW* 1:474).

Another concern of Wesley is to establish an evenly balanced relationship between justification and sanctification. In the following statement he is critical to the one-sidedness of Lutheran and Roman Catholic theology. Although he also presents a rather triumphalistic interpretation of the Methodist contribution to the history of theology, his theological position is obvious. Justification should be organically united to sanctification:

> Many who have spoken and written admirably well concerning justification had no clear conception, nay, were totally ignorant, of the doctrine of sanctification. Who has wrote more ably than Martin Luther on justification by faith alone? And who was more ignorant of the doctrine of sanctification, or more confused in his conceptions of it? In order to be thoroughly convinced of this, of his total ignorance with regard to sanctification, there needs no more than to read over, without prejudice, his celebrated comment on the Epistle to the Galatians. On the other hand, how many writers of the Romish Church (as Francis Sales and Juan de Castaniza in particular) have wrote strongly and scripturally on sanctification; who nevertheless were entirely unacquainted with the nature of justification. Insomuch that the whole body of their divines at the Council of Trent in their *Catechismus ad Parochos* totally confound sanctification and justifi-

cation together. But it has pleased God to give Methodists a full and clear knowledge of each, and the wide difference between them. (*WW*, 2:505-506)

Comparison

The differences between Luther and Wesley ultimately depend on two different paradigms for theology. Luther represents a soteriological and ethical system that is bifocal, because it circles around the doctrine of justification by faith alone and the doctrine of the two kingdoms. The first doctrine safeguards God's exclusive role in salvation. Because salvation is dependent on God's grace for Christ's sake and not on human merits, it is necessary to address the need of works in daily life. The second doctrine safeguards precisely that. By its distinction between the spiritual kingdom, in which God reigns with the gospel, and the secular kingdom, in which God reigns with the imperial law and its sword, he manages to hold creation and salvation separate without removing the world from God's reign. The basis of his interpretations of the Sermon on the Mount is almost exclusively the dichotomy created between the first two articles of faith, God as creator and savior. The work of the Spirit is not considered to the same extent.

Wesley establishes a theological unity of creation and salvation. God's salvific work is simply the continuation of the creation of cosmos, and salvation will end up in the creation of a new heaven and a new earth. He sees no contrariety between God's creating and saving works. Most significantly, his theology of salvation therefore begins in creation and ends in the new creation. God saves the world to fulfil the goals of creation and—primarily—not to overcome the fall in sin. The incarnation of God in Christ is not a necessity because of the fall but because of God's love in creation. A table may illustrate the differences between the theological systems of Luther and Wesley at this point; it is evident that they are rooted in different traditions:

	LUTHER (Western tradition)	**WESLEY (more of Eastern tradition)**
Starting Point in the Past	The human fall in sin	God's goals for creation
Salvation in the Present	The gospel is for comfort in waiting for heaven	The new birth: Inauguration of the new creation
Future Salvation	Entire change; complete break with the past	Completion of salvation as begun in the present

Because of Luther's roots in the Western and Augustinian tradition, his theology regards the Christian life under the perspective of *simul iustus et peccator*. The proper way to meet the promise of God's grace is to come back to the cross every day as a guilt-stricken sinner begging for pardon. By necessity, the righteousness of this world has to be distinguished from that of salvation, and the life of the Christian has to be viewed according to two different sets of rules, one for the secular life, another for the spiritual. Because the creation is conceived as completed before the fall, the orders of society are considered an eternal social structure to be sustained until the consummation.

For Wesley, the Christian life is viewed under the perspective of growth in grace, leading to a growth in love. The problem of guilt is solved—in principle—at the moment of justification, and the proper way of dealing with God's grace is now to live in it by being transformed by it. He agrees with Luther that the righteousness of the Christian actually is imputed by God from the beginning, but once given to the sinner it becomes real in the reborn believer. Describing the Christian religion as a way he implies that, to be a Christian means to be on this way, or rather to belong to the "way." This implies an existence that engages the person totally and therefore leads to a completely new life. His concept is similar to St. Luke's concept of the first Christians in the book of Acts, describing them as those who were or belonged to "the way," *tes hodou ontas* (Acts 9:2, cf. 19:9, 23; 22:4; 24:14, 22). Considering the fact that the term "Methodists" etymologically is derived from the Greek *met' hodos*, the preposition *meta* denoting to be in company with *tes hodou* or "the way," it is astonishing that Wesley never used this similarity in the Methodist propaganda.[17]

To Luther, a Christian exists in two spheres of life, one spiritual and one secular. In the spiritual kingdom, where God's saving work is performed, the gospel rules. According to it, the Christian is seen as completely righteous because Christ's righteousness is imputed by grace through faith. At the same time the Christian in this world remains a sinner. She or he is *simul iustus et peccator*, which implies that the Christian is saved from the guilt of sin but not from its power. In the secular kingdom, in which God sustains creation by help of the ordained stations and orders and where the persons are enlightened by civil law and human reason, the Christian may be actually righteous.

While Luther identifies Christ as the beginning of the new creation, Wesley teaches that the sanctified Christian should be considered to be a new creation. The consequences are dramatic. Luther conceives the Christian life as a life in comfort and hope for a future redemption, while Wesley encourages the people to expect an actualized redemption in the present.

Theologies of the World

Luther and Wesley both affirm that the world essentially is God's creation unceasingly sustained by the grace of God. The natural world is the foundation of human and social life. God's world is, however, threatened by sin and diabolic powers. It is therefore essential that the Christians engage their strength and powers on God's side in the struggle against evil.

Luther

As Luther sees the human world, it is ordered by God in certain social structures. These structures have an ontological significance to the world, for which reason they must be maintained. They cannot be evil, because they are created by God, and any person who intends to modify the social system is an evil-doer. Sin is primarily a personal concept, with secondary effects on social structures.

To Luther there are three basic orders which must be viewed as part of the created order (Althaus 1978:36-42; Harran 1985:210, cf. *WA*, 39^2:175): (1) Ministry (*status ecclesiasticus*) includes ecclesiastical orders but also administrators of the community chest, and their assistants and servants. (2) Marriage and economy (*status economicus*) includes the everyday life in the family, business, and economy; widows and unmarried persons are included along with parents, children, and servants. (3) The secular authority (*status politicus*) includes princes and lords, judges, civil officers, notaries, and their servants. These orders do not constitute separate compartments. No sphere is superior or inferior to the others, however, he sees the *status economicus*, with the family at its core, as the basis for the entire system. All persons are holding offices in one or more of these basic stations—a person can be both a judge and a father at the same time—for all of human life is comprehended in them. Precisely as holders of offices they are serving God and cooperating in the sustenance of creation, without which chaos would take over. He affirms that God declares, "these stations must remain if the world is to stand" (*LW*, 13:358). The preservation of humanity depends on them. For this reason his ethics of love becomes specific in the life of the stations. To love God and the neighbor means to be a faithful holder of one's office.

According to Luther, God has ordained the stations and the offices of the secular kingdom in a hierarchical structure for the sustenance of creation. When it comes to ethics, the basic Christian virtue is, therefore, to be faithful in the stations. The future eschatological character of the Christian existence gives him reason to reinforce the life in the worldly stations by identifying it with the calling of God. He is positive that the disloyalty to the social structure will inevitably lead to chaos. The authorities therefore have the "sword" as the main instrument for the protection of God's creation. The Christian's struggle against the evil powers therefore has, consequently, an essentially static character. Luther's reasoning explains why the attitudes recommended by the gospel in the Sermon on the Mount (meekness, non-resistance, enemy love, etc.) cannot be practiced in the secular kingdom. Human sin will take advantage of attitudes like that whenever practiced in the secular world. His dualism is coming to the surface here as well: The world is God's, but it is also the world of Satan.

Regarding social justice, Luther has the same concern for a just distribution of property as has Wesley, but the means they advise in order to accomplish this goal, differ. While Wesley trusts the regenerated Christian to take care of that, Luther affirms this task to be the obligation of the civil authority. When Luther here advocates social stability by strengthening the social hierarchy, the reason is not to protect the privileges of the rich. His conviction is that the hierarchical structure of society is the best protection against injustice.

The problem since Luther has been that, whenever his doctrine of the two kingdoms has become basic to the social structure of a nation, the rich classes notoriously have tended to forget the inherent social responsibilities of the doctrine, using their power to protect their privileges rather than to supply the poor. There is good reason to dispute, on historical grounds, his optimistic hope that "everything will be in good shape" if only the distinctions between ranks and persons are maintained. He should not be judged on the basis of modern social and political science, but on the basis of the insights of his own time. However, when the application of the doctrine is distorted by the privileged classes, it is possible to attack their positions on the basis of the doctrine of the two kingdoms, because its ethos is characterized as solidarity, and not selfish exploitation.

Wesley

Wesley's theology of the world is conceived dynamically. By the transformation of the believer, God creates channels for redeeming and renewing love to the world by creating new persons. Wesley at this point expects sanctified Christians to fight against evil in the personal, social, and natural spheres of life in the world. He anticipates the social and natural world to be transformed no less then the life of the persons. The instruments used for social change are, for instance, legislation, tax regulations, education, health work, employment, communal industries and trade, programs for human rights, waging of peace, etc. He interprets the search for "mammon" as an expropriation of the property of the creator. Proper stewardship is, on the other hand, "the practice of the agents of the new creation. It is giving creation back to the Creator" (Jennings 1990:154).

The concern for the poor is, to Jennings, actually fundamental to Wesley's theology of salvation: "our final relation to God depends on our relation to the poor" (Jennings 1990:130). The lack of concern indicates that a right relation to God, which is the basis of salvation, is not established. Christ preached a message of grace to the poor (Lk. 4:18), and Wesley makes the relation to the poor a criterion of salvation.

Comparison

Luther and Wesley both have a dualistic view of the world. After the fall, God's world is continuously invaded by Satan and ruled by diabolic and divine powers fighting against each other in a struggle which will not end until the *parousia*. In this struggle the Christian plays a role according to both.

To Wesley, the idea of the world as an arena of God's prevenient grace is dominating. Like Luther, he realizes sin in the world as a reality that needs to be limited. But different from Luther he realizes that sin can prevail in the social structure as such. Inspired by the words and deeds of Christ and also of the Hebrew prophets he identifies the social and economic systems of the nation as ungodly and corrupt. Most directly he addresses this concern on the issue of slavery, however, it is implied in his discourses on the Sermon on the Mount as well.

Fruits of Faith and Discipleship

Luther and Wesley equally affirm that the works of the Christian should be regarded as fruits of faith. They both quote Gal 5:6, affirming that "faith works by love". Christian ethics is primarily an issue of how to make love real in the world. When they come to the practical ethical level, however, they depart. While love, to Luther, is an ethical category, Wesley tends to understand love as coming out of the new being in Christ.

Luther

Luther makes ethics dependent on his doctrine of the two king-doms. Love should prevail in both kingdoms. The primary loyalty is always to God, however, in the secular kingdom the ethical norms come from reason and the imperial law, and the models for ethical conduct are implicit in the offices of society. According to him, this is not contradictory to God's will, for God has created the social order. The social offices and the hierarchical structures of society are sacred, because they are parts of God's created order. Consequently, the Lutheran ethics of calling is intimately connected to the obedience to superiors, taking responsibility of subjects as like a loving father, etc.

As observed, Luther in his interpretation of the Sermon on the Mount distinguishes between a specific Christian ethics for the Christian-in-person in the spiritual kingdom and a general ethics of the secular kingdom. The spiritual ethics is regulated by Christ's teachings and by the Sermon on the Mount in particular. In general, Luther affirms an absolutist interpretation of the precepts of the Sermon on the Mount as a basis for this specific ethics. The Christian-in-person does not become angry (*LW*, 21:83), does not look on the other sex with lust (*LW*, 21:86), does not divorce (*LW*, 21:94), does not swear (*LW*, 21:99), does not defend him- or herself when being attacked (*LW*, 21:108-109), gives money willingly when being asked (*LW*, 21:117), and loves her or his enemy (*LW*, 21:123). These regulations do not apply for the secular life, however, which is regulated by reason and the imperial law. For instance, in spite of his absolutist attitudes against divorce, Luther leaves this issue to the civil law, because marriage according to him is a secular arrangement. Though it is in opposition to his exegesis (*LW*, 21:96) he accepts divorce if the civil law accepts divorce.[18] In his discourses on the Sermon on the Mount he is more concerned to affirm what kind of ethical teaching the Sermon on the Mount is not, than to give explicit examples of the ethic in the spiritual kingdom. He is also concerned to describe the implications of the ethics of the secular world. His own ethical teaching is more directed to the affairs of the world.

There is no agreement among Lutheran theologians on the issue of the basis for Luther's ethics. According to Forell (1964:63) all ethics for Luther is based upon God's forgiveness of sin and not specific scriptures, neither the ten commandments nor the Sermon on the Mount. This is true of individual ethics as well as of social ethics. The point of reference for his ethics is always the relationship which follows from faith in God through the forgiveness of sins in love.[19]

On the issue of the place of ethics within theology, Luther's soteriology devalues good works (Rublack 1985:251). In his Sermon on the Mount discourses he is concerned more with the issue of right doctrine than with the issue of life (cf. Althaus 1981:420). The motive for this is to protect the doctrine of justification by faith alone. Within a soteriology hostile to works, there is little room for ethics. Such a soteriology could lead either to antinomianism or to a platonic rejection of works as a lower activity of human existence. But none of these is typical for his exegesis in general. In his interpretation of the Sermon on the Mount, his soteriology is combined with his theology of creation in a way that elevates works to be a significant part of God's calling. One example which he uses is the pious housewife:

> So a wife who is pious and faithful in her marriage can claim and boast that her station is commanded by God, that it is supported by the true, pure, and unadulterated Word of God, and that it heartily pleases God. Hence her works are all good fruit. Good should not be judged and evaluated on the basis of our

suppositions but on the basis of what God says and pronounces to be good. (*LW*, 21:262-263)

It can be affirmed, therefore, that "Luther changed the frame of reference: it was God's command to work: there was to be no longer any pious escape into monastic leisure: work and its profits had to be used to help the neighbor [*WA*, 10^2:236, 227]" (Rublack 1985:265). In his 95 Theses already (1517), he disconnects works from salvation and connects them with neighborly love instead:

> Christians should be taught that he who gives to the poor or lends to the needy has done better than by buying indulgences; Because a work of love increases love and by it a person becomes better, but by indulgences he does not become better, but only freer from penalty. (*LW*, 31:202)

Luther presumes these fruits of faith and Christian love to show up in two ways, first, in the spiritual kingdom, as the Christian-in-person's observance of the precepts of the Sermon on the Mount and, secondly, in the secular kingdom, as loyalty and obedience in the orders and stations.

To Luther, a general ethics instructed by the natural law, the imperial law, and human reason is applied to the secular kingdom, while the ethical commands of the gospel (the Sermon on the Mount) are not applicable to the world. The general ethical law is still considered to be the law of God and therefore valid for Christian ethical conduct. His general ethics is, consequently, an ethics of creation. He affirms, however, that the commands of the Sermon on the Mount are applicable to the Christian-in-person in the spiritual kingdom, which is ruled by a different and Christological ethics.

Luther's doctrine of salvation presupposes that works of love will follow as fruits of faith. This observation is supported by newer research. For instance Rublack maintains that Luther, since the early 1520s, "more and more stressed this second dimension of his theology of faith, namely works of love, the consequence of faith. His sermons addressed to his Wittenberg congregation strongly emphasize this aspect" (Rublack 1985, 266). On the other hand, he carefully distinguishes between works as fruits of faith in the two kingdoms. In the secular kingdom, they are described as obedience and faithfulness to the stations and offices. Because the civil orders are regarded to be a part of God's will of creation, a loyalty to the social system is presupposed, and this implies social stability as a fundamental virtue. In the spiritual kingdom, no stations and offices are implied. The love of God reigns in it without limitation. The ethical challenges are restricted to the Christian's relationship to the neighbor, however, both the Christian and the neighbor have to be "in-person." If one of them is "in-office," the secular kingdom is involved, and the ethics, consequently, are informed by the natural and imperial law. By this distinction, Luther eliminates God's love as a dynamic factor for social change. It remains as a nice disposition of the heart.

The result becomes an ethic which implies deep concerns for other people, however, without possibilities for efficient change of the causes of poverty, such as political oppression, and other social evils. Rublack's analysis of the significance of poor relief in the Reformation movement indicates that its philanthropy was carefully limited by Luther's ethics and the doctrine of the two kingdoms: "The poor were not to be advanced to rise in social status, but rather they were assisted to be able to stay where they were, in their station in life—just above a minimum standard of living. As there was no achievement by works in religious matters, so Luther did not advocate any achievement, advancement or improvement in social status or wealth" (Rublack 1985:266).

Luther's theology of creation and his theology of salvation both restrict the application of ethics. His theology of creation is a safeguard against applying the ethics of the Sermon on the Mount in the secular kingdom. His theology of salvation is a safeguard against using the ethics of the Sermon on the Mount in social relationships.

Wesley

Wesley by no means finds the ethical norms in the social structure; this structure rather should be altered for the reconstruction of a more just society. He finds the norms for ethical conduct in biblical models, like the examples of Jesus. More specifically, he points to scriptures like Lk. 4:18-19 (Is. 61:1-2), which he actually uses as a model for his own work as the leader of the Methodist movement (Meistad 1994:163-175). In his Sermon on the Mount discourses he also points to Mt. 25:34-40 as a model for activities like feeding the hungry, clothing the naked, etc., and to 1 Cor. 13 to indicate love as the basic ethical attitude.

The general frame of reference for Wesley's theology is the biblical vision of *shalom*. This is evident right from the beginning of his exegesis of the Sermon on the Mount (*WW*, 1:474). The dynamics as well as the goal of his soteriology is inspired by this notion. So is his ethics.

To be saved is to be regenerated by the same divine powers which rule the history of the world. It is also to be transformed toward the goal which God has set for creation and salvation. Salvation implies no less than the participation in the divine nature (2 Pet. 1:4), offered by grace through faith.

Christian ethics is, consequently, the fruits of this faith, or, the life in righteousness, joy, peace, and love (*WW*, 1:481). Through sanctified Christians God's love is given channels from the world of God to the natural, human, and social world, for the promotion of God's peace (cf. *WW*, 1:544).

It has been established that the distinction between Wesleyan theology and ethics is to some degree artificial. Ethical conduct is simply the human response to the experience of God's grace, and its spiritual energy is the experience of God's love. Love is the key concept describing the Christian's new *being* in Christ. Love is also the key concept expressing the Christian's *doing* in Christ (Hulley 1988:64-65, 68-69). Wesley affirms: "Immediately after faith He exhorts love and good works" (*NT-Notes*, 365). Provided that "self-realization" is understood religiously and not humanistically, Cannon's characteristics of Wesleyan ethics as "an ethics of self-realization" (Cannon 1946:236) is right to the point.

Wesley's concept of *imago dei* as the center of the perfection of the Christian is important to keep in mind, too. By using this concept as the goal of sanctification he roots deeply his theology of the way of salvation in the Eastern theological soil. On the one hand, this concept refers to the regeneration of the individual believer. On the other hand, it is frequently neglected that the concept of the image is not understood merely oriented from the individual by the Eastern fathers; it rather is a corporate concept. What follows from this observation is that the image of God concept is related to both personal and social regeneration, or, the personal regeneration finds its proper expression in the social and communal life with the neighbor as its object.

What kind of ethical conduct is expected by Wesley? His general answer is, works of love to the neighbor. He gives a number of suggestions exemplifying relevant expressions of love. One primary example is the "general rules," in which the Methodists are exhorted to do no harm, to do all possible good, and to use the means of grace (*WW*, 9:69-75). His intention is never to give detailed rules as casuistic regulations for all generations. They are suggestions for his contemporaries, not prescripts for all times and situations. However, he expected the rules to be observed in the actual context of the 18th-century. His emphasis is on discipleship interpreted dynamically and historically, not on doctrinal and ethical formulations: "It was in reaching out to others, in the working out of faith, that Wesley saw the true purpose of the church" (Watson 1985:20).

It has been demonstrated that Wesley emphasizes spiritual and ethical vitality rather than dogmatic orthodoxy. He establishes the primacy of love as the foundation of ethics. The love to the neighbor is the proper response of God's love to humanity as revealed through the Atonement of Christ, "[1 Jh. 4:19:] *We love him because he first loved us*—This is the sum of all religion, the genuine model of Christianity," he affirms (*NT-Notes*, 915). His aim is not to provide a dogmatic system but to indicate his solution to the basic question: What is the Christian religion? In his answers he focuses on the transforming experience of God's love rather than on theological abstractions; by "experience" he understands actual change of the person rather than emotions. No less than Calvin he insists that God is the supreme cause of salvation.

In the estimation of a British social-historian, Wesley "began a new chapter in the religious, social and educational history of the working class. This coincidence in time of Wesley and the Industrial Revolution had profound effects upon England for generations to come" (Trevelyan 1965:362). Contrary to other renewing movements in 17th-and 18th-century Britain, "Methodism, on the other hand, renewed the self-discipline and the active zeal without which religion loses its power and forgets its purpose; and this new evangelism was allied to an active philanthropy" (Trevelyan 1965:356). According to Trevelyan, "Methodism" is a term describing self-disciplined philanthropy rather than the Wesleyan movement.[20] This estimation says much about the way the Wesleyan-Methodist movement is viewed in the social history of Britain.[21]

Wesley was no social-ethicist in the modern sense of the word. The conditions for a modern social-ethical system did not exist at this time. On the other hand, he should be valued as a significant transitional person in a number of respects:

(1) Wesley's theology of salvation is clearly developed within a cosmological and social context.

(2) The effects of salvation are supposed to work within a social context. Significant goals of Wesley's theology of salvation are the establishment of flexible social ministries that are changing with different persons and societies. The purpose of these ministries is personal and social change.

(3) Wesley demonstrates a growing understanding of the necessity of changing society by the help of laws and other kinds of regulations no less than through the conversions of people.[22] Political actions are understood as fruits of faith and resulting from the love of the new being in Christ.

(4) Wesley points to specific goals for social change, for instance, a just distribution of social benefits like money, food, clothes, labor, and education, and he underscored human rights for

slaves and women. These goals are dominant to his interpretation of the Sermon on the Mount already.

(5) Wesley appeals for government action to secure human rights of the citizens (cf. *Thoughts on the Present Scarcity of Provisions*; *WW-J*, 11:53-59; cf. Hynson 1985:385).

(6) Wesley criticizes social evils in his own time and advocates for social reform, for instance, prison reforms.[23]

(7) Wesley accepts the possibility of social change by help of civil obedience and other similar actions when parliamentary methods are tried but do not succeed. He never, however, accepts the use of violence.[24]

A problem that contemporary Wesleyan theologians are much concerned with is that Wesley states that holiness is nothing but love. He affirms, but without being too specific, that holiness and love need to be expressed personally as well as socially. Some scholars object against him that he gives too few explicit instructions indicating how holiness ought to be applied to social structures in particular. My answer to this objection is that his vision of *shalom* as applied to this world actually functions as his model for social holiness, and he expects the same to be true for his successors. What brings peace with justice and happiness to people is the expression of love to one's neighbor. Because the work of Christ is essential to the establishing of love and peace, he may develop ethical implications from the doctrine of atonement; a person who is transformed by God's love will live in love and materialize love to her or his surroundings. The cosmological and social effects of atonement (Eph. 2) form a program for ethical action for him. Hassing concludes his discussion on Methodism and society: "Not only could the individual be regenerated and approach the image of God, society could also be transformed to approach the standards of the Heavenly City," and, Methodism was able "to produce a vision of a transformed world" (Hassing 1980:250-251). This is possible because of the eschatological nature of Wesley's soteriology. Based on his doctrine of the kingdom of God he presupposes sanctification to unfold in the midst of the world, thus transforming individuals, societies, and created nature.

To Wesley, Christian ethics is essentially trinitarian in its foundation but universally directed to persons, societies, and creation. The life in faith is personal and social at the same time. Religious experiences are personal but not individualistic, as genuine religious expressions reach out beyond the person to the social sphere. Ethical recognition and action are empowered by the Spirit. Wesley is concerned to regard every commandment of the law in light of the evangelical promises.

Wesley's conclusions lead to opposite results at this point. His approach to ethics is closely connected to his soteriology without being limited to strictly personal relationships. It involved social evils, too. As a matter of fact, Wesley's soteriology works toward the restoration of the corrupted cosmos conceived in its most comprehensive way. His theologies of creation and salvation, therefore, equally emphasize the transformation of individuals, societies, and nature, according to God's love.

Comparison

Luther and Wesley likewise reject antinomianism by referring to the fruits of faith as being the natural expression of the life in God. These fruits of faith are works of love to the neighbor. Wesley affirms readily Luther's description that the Christian lives in God by faith, and in the neighbor by love. The faith of the Christian will necessarily form love.

They strongly agree, too, that true faith will carry fruits. They as strongly disagree in their views on how fruits are coming forth. Because of Luther's distinctions between creation and salvation, secular and spiritual, law and gospel, his position is that the fruits of salvation first and foremost show forth in the secular kingdom. He is therefore thinking in terms of proper citizenship rather than discipleship. The fruits of faith (of the spiritual kingdom) will show up in the stations and offices of the world (the secular kingdom). The Christian is primarily accountable to superiors (who are in God's place) or subjects (to whom the Christian is in God's place), however, in cases of conflict of consciousness God should be obeyed rather than an evil superior. Wesley is thinking in terms of discipleship. To him, there is no distinction between spiritual and secular spheres of life. No part of the life in the natural or the social world is outside of the spiritual world. The Christian is therefore accountable to God alone.

Wesley anticipates that the fruits of faith be expressed to the Christian's neighbor. Luther will affirm this way of phrasing it. However, the difference is that Luther has his emphasis on the sustaining of the social structure while Wesley's emphasis is on the neighbor as person independent of any social structure. To Luther, the need to maintain the authority of civil orders and stations is always primary to the care of persons. To Wesley, the concern of persons is the primary concern.

Luther and Wesley agree that Christ in the Sermon on the Mount does not intend to lay the foundations of a general and universal ethics. The ethical implications of the message of the Sermon on the Mount are, consequently, directed to faithful Christians and not to humanity in general. Luther is positive that it is possible to develop a general Christian ethics which is universally applicable, because this general ethic is nothing but the content of the natural law. Wesley rejects the notion that Christian ethics ever can be the same as a universal ethic. His point is that the nature of Christian ethics is to be a discipleship in conformity to Christ, based upon the redemption of God and the outpouring of the Spirit and divine love to the human person. On the other hand, he opens up for a universal ethics based in his doctrine of prevenient grace, admitting that God's grace is at work in every person. The main point remains, the ethical basis is grace and not reason.

What is described as "Christian ethics" in Wesley's understanding, Luther would wholeheartedly affirm as the special Christian ethics, that is, for Christians-in-person and in the spiritual kingdom. He would reject the social implications of Wesley's "Christian ethics," however, indicating that Christian ethics by definition has to be an individual ethics.

From a Wesleyan point of view, the great weakness of Luther's ethics is that the special Christian ethic is withdrawn from the secular kingdom. Luther affirms, of course, that love is to reign in the heart of the Christian who is serving in office, but this cannot inform ethical conduct. The actual behavior is to be directed from reason and not from the inspiration of the Spirit. In this way, the most powerful ethical force seems to be lost. The promise of blessings offered by Christ is not received in its fullness.

To Luther, Wesley's ethical orientation is a result of a fundamental confusion between law and gospel, and the two kingdoms. It is therefore dangerous for the stability of a society. A Christian who is observing in society the admonitions of Christ for love of enemies, does not take the sin of the evil-doer and the demonic nature of his or her action into consideration. The evil powers will, therefore, inevitably lead to chaos.

In my opinion, it is not proved that Christ's interpretation of the antitheses of the Sermon on the Mount is impossible as guidelines for social action. Political leaders, who have tested them out in practice, have done so with considerable success. Outstanding examples are Mahatma Gandhi, Martin Luther King, Jr., and Nelson Mandela. On the other hand, the use of violence never has secured a lasting peace.

Discussion and Conclusions

In the science of religion a distinction often is made by priestly and prophetic functions (Clark 1969:291-306). The main concern of the priest is to preserve the values of the past chiefly by providing for them institutional and confessional expressions, while that of the prophet deals more with the rightness of living in a social context.

Luther's theology has a predominantly priestly orientation. His aim is the reconstruction of pure doctrine. His role in the history of Christianity should be characterized as prophetic. But once pure doctrine is reestablished, the aims of his theology are to conserve this doctrinal purity. For this reason his theology is priestly oriented. Because he relates theology to society, his theology also leads to the conservation of social structures.

The historical development of Lutheran theology confirms the general conclusion that the aims of this theological tradition are conservative. Certain theological manuscripts written by Luther and others have been given the status of confessional books or symbols that offer an authoritative expression of pure Christian doctrine. The Lutheran *Book of Concord*, first published in 1580, acknowledges nine symbolic books: The Apostles' Creed, the Nicene Creed (325; with the *Filioque*), the Athanasian Creed (451), Luther's two catechisms (1529), the Augsburg confession (*Confessio Augustana*, drawn up by Melanchthon, 1530), Melanchthon's Apology of the Augsburg Confession (1530), Luther's *Articles of Schmalcald* (1537), and *The Form of Concord* (1577). Next to the three ecumenical creeds the *Confessio Augustana* is generally esteemed to have a more prominent status than the other symbolic books (*Creeds* 1:221-222). Since the completion of the Confession, the primary enterprise of Lutheran theology has been to watch over the purity of doctrine according to this norm[25] of the theological issues of the 1500s. It accepted Luther's conservative view on the social structures, too. Not until this century, and particularly after the Second World War have Lutheran theologians managed to loosen the ties between theology and a hierarchical view of society.

Wesley's theology has a predominantly prophetic orientation. He makes theology an analytical instrument of a given historical and social situation, and a program for action as well. His aim is not to restore pure doctrine but the way of salvation as revealed in the Sermon on the Mount. This salvation is experienced in an actual human and social context. For this reason the theological issue is to analyze the meaning of salvation in light of this specific context. Because salvation is interpreted as a process toward full participation in God, change is made a significant category in Wesleyan theology. Social and political realities are supposed to change no less than persons, as God's will for salvation includes the entire cosmos.

These assessments do not intend to criticize Lutheran conservatism and hail Wesleyan social activism; the opposite could be argued for. I have observed that the average British Methodist largely gave up Wesley's radical approach to society when Wesley was still alive. He taught his followers to earn, save, and give away money, however, as they became rich, they abandoned the latter. As a result, the end of his theology was abandoned as well, as it aimed to make the believer an instrument for the salvation not of the individual soul alone but also of the world. For this reason Methodism—in the eyes of Wesley—has been corrupted as it has become a respectful and affluent church, made up by members with success.

This analysis of Luther's and Wesley's interpretations of the Sermon on the Mount has generally verified that: *Martin Luther's and John Wesley's interpretations of the Sermon on the Mount are different, because (1) their theological bases are paradigmatically different, and because (2) historical situations are different. The two paradigms are distinguishable by their various interpretations of the relationship between creation and salvation ("law and gospel"), the nature of salvation, and the nature of eschatology.*

Though Luther and Wesley interpret a number of details in a similar way, their basic understandings of the Sermon on the Mount are not easily compatible. The main reason for this is that their hermeneutics reveal that two different theological paradigms are basic to their exegeses. A direct comparison of Luther's and Wesley's interpretations is not possible without taking into consideration the foundational structures of their theologies. Detailed exegeses which appear to be similar or different, must be valued within the broader context of the systematic theological structures basic to the exegesis.

A summary of some theological variables will indicate how similarities and dissimilarities reveal the significance of acknowledging that Luther's and Wesley's theologies essentially belong to different paradigms. Their different ways of conceiving the relations between salvation and creation are probably the most fundamental reason for their theological concerns and, consequently, how their theologies are structured.

I have summarized the variables discussed in this chapter in the table below. The idea is to present how the theologies of Luther and Wesley are different in their presuppositions and implications.

That their theologies represent two different paradigms is evident from this table.

Summary of the Theologies of Luther and Wesley		
	LUTHER	**WESLEY**
Theological roots	*Western* tradition.	Predominantly *Eastern* tradition.
Eschatology	Future eschatology: The cosmos will be renewed after the final judgment.	Inaugurated eschatology: Renewal of persons, societies, and nature in the present.
Creation and salvation (gospel and law; epistemology)	Creation and salvation are separate works of God—God's sustenance of creation in the secular world and salvation in the spiritual world. Human reason and imperial law informs the ethos of the secular kingdom, and the gospel in the spiritual.	Creation and salvation are fundamentally united—salvation is a new creation of nature, humanity, and society. Human reason is corrupt but is informed by God's prevenient grace to recognize the calling to salvation as well as ethical norms.
Basic structures of theology	Based in the fall in sin: 1. The doctrine of justification by faith alone. 2. The doctrine of the two kingdoms.	Based in God's goal for creation: The way of salvation (from creation to the new creation).
	Theology and ethics are deduced from biblical sources; the Christian life is based in true (doctrinal) faith.	Theology and ethics are induced dialectically, from the actual new life given by God's grace, to the biblical sources.
Salvation as experienced in this world	Christ's righteousness imputed by grace through faith.	
	The Christian is saved from the guilt of sin and remains *simul iustus et peccator*.	The Christian is saved from the guilt as well as the power of sin and is renewed to the image of God (righteousness is imparted, too).

Summary of the Theologies of Luther and Wesley		
	LUTHER	**WESLEY**
Theologies of the world	Theological dualism: The world is arena of a metaphysical struggle between God and the devil.	
	Practical dualism: The evil threatens the order of society and the Christian's contribution is faithful loyalty in the stations, thus preserving the social structure against chaos.	Practical monism: Social structures are sinful, too, and the Christian's contribution is to remodel the world according to God's will.
Fruits of faith and discipleship	Works of love	
	Ethics of creation: The commandments of the Sermon on the Mount are not applicable to this world. Obedience to superiors and social structures: citizenship in civil orders and stations.	Trinitarian ethics: The commandments of the Sermon on the Mount are applicable to this world. Obedience to Christ: discipleship conceived as the imitation of Christ.
Conclusions	No human nor social change in this world: The Christian remains *simul iustus et peccator* and the social structures are created orders that should not be changed.	Human transformation after the image of God as well as social change according to God's vision for the world (*shalom*).

NOTES

[1.] See Wesley's, *The Present Scarcity of Provisions* (WW-J, 11:53-59); cf. his letter to the editor of the *Lloyd Evening Post* (WL, 5:350-354).

[2.] Wingren (1971:121-124) discusses what happens when a third use of the law, bringing Christian life into conformity with the law, is brought into Lutheran theology. If the full recognition of the law is made dependent on the revelation of Christ, as Calvin states (for instance, *Institutes*, 1:360; cf. Krusche 1957:184-190, 288-289; Niesel 1957:88-89; Jacobs 1959:108-109), the universal character of the law diminishes. The function of the law is then easily twisted to moralism, and it is used for the discrimination between better and worse people instead of providing a basis for solidarity. Wingren indicates that Reformed theology o the law has influenced Lutheran thought increasingly since the time of the *Concord formula*, and he argues that the notion of the true Church within the state church parish, made up by baptized but unconverted people, creates a need for criteria for judging between persons, which is foreign to Luther's thought. At the same time, the emphasis on the re-creating function of the law in the secular kingdom is displaced by the works of the regenerated believer, or the third use of the law. Luther's confidence in the civil person as a valuable citizen is thereby lost. According to the pietist, the human being has to be converted to be fully accepted. The gospel is not the enemy of the law any longer as it is to Luther. The conflict between the two is turned into a harmony. Wingren concludes that the focus is removed from the living and re-creating God to the final product, the perfected believer. Rather than being used in the constructive building of society, the civil law in the pietist state church system is used to protect orthodoxy against heresy.

According to Wingren (1971:129), the age of pietism represents a victory of Calvin and the spiritualists over Luther indicating that, to be a true Christian is not to be involved in secular business but to be separated from it. In Luther's theology there is a movement from the spiritual to the secular. In pietist theology the movement is the other way round. Luther's ethos is secular, the pietist ethos is spiritual. He observes with regret that practically all attempts of Lutheran renewal take place as a radicalization of pietist distinctives rather than as a revival of Luther's doctrines of creation and the law. The liberal theology, Kierkegaard, Barth, the Lunda theology, "all without exceptions, are *pietist.* ... In none of these ... theologies the theology of creation plays a significant role" (Wingren 1971:131).

Wingren here expresses a concern that is equally relevant to the revival of Wesleyan theology. Its ethos is personal and social at the same time. But Methodist revival movements after Wesley, in harmony with pietist theology, have been inclined to emphasize the personal perspective over against the social. The danger of turning the third use of the law into a casuistic moralism is definitely recognizable in the history of Methodism as well (for instance, Meistad 1984:36; Cameron 1961:218). According to my opinion, pietism in this form is distorting Wesleyan theology no less than Lutheran.

[3.] Watson affirms: "Wesley placed this perfection in a doctrinal context of *accountability*. Those pressing on to perfection were to wait for the gift of the fullness of love, 'not in careless indifference, or indolent inactivity; but in vigorous, universal obedience, in a zealous keeping of all the commandments, in watchfulness and painfulness. ... It is true we receive it by simple faith: But God does not, will not, give that faith, unless we seek it with all diligence, in the way which he hath ordained' [*WW-J*, 11:402-403]" (Watson 1985:122). "For what ultimately gave Methodist discipleship authenticity was Wesley's emphasis on faith and works alike as appropriate responses to God's gracious initiatives. To the great advantage of the Christian tradition, and in spite of the uninformed invective of enemies and the well-meaning excesses of friends, he never swerved from this twofold principle: True Christian discipleship can spring only from faith received by grace; and true faith in Christ can be sustained only by obedient discipleship in response to grace" (Watson 1985:144).

[4.] See particularly, "Predestination calmly considered" (*WW-J*, 10:204-259), and, "The Question, 'What Is an Arminian?' Answered, by a Lover of Free Grace" (*WW-J*, 10:358-361).

[5.] Logan argues: "Wesley, without resorting to some Thomistic or idealistic analogy of being, is able, nevertheless, to maintain the importance of the natural law of God, and, without minimizing the sinful condition of humankind, can at the same time maintain the possibility of some knowledge of that law. A genuine social ethic will either have to affirm forthrightly or boot-leg in by the back door something that resembles a natural law argument. ... The genius of Wesley lies, not in his originality, but in the synthesis whereby he is able to hold to an 'engraced' creation, and 'engraced' reason or conscience, and the divine revelation of the holy and just law of God. In terms of recent Protestant theological debate, Wesley is no less Christocentric in his theological epistemology than a Barth or a Brunner. The knowledge of the moral God of creation is gained through the benefits of the atoning death of Christ, that is, prevenient grace. In Wesley the doctrine of creation and the concomitant natural law rest no more upon a so-called natural theology than does it rest upon such in Barth or Brunner or, for that matter, in Jürgen Moltmann. In no wise, however, does this imply a rejection of the positive, constructive role which a rightly founded natural law can play in contemporary ethical deliberation" (Logan 1985a:365).

[6.] In Althaus's words: "man's natural religion constantly distorts and falsifies his relationship to God. He is ready to serve God only to the extent that God seems useful for his own purposes. He constantly sins against the First Commandment. What Feuerbach later characterized as the essence of religion is precisely what Luther sees as the constant form of actual distortion. Godliness is reduced to a means to an end rather than being recognized and desired as the highest good" (Althaus 1981:147-148; cf. Steinmetz 1986:24-27).

[7.] "In traditional theological terminology, this interpretation holds that God is first in the *ordo cognoscendi* as well as the *ordo essendi*. This is the consequence of holding, in accord with the Augustinian tradition, that God is the ground of all knowledge as well as the ground of all being. Knowledge of God, like the being of God, is not derived from knowledge of other things. This is the reverse of the traditional cosmological theistic proofs which begin with empirical knowledge of the world, or some aspect of it, and infer God's existence from this prior knowledge. The doctrine of prevenient grace as a principle of knowledge affirms that one's experience of the world raises the question of God because one is already aware of an impinging Presence. Knowledge of God is not secondary and inferential, but primary and direct" (Dunning 1985:54).

[8.] In Bornkamm's words: "Luther's two kingdom doctrine is so completely woven into his total theology that one can follow the threads in all directions: to his view of God, his doctrine of creation and preservation of the world, his Christology, his eschatology, his concept of the church, of reason, of justice, and so forth" (Bornkamm 1966:29). Bornkamm adds the following comment on the significance of Luther's interpretation of the Sermon on the Mount for his doctrine of the two kingdoms: "Thus Luther's doctrine of the two kingdoms cannot be understood without relating it to his understanding of the Sermon on the Mount" (Bornkamm 1966:30).

[9.] Luther's doctrine of the two kingdoms was in general supported by the Swiss Reformers, however, it was not given extensive significance by them. For instance, only two pages are dedicated to this doctrine in the 1,521-page edition of Calvin's *Institutes* (1:847-849); Calvin seems to be more apt to limit the doctrine to the personal domain than Luther: "There are in man, so to speak, two worlds, over which different kings and different laws have authority" (*Institutes*, 1:847). This statement supports Luther's concern that the division between the two kingdoms is to be found right in the midst of the life of any Christian.

In Barth's criticism of the doctrine he attacks Calvin and Zwingli as well as Luther for lack of Christological emphasis (Wingren 1971:113-114).

[10.] "It would be wrong to conclude from this, however, that the political implications of Luther's position in our present situation are what we now ordinarily think of as conservative. For him, it will be recalled, the proper ordering of the earthly kingdom cannot be deduced from Scripture. We must draw on reason and experience, not on the Bible, in attempting to discover the policies most likely to promote our neighbors' welfare in a given set of circumstances. Our world, however, is so vastly different from that of the 16th-century that it becomes idle to speculate regarding what he might now favor. His traditionalist conservatism is neither capitalist nor socialist in the modern senses of those terms. Both the major ideologies of the contemporary world are in a sense secularized forms of the messianic radicalism which Luther fought in the Left-Wing Reformation ... in any case he would insist that Christians are free to differ in politics" (Lindbeck 1985:16-17).

[11.] Spitz summarizes Luther's position: "To the extent that they are not fully sanctified, Christians, too, need the restraints of the law [...]. The law of love (*lex charitatis*) must be the guiding principle for the Christian citizen and love of neighbor should motivate people to public service" (cf. *LW*, 45:103-104). "The law of love should be the guiding principle of those in authority, but the government or state is not of itself a Christian authority. ... This view marks a distinct break with the medieval papal theory that the legitimacy of a government depends upon its subordination to the spiritual sword as embodied in the pope. Christian rulers should model their behavior after Christ and perform works of service and love toward their subjects. / Luther rejected any conception of the state as representing naked power lacking an ethical base and indifferent to the love of people or responsibility to God. He opposed all purely naturalistic accounts of the origin of government and of its legal foundation, for government is God's creature and ordinance. Good positive laws are rooted in a law which is inherent in human nature, but this law is not merely naturalistic but is theonomic, having a divinely obligatory character. From the Stoics to the end of the 18th-century the concept of natural law was generally understood to mean a body of principles which, resting on a divinely implanted endowment of human nature, underlie all good ethical precepts, just laws, and sound political institutions. This natural law (*lex naturae*) for Luther is a natural ethic as present among all peoples in all times, though not to be confused with a rationalistic-Enlightenment or democratic-revolutionary national law concept. ... Luther repeatedly identifies natural law and the law of love: 'Thou shalt love thy neighbor as thyself'" (Spitz 1985:142-144).

[12.] Steinmetz (1986:112, 124) attacks Reinhold Niebuhr for this conclusion and points to what is a common problem in the interpretation of Luther's doctrine of the two kingdoms, namely, that the kingdoms ought to be linked tightly together. If they are separated, the doctrine of the two kingdoms undercuts the ethical struggle for social justice; however, when the two kingdoms are held together, "it furthers that search [for social justice] by making the protection of the weak and innocent through the power of the state a function of that love of neighbor which faith spontaneously awakens" (Steinmetz 1986:125). He emphasizes the sayings of Luther underlying the importance of good works in the life of faith. What Christians are freed from is not good works "but false opinions concerning them [that they are meriting]. Christians are called to live in Christ by faith alone and in the neighbor by works of love. They do not perform good works in order to be justified but because they already are" (Steinmetz 1986:119). He quotes Luther for support: "I will do nothing in this life except what I see is necessary, profitable and salutary to my neighbor, since through faith I have an abundance of all good things in Christ" (Steinmetz 1986:119).

[13.] Watson (1985:39) observes that Wesley on this point "was primarily indebted to the English Protestant Tradition, which had resisted the radical Augustinianism of the continental reformers on the question of freedom of the will and irresistible grace."

[14.] Holifield formulates Wesley's position: "Wesley never elaborated a systematic theory of ethics, detached from broader theological assertions. When he addressed ethical issues or reflected on the ethical implications of eighteenth-century science, he returned always to a doctrine of creation and a distinction between two dimensions of God's graciousness. These dimensions Wesley called—using familiar and traditional Christian language—prevenient and sanctifying grace. His combination of the themes of creation and grace shaped his ethical vocabulary and permitted him to incorporate into his moral thought two themes that have often seemed to stand apart in Christian theology: love and law. The highest ethical possibility was the life of love. But Wesley never assumed that a loving disposition alone ensured morally appropriate behavior: Christian ethics required also the structure and wisdom of rules and laws" (Holifield 1986:109-110).

15. "Wesley operated with a tripartite understanding of the *imago Dei*: the natural image ('a picture of His own immortality; a spiritual being endued with understanding, freedom of will, and various affections'); the political image ('the governor of this lower world, having 'dominion over the fishes of the sea, and over all the earth') and the moral image ('righteousness and true holiness' [cf. Wesley's sermon no. 45, 'The New Birth,' *WW*, 2:188]). The pervasiveness of sin means that all three facets of the image are affected, corrupted, and distorted. In particular, however, the moral image has been turned completely from relationship with God and the divine law to the human self and a law-unto-ourselves. Somewhere Albert Outler has observed that while Wesley believed in total depravity, he did not believe in tee-total depravity. The image was defaced and severely distorted, but it had not been totally destroyed. Yet, even granting this qualification, the sinner still cannot discern the law of God" (Logan 1985a:365).

16. Hall is critical of Luther's interpretation of his own concept for logical reasons, because "for both [the concepts of sinfulness and righteousness] to be brought together in one statement as true and significant in respect to one and the same subject, and at the one and the same time (*simul*), it is necessary that they be clearly recognized as designations of the Christian man *seen from different viewpoints and evaluated on the basis of different presuppositions*. It is therefore absurd to couple them into a single phrase without indicating what the expressions individually signify and consequently from what standpoint they are to be seen and interpreted" (Hall 1963a:181).

17. Wesley comments on "The way" of Acts 19:2, "The Christian way of worshipping God" (*NT-Notes*, 471). To Acts 24:4 he sharply rejects that "the way" should be considered a sect: "A party or sect (so that word signifies) is formed by men; this way was prescribed by God" (*NT-Notes*, 494). This comment could be interpreted apologetically as a defence of the Methodist movement against popular accusations.

18. Althaus insists that, "Luther explicitly rejects a secularistic view of marriage." His idea, Althaus affirms, is that "Marriage is not subject to canon law and is to be regulated not by the ecclesiastical courts but by the officials of the government, that is, by the lawyers and not by the theologians" (Althaus 1978:88-89).

[19.] Forell partly bases his argument on the following quotation from Luther's comment to Gal. 5: "Afterwards, when I have apprehended Christ in faith and have died to the law and have been justified from sin and freed from death, devil, and hell through Christ—then I do good works, love God, give thanks and show love to the neighbor. But this love or the resulting works do not 'form my faith,' nor do they decorate it, but my faith forms and decorates love" (*WA*, 40^1:275, 12).

[20.] Trevelyan is so caught up with this position that he suggests the phenomenon "Methodism" actually was much older than the mission of the Wesleys, because Methodism "was a way of life devoted not only to religious observance but to self-discipline and work for others. ... 'Methodism' in one form or another inspired much of the philanthropic work of the century that ended with Wilberforce" (Trevelyan 1965:361).

[21.] Muelder offers a theological explanation: "It is well to lift up some of the Wesleyan motifs in theology which have had persistent social consequences, though it is not the function of this paper to deal with theological ethics systematically. The Wesleyan doctrine of grace is activist, personalistic, social, and perfectionist. The love of God calls forth human love for the neighbor in a universal context. When one who is converted to Christ confronts another person, no matter how wretched, one deals with such a one in a three-fold way: (a) as a person created by God in the divine image and likeness; (b) as a creature for whom Jesus Christ gave himself in self-sacrificing love; and (c) as a human being endowed with an immortal destiny, thus as a fellow pilgrim to eternal life. God is thus engaged in covenants with humankind in redemptive history, and there is no upward bound limit to human fulfillment short of the manifestation of the perfected image and likeness which all persons share with each other. The love of God includes but transcends justice; love requires justice and justice is fulfilled in love. It is inherent in the Wesleyan understanding of the kingdom of God that this is the kind of world that can be made better than it empirically is; for as God is active in love, and all God's children are to love their neighbors, so they ought to participate with a sense of self-worth in reforming society, despite their sinfulness and shortcomings. God's grace is sufficient for all; and the divine grace makes of each forgiven sinner a "somebody" equally precious in relation to every other participant in the realm of redemption. Such participation in history has radical social implications and consequences" (Muelder 1985:352).

[22.] Frequently it is stated that Wesley was a political "Tory" who supported the British monarchy. It is certainly true that Wesley rejected

Locke's position that political power comes from the people. In his tract *Thoughts Concerning the Origin of Power*, he points out that God is the only giver of power, and he explicitly rejects the idea of the people as the origin of political power: "Now, I cannot but acknowledge, I believe an old book, commonly called the Bible, to be true. Therefore I believe, 'there is no power but from God: The powers that be are ordained of God.' / The supposition, then, that the people are the origin of power, is every way indefensible" (*WW-J*, 11:47-48; cf. Hynson 1985:373). Though he never gave up this basic position on the issue of the origin of power, it is also a fact that his political attitudes to the issue of political means changed in his later years; Hynson states, concluding his fresh and penetrating studies on Wesley's attitudes to the state: "The politics of order was a constant factor for him, but there is a shift in the instrumental channels for maintaining order. From the belief in a divine monarchy to whom one offers the quiescence of passive obedience and non-resistance, Wesley moved to a firm affirmation of limited monarchy. Employing a Lockean form of the doctrine of an original compact, Wesley extrapolated a conservative, stabilized political order. ... However, Wesley seems to allow that revolution creates a political *tabula rasa* (not his term) in which persons, like the revolutionaries in America, enter into a new compact. Undergirding Wesley's concern, first through the Hanoverian limited monarchy's fight against revolution, and then, when the American revolt has succeeded, in the new providential situation in America, in his profound commitment to human rights—life, liberty, and property, and happiness which is synonymous with holiness" (Hynson 1985:374).

[23.] Cf. Trevelyan 1943:526; *WW*, 11:241. Wesley gives a number of references to prison conditions in his journal and his letters.

[24.] See my discussion on Wesley's interpretation of "On Violence (Mt. 5:38-41)".

[25.] This statement is made from a Scandinavian context, where the Lutheran churches are state churches. This privileged situation has allowed the conservative approach of Lutheran theology to remain almost undisputed. In general, Lutheran Scandinavian immigrants to the United States are also conservative theologically.

Bibliography

Primary Sources

Calvin, Jean
McNeill, John T. (ed.) (1960): "Calvin: Institutes of the Christian Religion." 2 vols. *The Library of Christian Classics*, vol. 20-21. Philadelphia: The Westminster Press.

Creeds, The
Schaff, Philip (ed.) (1983): *The Creeds of Christendom: With a History and Critical Notes*. 3 vols. Grand Rapids: Baker Book House, Sixth ed., 1931.

Fathers, The Church
Augustine: St. (1948): "The Lord's Sermon on the Mount." Translated by John J. Jegson with introduction and notes by the editors, in, *Ancient Christian Works: The Works of the Fathers in Translation*, vol. 5, Johannes Quasten and Joseph C. Plumpe, eds. Cork: The Mercier Press, Ltd.

Roberts, Alexander and Donaldson, James (eds.) (1981): *Ante-Nicene Fathers: Translations of the Writings of the Fathers down to A.D. 325*. Grand Rapids, Michigan: WM.B. Eerdmans Publishing Company. American reprint of the 1867 Edinburgh edition.

Schaff, Philip (ed.) (1981): *A Select Library of the Nicene and Post-Nicene Fathers of the Christian Church.* 14 vols. Grand Rapids, Michigan: W.M.B. Eerdmans Publishing Company.

Luther, Martin

Hjelde, Sigurd, Inge Lønning and Tarald Rasmussen (eds.) (1979-1983): *Martin Luther: Verker i utvalg* ("Martin Luther: Selected Works"). 6 vols. Oslo: Gyldendal Norsk Forlag.

Lerfeldt, Svend (ed.) (1977): *Lutherboken: Luthers liv og tanker belyst gjennom sitater fra hans verker* ("The Book on Luther: Luther's life and thoughts illuminated through quotations from his works"). Oslo: Lunde.

Luther, Martin (1981): *The Large Catechism of Martin Luther.* Translated by Robert H. Fischer. Philadelphia: Fortress Press, 1959, sixth printing.

Luther's Works (1955-). Helmut T. Lehmann, general ed. Philadelphia: Fortress Press and Saint Louis: Concordia Publishing House.

D. Martin Luthers Werke (1883-). Kritische Gesamtausgabe (*Weimarer Ausgabe*). Weimar: Hermann Bohlaus Nachfolger.

Meyer, Carl S. (ed.) (1963): "Luther's and Zwingli's Propositions for Debate: The Ninety-five Theses of 31 October 1517 and The Sixty-seven Articles of 19 January 1523." Vol. 30 in *Textus Minores*. Leiden: E.J. Brill.

Spiritual Fathers of John Wesley, and His Contemporary Interpreters of The Sermon on The Mount

The Works of James Arminius. The London Edition, translated by James Nichols and Williams Nichols, with introduction by Carl Bangs. 3 vols. Grand Rapids, Michigan: Baker Book House, repr. 1986 after the editions 1825 (vol. 1), 1828 (vol. 2), and 1875 (vol. 3).

Arndt, Johan (1881): *Sex Bøger om den sande Christendom, handlende om sande Christnes salige Omvendelse, hjertelige Anger og Ruelse over Synden, sande Tro og hellige Levnet og Omgjængelse*; Hvortil er føiet syv af den salige Mands Sendebreve samt hans Betænkning over den saakaldte tydske Theologi, hvori hans Levnetsløb og tvende Testamenter, tilligemed hans Paradis-Urtegaard ("Six Books on The True Christendom," etc. Horten: C. Andersens Forlag, printed after the first Danish edition of 1743.

Baxter, Richard (1649): *Aphorisms of Justification*. London: Francis Tyton.

Bengel, Johan Albert (1723): *Gnomon of the New Testament— with Original Notes Explanatory and Illustrative*. London.

----- (1859): *Gnomon Novi Testamenti, in quo ex nativa verborum vi simlicitas, profunditas, concinuitas, salubritas sensinium coelestium indicatur*. Tubingae: Editio tertia (First ed.: 1742).

Blackall, Offspring (1723): *Eighty Seven Practical Discourses upon Our Saviour's Sermon on the Mount*. 2 vols. London.

Bradford, John (1555): *The Writings of John Bradford, M.A., Fellow of Pembroke Hall, Cambridge, and Prebendary of St. Paul's, Martyr: Containing Sermons, Meditations, Examinations, etc.* 2 vols. Edited for The Parker Society by Aubrey Townsend. Originally publ. in Cambridge: The University Press, 1848 (vol. 1) and 1853 (vol. 2). Reprinted, Edinburgh, Scotland, and Carlisle, Pennsylvania: The Banner of Truth Trust, 1979.

Doddridge, Philip (1810): *The Family Expositor: Or, a Paraphrase and Version of The New Testament with Critical Notes, and a Practical Improvement of Each Section*. Vol. 1. London.

Edwards, *The Work of Jonathan*, with a memoir by Sereno E. Dwight, revised and corrected by Edward Hickman. 2 vols. Originally publ.: 1834, repr. from the 1974 edition. Edinburgh, Scotland, and Carlisle, Pennsylvania: The Banner of Truth Trust, 1986.

Kempis, Thomas A. (1963): *The Imitation of Christ*, translated by Betty I. Knott. London and Glasgow: Wm. Collins and Co. Ltd. / Fontana Books.

Law, William (1906): *A Serious Call to a Devout and Holy Life: Adapted to the State and Condition of All Orders of Christians.* Methuen Standard Library. London: Methuen and Co.

Peters, Edward (ed.) (1980): *Heresy and Authority in Medieval Europe: Documents in Translation*. Philadelphia: University of Pennsylvania Press.

Taylor, Jeremy (1789): *The Rule and Exercises of Holy Living and Dying*. Edited with Life, Introduction, and Notes, by F.A. Malleson. London.

Tyndale, William (1964): "Exposition upon the Fifth, Sixth, and Seventh Chapters of Matthew." *The Work of William Tyndale*, vol. 1, pp. 181-304, G.E. Duffield, ed., *The Courtenay Library of Reformation Classics*. Appleford, Berkshire, England: The Sutton Courtenay Press.

Wesley, Charles

Albin, Thomas R. (ed.) (1987): *Charles Wesley's Earliest Evangelical Sermons*. Six shorthand manuscript sermons now for the first time transcribed from the original by Thomas R. Albin and Oliver A. Beckerlegge. Wesley Historical Society.

Wesley, John

Baker, Frank (editor-in-chief): *The Works of John Wesley*. 34 vols. planned. Oxford: The Clarendon Press, 1975-. Nashville, Tenn.: Abingdon Press, 1984-.

Curnock, Nehemiah (ed.) (1938): *The Journal of the Rev. John Wesley*. 8 vols. London: The Epworth Press.

Heitzenrater, Richard P. (1984): *The Elusive Mr. Wesley*. 2 vols. Nashville, Tenn.: Abingdon Press.

Jackson, Thomas (ed.) (1984): *The Works of John Wesley*. 14 vols. Third edition complete and unabridged, reprinted from the 1872 edition issued by Wesleyan Methodist Book Room, London. Grand Rapids, Michigan: Baker Book House.

Outler, Albert C. (1964): "John Wesley." A *Library of Christian Thought*. New York: Oxford University Press.

Schoenhals, G. Roger (1987): *Wesley's Notes on the Bible*; one-volume abridgement of John Wesley's *Explanatory Notes on the Old Testament* and *Explanatory Notes on the New Testament*. Grand Rapids, Mich.: Francis Asbury Press / Zondervan Publishing House.

Sugden, Edward H. (ed.): *Wesley's Standard Sermons*. 2 vols. London: The Epworth Press. Vol. I: 4th ed., 1955; vol. II: 3rd ed., 1951.

Telford, John (ed.) (1931): *The Letters of the Rev. John Wesley, A.M.* Standard Edition, 8 vols. London: The Epworth Press.

Wesley, John (1970): *På Bibelns grund* ("On Biblical Foundation"). Wesley's Standard Sermons translated to Swedish by R. Eimir. Stockholm: Nya Bokförlags Aktiebolaget.

----- (1975): *Explanatory Notes upon the Old Testament*. 3 vols. Salem, Ohio: Schmul Publishers.

----- (1977): *Explanatory Notes upon the New Testament*. London: The Epworth Press, repr.

----- (1988): *Allein dieser Weg: Ein Gang durch die Bergpredigt*. Wesley's 13 discourses upon the Sermon on the Mount translated by Heinz Schäfer. Stuttgart: Christliches Verlagshaus GMBH.

Secondary Sources

Althaus, Paul (1978): *The Ethics of Martin Luther*. Translated and with foreword by Robert C. Schultz. Philadelphia: Fortress Press, 1972, 2nd printing.

----- (1981): *The Theology of Martin Luther*. Translated by Robert C. Schultz. Philadelphia: Fortress Press, 5th printing.

Askmark, Ragnar (editor-in-chief): *Nordisk Teologisk Uppslagsbok för hem och skola* ("Scandinavian Theological Encyclopedia for homes and schools"). 3 vols. Lund: C.W.K. Gleerups förlag, 1952-1957.

Aukrust, Tor: *Mennesket i samfunnet: En sosialetikk* ("Man in Society: Social Ethics"). 2 vols. Oslo: Forlaget Land og Kirke, vol. 1, 1965; vol. 2, 1986.

Bauman, Clarence (1985): *The Sermon on the Mount: The Modern Quest for Its Meaning.* Macon, Ga: Mercer University Press.

Bett, Henry (1937): *The Spirit of Methodism.* London: The Epworth Press.

Betz, Hans Dieter (1985): *Essays on the Sermon on the Mount.* Translated by L.L. Welborn. Philadelphia: Fortress Press.

Billing, Einar (1917): *Ett bidrag till frågan om Luthers religiösa och teologiska utvecklingsgång.* Inbjudning till Upsala universitets reformationsfest, den 31 oktober 1917 ("A contribution to the issue on Luther's religious and theological development. An invitation to the Reformation Anniversary at the University of Upsala"). Uppsala: The University of Uppsala.

Bligh, John (1975): *The Sermon on the Mount: A Discussion on Mt. 5-7.* Slough: St. Paul Publications.

Bockmuehl, Karl (1979): *Evangelicals and Social Ethics: A Commentary on Article 5 of the Lausanne Covenant.* Downers Grove, Ill.: Intervarsity Press.

Bonhoeffer, Dietrich (1963): *The Cost of Discipleship.* New York: Macmillan Publishing Co., Inc.; paperback edition.

----- (1965): *Ethics.* New York: Macmillan Publishing Co., Inc.; Paperback edition.

Borgen, Ole E. (1972): *John Wesley on the Sacraments: A Theological Study.* Nashville, Tenn.: Abingdon Press.

Borgen, Peder (1981a): "Fra Bibeltolkningens historie og aktuell debatt" ("From the History of Biblical Interpretation and Contemporary Debate"), in *Bibelen i brennpunktet for tro, historie og litteratur* ("The Bible in the Focus of Faith, History, and Literature), ed. by Peder Borgen. Trondheim: Tapir, 1981, 83-110.

Bornkamm, Heinrich (1966): *Luther's Doctrine of the Two Kingdoms in the Context of His Theology.* Translated by Karl H. Hertz. Philadelphia: Fortress Press.

Broch, Lisbeth (1954): "Fra de store oppdagelser til 1789." Bind 3 in *Aschehougs verdenshistorie: Fra antikken til våre dager*

("From the Great Discoveries till 1789." Vol. 3 in "Asche-houg's World History: From the Classic to Our Contemporary Times"). Oslo: H. Aschehoug and Co. / W. Nygaard, 1954.

Brueggemann (1987): *Living Toward a Vision: Biblical Reflections on Shalom*. New York: United Church Press, 1982, repr.

Cameron, Richard M. (1961): "Methodism and Society in Historical Perspective." *Methodism and Society*, vol. 1. New York: Abingdon Press.

Campbell, Ted (1984): "John Wesley's Conceptions and Uses of Christian Antiquity." Ph.D. dissertation, Southern Methodist University.

----- (1991): *John Wesley and Christian Antiquity: Religious Vision and Cultural Change*. Nashville, Tenn.: Kingswood Books / Abingdon.

Cannon, William Ragsdale (1946): *The Theology of John Wesley: With Special Reference to the Doctrine of Justification*. New York and Nashville, Tenn.: Abingdon / Cokesbury Press.

Carter, Henry (1951): *The Methodist Heritage*. London: The Epworth Press (Frank H. Cumbers), 1951, 2nd ed.

Cell, George Croft (1935): *The Rediscovery of John Wesley*. New York: Henry Holt and Company.

Ch'en, Jerome (1979): *China and the West: Society and Culture 1815-1937*. London: Hutchinson and Co (Publishers) Ltd.

Chiles, Robert E. (1983): *Theological Transition in American Methodism: 1790-1935*. Lanham: University Press of America.

Clapper, Gregory S. (1985): "True Religion and the Affections: A Study of John Wesley's Abridgement of Jonathan Edward's *Treatise on Religious Affections*." In Theodor Runyon (ed.): *Wesleyan Theology Today: A Bicentennial Theological Consultation*. Nashville, Tenn.: Kingswood Books / The United Methodist Publishing House, 416-423.

----- (1985a): "John Wesley on Religious Affections: His Views on Experience and Emotion and Their Role in the Christian Life and Theology." Ph.D. dissertation, Emory University, Atlanta. University Microfilms International, 8516564.

----- (1985a): "John Wesley on Religious Affections: His Views on Experience and Emotion and Their Role in the Christian Life and Theology." Ph.D. dissertation, Emory University, Atlanta. University Microfilms International, 8516564.

Clark, Walter Houston (1969): *The Psychology of Religion: An Introduction to Religious Experience and Behaviour*. Toronto: Macmillan, 10th printing.

Conn, Robert (1979): *Journeys: A Christian Approach to Sexuality*. Nashville, Tenn.: The United Methodist Publishing House.

Cubie, David L. (1985): "The Theology of Love in Wesley," in *Wesleyan Theological Journal*, vol. 20 (1:1985), 122-154.

Cushman, Robert E. (1989): *John Wesley's Experimental Divinity: Studies in the Methodist Doctrinal Standards*. Nashville, Tenn.: Kingswood Books.

David, J.C. (1992): "Religion and the Struggle for Freedom in the English Revolution," in *The Historical Journal*, vol. 35 (3: 1992), 507-530.

Deschner, John W. (1960): *Wesley's Christology*. Dallas, Texas: Southern Methodist University Press.

Dodd, C.H. (1961): *The Parables of the Kingdom*. New York: Scribner's.

Doughty, W.L. (1955): *John Wesley: Preacher*. London: The Epworth Press.

Duling, Dennis C. (1979): *Jesus Christ through History*. New York: Harcourt Brace Jovanovich.

Dunning, H. Ray (1985): "Perspective for a Wesleyan Systematic Theology," in *Wesleyan Theology Today: A Bicentennial Theological Consultation*. Theodore Runyon, ed. Nashville, Tenn.: Kingswood Books / The United Methodist Publishing House, 51-55.

Edwards, Mark U., Jr. (1975): *Luther and the False Brethren*. Stanford, Cal.: Stanford University Press.

Forde, Gerhard O. (1983): "Law and Gospel in Luther's Hermeneutic," in *Interpretation*, vol. 3 (1983), 240-252.

Forell, George W. (1964): *Faith Active in Love: An Investigation of the Principles Underlying Luther's Social Ethics*. Minneapolis, Minnesota: Augsburg Publishing House, 4th printing.

Gills, Frederick C. (1954): *The Romantic Movement of Methodism: A Study of English Romanticism and the Evangelical Revival.* London: The Epworth Press.

González, Justo L. (1989) *Christian Thought Revisited: Three Types of Theology.* Nashville, Tenn.: Abingdon Press.

Greenslade, S.L. (ed.) (1963): *The Cambridge History of the Bible.* Vol. 3: "The West from the Reformation to the Present Day". Cambridge: The University Press.

Gritsch, Eric W. (1983): "The Cultural Context of Luther's Interpretation," in *Interpretation*, vol. 3 (1983), 266-276.

Gustafson, James M. (1968): *Christ and the Moral Life.* New York, Evanston, London: Harper and Row, Publishers.

Haendler, Gert (1981): *Luther on Ministerial Office and Congregational Function.* Edited with an introduction by Eric W. Gritsch; translated by Ruth C. Gritsch. Philadelphia: Fortress Press.

Hägglund, Bengt (1963): *Teologiens historia: En dogmhistorisk översikt* ("History of Theology: A Survey of the History of Doctrines"). Lund: C.W.K. Gleerups förlag, 2nd rev. ed.

Hall, Thor (1963): "The Christian's Life: Wesley's Alternative to Luther and Calvin," in *Duke Divinity School Review*, vol. 28 (2:1963), 111-126.

----- (1963a): "An Analysis of Simul Iustus et Peccator," in *Theology Today*, vol. 20 (2:1963), 174-182.

----- (1988): "Luther, Calvin and Wesley on the Christian Life: Exploration of Theological Types," in "Context: Essays in Honour of Peder Borgen." Peter Wilhelm Bøckman and Roald Kristiansen, eds. *Relieff*, publications of the Department of Religious Studies, University of Trondheim, vol. 24. Trondheim, Norway: Tapir, 45-60.

----- (1988a): "Wesley og hans kvinner" ("Wesley and His Women"), in *Teologisk forum*, vol. 2 (2:1988), 43-65.

Harmon, Nolan B. (ed.) (1974): *Encyclopedia of World Methodism.* 2 vols. Nashville, Tenn.: United Methodist Publishing House.

Harran, Marilyn J. (1985): "Luther and Freedom of Thought", in, *Martin Luther and the Modern Mind: Freedom, Conscience,*

Toleration, Rights, edited by Manfred Hoffmann. Vol. 22 in *Toronto Studies in Theology.* New York and Toronto: The Edwin Mellen Press, 191-236.

Hassing, Arne (1980): *Religion and Power: The Case of Methodism in Norway.* Waynesville, NC: General Commission on Archives and History (The United Methodist Church) / The Mountaineer.

Hendricks, M. Elton (1983): "John Wesley and Natural Theology," in *Wesley Theological Journal,* vol. 18 (2:1983), 7-17).

Heitzenrater, Richard P. (1972): *John Wesley and the Oxford Methodists, 1725-1735.* Ph.D. dissertation, Duke University.

----- (1984): *The Elusive Mr. Wesley.* 2 vols. Nashville, Tenn.: Abingdon Press.

Hendrix, Scott H. (1983): "Luther against the Background of the History of Biblical Interpretation," in *Interpretation,* vol. 3 (1983), 229-239.

Hildebrandt, Franz (1951): *From Luther to Wesley.* London: Lutterworth Press.

Hoffmann, Manfred (1985): "Reformation and Toleration," in, "Martin Luther and the Modern Mind: Freedom, Conscience, Toleration, Rights," Manfred Hoffmann, ed. Vol. 22 in *Toronto Studies in Theology.* New York and Toronto: The Edwin Mellen Press, 85-124.

Holifield, E. Brooks (1986): *Health and Medicine in the Methodist Tradition.* New York: Crossroad.

Hulley, L.D. (1988): *To Be and to Do: Exploring Wesley's Thought on Ethical Behaviour.* Pretoria: University of South Africa.

Hygen, Johan B. (1971): "Reformasjonens venstre fløy" ("The Left Wing of the Reformation"), in *Etik och kristen tro* ("Ethics and Christian Faith"). Gustaf Wingren, ed. Lund: CWK Gleerup, 148-161.

Hynson, Leon O. (1985): "Implications of Wesley's Method and Political Thought," in *Wesleyan Theology Today: A Bicentennial Theological Consultation.* Theodore Runyon, ed. Nashville, Tenn.: Kingswood Books / The United Methodist Publishing House, 373-388.

----- (1985a): "The Wesleyan Quadrilateral in the American Holiness Tradition," in *Wesleyan Theological Journal*, vol. 20 (1:1985), 19-33).

Imsen, Steinar (1984): *Senmiddelalderen: Emner fra Europas historie 1300-1550* ("The Late Medieval Ages: Issues from the History of Europe 1300-1550). Oslo: J.W. Cappelens forlag A.S.

Ives, A.G. (1970): *Kingswood School in Wesley's Day and Since.* London: Epworth Press.

Jacobs, Paul (1959): *Theologie reformierter Bekenntnisschriften.* Neukircken.

Jennings, Theodore W., Jr. (1990): *Good News to the Poor: John Wesley's Evangelical Economics.* Nashville, Tenn.: Abingdon Press.

Joy, Donald M. (1985): "Some Biblical Foundations and Metaphors of Vocational Ideals in the Wesleyan Tradition," in *Wesleyan Theology Today: A Bicentennial Theological Consultation.* Theodore Runyon, ed. Nashville, Tenn.: Kingswood Books / The United Methodist Publishing House, 299-305.

Källstad, Thorvald (1974): *John Wesley and the Bible: A Psychological Study.* Stockholm: Nya Bokförlags Aktiebolaget.

Kelly, J.N.D. (1978): *Early Christian Doctrines.* New York, Hagertown, San Francisco, London: Harper and Row, Publishers, reprinted.

Kierkegaard, Søren (1977): *Philosophiske smuler* ("Philosophical Fragments"). Publ. with introduction and comments by Niels Thulstrup. København: C.A. Reitzels Boghandel A-S.

Krusche, Werner (1957): *Das Wirken des Heiligen Geistes nach Calvin.* Göttingen.

Lean, Garth (1964): *John Wesley, Anglican.* London: Blandford Press.

Lindbeck, George A. (1985): "Modernity and Luther's Understanding of the Freedom of the Christian," in "Martin Luther and the Modern Mind: Freedom, Conscience, Toleration, Rights," Manfred Hoffmann, ed. Vol. 22 in *Toronto Studies in Theology.* New York and Toronto: The Edwin Mellen Press, 1-22.

Lindström, Harald (1961): *Wesley and Sanctification: A Study in the Doctrine of Salvation*. London: The Epworth Press, repr.

Locher, Gottfried W. (1981): "Zwingli's Thought: New Perspectives." *Studies in the History of Christian Thought*. Heiko A. Oberman, ed. Vol. 25. Leiden: E.J. Brill.

Lockyer, Thos. F. (1922): *Paul: Luther: Wesley: A Study in Religious Experience As Illustrative of the Ethic of Christianity*. London: The Epworth Press / J. Alfred Sharp.

Logan, James C. (1985): "Baptism — the Ecumenical Sacrament and the Wesleyan Tradition," in *Wesleyan Theology Today: A Bicentennial Theological Consultation*. Theodore Runyon, ed. Nashville, Tenn.: Kingswood Books / The United Methodist Publishing House, 323-329.

----- (1985a): "Toward a Wesleyan Social Ethic," in *Wesleyan Theology Today: A Bicentennial Theological Consultation*. Theodore Runyon, ed. Nashville, Tenn.: Kingswood Books / The United Methodist Publishing House, 361-372.

Maddox, Randy L. (1984): "Responsible Grace: The Systematic Perspective of Wesleyan Theology," in *Wesleyan Theological Journal*, vol. 19 (1:1984), 7-22.

----- (1990): "John Wesley and Eastern Orthodoxy Influences: Convergences and Differences," in *Asbury Theological Journal*, vol. 42 (2:1990), 29-53.

----- (1994): *Responsible Grace: John Wesley's Practical Theology*. Nashville, Tenn.: Abingdon Press / Kingswood Books.

Madron, Thomas W. (1981): "John Wesley on Economics," in *Sanctification and Liberation: Liberation Theologies in Light of the Wesleyan Tradition*. Theodor Runyon, ed. Nashville, Tenn.: Abingdon, 102-115.

Marquardt, Manfred (1977): *Praxis und Prinzipien der Sozialethik John Wesleys*. Vol. 21 in *Kirche und Konfession*. Göttingen: Vandenhoeck and Ruprecht.

----- (1988): "Gewissheit und Anfechtung bei Martin Luther und John Wesley," in *Theologie für die Praxis: Aus dem Theologischen Seminar der Evangelisch-methodistischen Kirche*, vol. 14 (1:1988), 14-28.

McArthur, Harvey K. (1960): *Understanding the Sermon on the Mount*. New York: Harper and Row.

McCormick, K. Steve (1991): "Theosis in Chrysostom and Wesley: An Eastern Paradigm on Faith and Love," in *Wesleyan Theological Journal*, vol. 26 (1:1991), 38-103.

Meistad, Tore (1983): *John Wesleys tolkning av Bergprekenen* ("John Wesley's Interpretation of the Sermon on the Mount"). Oslo: Norsk Forlagsselskap.

----- (1984): "Die Zukunft des Methodismus im heutigen Europa und wie dieser Herausfordering zu begegnen ist: Geistlich, Theologisch, Etisch," in *Die Zukunft des Methodismus in Europa*, Karl-Heinz Vogt, ed. Arbeitsmaterial von der Europäische Theologischen Tagung in Reutlingen vom 25. Februar vis 2. März 1984 anlässlich des 200jährigen Jubiläums der EmK. Stuttgart: Bildungswerk der EmK-S.

----- (1985): "John Wesleys bruk av Bibelen" ("John Wesley's use of the Bible"), in *Bibel og forkynnelse* ("Bible and Preaching"), Tore Meistad (ed.). Bergen: Metodistkirkens teologiske seminar / Metodistkirkens Utdannings- og Opplysningsråd, 84-109.

----- (1989): "To Be a Christian in the World: Martin Luther's and John Wesley's Interpretation of the Sermon on the Mount". Ph.D. dissertation. Department of Religious Studies, University of Trondheim, Norway.

----- (1994): "Studier i wesleyansk teologi" ("Studies in Wesleyan Theology"). *ALH-forskning* (the research series of Alta College of Education), 1:1994, 155-177.

Minor, Rüdiger (1988): "Being a Christian Calls Us to Faithfulness: What Hinders Us on Our Way As Christians." Sermon given at the Faith Conference in Hollabrunn, Austria, July 21, 1988.

Moltmann, Jürgen (1981): *The Trinity and the Kingdom*. San Francisco: Harper and Row.

----- (1985): "Reformation and Revolution", in *Martin Luther and the Modern Mind: Freedom, Conscience, Toleration, Rights*. Manfred Hoffmann ed. Vol. 22 in *Toronto Studies in Theology*. New York and Toronto: The Edwin Mellen Press, 163-190.

Muelder, Walter George (1985): "The Methodist Social Creed and Ecumenical Ethics," in *Wesleyan Theology Today: A Bicentennial Theological Consultation*. Theodore Runyon, ed. Nashville, Tenn.: Kingswood Books / The United Methodist Publishing House, 351-360.

Niesel, Wilhelm (1957): *Die Theologie Calvins*. München: 2nd ed.

Nilsen, Einar Anker (1952): "The Idea of God and Personality Integration with Special Emphasis on Self-Evaluation As a Deciding Factor—an Historical, Clinical, Experimental Approach." Ph.D. dissertation, Northwestern University, Evanston.

Outler, Albert C. (1975): *Theology in the Wesleyan Spirit*. Nashville, Tenn.: Discipleship Resources.

Pelikan, Jaroslav (1959): *Luther the Expositior: Introduction to the Reformer's Exegetical Writings*. Companion volume to *Luther's Works*. Saint Louis: Concordia Publishing House.

Plumb, J.H. (1963): *England in the Eighteenth Century*. Vol. 7 of *The Pelican History of England*. Harmonsworth: Pelican Books Ltd., repr. 1978.

Prenter, Regin (1979): *Skabelse og genløsning: Dogmatik* ("Creation and Redemption: Dogmatics"). København: G.E.C. Gads forlag, 1967, 7th ed.

Prince, John W. (1926): *Wesley on Religious Education: A Study of John Wesley's Theories and Methods of the Education of Children in Religion*. New York: The Methodist Book Concern.

Ravindratas, Paramanathan (1987): "Wesley og økumenikk" ("Wesley and Ecumenism"), in *Teologisk Forum*, vol. 1 (2:1987), 6-19.

Rublack, Hans-Christoph (1985): "Reformation and Society", in *Martin Luther and the Modern Mind: Freedom, Conscience, Toleration, Rights*. Manfred Hoffmann, ed. Vol. 22 in *Toronto Studies in Theology*. New York and Toronto: The Edwin Mellen Press, 237-278.

Runyon, Theodore (1981): "Wesley and the Theologies of Liberation," in *Sanctification and Liberation: Liberation Theologies in Light of the Wesleyan Tradition*. Theodore Runyon, ed. Nashville, Tenn.: Abingdon Press, 9-48.

----- (1985): "What Is Methodism's Theological Contribution Today?" in *Wesleyan Theology Today: A Bicentennial Theological Consultation*. Theodore Runyon, ed. Nashville, Tenn.: Kingswood Books / The United Methodist Publishing House, 7-13.

Rupp, Gordon (1983): *John Wesley und Martin Luther: Ein Beitrag zum lutherischen-methodistischen Dialog*. Vol. 16 in *Beiträge zur Geschichte der Evangelisch-methodistischen Kirche*. Karl Steckel ed. Stuttgart: Studiegemeinschaft für Geschichte der Evangelisch-methodistischen Kirche.

Scharffenorth, Gerta (1982): *Den Glauben ins Leben ziehen: Studien zu Luthers Theologie*. München.

Schmidt, Martin (1966): *John Wesley*. 3 vols. Zürich: Götthelv Verlag.

Semmel, Bernard (1974): *The Methodist Revolution*. London: Heinemann.

Siggins, Jan D. Kingston (1970): *Martin Luther's Doctrine of Christ*. New Haven: Yale University Press.

Skirbekk, Gunnar (1985): *Filosofihistorie I: Innføring i europeisk filosofihistorie med særleg vekt på politisk filosofi* ("The History of Philosophy, I: Introduction to the History of Philosophy in Europe, with Special Emphasis on Political Philosophy"). Bergen: Universitetsforlaget AS, 3rd ed., 3rd publ.

Snyder, Howard (1980): *The Radical Wesley and Patterns for Church Renewal*. Downers Grove, Ill.: Inter-Varsity Press.

Spitz, Lewis W. (1985): "The Christian in Church and State", in *Martin Luther and the Modern Mind: Freedom, Conscience, Toleration, Rights*. Manfred Hoffmann, ed. Vol. 22 in *Toronto Studies in Theology*. New York and Toronto: The Edwin Mellen Press, 125-162.

Steinmetz, David C. (1983): "Scripture and the Lord's Supper in Luther's Theology," in *Interpretation*, vol. 3 (1983), 253-265).

----- (1986): *Luther in Context*. Bloomington: Indiana University Press.

Stendahl, Krister (1977): *Paul among Jews and Gentiles and Other Essays*. Philadelphia: Fortress Press.

Streiff, Patrick Philipp (1985): "Der ökumenische Geist im frühen Methodismus: Mit besonderer Berücksichtigung der Kontroverse zwischen calvinistischen and wesleyanischen Methodisten im 18. Jahrhundert," in *Hoffnung der Kirche und Erneuerung der Welt: Beiträge zu den ökumenischen, sozialen und politischen Wirkung des Pietismus; Festschrift für Andreas Lindt*. Robert Herren and Herrmann Kocher, eds. in cooperation with Alfred Schindler, Rudolf Dellsperger, and Martin Brecht. Göttingen: Vandenhoeck and Ruprecht, 59-77.

Trevelyan, George Macaulay (1943): *History of England*, with maps; A new and enlarged edition. London, New York, Toronto: Longmans, Green and Co., 2nd ed., rev., new impression.

----- (1965): *English Social History: A Survey of Six Centuries: Chaucer to Queen Victora*. London: Longmans, Green and Co Ltd, 3rd edition, new impression.

Tuttle, Robert G., Jr. (1978): *John Wesley: His Life and Theology*. Grand Rapids, Mich.: Zondervan Publishing House.

Tyerman, L. (1880): *The Life and Times of the Rev. John Wesley, M.A., Founder of the Methodists*. 3 vols. London: Hodder and Stoughton, 5th ed.

Walls, Jerry L. (1986): *The Problem of Pluralism: Recovering United Methodist Identity*. Wilmore, Ky: Good News Books.

Warner, George Townsend (1958): *A Brief Survey of British History*. Revised and enlarged by R.L. Mackie. London and Glasgow: Blackie and Son Limited, new ed. 1938, reprinted.

Warner, Wellman J. (1930): *The Wesleyan Movement in the Industrial Revolution*. London, New York, Toronto: Longmans, Green and Co.

Watson, David Lowes (1985): *The Early Methodist Class Meeting: Its Origin and Significance*. Nashville, Tenn.: Discipleship Resources.

Weber, Max (1976): *The Protestant Ethic and the Spirit of Capitalism*, translated by Talcott Parsons; with introduction by Anthony Giddens. New York: Charles Scribner's Sons.

Williams, Colin W. (1962): *John Wesley's Theology Today.* London: The Epworth Press, 1960, repr.

Williams, George Huntston (1962): *The Radical Reformation.* Philadelphia: The Westminster Press.

Wilson, Charles R. (1977): "The Relevance of John Wesley's Distinctive Correlation of Love and Law," in *Wesleyan Theological Journal,* vol. 12 (1:1977), 54-59.

Windisch, Hans (1951): *The Meaning of the Sermon on the Mount: A Contribution to the Historical Understanding of the Gospels and to the Problem of Their True Exegesis.* Philadelphia: Westminster Press.

Wingren, Gustaf (1948): *Luthers lära om kallelsen* ("Luther on Vocation"). Lund: C.W.K. Gleerups förlag, 1942, 2nd ed. (German ed., Münich: 1952; American ed., Philadelphia: 1957.

----- (1971): "Reformationens och lutherdommens ethos" ("The Ethos of the Reformation and the Lutheran Church"), in *Etik ock kristen tro* ("Ethics and Christian Faith"). Gustaf Wingren, ed. Lund: CWK Gleerup, 112-147.

Wisløff, Carl Fr. (1983): *Martin Luthers teologi: En innføring* ("The Theology of Martin Luther: An Introduction"). Oslo: Lunde forlag.

Wogaman, J. Philip (1976): *A Christian Method of Moral Judgment.* Philadelphia: Westminster Press.

Woodward, Max W. (1983): *One at London: Some Account of Mr. Wesley's Chapel and London House.* London: Friends of Wesley's Chapel, 2nd ed.

Scriptural Index

Index of Names and Subjects

About the Author

A United Methodist minister in Norway, Dr. Tore Meistad has served as a church pastor, dean of a Methodist boarding school for young adults with various handicapping conditions, and dean of the UMC theological seminary. In 1990 he was appointed to his present position as associate professor of Finnmark State College of Higher Education, Alta, teaching religion.

Dr. Meistad's extensive research has been performed mainly within three areas: (1) the history of the ideas of the Wesleyan movement, (2) the history of the free church movements in Norway, and (3) the analysis of how the Christian religion has penetrated the Norwegian culture and society, particularly in northern Norway. He has worked with these issues in the context of the training of ministers as well as of teachers' education.

For many years Dr. Meistad has been active in initiating research projects. For instance, in 1993-1996 he organized and directed a research network including more than 20 scholars from a number of universities and colleges. The projects of the network focused on how the religiosity varied in the different regions of Norway. This research, which initiated the study of regional religiosity in Norway, was financed by the Norwegian Council of Research.